D1247919

The Library of
Southern Civilization

THE LIBRARY OF
SOUTHERN CIVILIZATION
Lewis P. Simpson, Editor

Southern Women
in the Recent
Educational Movement
in the South

SOUTHERN WOMEN

IN THE RECENT

EDUCATIONAL MOVEMENT

IN

THE SOUTH

A. D. MAYO

Edited with an Introduction by
Dan T. Carter and
Amy Friedlander

LOUISIANA STATE UNIVERSITY PRESS
BATON ROUGE AND LONDON

LIBRARY OF CONGRESS CATALOGING IN PUBLICATION DATA

Mayo, Amory Dwight, 1823–1907.
    Southern women in the recent educational movement
in the South.

    (The Library of Southern civilization)
    Reprint of the 1892 ed. published by the Govt.
Print. Off., Washington, as Circular of information,
1892, no. 1, of the U. S. Bureau of Education.
    Includes bibliographical references and index.
    1. Educational—Southern States—History.
2. Afro-Americans—Education—Southern States—
History. I. Carter, Dan T. II. Friedlander, Amy.

III. Title. IV. Series: United States. Office
of Education. Circular of information; 1892,
no. 1.
LA230.5.S6M38   1978   370'.975   78–1554
ISBN 0–8071–0466–3

Contents

Preface

Amory Dwight Mayo's work speaks for itself. In our brief introductory essay we have not summarized all of his many observations, nor have we restated the conclusions he reached in *Southern Women in the Recent Educational Movement in the South*. We have sought to furnish enough biographical and intellectual background to place Mayo in the intellectual context of the late nineteenth century and to show how his ideas evolved during his forty years of active public service.

The index is designed to help the reader examine Mayo's ideas, concepts, and attitudes as well as to locate the names and places mentioned in his book. In annotating the text itself, we have tried to avoid overdocumentation while still providing enough information to make the work useful to general readers and researchers in the field. Major figures who influenced Mayo or shaped educational ideas in the nineteenth century are briefly described. Whenever possible, we have also identified secondary figures mentioned in the text, but complete identification has been impossible since Mayo sometimes mentioned by last name individuals working in isolated schools of the Deep South.

Introduction

In his final state of the union address in 1880, President Rutherford B. Hayes implicitly acknowledged the failure of political Reconstruction. Mass public education, not legislative coercion was the "best and surest guaranty of the primary rights of citizenship," argued Hayes. Wherever the public school house existed, "peace, virtue and social order prevail and civil and religious liberty are secure."[1]

A handful of former abolitionists condemned Hayes for abandoning the freedmen to their former masters, but the president's emphasis upon education reflected a significant shift in the nation's mood. Discouraged by the apparent failure of the Reconstruction regimes and often embittered toward the freedmen and women of the South, many wartime abolitionists retreated from their earlier reform commitments. Even before the Reconstruction regimes collapsed in South Carolina, Florida, and Louisiana, James Russell Lowell—one-time poet of the antislavery movement—ruefully recalled the naïveté he had shared with many contemporaries. He had foolishly believed that "human nature is as clay in the hands of a potter." Now he had come to see it as the "result of a long past & only to be reshaped by the slow influences of an equally long future."[2] Sidney Andrews, a New England abolitionist whose postwar account of the South had fueled Radical Reconstruction, was more bitter than reflective. Instead of improvement in the conditions of southern blacks, emancipation had brought "indolence" and "dissipation." Blacks would have to learn the "lesson taught of all time—that growth and sure advancement are the reward of individual purpose and endeavor." The time had come for blacks to be left to work out their own destiny—regardless of the outcome.[3]

Amory Dwight Mayo did not share Andrews' bleak outlook, nor

1. James D. Richardson (ed.), *A Compilation of the Messages and Papers of the Presidents* (11 vols.; Washington, D.C.: Bureau of National Literature, 1897–1911), VI, 4554.
2. Quoted in Martin Duberman, *James Russell Lowell* (Boston: Houghton Mifflin, 1966), 276.
3. Boston *Advertiser*, May 16, 20, 1867; May 23, 1870.

did he dismiss the achievements of the Reconstruction era. But he had skeptically concluded by the 1880s that politics was "no cure for any evil in this Republic." Education alone could "permanently cure any disease of the body politic in this Republic; because education means the fashioning of the men and women who fashion the state." Thus, in 1800, he enthusiastically endorsed President Hayes's suggestion that the time had come for the "soldier to give way to the schoolmaster in the complete reconstruction of national affairs."[4]

As he wrote these words, Mayo was on the brink of a twenty-year career as an educational missionary to the South. From 1880 to 1900 he would visit hundreds of towns and hamlets from Virginia to Texas, spreading the gospel of personal and social regeneration through the "new education."

Mayo's growing involvement in the educational movement of the South came at a critical time, as the region moved from the social and political upheavals of Reconstruction to the repression of the late 1890s. The "redeemer" campaigns of the 1870s had dramatically reduced the limited black participation in the Reconstruction governments, but Negro voters remained a critical element in the politics of several southern states. And even though segregation had become the most common social practice of the era, uncertainty and fluidity existed in black-white relations. The 1860s had seen (in the context of a slave society) a revolution in race relations with blacks transformed overnight from slaves to citizens. Without the gift of foresight, Mayo and his fellow reformers believed they were on the brink of a second revolution in which the creation of an adequate educational system would painlessly transform society.

The failure of that vision with the bleak outcome of the disfranchisement conventions of the 1890s and the final triumph of legal segregation may have led us to ignore some of the factors that gave hope in the 1880s. Perhaps it is time to look at one of these often-criticized men from his own perspective as well as from the critical vantage point of hindsight.

In many respects, Mayo typified a generation of mid-nineteenth century reformers. Born in 1823 to a comfortable Warwick, Massachusetts, family, he first found his "calling" in life as a Unitarian minister. Even as he avoided partisan politics, he enlisted in a vari-

---

4. Amory Dwight Mayo, "The President's Speech," *Education*, I (1880), 84.

ety of popular reform movements in the 1840s, supporting the peace movement, prison and hospital reform, temperance and abolition. "Numberless as are the evils which afflict the earth," he wrote in 1847, "they yield to the number of human remedies." The ancient abuses of human society were "fleeing to the mountains."[5]

But it was the educational reform movement of the 1840s and 1850s that increasingly drew Mayo's commitment. As a young man he had argued that the "education and the reformation of many is the great purpose appearing in every relation of Providence to the world." Although he continued to serve as a Unitarian minister through the 1850s and 1860s, he became increasingly involved in supporting the public school movement, serving on school boards in Cincinnati, Ohio, Springfield, Massachusetts, and Albany, New York.[6]

Between the 1840s and his travels in the South, Mayo's ideas on education had matured in the direction of what he called the "new education." Part of a series of changes in the late nineteenth century that extended from elementary to higher education, this loose-knit body of ideas had at its center the work of Francis Wayland Parker. Parker instituted far-reaching innovations in the school system of Quincy, Massachusetts, in the 1870s and further refined his theories at the Cook County Normal School in the 1880s. Parker was typical of other American intellectuals in his willingness to borrow European ideas, and like other educators, he built primarily upon the experiments of Johann Heinrich Pestalozzi.[7]

The thrust of Pestalozzi's pedagogy consisted of teaching the child in a manner he believed was consistent with the "natural" learning process. A child, he argued, learned by experience. The teacher should begin, therefore, with familiar concepts and gradually progress to unfamiliar ones. Instructing by use of the "object-lesson" thus became a hallmark of Pestalozzian thought. His school at Yverdun, Switzerland, itself became an object-lesson as well as a laboratory for

5. Amory Dwight Mayo, *The Balance: Moral Arguments for Universalism* (Boston: Mussey and Tompkins, 1847), 142.

6. *Dictionary of American Biography* XI, 461–62; "Who's Who in Education. Rev. A. D. Mayo, LL.D.," *Journal of Education*, LXV (March 14, 1907), 297.

7. For an overview of the influence of Pestalozzi and his followers see John Alfred Green, *The Educational Ideas of Pestalozzi* (New York: Greenwood Press, 1969); Lawrence Cremin, *The Transformation of the School: Progressivism in American Education, 1876–1957* (New York: Alfred A. Knopf, 1961), 218–35; Merle Curti, *The Social Ideas of American Educators* (Totowa, N.J.: Littlefield, Adams, 1971), 101–68; Frank Pierrepont Graves, *Great Educators of Three Centuries: Their Work and Its Influence on Modern Education* (New York: Macmillan, 1912), 122–66; Russel Blaine Nye, *Society and Culture in America, 1830–1860* (New York: Harper and Row, 1974), 373–76.

those interested in his ideas, and his most enduring object-lesson was his novel *Leonard and Gertrude* (1781). Reflecting Pestalozzi's faith in the regenerative moral power of a woman's influence, Gertrude reformed her husband by her virtuous example. Their exemplary conduct in turn reformed the village, and the village had a similar effect upon the state.[8]

Leonard and Gertrude also reflected Pestalozzi's interest in individual and social improvement. His work, in this regard, found a receptive audience among American antebellum reformers who were concerned about the education of the citizens of a democracy. Horace Mann and Henry Barnard were only two of several reformers familiar with Pestalozzian ideas. A generation later, Parker shared their belief in the social benefits to be derived from education. He considered character the ethical purpose of education, but character was "a vague word, unless translated into concrete terms of action. Such terms are found in the true meaning of citizenship and the qualities of citizenship are interpreted by the needs of community life." Knowledge, he went on to say in the same passage, was as essential to the mind as blood, breath, and food to the body. "But there is an immeasurable difference between knowledge as an end and knowledge as a means. Citizenship demands fullness and richness of knowledge, but it also determines the kind and the nature of the truth to be applied through self-expression or skill."[9]

Parker had been invited to Quincy in 1873 after members of the school board conducted the annual examinations personally only to discover that students could recite the rules of grammar and could speed through prescribed word lists but could neither write an ordinary letter nor read unfamiliar sources easily. The changes that Parker instituted were reminiscent of Pestalozzi's ideas in their effort to reach children "as human beings," rather than by merely applying the texts of the traditional curriculum to children's minds like paint on the wall. "Each child," he later wrote, "has his own individuality, his stream of thought, his desires, his hopes and fears, his grief and joy." At Quincy, "we tried to make the children happy, so happy that they should love to go to school."[10]

8. The only English edition of *Leonard and Gertrude* available to most Americans was a translation by Frederick B. Perkins of the first part of the work in an 1859 issue of the *American Journal of Education*.

9. Francis W. Parker, "An Account of the Work of the Cook County and Chicago Normal School from 1883 to 1899," in U.S. Department of Interior, Bureau of Education, *Report of the Commissioner of Education for the Year 1902* (Washington, D.C.: Government Printing Office, 1903), I, 253.

10. Francis W. Parker, "Address on the Quincy Method," *ibid.*, I, 239–40.

His innovations ranged from abandoning the traditional curriculum and rote memorization to instituting field trips to study geography, introducing drawing as an exercise in manual dexterity and individual expression, and using newspapers and magazines rather than readers. When he took over the principalship of the Cook County Normal School, he expanded these programs in its practice school. Modeling and painting as well as drawing, nature trips, elementary laboratory work in biology and physics, music, drama, physical education and hygiene took their places in a curriculum designed to educate the whole child. The separate subjects were integrated so that a field trip might become the subject of an essay or drawing, both of which were designed to develop the child's ability to articulate his thoughts.[11]

Parker's brand of education was not without critics. Charles H. Levermore believed that the "new education" had "run mad" at Harvard where, under the presidency of Charles Eliot, the elective system and student participation in university government had undermined necessary grounding in the traditional curriculum and resulted in half-trained minds. Even devotees of the new education discussed it at length since Parker, its apostle, never formalized his ideas into a coherent corpus of theory. Indeed, the essence of his method was "a spirit of study" and "everlasting change."[12]

Whatever its limits as a coherent philosophical movement, the "new education" was tailor-made for the reformers of the mid-nineteenth century. By the time Mayo began his travels in the South he was able to summarize what he believed to be the four principles of this educational philosophy. In a democratic society, education should seek to develop the "ability and natural endowments" of every single child; there was no place for caste and class in American society. The purpose of education was not to indoctrinate the pupil with useless facts and unrelated knowledge, but to "implant the love of truth and to train the faculties to find it by vital contact with nature, humanity, literature and art." No education was complete without implanting in the child the character traits associated with the "Christian method of love," and finally, skilled and trained teachers committed to no single philosophy of pedagogy should constantly change their methods of instruction to suit the needs of individual children.[13]

11. Amory Dwight Mayo, "The New Education and Col. Parker," *Journal of Education*, XVIII (1883), 84–85.

12. Charles H. Levermore, "The 'New Education' Run Mad," *Education*, VI (1886), 290–98.

13. Mayo, "The New Education and Col. Parker," 84–86.

Such were the lofty goals that Mayo proclaimed. Viewed from a later historical perspective, this emphasis upon gradual (and painless) educational reform rather than on basic economic and political change seems a form of intellectual escapism. With the apparent failures of Reconstruction politics only a recent memory for Mayo, however, the notion of social reformation through education seemed a way around the self-defeating conflicts of the politics of the 1860s and 1870s.[14]

Nor can it be said that Mayo failed to understand the many obstacles to change in the late nineteenth-century South. Even as he employed the soothing vocabulary of the patient reformer, he ridiculed the optimistic bombast of New South spokesmen who insisted that the South's educational system was sound. In his many reports for the Bureau of Education, he alternated his hopeful prescriptions with a sobering catalogue of the region's many cultural and economic deficiencies.

His healthy skepticism can be seen in his discussion and analysis of the concept of industrial education. Vocational and industrial training was the most popular panacea in the late nineteenth-century South. It meshed neatly with the era's rhetoric of societal advancement through industrial development, and above all else, it seemed to offer a solution to the vexing problem of educating the Negro. Industrial education disarmed the fears of conservative southern whites who believed the classroom would "spoil" black laborers. To some blacks like Booker T. Washington, it seemed to offer prospects for a secure, albeit inferior, position for blacks who were threatened with economic destruction. For white reformers interested in the "uplifting" of the postwar Negro, vocational and industrial training offered much in the way of "character building" for the former slaves. All of these factors appealed to Mayo, none more than the role this training would play in instilling inner habits of social discipline among the blacks of the South. Viewed by late nineteenth-century standards, Mayo was remarkably "liberal" in his racial views. But the plain fact of the matter is that Mayo—like most of his contemporaries —occasionally had deep misgivings about the cultural maturity of the Negro.[15]

14. For a discussion of the shift of emphasis from political to educational reform in the South see James M. McPherson, *The Abolitionist Legacy: From Reconstruction to the NAACP* (Princeton: Princeton University Press, 1975), 143–298.

15. With other reformers of the mid-nineteenth century, Mayo shared what George Frederickson has called the "Romantic-racialism" of the era. In his most hopeful moments, Mayo saw the gentle and forbearing blacks of the South as a vital antidote to a vulgar, power-hungry Anglo-Saxon civilization. Frederickson, *The Black Image in the White Mind: The*

In practical terms, concluded Mayo, the Negro was the "child race of Christendom," the last people to step "over the threshold of modern civilization." Thus, it was not surprising that southern blacks were subject to the moral and intellectual infirmities of a "backward" people.[16] The license which had followed in the wake of slavery made it absolutely essential that a sense of firm discipline be established over a people not yet schooled in the habits of inner self-control.

The Massachusetts clergyman, like many of his Victorian contemporaries, seems to have been particularly repelled by the evidence of "sexual degradation" which he saw on every hand. Although he blamed this lack of chastity among southern blacks on the double inheritance of "savage Africa" and the sexual license of the slave quarters, he brooded over the consequence of a generation of black boys and girls raised in this unhealthy environment. At several points in his pleas for better conditions for blacks, he used unusually vivid metaphors to illustrate his deep concern. Unless dramatic improvements were made, he concluded in 1894, parts of the black community would remain a "great American sewer under the back windows of every respectable home," a "black slough at the bottom of American Society [which] would make Republican government a chronic conflict." Industrial education held out the prospect of offering structure and discipline to a people who badly needed both.[17]

And yet, the gentle Unitarian refused to allow his fears and misgivings to lead him into an unqualified endorsement of this new fad. In 1888 when he prepared a booklet on industrial education in the South he warned against making such a program compulsory for blacks (and poor whites). "It is important that . . . we steer clear of that narrow idea which would make the common school, like the English public school, an arrangement for the 'working classes,' with the poor consigned to learning repetitive manual skills while the upper class is instructed in the traditional 'higher' curriculum."[18] As he

---

Debate on Afro-American Character and Destiny, 1817–1914 (New York: Harper and Row, 1971), 97–129.

16. Amory Dwight Mayo, "Progress of the Negro," *Forum*, X (1890), 336.

17. Amory Dwight Mayo, "The Women's Movement in the South," *New England Magazine*, V (1891), 249–60. See also, Amory Dwight Mayo, "The Negro American Citizen in the New American Life" (N.p., 1891), 9; *The Colored American Working Man of the New Time: An Address Delivered Before the State Agricultural and Mechanical College for the Colored Race at Greensboro, N.C., May 26, 1898* (Hampton, Va.: Press of Hampton Institute, 1898); *The Opportunity and Obligation of the Educated Class of the Colored Race in the Southern States: An Address Delivered Before the Agricultural and Mechanical College for Negroes at Normal, Alabama, May 29, 1899* (Normal, Ala.: n.p., 1899).

18. Amory Dwight Mayo, *Industrial Education in the South*, U.S. Department of Interior, Bureau of Education (Washington, D.C.: Government Printing Office, 1888), 29.

would later argue in *Southern Women* in a way that foreshadowed W. E. B. DuBois, "no people can get on without a head; a genuine aristocracy of character, intelligence and executive power." Mayo never lost his faith in the curative power of mass education, but he refused to accept the workshops of Tuskegee and Hampton as the ultimate solution to the South's economic, educational, and racial problems.

Moreover, despite his occasional misgivings, Mayo remained basically an optimist insofar as the future of southern blacks were concerned. In observing the failures and accomplishments of the South's former slaves, Mayo implicitly (and sometimes explicitly) compared their progress with that of the southern Europeans who had begun to pour into the urban areas of New England. In virtually every category he found the black southerners preferable. Embittered by repeated conflicts with Catholic leaders over the concept of public education, he found comfort in the Protestant, evangelical make-up of the black community. Here there were no meddling priests or bishops to thwart programs for public education. And if whites sometimes ridiculed the blacks' "amiability, habit of imitation, love of approbation, and desire for a front seat"—these were essential ingredients in the adoption of American civilization. Better this than the sullen withdrawal into their own culture of the "insolent naturalized foreign element that now dominates our Northern industrial centers." Even the much vaunted "immorality" of the southern Negro was far less serious than the "vices of the lower class of the south of Europe people" who were "swarming" the shores of the United States.[19]

If Mayo did see education as a panacea for the ills of the South, his conception of reform was broad and far-reaching. With gentle but unmistakable criticism, he chided southerners for their parsimonious attitude toward government services and he shrewdly recognized the way in which the taxpayer revolts of the Reconstruction era and the governmental retrenchment of the 1870s and 1880s crippled any hope for improving the backward educational system. "The South has yet to learn the fundamental fact of American society," he said at one point, "that just and even generous taxation in this Republic is not 'tyranny.'"[20]

19. Mayo, "The Negro American Citizen," 9.
20. Amory Dwight Mayo, "Some Present Aspects of Education in the South," *Education*, XVI (January, 1896), 257–66.

Even if this "pestilential heresy" was exploded, however, Mayo recognized that the poverty of the former Confederate states made the creation of an adequate public system impossible. Thus, he reserved his angriest attacks for his fellow northerners. The failure of New England senators to support national aid to education was an indictment of the region's statesmanship far greater than any critic, "however malignant," concluded the native of Massachusetts. Any opponent of the Blair bill for national aid to education should be entitled to a "retirement from power for a quarter of a century on the ground of political incapacity."[21]

A significant cause for optimism was the emerging role that an all-wise providence had designed for the southern woman in the uplifting of the South. From Pestalozzi and the exemplars of the "new education" Mayo became convinced that women, when properly trained and motivated, were the best teachers possible. In this conclusion he shared the views of other important educational reformers. Women teachers were best suited for molding the "childhood and youth of the nation," concluded Horace Mann in 1845. "Here is the replenishing of the world; here is a new wave of existence. From these little children will be selected the judges and statesmen of the next half century." Teachers and primarily women teachers were literally the "creators of a world destiny . . . moulding the elements of a coming society."[22] To nineteenth-century reformers, the mother/teacher was granted an awesome duty and responsibility; the future of a democratic society literally rested in her delicate hands. As Catherine Beecher had argued in 1844, it was an iron chain of interconnecting ideas. The success of democratic institutions rested upon the "intellectual and moral character of the mass of the people." And the formation of this "moral and intellectual character" was committed to the "female hand." The "mother forms the character of the future man."[23] And the role of the teacher was to extend this benevolent regime throughout the formative years of childhood.

The problems wrought by emancipation made the need for southern women even more compelling. Like most of his contemporaries —North and South—Mayo accepted the notion that the southern plantation had been a "school for civilization" which had brought the

21. Amory Dwight Mayo, "The Third Estate of the South," *New England Magazine*, III (November, 1890), 307.

22. Horace Mann, "Editor's Address," *Common School Journal*, VII (1845), 3.

23. Anne L. Kuhn, *The Mother's Role in Childhood Education: New England Concepts, 1830–1860* (New Haven: Yale University Press, 1947), 181–82.

blessings of civilization and Christianity to the millions of southern slaves. The Civil War had ended slavery, but that same war had wrought a revolution in the role and status of southern women—a revolution that providentially furnished a new kind of leadership and direction more suited to the age. Under the pressure of the war, with most southern men at the front or disabled, southern women had stepped out of their confined roles and onto the larger stage of southern society. These women, a kind of natural elite schooled in the races and culture of the Old South, held the potential for the vital function of training young, emancipated blacks. Southerners had never understood, said Mayo, that the most "genuine worship of women is shown by the large appreciation of her nature and her place in the modern world."[24]

A careful observer of the educational scene in the South, Mayo was one of the first individuals to point to the revolution taking place in the composition of the South's teaching corps. Regretfully, he noted in 1884, "too few, by far, of the foremost young men of the South will be persuaded to serve for the scanty pay of the schoolmaster." But he expressed hope that the women of the South—"looking for some honorable means of livelihood"—would take their place in the schools.[25] His optimism was well founded. Before the Civil War southern women composed less than 25 percent of the region's teaching force, a figure that changed little throughout the 1860s and 1870s. But the 1880s marked a dramatic shift; the number of women in the profession increased 100 percent whereas the number of men declined significantly. As a percentage of the teaching force, women grew from less than one-third to nearly 60 percent, and in some states the changeover was even greater. A similar transition had taken place in New England and the Midwest from the 1820s through the 1850s, but the rapidity of the transformation was four times greater in the

24. Although Mayo welcomed the decline of "exaggerated Southern Chivalry" for intellectual reasons, southern writers—male and female—were far more likely to note the same development with regret. In 1889 one Georgia woman noted that southern women had been forced into the marketplace for jobs because "Southern chivalry has failed to remedy the curse of poverty." Atlanta *Constitution*, July 4, 1889. As the southern educator Atticus Haygood concluded, the struggle for economic survival, quite apart from any theoretical questions of women's rights, had led southern women into the work force of the region. Haygood, "The South and the School Problem," *Harper's New Monthly Magazine*, LXXIX (1889), 227. See also Walter Fisk Tillett's "Women as Affected by the War," *Century Illustrated Monthly Magazine*, n.s., XXI (1891), 9–16.

25. Amory Dwight Mayo, "Building for the Children in the South," *Education*, V (1884), 10–11.

South than in the North. By the census of 1900 there was little difference between North and South.[26]

The "new education" called for trained teachers, and entrance into an increasingly professionalized teaching force held important implications for women. At the very least, it represented an expansion of roles beyond the traditional wife/mother. Mayo was clearly aware of these social ramifications.[27] Yet he assured himself and his audience that a public role as teacher did not mean political activism. "The enthusiastic advocate of 'Woman's Rights' may fancy I am about to announce a grand rally to the standard of woman suffrage, and all things inscribed on that banner, among the southern sisters," but, in fact, when Mayo spoke of the southern women's movement, he meant "the movement of all women in the South who 'having eyes, see, and having ears, hear.' and having souls welcome the call of God and go forth, ofttimes under a cloud of local prejudice, but more and more coming to be known as the leaders of the higher society in every state."[28] Despite his pointed linking of changes in the postbellum South to changes in the status of women, he continued to see these in the limited context of a Reconstruction reformer's desire to bring southern institutions in line with national norms. Thus, it was "little short of providential interposition" that the Civil War had created the setting for a massive movement of the "better class" of southern women into the black and white classrooms of the South. These "consecrated" young women would become a "beautiful object lesson" in uplifting the region's backward people and joining them to the larger nation in an "enduring social bond."[29]

When he completed *Southern Women* in late 1891, Mayo foresaw gradual and continuing improvement in the racial and economic life of the South. If his viewpoint was sometimes overly optimistic, it was nevertheless grounded in a perceptive assessment of the South

26. U.S. Department of Interior, *Report of the Department of Education for the Year 1903* (Washington, D.C.: Government Printing Office, 1905), I, 88–89; U.S. Department of Commerce and Labor, Bureau of the Census, *Special Reports, Supplemental Analysis and Derivative Tables, Twelfth Census of the U.S., 1900* (Washington, D.C.: Government Printing Office, 1906), 485–87; U.S. Department of Commerce and Labor, Bureau of the Census, *Statistics of Women at Work: Based on Unpublished Material Derived from the Schedules of the Twelfth Census, 1900* (Washington, D.C.: Government Printing Office, 1907); U.S. Department of the Interior, Census Office, *Compendium of the 10th Census, June 1880* (Washington, D.C.: Government Printing Office, 1883), 1640–1641.

27. See especially *Southern Women*, 52–54.

28. Mayo, "The Women's Movement in the South," 250, 256.

29. *Ibid.*, 258.

he had come to know so well. Instead of progress, however, Americans of the 1890s witnessed a decade of racial turmoil and violence culminating in the total domination of whites over blacks in southern society. The political conventions that completely disfranchised blacks in the 1890s were the capstone to a momentum of regression rather than progress. It was hardly the future Mayo had predicted.

When faced with this deterioration in southern race relations, Mayo followed a path which was to be taken by many of his fellow reformers. He first retreated to an emphasis on self-help black economic development, and in a series of addresses at Negro institutions in the late 1890s he warned blacks against concerning themselves with political issues and pointless demands for more "rights." By the time he spoke to the graduating class of Alabama A & M in May of 1899, his advice had become a pale echo of Booker T. Washington at his most conservative.[30]

At the same time, his emphasis shifted from the discrimination exercised by white society to the failure of blacks themselves. Few documents are more revealing in this respect than an 1898 essay Mayo published in *Education*. The aging minister warned of the national dangers posed by the "ignorance, superstition, shiftlessness, vulgarity and vice" of the uneducated masses of the North and South. He pleaded for the enactment of a rigid educational test for the new immigrants who crowded Ellis Island and he called for strict new controls on the number of immigrants admitted to the United States. "We must stop the inflow from everywhere that, in one generation would make this Republic the mental and moral sewer of all nations,' concluded Mayo. Gone was any attempt to contrast the problems of the new immigrants with the potential of the former slaves of the South. Together they were linked as a common peril to the Republic. The various disfranchisement provisions enacted by the southern states, the tightened election laws in New England, and the proposals to restrict immigrants were a "simple, sensible, American attempt to prevent that massing of the forces of illiteracy which . . . in every city and in the most cultivated states of the North, no less than in the Black Belt and the mountain wilderness of the South, has already become the peril of the Republic."[31] The South was no longer the nation's problem; it was the solution.

---

30. Mayo, *The Colored American Working Man*; Mayo, *The Opportunity and Obligation of the Educated Class*.

31. Amory Dwight Mayo, "The Significance of Illiteracy in the United States," *Education*, XIX (1898), 34–36.

Although Amory Mayo lived for another decade and continued to write on issues of the day, he never again discussed the South or its people, subjects that had once constituted his life's work. In the absence of other materials on Mayo's activities during the 1890s we can only speculate upon the factors that led to this transformation in his thinking. What seems certain, however, is that his tenacious emphasis upon the "reformative" power of education—a faith that had shielded him from the disillusionment of many Reconstruction reformers—blinded him to the limitations of his own outlook and philosophy. Mayo's vision of a South reborn through the saving grace of public education had proved inadequate to the monumental task of racial readjustment and postwar Reconstruction.

The ultimate failure of this kindly New Englander as a prophet and as a social analyst is a double tragedy, for it reflects both his misjudgment and that of a generation of intelligent, well-intentioned reformers who believed that all things were possible and that social progress was inevitable.

[*Whole Number* 186

BUREAU OF EDUCATION
CIRCULAR OF INFORMATION NO. 1, 1892

SOUTHERN WOMEN

IN THE RECENT

EDUCATIONAL MOVEMENT

IN

THE SOUTH,

BY

REV. A. D. MAYO, M. A.

WASHINGTON:
GOVERNMENT PRINTING OFFICE.
1892

ANALYSIS OF CONTENTS.

PART I.

SCHOOLS FOR THE EDUCATION OF SOUTHERN WHITE GIRLS.

PART II.

NORTHERN AND SOUTHERN WOMEN IN THE EDUCATION OF THE NEGRO IN THE SOUTH.

PART III

Southern Women in the Southern Common School.

LETTER OF TRANSMITTAL.

DEPARTMENT OF THE INTERIOR,
BUREAU OF EDUCATION,
Washington, D. C., January 14, 1892.

SIR: I have the honor to present herewith for publication as a circular of information a work on the subject of the Southern Women in the Recent Educational Movement in the South. It has been prepared by Rev. Dr. A. D. Mayo, who has traveled through the various sections of the South for some twelve years, visiting educational institutions of all kinds, and acquainting himself with the labors and results of the various educational forces. A circular letter has been sent to various authorities soliciting information, and the replies received have been very numerous and satisfactory.

This treatise includes the work of the Southern schools for the education of girls; secondly, the work of Northern and Southern women in the superior schools for colored youth; and thirdly, the common school. It is a notice of the labors of many noble women. Inasmuch as education in our time is coming more and more largely into the hands of the women, the phase herein treated is becoming more significant every year. The body of the treatise relates to the foundation and management of that class of schools which exercises a molding effect on the entire elementary education; for the secondary schools of the South are doing most of the work of educating the teachers. In the case of the colored schools one may say that the secondary schools educate also the preachers who are doing the best work.

Of Dr. Mayo it is not necessary to speak, as he is well known to the literary world and to the educational world as a thoughtful writer on the subject of the social questions branching out from education as a center. He is skillful in literary style of presentation and has himself been for a long time a great power for the uplifting of the teacher and the school. It gives me pleasure, therefore, to transmit for publication this circular of information.

Very respectfully,

W. T. HARRIS.

Hon. JOHN W. NOBLE,
Secretary of the Interior, Washington, D. C.

SOUTHERN WOMEN IN THE RECENT EDUCATIONAL MOVEMENT IN THE SOUTH.

INTRODUCTION.

Early in January, 1891, the United States Commissioner of Education, Dr. William T. Harris, caused the following circular letter from the United States Bureau of Education to be widely distributed through the Southern States of the Union. In this document, as here repeated, the original intention of the author of the present circular of information was fully set forth.

DEPARTMENT OF THE INTERIOR,
BUREAU OF EDUCATION,
Washington, D. C., January 5, 1891.

DEAR SIR: A circular of information is now in course of preparation, entitled "Southern Women in the Recent Educational Movement in the South," by Rev. A. D. Mayo. The object of this publication is to direct attention to the services, especially in the recent elementary and secondary education of Southern children and youth during the past twenty-five years, rendered by the women of our Southern States, who as teachers and friends of this educational movement deserve the approbation of the American people.

This circular will treat of the schooling of Southern children and youth in all varieties of institutions under the direction of Southern women; of schools for the special instruction of girls of all descriptions; of the service of Northern women, especially in the instruction of the colored people; of the growth of recent Southern literature, by female writers; noting the development of associations of women for the promotion of literature, music, and art, with special emphasis on the branch of industrial education bearing upon domestic economy; and whatever social movements may be interesting as an indication of the interest and activity of Southern women in the general intellectual, moral, and religious uplifting of the present generation.

It is earnestly desired that all persons who may receive this letter will at once signify their interest in its object by contributing information bearing upon any portion of this work. All communications should be sent to this Bureau.

Hoping for an early response to this request, I remain,

Respectfully, yours,

WM. T. HARRIS,
Commissioner.

CHARACTER OF INFORMATION DESIRED.

1. Catalogues of all private, corporate, and denominational schools for girls, accompanied with any documents that will throw light on the history of such institutions.

2. Reports of local public schools and State institutions, either for girls or coeducational.

17

3. Information concerning libraries.

4. Literary associations and arrangements for industrial and art education.

5. Reminiscences of prominent female seminaries, celebrated teachers, and educational methods in such institutions previous to 1860.

6. Information concerning the activity of women in the temperance reformation and Sunday-school work.

7. Contributions of fact, or suggestions concerning the preparation of the circular are respectfully solicited.

In response to this invitation, there have been received at the United States Bureau of Education some two hundred catalogues of schools established for the education of white girls in the sixteen Southern States; also an almost complete list of the catalogues of the more important institutions for the training of colored youth, especially those established and managed by the educational boards of the various Protestant Christian denominations in the Northern States. From the schools of the Catholic Church no returns were received. Our own observation, during the past twelve years of a ministry of education in the South, including every State, enabled us to make a considerable addition to this collection of documents. We are aware that these printed sources of information furnish no very reliable basis for an undertaking so broad as outlined in the circular letter of the Bureau. Only such a personal acquaintance with a large number of these seminaries as we have been able to form, during the past twelve years, has enabled us to speak of the system of education for girls represented by this collection of documents with the intelligence and discrimination that gives any value to our undertaking. Whatever of truth in this description, or wisdom in the accompanying suggestions concerning educational affairs in the South, may be found in the present essay is largely due to the unusual opportunity enjoyed by the author for the careful study of the schools, and a friendly and often intimate acquaintance with their managers and instructors and the educational authorities of all these States.

But it soon became evident that our original plan, as set forth in the circular letter, was quite impracticable. No information was received on any topic outside the ordinary line of school work. And although we had gone through all the States of the South during the past twelve years with an eye open to the observation of these matters, yet it seemed unwise, in a period so unique, amid the rapid transition of social customs, to even attempt a simple statement of the rapidly growing influence of Southern women in the various directions indicated in the circular letter. All that could be done in this direction was to treat the general educational question in connection with the environment supplied by the present state of Southern affairs; especially as modified by the Woman's Movement, which is such a notable feature of the present life of all these States.

It therefore became necessary to somewhat change the original plan of this circular of information. On further reflection, it seemed that au honest and careful delineation of the entire realm of educational life represented by the schools for girls in the South, with the peculiar relation of Southern women thereto, as these matters have appeared to the author, would be the most valuable contribution to the cause of Southern education possible under the circumstances. The great need ot our American schools is that this entire realm of the national life should be brought out from the mirage of personal, ecclesiastical, local, provincial, and patriotic laudation, by which our educational estab- lishments are at once magnified to the world and obscured from the truthful judgment of a fair-minded and progressive educational public. The educational affairs of the South, owing to causes apparent to all, are in special need of this treatment. We have honestly endeavored to tell what we have seen ; not as the representative of any pedagogic theory, but as a friend of universal education, equally interested in the work of the teachers and the welfare of the children in every portion of the Republic; more desirous of giving hearty encouragement to sin- cere and capable effort, and bearing generous testimony to what has been achieved, than to emphasize defects that can only be outgrown by a gradual development of what is already well begun.

This circular is therefore little more than a somewhat elaborate review of what we have seen and learned in the twelve years wholly given to a ministry of education in the South, which has included every variety of school, both races, and all classes, in its observations and labors; with the study of all available literature, educational, historical, and social, bearing on this central theme.

As the educational public of the South, so far, has not seriously con- sidered the higher education of woman, either in the woman's college, the annex, or the coeducational university, and the coöperation of women as instructors and managers in this department is very limited, there has been only such reference to this portion of the school life of the South as the arrangements already existing would justify.

The three main divisions of this essay are, first : Southern schools for the education of girls ; second, the work of Northern and Southern women in the superior schools for colored youth; third, the common school. In all these departments of educational activity the women of the South are every year becoming more broadly and vitally interested, and here must we look for the most important manifestation of the in- fluence of woman, through education, upon the unfolding social status of this portion of the country.

In furtherance of the general purpose of the circular it has been deemed advisable, at the suggestion of the United States Commissioner of Education, to include in an appendix several essays, originally pre- pared as lectures or magazine articles, bearing upon the subject of education in the South. All of these are either now out of print as fugitive pamphlets, or hitherto unpublished. These were all addressed to a Northern public, with the hope of giving more intelligent and encouraging information upon Southern affairs than could be gathered from the partisan political press, or is accessible to the occasional visitor to these States. They were written under the impulse of actual observation, and inspired by the spirit of hopefulness that inevitably follows an extended acquaintance with the recent educational movement in the South.

As the only intent of this circular of information is the just appreciation and encouragement of the efforts of the Southern educational public, teachers, and school authorities to face the mighty problem of the fit training of the coming generation of 6,000,000 Southern children and youth for good American citizenship, the author will be grateful for intelligent and sympathetic criticism, corrections of misinformation, and contributions of material that will make a subsequent review of the present essay, or any future work upon the same theme, more worthy of attention.

A. D. MAYO,
25 Beacon St., Boston, Mass.

PART I.

SCHOOLS FOR THE EDUCATION OF SOUTHERN GIRLS.

I.

Under the lofty aspiration for the restoration of National Unity in the years immediately following the close of the great civil war, the people of the Northern, with the formal assent of the Southern, States placed several amendments in the Constitution of the Republic. In their logical and practical application these amendments were a full generation in advance of the actual life of the Northern, and, under existing circumstances and·conditions, for a long time, could only be an ideal to Southern society. No reflecting man can doubt that these ideals will remain and, as the years go on, become a vital element in the life of the whole Republic. But the average Statesman of the most advanced portion of the Union, cradled in the fierce conflicts and demoralized by the doubtful practices of local partisan politics, can not be expected to recognize the fact that, only by a slow and tortuous process of education has the country been lifted to the vision of such an ideal, and only by the evolution of the republican consciousness during successive years, perhaps generations, can this strangely compounded American people be brought to the consistent practice of what has been placed in the fundamental law of the land.

The steadily growing confidence of the most reliable portion of the American people in the progress of the Southern States towards the American order of affairs is not founded on the fluctuations of political parties or the periodical triumphs of partisan platforms. The three radical issues, on whose decision hangs the future of the Republic, are: First, the limit of National obligation to educate American youth for American citizenship; second, the corresponding obligation to legislate for the moral development of the people, as illustrated in the present movement for Congressional action concerning temperance, marriage, divorce, &c.; third, the attitude of the National Government towards the vast and involved demand for the readjustment of labor from the European to the American order of affairs, including the entire questions of tariff, currency, and the claims of the socialistic scheme. Beneath these mighty issues of the near political future, already looming on the horizon and darkening the heavens above the venomous warfare of the political párties, our present partisan conflicts appear petty, superficial, and fragmentary.

The conditions and materials for the consideration of these momentous questions are now being prepared, in all portions of the country; perhaps nowhere more decisively than in the sixteen former slave States. To the very foundations of society; to the readjustment of labor; the development of better home life; and the placing on the ground a complete and effective system for the schooling of all children and youth in the elements of knowledge and discipline essential to good American citizenship, must we look for the most hopeful evidence of this movement through all these Commonwealths.

No proof of the essential American character of the white populations of the sixteen Southern States is so conclusive as the way in which they have grappled with these fundamental questions, with whose solution the very existence of National life is bound up. Essentially Anglo-Saxon in its present constitution; not largely implicated in the difficult problem of educating several millions of recent European immigrants, chiefly of the humbler classes of the Old World, into accord with American ideas and habits; not yet demoralized by the wonderful influx of material prosperity, which has already lifted whole classes of our people to a state of physical comfort and social aspiration hitherto unknown in Christendom and massed wealth in vast combinations that prophesy a new aristocracy in the heart of the Republic; its less-favored class, of both races, in a condition that will allow reasonable time for gradual uplift and adjustment; the Southern people, under a singularly astute and persistent leadership in public affairs, has gone about this work in the historical and conservative method of the great British civilization over the sea. It has resisted, with growing success, every premature attempt to deal with the political and social aspect of Southern society. While some of the methods by which this has been accomplished can not be defended, the ultimate issue of this contention is already apparent. The last outcome of an uplift of any modern people, continued through generations, is the full bestowment of free manhood suffrage and the breaking down of old barriers of pagan caste, by which the mass of mankind has been fenced off from the enjoyment of the upper regions of social life. It was not till the American Republic bestowed the greatest opportunity of modern civilization, manhood suffrage, on the emancipated slaves, that the mother country took the final step toward placing the ballot in the hands of every Englishman. The social emancipation of British society is still a dream of the far-off future. In notable correspondence with the movement over the sea, in the home of Constitutional government, the powerful and able class that, up to the present year, dominated Southern society, has insisted on elbow-room, space, time for that gradual and substantial growth of the educational, industrial, and domestic realms of Southern life, without which all partial and premature adjustments of the political and social problems would only bequeath new embarrassments and perils to future generations.

II.

At last, out from the drifting mists, even amid the rifts of the political storm-clouds, have emerged two realms of the new continent of our Southern life. The attention of the Nation has first been attracted to the fact that, during the past generation, since 1865, the South has been growing a pair of sturdy financial legs and getting a business head on its shoulders. Underneath the inflated rhetoric of the Press, the land agents, and the investors of capital in " booming " towns, have appeared these solid facts: First, that the natural resources of this vast country are a permanent addition to the world's stock of raw material; second, that capital from all the great centers of civilization is steadily flowing Southward for permanent investment; third, that at present a larger proportion of the Southern people is engaged in productive labor than at any previous year in the history of the South.

It is not strange that great statesmen, in their legitimate anxiety that the Negro-American citizen should come into the complete exercise of the suffrage, should hardly appreciate to what an extent he has improved his more radical opportunity of free labor. With the single exception of operative work in the new cotton mills, the Southern colored man and woman are now well on the way to a self-supporting participation in every branch of productive industry. More and more does the negro monopolize agricultural labor and only awaits a better training in methods of farm work and economy to become the owner and cultivator of vast areas of the old South, with a fair share in the possession of its new lands. Through the splendid benevolence of the North he has already received an impetus in the education for the various mechanical trades which has opened the door to this entire realm of profitable labor. The foremost leader of industrial education in one of our most progressive Southern States two years ago told a legislative committee that, unless they speedily went about the generous support of a State school of technology, they must be prepared to hand over the leadership in mechanics to the graduates of these great schools for the instruction of colored youth. Already is the negro woman in full possession of the department of domestic service in the Southern home, and, with the training inaugurated in many Southern schools in skilled housekeeping, she may become the most valuable serving woman in Christendom. An increasing multitude of bright colored boys and girls in all these States are learning a variety of trades and occupations which will fit them to be successful competitors for many of the operative and even skilled industries, in a few years to be fully established.

But the white boy and girl of this region are not idle. In every great educational center of the South the arrangements for industrial education are being considered or placed on the ground for both sexes. At present the Southern boy leaves school at twelve to face the world, and his sister is getting the modern woman's share of the secondary and higher education that, under modern methods of instruction, will develop her capacity for all varieties of skilled profitable work.

In short, the Southern people, of all classes and both races, are making steady progress in the art of getting an honest living and making money—according to Dr. Johnson one of the most religious of human occupations—and are working towards the new industrial civilization with an assiduity and success that compel the attention of the country and the world. And into whatever vagaries of financial speculation and disastrous experiment the masses of the South may be inveigled by ignorant and ambitious political leaders, it can be safely predicted that our Southern American States are in the line of a steady progress towards a powerful industrial civilization that will develop the amazing material resources of their extended country.

III.

Along with this gradual uplift in the field of industrial occupation, we note a decided advance in comfortable living and an improved home life, especially for great numbers of the humbler sort of folk in every portion of the Southern States. It was never understood, outside the limits of the Confederacy, what a complete wreck of Southern private fortunes, amounting to a widespread practical bankruptcy, was wrought by the war. An interesting literature has sprung up during the past ten years, revealing the almost incredible privations of multitudes even of the better sort of Southern families during these dreadful years. We have never been able to put out of mind the fearful spectacle of the crowds of poor white refugees from the border States that, during these years, swarmed the northern shore of the Ohio River, to say nothing of the cloud of "contrabands," all fleeing from actual starvation. This great disaster could be compared to nothing more fitly than the reduction, in a State like Massachusetts, of every family worth $5,000 and upward, to absolute destitution of the means of living, as far as available property is concerned. The noble qualities of this population came out in the heroic endurance of this overwhelming calamity of personal bereavement, poverty, and the failure of a cause which, certainly to the vast majority, seemed worthy of all consecration and sacrifice. The devotion of the slave population during the war, not from fear, but largely with remarkable intelligence of what was going on for their interest, to the defenceless families of women and children, is a bond of gratitude apparent to every observer of Southern society.

Even through the prolonged war of politics which in some of these States held on until 1876, the mass of the Southern people, especially the superior families, were largely absorbed by the problem of self support. If the women of these States ever gave cause for the imputation of laziness, it has been thoroughly disproved by the experiences of the past twenty-five years. Thousands, it is said a full million, of Southern young men, during this period, have left the old plantation life, seeking their fortunes in the new Southwest beyond the Mississippi; the growing towns of the new Northwest, and the cities of the border from New York to San Francisco. The "burden and heat" of this new day has been borne by the devoted mothers and daughters of the rural districts. Amid the distractions of a disordered domestic service, often with destitution of the means of comfortable living, and the confusion of the readjustment of labor—trials that would appal any class of women with less nerve and native cheerfulness—they have gradually brought order out of chaos, and every year are living with somewhat more of comfort, looking to "a good time coming" for the children. The new village and city life that has come up in the true American style, especially in the border and South-western States, is steadily receiving a valuable element of population; the enterprising, ambitious, and aspiring Southern families who desire for themselves and their children all the opportunities of the present American life. Already is one-third of the population of Texas, the latest and most prosperous of all these States, collected in villages and cities. The rapid growth of scores of these new and old centers of prosperity is a surprise, even to our Northern and Western people, accustomed to miracles of similar development.

Meanwhile, thousands of the humbler sort of the white folk, who, under the former dispensation, even in the oldest States of the South, were living in ways for which there was no parallel amid our native American population, have been able to procure land and improve their condition. The poor country school is a boon to many of their more promising youth, awaking a spirit that has led the bright boy or girl out from the shut-up domain of childhood to the wonder land of the new Southern life. In the Gulf States, especially in the old plantation country, the farmers are still greatly oppressed by the intolerable "lien system," whereby the growing crop is mortgaged to the factor in town and the family is compelled to buy its necessities, often at exorbitant rates, of the man who holds it by the throat. This condition of affairs of itself is enough to explain the recent uprising of the Farmers' Alliance and the bitterness of recent political contests in several of these States. It is to be feared that the wild and dishonest schemes of a class of the leaders of this important movement—amounting to a practical policy of wholesale repudiation of debts and scuttling the credit of States and the Nation—will leave multitudes of these honest and credulous people worse off than before. But nature is bountiful in this favored Southland. For the past twenty-five years the people of whole districts of this portion of the country have been living under conditions which would have driven the farmers of any Northern State to desperation, carried through in the arms of the bounteous Southern mother, nature.

IV.

The growing manufacturing and mining enterprises of the South have also afforded the means of improved living to many thousands of the poor white as well as colored people. In all these avenues of labor, the colored folk have a full share of opportunity, with the exception of the cotton mills, which are still operated by the poorer whites. Nowhere is the better side of manufacturing industry, considered as an agency for the elevation of a degraded and poverty-stricken class, so forced upon the attention as in many of these manufacturing villages, in neighborhoods a generation ago inhabited by " poor white trash," squatters, and tramps, living in indescribable ignorance, squalor, and vice. Now these people are gathered into villages, where steady labor has wrought its great reformation ; decent housing has broken up the disgusting huddling of the old shanty life; and good schools and churches, generally supplied by the corporation, have offered to the children the first real opportunity of mental, moral, and social training. Such villages as Graniteville, S. C., Anniston and Girard, Ala., scores of new places in the country, and whole districts in some of the most prosperous cities attest the wonderful improvement of this class.

The numerous agencies of household machinery now being introduced into Southern home life are bringing the facilities for respectable living where it was an impossibility before. The railroad—the American John the Baptist in the wilderness, sounding forth the oncoming of a Christian civilization—is now penetrating the vast mountain realms of the old central South. New towns and settlements are springing up along its path, good families are coming in, and all the uplifting agencies of civilization are found where solitude or a life merging on barbarism had prevailed. The present census will show a decided advance in the valuation of the majority of these States and a corresponding increase of comfort in family life. Yet, multitudes of American citizens—of the less-favored whites and a large portion of the negroes—are still abiding in a slough of physical, mental, and moral despond, a standing reproach to a Christian country, which pours forth its treasures and sends its missionaries to the ends of the earth, while the most dangerous heathen in the world are at its own doors.

V.

Of course, this gradual improvement in the means of living is accompanied by a corresponding advancement in the *morale* of the Southern home. The family life of the superior class of the Southern people has long been their boast. Certainly, in a beautiful personal frankness, social freedom, helpfulness, and the ability to get the most out of the least promising environment, this claim is still borne out. The social ambition, enterprise, and love of elegance in all matters affecting family life will develop a state of society in coming years which will make our American Southland one of the favored spots of Christendom.

But the most evident growth in the upper story of the Southern home is in the improved circumstances, opportunities for education, and social refinement enjoyed by thousands of families who, since 1865, have had their first outlook upon the new world of American aspiration. It is only an ignorant or hopeless view of the fact that still denies the steady improvement in " gentle manners and good morals," even among the average class of the colored folk. Our Southern friends are sometimes too apt to forget the increasing number of these families who are living in respectability, morality, even with many of the refinements and most of the decencies of a Christian home. Swarmed upon as are all the centers of Southern population by the idle, vicious, and shiftless of this race; driven to desperation by the difficulty of obtaining honest and effective house-service; exasperated by the silly and mischievous crowd of " big-headed " youth, whom a little schooling has spoiled for the faithful working habits of their ignorant parents; it is not strange that many of the best Southern friends of the Negro almost despair of the situation. But a more careful and wider view corrects this partial estimate and sees in the steadily increasing number of the better sort of families, in all these States, the formation of that genuine upper class on which the masses below must more and more depend for their uplift into a better social life. It is through this class that the friendly white people of both sections can best serve the masses of the freedmen and contribute to the solution of what is called " the race question." This solution is simply the process of elevating the majority of the colored people to a condition of intelligence, morality, profitable industry, economy, and good home life, where all the higher influences of American civilization can be brought to bear upon their future.

What this enlargement of the Southern home in all classes during the past twenty years signifies, and what it prophesies for the swifter years to come, can be best appreciated by one who, like the writer of this essay, has lived for twelve years in the homes of the people, of "all sorts and conditions," in all these Southern States. During the coming twenty-five years all these good agencies and influences will work with tenfold power towards the day when the full problem of Southern society can be taken up and considered with an intelligence, calmness, absence of local susceptibility, and a breadth of sympathy by the whole American people which is now impossible.

VI.

If we have seemed to linger unduly upon these fundamental conditions of the present Southern life, it is because nowhere are the industrial and home interests of a people more vitally interwoven with all their higher interests than in these States, especially those which suffered most in the ruin of the civil war. And nowhere so notably in this country as there, is that peculiar educational influence dependent on the imperative direction and watchful control of a population just

emerging from a state of servitude, confused between the decay of the
old-time habits and the impractical and inflated expectations born of
the mighty and perilous gift of full American citizenship. There is
little doubt that the cultivated youth of our Northern States often suffer
from lack of the peculiar discipline of this habit of command; the imperious necessity of the direction of an inferior people dependent in a
thousand ways on a superior class. In the Northern States this office
is largely assumed by the Catholic priesthood for a large section of the
humbler class of late European descent. So thousands of our cultivated Northern youth of the better sort are never brought in contact
with any set of people in a relation similar to that which is forced upon
every Southern youth of good family. No education so develops a premature manhood and womanhood—most hateful and offensive if without
good culture and Christian character, but, allied with the better qualities, most attractive, powerful, and largely influential in all realms of
life.

The care of the home, especially in the country during the civil war,
was a great university to the women of the South. The amazing difficulties of the home situation, even to the present day, has trained multitudes of young girls into a womanhood of great promise. The Southern boy who steps out from his brief school life at 12 or 14 to face the
world, amid his peculiar environment gets an educational discipline
that might often be envied by the graduate of the noblest university.
If the most favored lot of any American youth is to be born and reared
where the demands for an effective and noble manhood and womanhood
are most apparent and the horizon is crowded with opportunities for a
worthy success, then is the young man and woman of our Southland in
no condition to be pitied; rather to be congratulated and aided by the
human sympathy and friendly rivalry of his companions in every section of the Republic.

Emphatically true is this of the better class of the colored youth. It
is enough to discredit any young colored man or woman who has enjoyed the opportunities now offered to thousands of the race for a good
education, to be seen hanging about a Northern city, whining and making parade of race disabilities. All disabilities in this life have their
compensations. If this young graduate of Fiske, Hampton, or Howard
can not go to the white man's social entertainment, sit in the parquet
or private box at the theater, and is shut out from the questionable
opportunities of the upper world of fashion, he has yet the supreme
opportunity of manhood; to be the missionary of the higher American
civilization to 7,000,000 of his own people, twice the number of the constituents of George Washington, first President of the United States;
a relation so peculiar that no other American man or woman, sacred or
secular, has anything that quite resembles it.

In these directions must we look for a great educational influence
peculiar to our Southern civilization, if reënforced with good culture

and broad charity—furnishing a university of manhood and womanhood full of rich compensations for the lack of numerous advantages which, without this central discipline, are of doubtful utility.

VII.

In short, it is impossible to obtain a fair estimate either of the recent educational movement in the South or the relation of Southern women thereto, without a careful consideration of the whole environment of industrial, domestic, social, ecclesiastical, and political life amid which this remarkable awakening has taken place. And then, after a tolerably correct overlook of the general features of Southern society has been obtained, there must be taken into consideration the differences in State, local, and even county and neighborhood society. The enthusiastic admirers of the old-time civilization who still demand a distinctively "Southern" education, literature, and manners, obtain little response outside the domain of partisan politics. Even this unity of political action through sixteen States will disappear with an adjustment of the race question, which is steadily coming to pass by the action of agencies over which politics has little control.

There is notable significance in the Gulf State habit of speaking of the border and Piedmont region of the old South as "the North." Northern in any provincial sense these great Commonwealths will never become. Even a much larger immigration of Northern people than now seems probable will not essentially change their peculiar characteristics. But there is a steady growth, in all the more prosperous regions of the South, into an Americanism that, preserving the most valuable characteristics of the old home life, will, as the generations go on, be polarized by the thought that the name "American citizen" is the noblest earthly title and the opportunities of the new national life a powerful stimulant to the loftiest human ambition. Outside a persistent though somewhat wavering devotion to the platform of one political party in national affairs, there are as radical differences between these States as among those beyond the old Mason and Dixon line. These diverse conditions plainly appear in the different measures of zeal and efficiency in the support of the people's common school; proceeding with remarkable vigor in the new Southwest—Texas, southern Missouri, and western Arkansas—but still lagging in the old cotton kingdom, from Charleston, S. C., to the Sabine River. All these considerations must be regarded in any correct estimate of the present educational situation in the South.

VIII.

The large class of illiterate white people that is still found, even in the oldest of these States, must be studied in connection with its history and surroundings in order to obtain a just estimate of this element of population. The old Northern and several of the new Western States have no appreciable illiterate class of the original "native-American" descent. The considerable number of white people that figure in the educational statistics of these States as "illiterates" are almost entirely of recent European or Canadian origin, and their children are rapidly being lifted out of this "slough of despond" by the common and parochial schools. But ignorance of letters implies a special condition of mind in a family shot into American life from the lower strata of Italy, Russia, Hungary, or even the Teutonic civilization of northern Europe, and from the most foreign of all countries, the French provinces of the Dominion of Canada. This family comes to the country with no outfit of knowledge, experience, or ability to get in range of the new American life, and when it is captured, at once, by a political or ecclesiastical "boss" and enlisted in a "grand army," under orders as despotic as the European military service, the chances of a broadening view of American affairs are small. The deliberate vote of a decided majority of the voters of one of our most progressive Northwestern States against the compulsory teaching of the English language in all schools may well be taken to heart by the American people. To this whole class of illiterates the lack of ability to use the language of the country in reading and writing is like a sentence, perhaps for life, to a prison, with no outlook beyond.

But the illiterate farmer of the Southern Piedmont realm, or the ignorant mountaineer, as seen on court day crowding the public square of a Southern upland county town, is a man of another sort. Unless a confirmed tramp, a member of the declining order of "poor white trash," or a criminal, he is a genuine product of the soil, and bears, in every trait of character and mental peculiarity, the stamp of a historic orgin. His grandfather shouldered the "queen's arms" in the Revolution; tramped the awful journey, through pathless woods and mountain gorges with Boone and Sevier, to settle the new Southwest; waded through a generation of bloody warfare to suppress the savage; followed on the heels of "Old Hickory" from the Ohio River to New Orleans; saved the wild Northwest from British occupation, while Washington and the soldiers of the old Northeast were facing the armies of the greatest Empire on the globe upon the Atlantic seaboard. His father was educated by the rough and shut-in life of the upland Southern region, before 1860, when the traveling preacher and backwoods politician were the schoolmasters in the two departments of the American university open for his instruction. Later came along the mighty whirlwind of the war of the sections, marshaling on opposite sides himself and his neighbor; as the conflict swept on, flaming out into neighborhood, family, and local hatreds that even yet burst out all over this vast realm on the least provocation, like half-smothered fires.

To such a man, to whom the title of "free and independent American citizen" is the most precious inheritance; often a sharp trader, a violent lay theologian, and local "ring" politician; not unfrequently a man of substantial native mental and moral worth; the suggestion of disfranchisement for illiteracy would come like the proposition to take the suffrage from the descendants of the Warrens and Adamses of New England, the Clintons and Jays of New York, the Jeffersons and Lees of Old Virginia. Whatever the Southern people may be persuaded or driven to do by the perils of an incompetent citizenship, there will be no serious attempt to separate the white native people on a literary line. The most that can be expected in this direction is, that when the Southern country common school has become as common and as effective as in the North—poor enough even there—a rigorous suffrage law may act as a sharp goad to impel the lazy-going crowd of the ignorant and shiftless to educate their children for good citizenship.

IX.

There are several millions of the Southern Negro population to whom the American epithet of most contemptuous import, "ignoramus," can be applied in no similar sense. Above the lowest strata, still in the bonds of semibarbarism, is a great multitude, mightily stimulated by the aspiration to throw off the incubus of ignorance, looking to education as the magic key that shall unlock the shining gates of a full and free American citizenship. Could the story of the hopes and longings, the prayers and toils and sacrifices of this great body of new-made citizens for the schooling of their children, as we have seen it even in its later phases during the past twelve years, be written out, much more as displayed under the pathetic conditions of the days of early emancipation, it would forever shut the mouth of every man worthy the American name who might be moved to resist, ridicule, or in any way obstruct this wondrous uprising of a race. Whatever may be truly said of the lamentable inefficiency of the average school for the two millions of our colored children and youth; however melancholy the result of the sham education of thousands who have only come in sight of "the little learning" which is "a dangerous thing," still this great movement to lift upward seven millions of American citizens, only a generation ago emancipated from two hundred years of bondage, is one of the most memorable in the history of any country. Especially honorable is it to that portion of the Southern people who have entered into and persisted in this movement in the face of ancient prejudice, financial embarrassment, political distraction, and sectional misunderstanding.

X.

From these lowlands of Southern life, where a full third of its 20,000,000 of people still abide, up through the intermediate realm, even to the cultivated classes, these modifying circumstances already presented, and others hereafter to be pointed out, must be taken into consideration if the student of the recent educational movement in the South is to

come to any reliable conclusion. Outside a small though gradually
enlarging class of the sons and daughters of the more favored in worldly
means, to the vast majority of the children and youth of the respectable
white folk of these States, the pursuit of a good education still remains
a sharp climb up "a steep and rugged way." To appreciate it we must
go back a full half century in the Northeast and a long generation in
the Northwest, and recall the exhausting toils, painful economies, and
patient sacrifices of the country people to save for the growing boy and
girl; the long daily journey to the little district school; the occasional
term at the local academy; the entrance to college with meager outfit
of scholarly preparation and 'the sinews of war;' the weary winter and
summer schoolkeeping to " keep the pot boiling." We have been living
for the past twelve years among people in all these sixteen Southern
States who are carrying on the work of educating their families with
a persistence, self-denial, even a waste of life energy, that kindles the
humblest station with a bright gleam of honor and prophesies all good
things for the future. Even yet a full third of the children and youth
of legal school age—and the mass of Southern youth from fourteen to
eighteen are as surely in need of good schooling as those of more
favored sections from ten to fifteen—are in no useful connection with
anything deserving the name of school. The periodical outbreak of
impatience from the most competent Southern educators over the inefficiency, often the worse than uselessness, of the country district school
through whole States does not exaggerate the fact that, after twenty
years of prodigious effort, multitudes of the children of this section are
not getting even a tolerable allowance of the common heritage of every
American youth—the meager elementary education which will set ajar
the gates of competent citizenship.

So, when the inspector, Northern or Southern, going around reviewing
the present educational facilities of these States with the pedagogical
yardstick of the expert, vents his disgust or indignation at their defects and brands the people as " illiterate" in the sense of that word
at the centers of culture at home and abroad, he misses the very heart
and pith of the whole matter. For this colored boy or girl that works
all day at Hampton school for the privilege of keeping awake to study
after sundown, and, then, after a year of this schooling, must go off to
toil or teach with the fond hope of coming again and again—trying
to do the school work of two years in five—is getting out of that " holy
war" a discipline of manhood and womanhood which many a rich man's
son or daughter, sent to Europe for a " finish," might envy. This tall,
gaunt mountaineer, who " shows up" at Berea or U. S. Grant University without shirt collar, trousers tucked into his muddy boots, leading his blushing sister, cousin, or sweetheart, there to " begin at the
beginning," working up from the second reader and multiplication
table; off and on, going home to work on the new railroad, chop wood,
peddle books, or, like George Washington's old schoolmaster, teach

the little mountain boys and girls all he knows, is in the very state of vital reception which would be the ideal of Pestalozzi; a state where 1 every sort of knowledge sticks, and mind, heart and soul concentrate into the same desperation of purpose whereby Horace Mann fitted for 2 college in three months, Hugh Miller dug his way down to the old red 3 sandstone, and thousands of the world's bravest and best have "taken the kingdom by force."

As we stand before the curious and eager crowd in the Southern graded village school or the country academy to tell anew our "story without an end," we mark the quick rebound of emotion from the seats, the flashing eye of this pale-faced boy, the kindling cheeks of this generous girl, and feel the ebb and flow of the tide of aspiration, hope, and high resolve from soul to soul. That boy is here because a whole family has been denying itself new clothes, home comforts, journeyings, more things than they tell each other, that the promising son may have his chance. That girl will go home to pull up her younger sister or teach a country school, three miles off, through winter mud and summer blaze, to keep her brother in college. These teachers, often of the best families in the county, are living on salaries that would be scorned by the proud *"bonnes"* that swarm the Central Park of New York, or the stylish cooks and chambermaids that march in stately procession to Sunday morning service in Chicago; lending of their little store to the promising scholar of the school, ever turning about in their shut-up life like a tired man in bed to find an easier spot to lie. Three-fourths of the children and youth in a dozen of these States who really think of gaining an education are getting their schooling amid circumstances that are, in themselves, a most stringent and, if rightly understood and used, a most valuable university of American citizenship.

XI.

And to thousands of families, this discipline of toil, economy, and sacrifice for the children is itself the most precious "supplemental educational course;" in middle or even advanced life opening a new realm of observation and experience. The most favored class of Southern students are not exempt from the peculiar influences of the new Southern life; if not stinted in money, often shut in by walls of local and home environment which tell on their entire future. Nowhere in Christendom are 6,000,000 children and youth, the younger third of a great population, coming up to responsible manhood and womanhood through a personal, domestic, neighborhood, and historical experience so notable, in some ways so valuable, in all ways so essential to a just understanding of the educational situation—as in these sixteen States we once called the Southern American Commonwealths. Could the whole story of the Southern educational situation have been disentangled from the everglade of misunderstanding and misrepresentation, cultivated theorizing, and political malignity in which it has been obscured even from the view of the average honest and intelligent observer, no statesman looking to the verdict of history would have put his name on record with the fatal annex, " No," over against the wise and patriotic scheme of National Aid to Southern Education which was finally rejected by the Senate of the United States in the spring of 1890. The name and fame of the men who projected and, to the last, held fast to that great conception are secure and will come forth from the little cloud of present obscuration to lead the way to some even more comprehensive and radical movement of the whole American people to stamp out the illiteracy which is the bottom peril of every American community, from metropolitan New York to the most remote ranch of New Mexico or the glacier slopes of Alaska.

XII.

In no way has the United States Bureau of Education more decisively vindicated its importance than by its persistent effort to make the Southern people acquainted with their own educational history, progress, and present necessity.   Twenty-five years ago it seemed almost a hopeless task to understand the condition of educational affairs, before 1865, even in the oldest of these States.   Probably a large amount of valuable material for such a record had been destroyed during the Civil War.   There were no reliable educational collections in the State archives and even the college and university libraries were scantily furnished with catalogues and historical memorials of the higher class of schools.   We do know enough of the state of education among the lower masses of the white people to discredit the estimates then or subsequently made concerning popular illiteracy.   By the unwearied labors of Henry Barnard and John Eaton, the two first United States Commissioners of Education, a considerable mass of material was accumulated in the library of the Bureau and arranged by its indefatigable librarian, Mr. Henderson Presnell, in a way that, while it inspired gratitude for the immense labor implied in the collection, did little more than reveal its amazing deficiencies.   Under the administration of Hon. N. H. R. Dawson a series of excellent monographs on Southern education, previous to 1860, has been issued, which, fragmentary as they are, have the great merit of directing the attention of Southern school men and statesmen to this interesting field of home inquiry.   It would be a great service both to American education and civilization could the historical department of Johns Hopkins University, to which the Bureau of Education is already so indebted, push these investigations to their last possible result and give the country a truthful history of the school life of the fifteen Southern States before the great war.

Not even the most powerful Northern State, with its large facilities for accumulating statistics through its public-school department, had arrived at any very satisfactory understanding of its own condition in this respect previous to 1860.   But in the fifteen Southern States all the

educational and social tendencies and habits of the people were unfavorable to such an effort.   Outside a dozen State universities and the
free schools of a few of the more prominent cities, there was no organization of the public school system that claimed the attention of legis-
lators through yearly reports of the true educational condition of the
people.   The Southern educators as a class had taken to heart the venerable fallacy that education proceeds downwards from the summit towards the base of society.   It is true, no less in education than in every
realm of human affairs, that the few inspired, highly endowed, and
amply furnished leaders of the race are the guide posts of civilization.
But it is a painful fact that in no age or land has a superior cultured
class been strongly moved by its own impulse to hand down the torch
of good learning to the mass of mankind.   The innate selfishness of our
obstinate human nature is easily satisfied with any superiority of the
individual or a favored class, and finds a thousand plausible arguments
for withholding the inalienable rights of our common humanity from
the majority of mankind.   Thus, while in every country, ancient and
modern, the movement for universal education has doubtless been led
by a devoted group of eminent scholars and thinkers, the organized
higher education of the country has always been the most formidable
obstacle to the reformer.   No illustration of this fact is more striking than England.   With a famous university system dating back
through centuries, a glorious literature, a cultured clergy, a trained
statesmanship, and a habit of constitutional government that led the
old world, even in 1860 there was nothing in England that deserved
the name of a public-school system, and the secondary schools at a later
date, as a class, were declared by the evidence of experts unworthy of the
country.   Until the legislation of the present year no Englishman could
obtain free elementary public schooling for his children without the last
humiliation of poverty—a sworn declaration of inability to pay the
small tuition fee of the present system ; and the House of Lords and the
concentrated interest of the great secondary and collegiate system for
generations barred the way to the establishment of a free public high
school.   It can not be denied that the intelligent masses of the people
in every country have wrested popular education from the powers
above by direct political action upon the Government, as in Great
Britain and the United States, or by an imposing demonstration of the
perils of illiteracy to national existence, as on the Continent.

XIII.

Doubtless our Southern United States had weighty reasons for withholding the free school from even the majority of their white population
in the very constitution of Southern society previous to 1860.   Their industrial system concentrated power and opportunity of all sorts in a
small and extremely able class.   The arrangements for the educational
training of this portion of their people were, all things considered, rea-

sonably adequate to the demands of society. The collegiate and academical schools of these fifteen States were, with few exceptions, denominational, and largely under the influence of the leading Protestant clergy. Many of these were satisfactory to their patrons and some of them of national reputation. The isolation of plantation life made home instruction, through resident tutorship, a favorite resort, or gathered little groups of children in neighborhood private schools. The wealthy families often sent their children to the North or to Europe for superior training. The attempts at an effective system of common schools for the humbler white people were spasmodic and never very satisfactory. The chronic jealousy of concentrated power, even in a State government, paralyzed the efforts of the more zealous and enlightened public schoolmen who urged the dire necessity of universal education upon the legislatures. The growing alienation of the great leaders of political affairs from the Northern policy told strongly against an imitation of the common-school system of that portion of the country. Although the persistent appeals of an influential class of writers, in journals like De Bow's Review, in disparagement of Northern schools, teachers, and educational literature for Southern youth, seemed to have failed to estrange the more intelligent class from the connection with this source of educational supply, there was yet little probability that any of these States would follow the educational lead of the old Northeast or the new Northwest.

To these and other causes must we look for the singular lack of valuable information concerning the educational affairs of the South before 1860. Indeed, the more earnestly the effort is made to obtain a truthful account of this period the more uncertain are the results. This uncertainty is the prime cause of the habit of mutual exaggeration in the attempt to picture the actual state of affairs during this period. On the one hand, the Northern educator and statesman, disheartened at the dearth of reliable data, is inclined to exaggerate the illiteracy of the Southern masses, and depreciate the quality and quantity of the educational facilities in actual operation. On the other hand, a class of Southern educational and popular leaders, who hold to the amiable policy of claiming all things for their civilization in the golden age before the flood, obscure the truth and mislead the public mind by a boastful exaggeration as unreliable and far more mischievous than the opposite. The South can afford to face the plain truth concerning itself at any period of its history. The Southern historian who will patiently and conscientiously gather up the previous movements of its educational life, from the colonial days to the breaking out of the Civil War, will not only confer a lasting benefit on his own section, but enrich the National educational literature with the record of a great people struggling against the disabilities of a vast new country and a peculiar industrial system, slowly feeling its way towards the American idea of universal education; meanwhile, training a superior class which, in executive faculty, in public affairs and social influence, for a time held the acknowledged leadership of the Republic.

XIV

No part of this record would be more valuable than such a picture as might be truthfully drawn of the efforts to educate the entire white population of these fifteen States during the seventy-five years from the revolutionary era to the beginning of the Civil War. Even before the revolt of the thirteen colonies from Great Britain the leading minds of Virginia, with sympathy in other colonies, had fully apprehended the imperative necessity of a public system of schooling for the white people. Thomas Jefferson went further, and outlined in his remarkable scheme a plan for the emancipation of the slaves and their training, by industrial education, for their duties as freedmen, or removal from the country. His comprehensive plans, set before the people of Virginia 8 previous to the Revolutionary war, were substantially approved by the dozen foremost minds of that epoch. Washington, Madison, Cabell, and Marshall, with a heroic following, labored for an entire generation to convince the people of the old Dominion of their necessity. But the gulf between the foremost and the average comprehension of republican society was too deep and broad to be spanned. The ecclesiastical interest concentrated in the leading denominational seats of learning was opposed from the first. The average planter was either too well satisfied with what he could buy for his own household or too skeptical concerning the result of educating "the common herd," to favor such an uncertain experiment. The result of this protracted struggle, one of the most interesting and instructive in American educational annals, through the first generation of the Republic till 1820, was the virtual defeat of Jefferson's plan, with the sole exception of the University of Virginia, the capstone of the edifice. Even this great school was imimpossible in the older part of the State, and the new university arose on its western edge, a prophetic suggestion of the future development of a State university system towards the sunset, even to the remote Pacific coast. Virginia, then as now, was the educational leader of the South, and the history of public schooling in the remaining fourteen States, till 1860, was a repetition of the conflict in the mother Commonwealth.

But it was not without frequent and partially successful efforts, for a broader policy that these States were all found, in 1860, tied fast to the old British system of public education, as far as it could be applied to a new country and circumstances in many ways so diverse. All these Commonwealths, in 1860, were supplied with a State university or denominational colleges of respectable standing, according to the ideas of that educationally far-off period. There were a sufficient number of academical schools, chiefly of the sectarian Christian type, to supply the demand for the secondary education. Of course, in the dearth of common-school opportunities and the low grade of numbers of the private or neighborhood facilities, these secondary schools, though often dignified with the title "college," were largely given to what is now regarded the higher-elementary and grammar-grade instruction in a good Southern graded school. It is impossible to learn the number of pupils sent to the North, instructed by northern or European teachers at home, or educated abroad; but from occasional statements, especially in the older States, it must have been considerable.

XV.

But the most interesting, as well as the most obscure, portion of this record is the persistent effort of leading educators in all these States to establish an effective system of public elementary schooling for the masses of the white people. The glimpses into the dark realm of lower-class illiteracy which opens in twilight vistas along the journey traversed by the historical student are painfully suggestive of an educational destitution not known or not recognized by the educated class. The persistent effort of an eminent group of educational reformers, of whom President Thornwell of South Carolina, Dr. Breckinridge of Kentucky, and Dr. Wiley of North Carolina were illustrious examples, to arouse the public mind to the danger of such a condition, drew a broad avenue of light through the twilight of popular intelligence up to the very year of the war of secession. No volume of greater interest and value to the present condition of the South could be published than a collection of the addresses and a record of the important meetings called in every Southern State by distinguished men for the furtherance of this style of public education.

The Southern free school of this period did not propose to be a "common school" for "all orders and conditions of people." Like the English board school, it was professedly a limited elementary system of public instruction for the large number of children and youth unable to incur the expense of the established collegiate and secondary institutions. In several of these States, in Virginia, Tennessee, North Carolina, South Carolina, Alabama, Missouri, Georgia, and Louisiana, an intermittent, sometimes, as in the case of North Carolina for a few years before 1860, a hopeful success, was achieved. But the whole tide of political policy and the established habit of society worked against the permanent establishment of such a meager system of public education. The schools were so often poor and the conditions of lower caste life so oppressive that they were avoided by the very people for whom the system was established. An American citizen may be ignorant, degraded, full of the prejudices and vices of illiteracy, but the one thing he will not abide is the imputation of "sitting down at the second table" in any public arrangement. Against this and other equally serious impediments this system struggled, swamped in failure or achieving a spasmodic success even more discouraging to the intelligent friends of universal education.

But in several of the foremost cities of the South, in Charleston, S. C., Mobile, Ala., Savannah, Ga., and New Orleans, La., in Nashville and Memphis, Tenn., with greater success in Baltimore, Louisville, and St. Louis, on the border, a city system of public instruction was established, of efficient character, frequently under the direction of eminent teachers from the North, which included large numbers of the more favored class of the population and laid the foundation of the present excellent public schools of all those cities. Especially to this movement in Tennessee and North Carolina is the South indebted for a numerous body of superintendents in the new graded schools in all the Southern Atlantic States, as Virginia still furnishes a large contingent of the professors and presidents of the leading colleges of the Southwest.

XVI.

But it is not to this imperfect ante-bellum system of public education that we are to look for the schooling of Southern girls in the last generation. Up to 1865 there was no coeducational State university in the South. The intermittent and feeble free schools of the open country offered small attraction even for the daughters of the poorer classes. Twenty years ago, visiting a public school in Sheffield, England, I observed with astonishment the inferior dress and general appearance of the girls, for which the characteristic explanation was given by the master; " You must know, sir, that an Englishman, of the class that patronize these schools, gives all he has to the boy of the family and leaves the girl to get on as she can." The lot of the girl of the humbler classes of white people in our Southern States, a generation ago, did not include even the small allowance of schooling granted to the boy. The exception to this habit was the large attendance on the new public schools in a few Southern cities. In each of these an excellent public high school for girls was established. Indeed, one of the most significant results of this movement was the coming to the front of a large class of enthusiastic girls, already waiting for the opening act of the inspiring drama of woman's free education in the Southland.

The secondary schools of these States, established by the different religious bodies, sometimes by private or even municipal associated enterprise, were, during the period that closed in 1860, the chief dependence of the Southern girl who aspired to more than the ordinary home or neighborhood training and was not able to go to more ambitious seminaries in the North or study abroad. In another place we shall endeavor to give a list of the more celebrated of this class of schools which, under the numerous titles, "female seminary," "college," "institute," were multiplied through all the fifteen States south of Mason and Dixon's line, up to the memorable opening year of the great conflict. Here again, the unfortunate lack of valuable statistics prevents a satisfactory estimate of the number, quality, or influence of these numerous and highly appreciated seminaries. A few of the best have preserved interesting records. The grateful recollection of numbers of good women trained in them, and the States and localities blessed by the labors of their more celebrated teachers, might be drawn upon for a memorial of what is rapidly passing out of public remembrance. One of these institutions, the Wesleyan Female College, of Macon, Ga., claims the honor of being the first in the United States to bestow college degrees on young women.

The character of these schools probably did not differ essentially from the same class of schools for girls in the Northern States, although, in the North, there were a large number of coeducational academies. The old-time academy of New England, attended by the ambitious boys and girls of the neighborhood, was the suggestion and model of the American coeducational college. There is no doubt that the instruction in this class of secondary schools was more thorough than in the female seminaries of similar rank ; for the presence of a considerable class of young men, preparing for college, was an incentive to their friends of the other sex. But it must be recollected that the present advanced opinions and elaborate arrangements for the secondary and higher education of girls, in the Northern States, largely represent an educational movement of the past thirty years. A few really superior schools for young ladies, mostly too expensive for general attendance; a smaller number of less expensive colleges or higher class academies, like Oberlin, Ohio, and South Hadley, Mass.; two or three colleges, somewhat reluctantly opened for the admittance of female students; and the new State Normal School of the East, blazed the route of the splendid highway along which the American girl now walks amid the observation and applause of the educational public in both hemispheres. The best arrangements for a general superior training of young women up to 1860, were perhaps found in the upper grade of the State normal schools of Massachusetts. Here was introduced a method of instruction that was destined to supersede the regulation female seminary type of superficial cramming in the solid and rapid " shamming " in the ornamental branches. Some of these Northern schools attracted large numbers of Southern girls. Of these, the celebrated Troy, N. Y., Female Seminary, established and presided over with great executive ability by Madame Emma Willard, was the most celebrated. Even up to the year 1860, as we recall, this school was crowded with the daughters of leading families from all the States of the South.

Some of the home schools of this description were established and taught by Northern educators, like the Central Female College at Clinton, Miss., by Dr. Hillman and others hereafter to be named. Others were under the direction of teachers greatly prized and affectionately remembered at home. But few of them were under the entire control of women. The Southern Protestant clergy during this period were as influential in the direction of the academical and college education of the South as the Catholic priesthood of any European

nation to-day. Especially was the "female college" a special professional preserve. The labors, sacrifices, and devoted services of many
of these men endeared them to this generation of Southern women,
and their affectionate appreciation of their spiritual leaders has hindered the development of the higher grades of the public schools and
largely aided in the rebuilding of the old-time seminary for girls overthrown by the war.

XVII.

The lack of good preparatory home schools and the isolation of family life in the country were a great obstacle to the success of this class
of institutions and hindered the solid education of the Southern young
women during all these years. Even now thousands of these good
girls, eager for educational opportunity, are compelled to come to the
academy so imperfectly prepared in the elements that a thorough secondary education, in the brief period of attendance, is a virtual impossibility. In these earlier years the hindrances must have been even
more formidable than at present. But with all these drawbacks there
was a fair amount of excellent work going on in these numerous female
colleges and seminaries, as the large class of intelligent and accomplished Southern women of that day, trained exclusively in them, at-
tests. One of the peculiarities of the old-time Southern education was
the large number of English, Scotch, and Protestant Irish teachers in
all these schools. Many of them were men of eminent ability. Some
of the Catholic schools of these States, especially those of Maryland
and Louisiana, are said to have had unusual merit. There were also
in every city of the South, and now and then in the villages, schools
of especial value, semiprivate, generally a small number of select students grouped about a teacher of rare ability and notable womanhood.
Would that a picture of this deeply interesting world of the old-time
school life of the Southern girl could be reproduced even as vivid and
vital as is possible for the similar realm of culture in the Northern
States. No occupation should be more attractive to a large number of
young literary aspirants in the South than the gathering up of these
memorials of the dear old days of the mothers and grandmothers, and
presenting them in the simple garb of honest and truthful histories
for the reverent recollection and encouragement of the wideawake
young Southern womanhood of to-day.

XVIII.

But it must be evident to every careful observer of Southern affairs,
for the past generation, that the school life of these States previous to
1860 does not sufficiently explain the remarkable revelation of Southern womanhood subsequent to that critical epoch. Valuable as some
of these schools may have been, and much as a limited class may have
availed themselves of larger opportunities elsewhere, still the question

forces itself upon the observer, to what must we attribute the wonderful display of ability, industry, and patient endurance of the greatest earthly trials by multitudes of Southern women during the war? How account for the marvelous rebound of ambition and energy that, in the twenty-five years since its close, have virtually placed the younger womanhood of all these States in control of the upper story of the new order of Southern society? Now that the old-time assumption of a hereditary social superiority, dating from the colonial era, has been relegated to the domain of romance, the reasons for this condition must be sought in the environment of the woman's lot during the generations before this flood. There must we look for "the hiding place of power" in this episode of the social history of the South.

Our human nature, in spite of its "natural and acquired depravity" and its "often infirmities," has a wondrous facility in adjusting itself to inflexible conditions. What can not be had through the ordinary channels of supply will "by hook or crook" be secured, at least in a partial degree, often by the most circuitous route and in ways incomprehensible to the social and educational pedant. No people on earth has displayed the practical ability to wrench the best things of life out of the most uncompromising surroundings to such an extent as the energetic and aspiring race that formed the bulk of the settlers of the old thirteen American colonies. Neither the southern nor northern Atlantic coast has any special reason to boast of the current of "gentle blood" from the old world mingled with its population previous to the Revolutionary war. In the South it was oftener a hindrance than a help. The leading patriotic class in each of the Atlantic colonies, that seized the reins of public affairs at this crisis and dragged an often reluctant following at its heels through the terrible eight years of conflict, was everywhere composed of the intelligent, progressive "middle interest" that has made the larger Great Britian of to-day. Such a people divines by a swift instinct the essentials of success in education and drives at the heart of the matter through methods inscrutable to the cultured classes.

Nowhere in any civilized country has been seen a spectacle like the career of the women of New England from the landing on Plymouth Rock to the edge of the present half century. For more than two hundred years these women, not inferior to any in the world in the capacity for the noblest culture, devoutly religious, the best blood of the great middle class of the British Islands, worked at the development of one of the most difficult countries ever subdued by civilized man. Exposed to the hardships of a savage climate and a bleak and stubborn soil; with no servant class; compelled to build up their home life from the foundation by the work of their own hands;—such a record of toil, hardship, sacrifice, and suffering, so patiently and silently endured that no adequate picture of it has yet passed into the literature of New England, is without parallel in the annals of any superior race. But out of the heart of this bitter struggle with a hostile environment came the New England womanhood which, more than any other influence, accounts for the astonishing success, in all realms of our American life, of that little corner of the Republic. Those women, out of the meager district school and the county boarding-school, deprived of access to the higher region of liberal culture, conquered the situation. Half a century ago they had become the best informed and most aspiring body of women in Christendom. And when Providence came to the rescue, with the reënforcement of the Irish peasant girl, and labor-saving machinery relieving the awful strain of two centuries on her physical energy, she charged upon and captured, one by one, the most vital opportunities of the new age. She found out three hundred and fifty ways of getting an honest living. She took, as her right, nine-tenths of the positions as teacher in the common school. She thronged the academy, free high and normal schools, and, later, developed a group of the most thorough institutions for the higher education of woman, and persuaded successive legislatures to declare her a voter and holder of office in State, city, and township school affairs. And now, flushed with success, she has placed even Harvard University in a state of siege. The Woman's Annex of that institution "has come to stay"—planted before its gates—till the last American stronghold of exclusive masculine opportunity in university education strikes the flag and the woman's victory is won.

XIX.

We shall never do justice to the Southern sisterhood of the Republic till we recognize in the women of these sixteen States the capable and aspiring native type of character so magnificently displayed in the women of New England and the North. In the South, society, less modified by recent foreign admixture than even the New England of the past generation, was more strongly dominated by obstinate laws of caste than even in the mother country. With no hereditary civil or social privilege, the old-time industrial system of itself drew a practical landmark of social separation, even more difficult to overleap than the wavering line of what Richard Cobden called "the Chinese social caste of Great Britain." Nowhere was the opportunity for educational and social development more persistently withholden from the majority of women of the lower orders than in the older Southern States previous to 1860. Yet nowhere was there to be found a greater body of the sex, of good natural parts, with all the capabilities of womanly advancement, in a condition so unpropitious. On the other hand, the old plantation life, though in some respects favorable to the training of a superior womanhood, was heavily weighted with occasions for despondency, discouragement, and all the temptations that besiege the home of a more favored class. Unfortunately the outside world too often came in contact with that sort of Southern woman which misrepresents any community—the pleasure hunting, selfish, ultra fashionable set, on which all unfavorable influences tell most visibly. The result was that the North, several generations before the war, came to regard the most demonstrative class, the Southern visitors at its summer resorts, as the type of the superior woman of the fifteen Southern States.

XX.

Even in the twilight of the partial acquaintance of the present, one is amazed at the grotesque misapprehension of Southern womanhood that in the generation preceding the civil war prevailed everywhere outside of special circles, especially in the Northeastern States. The day of the omnipresent society editor of the metropolitan journal had not dawned. The growing estrangements of public policy and the preoccupation of the political press with exasperating differences really shut off these fifteen States from the great mass of respectable people through the entire North. The only class of Southern women that was spoken of was the society based on the life of the slave plantation, with the professional classes that at once served and represented it.

The peculiarities, individual, domestic, and temperamental; the local and provincial habits of social life; the lights and shadows of this far-off realm were magnified and distorted, till a notion of Southern womanhood as misleading as the corresponding caricature of what was styled the Puritan society of New England became the established conviction north of Mason and Dixon's line. The eccentricities of individuals, conceits of cliques, and antics of visiting adventurers in Washington and the summer resorts of fashion were transferred to the entire class.

The Southern woman was pictured as an object lesson of feminine self-indulgence and laziness—a sort of barbaric queen, surrounded by her dusky satellites, who anticipated her every whim. Her pet activities were furious secession politics, ultra fashionable excesses, with an occasional cyclone of jealousy or passionate rage over one of the inevitable outbreaks that, like tropical earthquakes, relieved the stagnation of her monotonous home life. With occasional brilliant exceptions ignorant of letters, art, and music, with no capacity for literary production or interest in the great movements for the elevation of humanity that so profoundly excited the serious society of other States and nations, she was pictured rather as the heroine of the sensational novel, or the leading lady of the stage, than as the descendant of Martha and Mary Washington and the group of notable and patriotic Southern dames and damsels of an earlier epoch.

And still, although the opportunities for intimate acquaintance between the people of the different sections are wonderfully enlarged, in the face of the annual march of the army of tourists to "the sunny South" and the growing habit of visitation to the Northern cities, at all seasons, by crowds of eager young Southern women, the old-time notion of the personal and social status of the Southern women remains "a delusion and a snare." I am perpetually questioned, by intelligent and influential people in all parts of the country, concerning the Southern woman of the period in a way that is at once an amusement and an amazement. At the bottom of this misconception is found the extreme difficulty of an impartial and just estimate of an aristocratic and democratic order of society from mutual observation ; and when, as in the present case, the difficulty is exaggerated by the fact that society in the South is an aristocratic in a state of rapid transformation to an American democratic order of affairs, we need not wonder at the popular misapprehension on both sides of the line.

XXI.

But, even at this distance of time, under the greatly changed condition of affairs in the Southern country life, it is possible for a sympathetic and just observer to picture to himself the life of the great body of good Southern women of the old time; the class which in every community deals with the common interest and keeps society alive. The plantation "house-mother" of the years before the great Revolution was, in fact, a most laborious, sorely tried woman, burdened with weighty responsibilities. Instead of the oriental queen, attended by her handmaids, she was the responsible head of a family, made up of all the elements that "try women's souls," in a position requiring the best administrative talent and unflagging tact. The situation, all the time, appealed to her deepest sympathies and taxed to exhaustion the resources of an intelligent and forcible womanhood. Her husband's slaves were a crowd of exacting and dependent children, always at hand, looking to her as the comforter in trouble, the kind mediator in every difficulty, the Lady Bountiful, from whose generous hands descended perpetual showers of the good things that made the condition tolerable and wreathed its darkness with such rainbow hues as its fearful possibilities would admit. How she bore herself during that long period amid the duties of her common life, outside the surface realm of her private opinion, prejudices, and natural preference for her own style of life, is only to be learned, at present, by one who has lived with her now these dozen years, and through the sacred confidences of numberless families has been able to reconstruct that fabric of old-time society that, seen through the lurid splendors of a mighty revolution, now appears the golden age to the imaginative maiden in the seminary or to the grandmother in the dilapidated mansion, sinking away from this life through dreams of the dear old days that can never return. The life of the vast majority of the best women of the South, then as now, was lived far from cities, outside the attractions and temptations of the fierce and splendid metropolitan living of to-day, on the plantation in the country, or in little villages, which were mainly collections of well-to-do people brought together by the public necessities of the county affairs of that far-off period.

XXII.

This country and village life was the real university where was trained the womanhood which was the best product of the old South. The absence of the magnificent opportunities of the aristocratic life of Europe drove the boy of the plantation into the temptations that always beset a leisurely class in a new country—rough sports, a sensual and despotic personal habit, and a perilous opportunity for the abuse of irresponsible power. But, because of this peril from the whole world outside the home, the wife and mother drew closer the cords of restraint upon the daughters of the house. Here was the very heart, the " saving grace" of the old Southern life; the mistress and mother among her daughters and handmaids in her own country house. Though shut up by the inflexible law of the old-time American society from much that is now open to her granddaughter, she did assert and maintain a singular personal independence in her own little domain. What she could not do with the men, she did achieve, all the more surely, with the women of the household. No set of girls in Christendom were watched with more vigilant eyes; more carefully guarded from the sight or even the knowledge of much that was going on about them; more persistently urged by the Christian mother and clergyman to take fast hold on the solemn realities and rely on the divine consolations of religion; in all ways more surely girdled about, as with a wall of fire, from the sensual temptatious of society, at home and elsewhere, than the Southern young women of the more favored sort in those early days.

Many of them were educated entirely at home, often by teachers of superior merit. Large numbers of the most eminent men of the North, among whom in their student days were William H. Seward, Dr. William Ellery Channing, and James G. Blaine, served an apprenticeship as teachers and tutors in Southern families. In our journeyings through the Southern States we often come upon an excellent family whose mother or grandmother came South as a teacher of girls and remained and cast in her lot with the people of the section. And when the daughter of the household came home for her brief outing from school,—after a short run in society, she almost invariably succumbed to the common fate of an early marriage and joined the procession of hard-working, heavy-laden wives and mothers who were the heart and soul of her dear Southland. This life, with all its drawbacks of a narrow sphere of outward activity, inevitable provincial and class prejudice, its terrible strain on the physical energies, and constant trials to the higher moral and artistic sensibilities, had the compensation of a genial social spirit, a proverbial hospitality, a charming personal frankness of manner, and a quick sensibility to exalted sentiment and noble enthusiasm that gave the better sort of our American Southern women an enviable place in society at Washington and opened doors of welcome in every civilized land.

Here, in this peculiar life, destined by its very nature to be temporary—always threatened with the perils of insurrection from below or aggression from outside—did the Southern woman of the dominant class of half a century ago find her real university. Here did she concentrate her native power and plume her restless aspirations. And here did she so prevail in her own sphere of influence that the best manhood of the South fell down and worshiped at her shrine; so that the heroine of the new Southern literature is the woman of the old time, the house-mother, the queen of society, the peacemaker of the neighborhood, the saint of the church.

XXIII.

But the environment of the old social order found its inevitable close. Into this woman's kingdom of the old Southern country life burst the storm of the greatest civil war of modern times, a conflict burdened with more radical changes of the basal structure of society than any in the chronicles of time. As by a terrible black hand, the country in eleven States was swept clean of its effective fighting manhood, leaving the women, children, and slaves in virtual possession of the land. No period of American history is so rich in the materials for a national literature as the condition of these States during the progress of the four years' war. Still largely hidden from popular knowledge, this period abides in the memory of the Southern people of both races with a tenacity that no argument or experience of other conditions can efface.

During these terrible years the Southern woman came to the front as never before, and, like American womanhood in every great emergency, revealed qualities not only of endurance, but of great executive capacity. As the years go on all this will come out in literature, in the recollections of families, in the gathering of local historical materials, but most of all in the impression left upon the generations by this great uprising of the mothers. For this was the awful day of decision, whether the Republic should lose the treasures of womanhood garnered through two centuries of Southern life, now being revealed amid the perils of revolution in such prodigious force of character, henceforth to be evolved into new excellence through the long centuries of constructive American civilization. This episode was the fit culmination of the peculiar style of life which had been the university of the Southern woman from the early settlement of the southern Atlantic coast till the close of the " war for the independence of the South." Happily for the cause of republican society, for the uplift of man through all coming time, an all-wise Providence decreed that only through the living together of the whole American people in " liberty and union, one and indivisible, now and forever," could be realized the highest form of local independence consistent with a Christian nationality in the present age of the world.

XXIV.

During this entire period, the four years of conflict and in large measure through the ten years from 1860 to 1870, the majority of the academical schools for Southern girls were closed. Many of the most celebrated of them, like the colleges for young men, lost their endowments. Their buildings were often either left in ruins or dilapidated; their teachers scattered ; in some cases their properties confiscated or purchased for the new schools of the freedmen. The great majority of this generation of girls, of the best families, in early childhood or born during this decade, came up to young womanhood with only the scholastic training picked up amid the cares, toils, alarms, and conflicts of that terrible time.

Probably a large number of the girls at home obtained something resembling an education, in its way superior to that of their brothers, since the latter were far more-demoralized by the war spirit and more engrossed by the demand of home work. One of the most serious drawbacks to the progress of the South in its upper-story life to-day is the lack of a good common schooling, almost the lack of any schooling at all, by a large class of men who represent this generation of stay-at-home boys. Deprived of the invaluable training that made the intelligent Confederate soldier the most valuable citizen in the reconstruction ; most deeply impressed with sectional and race prejudice; never quite reconciled to the evil fate that deprived them of the glories and sufferings of the fighting days, these people often seem to await a discipline which will open their eyes to what is evident to any thoughtful Southern man who faced the majestic Republic in arms and came home not only satisfied, but in his heart rejoicing, that here was a power impossible to be overset, flanked or warped to any other destiny than the union of all States in a mighty brotherhood of the freedom of all men and the complete enjoyment by all of every essential opportunity of American life.

XXV.

With the close of this bitter conflict came in another era, no less trying to the womanhood of the South; a virtual prolongation of the war in the humiliations, sufferings, exasperations, and despair of the early period of reconstruction. The entire body of slave-owners of the Southern States in 1860 probably did not equal the present population of the city of Boston; and the whole mass of people directly concerned with the institution included scarcely a third of the white population of the section. But no class so few in numbers was, for all practical purposes, so powerful in any Christian nation. It had virtually dictated the political policy of the Republic from the accession of Thomas Jefferson to the Presidency and was all powerful in each of the fifteen slave States. In a brief four years this class, in the full conviction of the truth of its own theory of government and with no doubt of its essential superiority, aspiring to the establishment of a new nationality, was more completely overthrown and permanently disintegrated than any aristocracy of modern times. It is not necessary to recall the doleful era of the transition, from the close of the war in 1865 to the resumption of full political activity by the reconstructed States in 1876. Enough to say that the women of the South, in this as in former trials of the war period, bore the heavy end of the home burden; to the exhausting duties and crushing sorrows of the household life adding the task of comforting and encouraging the returning soldier and toiling for the fit education of the children.

It would seem incredible that, during this period, from 1860 to 1876, including the school age of an entire generation, amid all the discouragements and distractions of Southern life, there still went on a sort of prolongation of the old-time system of education for the boys and girls. But the reader of any one of a score of the memorials of life in the South during the fighting years, describing the marvelous fertility of resource by which that life was made endurable, may picture the devices and schemes for schooling the children through which the old love of letters was maintained. Unhappily, too many of the boys came out of this period with little preparation for the state of affairs that confronted the manhood of the South in those critical years. To this lack of good training in the school and the inevitable demoralization of children in the home incident to a revolutionary epoch must be ascribed, in large measure, the melancholy exhibitions of disorder, especially in dealing with the race question, which still appear in more than one of these States. A portion of the old schools for girls were revived. Others were extemporized. In Virginia and several of the more progressive States the common school was inaugurated as early as 1870, and much more was done than would seem possible to meet the sharp demand even for the limited opportunity of school life enjoyed by the mothers.

But to another class of the white children of the South this experience came, not as the downfall of a lofty ambition and the destruction of a social order, but as a new era of hope. The nonslaveholding white population of the South in 1860 was twice as large as the class we have already described. To multitudes of these people the opportunity of an education in the elements of knowledge was now for the first time afforded. The common schools established by the temporary governments during these years were for them an open door to the temple of instruction. Many of their more promising young people became teachers. From that day has gone on the steady growth of "the third estate of the South," now rising to the political control of every Southern State, and a most notable element in the material prosperity of this section.

Yet to this class the hope of an educational uplift has so far been of small realization. The best common schools of the South are still in the cities and towns. In no State is there yet established a system of country schools satisfactory to any family really moved with educational aspiration for its children. The academies and colleges for white youth, though administered often at a great sacrifice to their teachers and managers, and doing about all that can reasonably be expected for this class of pupils, are still inaccessible to the majority of girls. There are few arrangements for student aid to this class; indeed less, by far, than for the more aspiring youth of the colored race. The problem that now weighs on the hearts of the noblest educators of the South is the establishment of a system of secondary schooling, at once good in itself and cheap enough to attract large numbers of these, the future women of these States, many of whom in time will enjoy material prosperity and, by native force of character and self culture, become influential leaders in society.

I wish it were allowed to print a letter received by the writer of this circular of information from Bishop Atticus Haygood, setting forth the longing desire and imperative need of thousands of the girls of this class in the Southwest and the great hope of his noble heart to establish, somewhere on the border between the lowland and upland realm of the South, a great school of all work, adapted to their limited means and amply furnished for their especial needs.

XXVI

It is therefore easily understood why from the women of its more favored class, who thirty years ago were alone competent to teach, there should have come to the front a remarkable body of instructors in response to the call of these States for the rehabilitation of its old-time system of education for girls. For several years, in some of the States till 1876, the reconstruction governments labored with zeal and a commendable purpose to establish the Northern system of free common schools for both races. In another place we shall trace the beginnings of the great and good work that, inaugurated amid the confusion and perils of civil war for the past generation, has been carried on by the Christian people of the Northern States, through church and private organizations, for the education of the freedmen. It was not strange that neither this nor the corresponding effort of the reconstruction governments for the establishment of the free common school for both races should at first be appreciated by a people in the condition of the population of the eleven ex-Confederate States. The people's common school first came to the South as a part of an overwhelming revolution that had forever destroyed the old order of Southern society, reduced its educated and leading class to poverty, and forced upon a dozen proud American commonwealths a government by their own freedmen, upheld by the national authority alone. The war for the Union really continued more than ten years, and was not closed till the final restoration of self-government to all the revolting States in 1876. A good deal of preliminary work was done, some of it well done, by the temporary masters of the situation, in the establishment of schools for both races, the building of schoolhouses, the expenditure of large sums of money, and the labors of devoted men and women, whose memory is precious at home and compels the admiration of the Christian peoples across the sea. The Peabody educational fund, under the energetic and conciliatory administration of its president, Hon. Robert C. Winthrop, and secretary, Dr. Barnes Sears, was planting the beginnings of the people's common school all over the South. 15

But the special interest of this circular of information is concerned with the beginnings of that great revival, which is described in its title as "The Recent Educational Movement in the South." This naturally began as an attempt to revive the old schools, prostrated or suspended by the war, and to establish, by private effort or the cooperation of the different churches, new institutions to meet the imperious call for the schooling of the youth. The imminent danger in 1865 was that a whole generation of children, rapidly passing into or out of the ordinary school age, would come up without the ordinary opportunities of elementary education; even that the sons and daughters of good families would be flung back a full half century in educational opportunity.

XXVII.

When Gen. Robert E. Lee bade farewell to his defeated soldiers, saying, "Go home and cultivate your virtues," he struck the keynote of the higher American civilization through sixteen great States. When he quietly assumed the presidency of the college established by the bounty of Washington, and linked his own name with that of the Father of his Country in its reorganization, he became an illustrious object lesson of the fundamental need of his section, and set forth the only practical way by which these States could be finally brought into perpetual and patriotic union in the new Republic. Wisely avoiding the stormy realm of politics, he reorganized this institution of learning on the basis of the advanced university education, and gathered about him a faculty several of whom have gone forth to become leaders of the higher education in all the Southern States. Dr. E. S. Joynes, the veteran advo- 16 cate of the public school and the wisest illustrator of its best methods of organization, discipline, and instruction, among the college men of the South; William Preston Johnson, foremost of the university presi- 17 dents of the Southwest, and broadest of all its educators in his wise and profound comprehension of all educational forces in the training of a Southern Commonwealth, with others only less earnest and able, went out from Washington and Lee. And all over the South the most eminent of the surviving military men, who wisely looked to the silent upbuilding of the new Southern life through the educational training of a new generation, followed the example of their venerated commander.

The country has yet to learn its indebtedness to this demonstration of the "brigadier" in the schoolroom. Many of these elderly men were graduates of West Point or Northern colleges before the war. They were found everywhere, from Delaware to Texas, the ablest leaders of the new educational movement, as far as it included the young men seeking the higher and secondary instruction through all these States.

In like manner did the corresponding class of educated women now appear as leaders in the revival of the seminaries for the training of Southern girls. Hundreds of the most cultivated and distinguished women; many of the widows, daughters and sisters of men once eminent in civil and military affairs before and during the great conflict; found their way to the schoolroom. It would be easy to show that almost every celebrated family in the old Atlantic Southern States was represented there by some woman of high social standing, good culture, and eminent character. A list of names that have fallen under the observation of the author of this circular during the past twelve years of his ministry of education through the South would suggest the entire history of these sixteen Southern States for the past half century. The first State institute of the teachers of Virginia, held in the summer of 1880, at the University of Virginia, numbered among its 500 pupils and instructors a representative as complete of the historical families of the Old Dominion as could have been furnished. Some of the best private and public schools of New Orleans have been and are still under the direction of ladies representing the families of Jefferson Davis, Governor Humphrey, Bishop and Gen. Polk, Sargent S. Prentiss, Gen. Beauregard, and others only less eminent. The widows of several Confederate governors and generals were found teaching in private or public schools in all the Southern States. The largest public school for colored children in Charleston, S. C., with its 1,500 pupils, was in 1882, officered by a Southern brigadier, with a full corps of women teachers, of native birth, representing good families in Charleston before and since the war. The widows of Gen. J. E. B. Stuart and the brave Gen. Pickett, who led the final charge at Gettysburg, have been at the head of seminaries for girls in Virginia. Indeed, this feature of the recent Southern school life is so common, that, except for illustration, it would be useless to print the long catalogue of excellent women who, in the hour of educational emergency, obeyed the call of their people; a splendid volunteer army, standing in their places, doing the work and biding the time when the South can put on the ground a complete arrangement for training the teachers of its growing system of elementary and secondary schools.

XXVIII.

It can readily be seen what an elevating and powerful influence this must have been in the opening era of this work of rehabilitation, twenty-five years ago. It brought the highest religious, literary, and social womanly culture in these States in contact, not only with the daughters of the superior families, but often, in the new private and public schools, with the children of both sexes and all classes, gathered in from the highways and byways. In several of the Southern cities—largely in Baltimore, Richmond, New Orleans, and Charleston—the new public schools for colored children and youth were taught by women of Southern birth and training; in some instances by women who had presided as the mistress of the "old plantation home" in the old time. The widow of ex-President John Tyler spent her later years as the matron of the Louise Home for reduced Southern gentlewomen in Washington; and the youngest son of the old statesman is now president of old William and Mary College, revived as a normal college for the training of common-school teachers, with a larger attendance of students than in its most flourishing days of the past. To realize this feature of the great educational movement of the Southern people after the war, we must imagine a region like the New England States suddenly reduced to poverty by the overthrow of its great material interests and the wreck of all private fortunes, with the drift to the schoolrooms and all the benevolent institutions of multitudes of the most cultivated women, to engage in the work not only of supervision, but of ordinary instruction, for an entire generation.

Of course, this feature of the new Southern educational situation is temporary, and will disappear as these States are able to put an effective system of common schools on the ground and rebuild and endow their secondary and higher seminaries and colleges. Already have all these States either actually established or proposed to put on the ground the modern State and city normal school, with its annex, the teachers' institute and Chautauqua Assembly for the summer training in pedagogy. But it will always be held by the educational historian of the South a signal "dispensation of Providence" that in the hour of its greatest need this army of good women rose up and "held the fort" till the people could come to their relief. And this army of "elect ladies" was enrolled from the graduates of that university—the home and family life of the superior class of these fifteen States in existence for a century before the war.

It was from this deep fountain of womanly character, intelligence, and worthy ambition, so long pent up within the limits of the plantation and the parish church, with its chief outlet into the realm of social success, that issued this "woman's movement" of which we write. It was an original movement; as far as any local influence can be said to originate anything of the sort in our country, quite inevitable under the new situation. No body of superior women ever lived faster than the women of the South through the ten years from 1860 to 1870. During the actual continuance of the war they shouldered the upper side of civilization in the eleven Confederate and largely came to the front in the four border States. For the first time in the history of this portion of the country had its women been called to any similar assertion of personal independence, varied executive activity, and supreme responsibility. During the years immediately following the suspension of the conflict of arms the men were so absorbed by the problem of self support, the adjustment of industries and the exasperations and humiliations of the civil interregnum, that this habit of the household went on unchecked, even supported by the gratitude and chivalric enthusiasm of the other sex.

XXIX.

So, at the end of the ten swift years from the close of the armed strife, it was evident to every careful observer that a new woman's day was dawning in the Southland, to become an element of Southern society as permanent as the emancipation of the slave or the upheaval of the mass of nonslaveholding white folks that has so thoroughly agitated the political affairs of the section within the past two years. The movement did not assume at first, and has not yet assumed, the type of the Northern progressive American woman's demand for equal civil rights and opportunities with men. It rather worked along the channels already worn by the older Southern society; at first, through the demand for a broader and more thorough education for the new generation of girls; next, the assumption of a more decided influence in the church; then a deep interest in the moral purification of society through the temperance reformation, and a final push towards the capture of a whole class of industries for women, hitherto unknown to or neglected by the sex.

The beginning of this great movement that has already wrought such powerful changes in Southern society was naturally a demand for the restoration of the old and the establishment of new educational opportunities for the girls. As fast as possible, the old schools, prostrated or suspended by the war, were revived, put on their feet, and filled at once with a crowd of students. The dearth of good elementary schools in the country compelled many of these young women to come to the seminary with small preparation for real academical work, and the lack of means too often gave them but scant time even to get on their educational feet. Of course there was the usual amount of superficial, pretentious, and practically useless instruction in many of these institutions, dignified with high sounding names. But it gradually became known that " the power behind the throne," the thoughtful women in every community, was insisting on a better style of instruction, more solid acquirements, an education that would graduate the daughter better able to teach, to make her own way in the world, to walk abreast with the young women of other portions of the country. Although these schools were still largely officered, and, in their executive details, managed by men, it was apparent that the day when the father of the house and the parish minister could draw a hard and fast educational and social diagram of the Southern woman was passing. The room teaching in these schools was largely monopolized by women. The growing demand for skilled teachers in some cases was bringing in trained instructors from the North; but, oftener, sending the home teachers on their travels during the summer to observe, study, make valuable acquaintances, and return with new and more comprehensive ideas of their work. The seminaries that were managed by eminent women, or in which advanced methods of instruction and more exalted ideas of womanly culture prevailed, received the best material for student life from all portions of the South.

The real impetus of this important movement was in a thousand homes, where the mother, grandmother, and maiden aunt, who had lived through the life of the awful revolutionary epoch, were toiling, saving, scheming to keep the elder daughter in the best school and impress upon her the fact that at the earliest opportunity she must join the ranks of the helpers to lift up the younger sisters, possibly the brothers of the family. These women were probably in no special mood of repentance for the past, and loved the dear old days with all the fervor of an attachment to what is forever lost. Perhaps the full import of what they were doing was not always so apparent to them as to an appreciative and fair-minded looker on; but they felt, in the way a wise and forward-looking woman always does feel, with the force of her entire womanhood, that the past was past and could never return; that the present, with all its drawbacks and disappointments, was not a field strewn with the ruins of a decaying, but a wide lot, piled high with the materials for a coming order of affairs, better and nobler in all opportunities for the mass and not inferior in its ideal for the loftier style of womanhood.

If we were to name the one feature of Southern life, which, during a twelve years Ministry of Education that has been a virtual residence with and study of Southern society, has most compelled our attention, we should, without hesitation, indicate this, *the push to the front of the better sort of Southern young womanhood, everywhere encouraged by the sympathy, support, sacrifice, toils, and prayers of the superior women of the elder generation at home.* We are aware that this will be denied by the loud and blatant class who seem to regard every suggestion of progress in Southern affairs as an imputation on the past or an assumption of superiority by other portions of the country. It is doubtless deplored by a diminishing class, who look on any departure from the ancient order as a step towards social degeneracy. It is not always understood by the people who should be in the most complete sympathy with the movement, especially in the western States, preoccupied with their own prodigious advancement and almost oblivious of what is going on east of the Alleghenies and south of the Potomac and Ohio. It is not fully comprehended by thousands of noble women who are wearing out their life to bring in this new day of the Lord. But coming it is, more rapidly than ever was known in the development of any society so large and complex, with bright omens of hope and cheer not only to the young womanhood of the South but laden with a benediction to American life.

Returning to the special direction of this movement in the rehabilitation of the arrangements for the secondary and higher schooling of young women, we note several characteristics of progress especially observed in the better class of these institutions that have come under our observation during the past twelve years.

XXX.

First. An increasing demand for superior methods of instruction in the common English studies, and a more thorough grounding in the essentials of a solid elementary education. The weak side of our American schooling for girls has always been the neglect of the essentials of scholarship and the furious rage for "high things;" a cheap training in languages, a laborious trifling with the so-called "accomplishments," poor music and unæsthetic art. The South, from its peculiar temptation to make social success the chief end of woman outside the home, has suffered most of all from this educational.heresy. The Northern common school, with all its defects, has kept alive in the mind of the girl, no less than the boy, the importance of making this grounding in the elements the fundamental condition of education. The free high and normal schools have reconstructed the "female seminary" for the last generation, and mightily exalted and broadened the whole realm of school culture for young women. In the South it has only been within the past twenty-five years that, even in the cities and large towns, a substantial system of public graded schools has introduced the natural methods of instruction which so differentiate a superior school of to-day from the past. In the country, outside of favored localities, there has been a lamentable failure to bring these schools up to the needs of the people who really desire a good education for their children. It is often said that the present situation, for this class, is less favorable than the past; since the better sort of families often have not the means to send their daughters from home, and the district school of the neighborhood is of little use. In this emergency, there has been a decided pressure upon many of the leading private and denominational seminaries for girls for a style of organization, discipline, and instruction abreast of the foremost opportunities of the country.

Of course this demand is first responded to by an eruption all over the country of pretenders, shouting the names and the methods of the best at home and abroad. Adventurers from everywhere who could not obtain a respectable engagement at home, cranks and charlatans and educated trumpeters from all lands, have swarmed in upon this portion of the country. A little group of children in a noisy nursery in the home of an impecunious lady hangs out the sign, "Kindergarten." The old-time private school is rechristened, "Normal." Rival denominational seminaries for girls, at best poorly organized primary and grammar academies, confront each other as " Female Colleges," and print diplomas that would astonish Smith, Vassar, Wellesley, and the Harvard Annex. The most lamentable display of this mischievous tendency seems to be in the pretensions of a noisy crowd of foreign musicians, who, with the most sublime assumption, slaughter the time, spend the money, and torment the people with the antics of the musical pupil; unless the portentous development of the regulation "Art Department" may be a rival. But this is an evil that subsides with the progress of sensible home ideas and acquaintance with real schools, where the ambition is to thoroughly work out a moderate curriculum and send forth ? young woman able to help herself along the broadening highway of American culture.

One of the most cheering indications in this department of Southern educational activity is the steady improvement in the better class of these schools for young women, and the increasing patronage of the institutions that have resolutely given in their adherence to this upward movement. Our great Northern cities are swarming through the summer with bright and energetic Southern teachers, often at sacrifice of time, money, and health, spending their vacation in study. They abound at the Summer Normals, Chatauquas, Institutes, and often prolong the visit for a round of observation among the most celebrated schools of these communities. The ablest leaders of these summer schools of instruction in the North are often brought down to the Southern institutes, and come back eloquent with the inspiration of their hearty welcome and full of praise for the splendid enthusiasm, especially of their young women pupils. Several of the best Southern seminaries now arrange a foreign summer tour for their teachers, and an increasing number of young women are now preparing, in the best European and American centers of learning, for work at home.

The new State and city normal schools do better work, each year, and every attempt, by a reactionary political squad, to abolish or cripple this side of the public-school system results in their more complete establishment. Two States, Mississippi and Georgia, have established, and South Carolina is contemplating the establishment of a peculiar seminary for girls, which, under the name of " Industrial and Normal College," under State control, offers freely or at reduced charge, in one institution, opportunity for Academical, Industrial, and Normal training. We have rarely visited a Southern academy for girls during the 18 past ten years that did not have at least one, often more than one, superior woman in the class room, full of zeal and appreciation for the best ways of doing the most thorough and practical work. This tendency was never so evident as at present, and it is full of promise for this department of the new education in the new South.

XXXI.

Second. The inevitable result of this reform in respect to a good elementary training is the modification of the old-time curriculum, in which the energy of a crude mind was exhausted in a tussle with boarding-school Latin; while our glorious mother tongue, with its literature, science, history, and geography, philosophy and pedagogics, were pushed aside for a waste of precious years over a flirtation with opera music and the regulation picture painting, miscalled art. The cornerstone of all valuable studies is a good foundation in " the three R's "; good reading, spelling, grammar, writing, and arithmetic. Much of the so-called higher education in the girls' college of the past was a shirking of real culture from this lamentable inefficiency in the elements. We note a strongly growing appreciation in these seminaries of the value of the broader culture that places a young woman in vital connection with the age in which she lives, the country of which she is a citizen, and the new social condition of which she is a part.

An introduction to the realm of nature-knowledge opens the gates of a wonderland, more enchanting than all the idle vagaries of romance. A taste for good literature is, in itself, a great education. With the present ease of access to books, in connection with this instruction in English and American literature, we mark the growth of the school library, the nucleus of the free public library of the future.

History and geography, combined with the structure of American civil government and political economy, will alone qualify the young woman of the South to realize the true significance of the social problems in which she is involved and save these States from an era of the ignorant and destructive experimenting of machine partisan politics.

In place of the superficial trifling with "high art," we hail the coming in of a genuine training in free hand, industrial, and decorative drawing, with design, which will at once enlarge the popular intelligence in all matters concerning architecture, home building, and the ornamentation of life, and open the door to a career of industrial activity so essential to multitudes of young women in the South. Why the Southern girl should flounder on through humiliating dependence and straitened means into the vortex of a half-enforced early marriage, the greatest social disability, while her sister of the North has at command 350 ways of gaining an honorable self-support until the day when she can deliberately and with womanly independence choose her lot in life, is a vital question. The answer is already being rendered in the steady drift away from that style of female education which lands the girl on the edge of womanhood, a helpless mush of morbid sentiment and a pathetic object lesson of practical inefficiency, a child-woman cast into the arms of the man to whom her life is linked for support and direction in all the great emergencies of life, towards a broad, sound, mental and industrial training, which shall bring to her husband a "help meet for him" and give to society its essential ballast of womanly wisdom and character.

The study of philosophy in connection with physiology, and the application of both to the conduct of life, with the introduction of pedagogy, not only the art of " school-keeping " but of training the young American of the day for American citizenship, is a new departure of inestimable value. In connection with a genuine Christian education; a training in self-control, moral discernment, and " the common Christianity " of the Golden Rule, the Sermon on the Mount, and the law of love; we must look to this for a reform in the go-as-you-please type of family discipline which is casting upon society, at the perilous epoch when the social relations of different races and the blending of all local activities into a new nationality are to be determined, multitudes of undisciplined boys and capricious girls, food for the bigot and the demagogue, a chronic peril to American civilization.

XXXII.

No praise can be too great for the wise educators who are resolutely and persistently shaping the curriculum of the woman's college and seminary in this direction. Their work is really the exaltation of the home education that molded the superior woman of the past, to a broader recognition and a permanent organization in the school life of the country. And not the least advantage of this movement will be its result in bringing the higher education of Southern women into sympathy with the best ideals and methods now prevailing in all civilized lands. The most mischievous obstruction to such education to-day is the narrow crotchet which demands a special education for the South; as if human nature in these sixteen American States were so out of gear with Christendom that its manhood and womanhood must be sentenced to a new century of provincialism. The young Southern American woman of to-day will not and ought not to be satisfied with anything less than a free range through the entire field of the noblest culture of her sex. Thus, with a womanhood so trained, she will best learn the application of the broadest ideals of American society to the peculiar demands and exigencies of her special lot at home.

XXXIII.

Third. Along with this we note with great interest the admirable notions of social training in many of the good women who direct the leading schools for Southern girls. Probably the worst use an American well-to-do family can make of its money is to send a daughter to the regulation "finishing school" as a preparation for "coming out" in polite society. As far as our observation extends, this absurdity is not yet fastened upon the best seminaries for young women in the Southern States. The true leaders of the coming Southern society are now found in the group of wise, cultivated, Christian women who are guiding thousands of girls into an ideal of social life which will save the coming generation from the wild and senseless riot to which our new American wealth is the temptation. In place of the old-time fashionable boarding school, where a girl was " groomed " for a race of social folly, with a " finish " in the sort of marriage to which this life is the prelude, we see in many of these seminaries, in the discipline, instruction, and entire conduct of affairs, the ideal of an education for a genuine American life which prophesies good things for the perilous years to come.

The ideal of social superiority will have more to do with the future of the South, under its present rising ambition for wealth and every sort of enjoyment, than the wrangles of legislatures or the disputations of sectarian theologians. The young educated Southern woman is coming into her own right of mistress of society, and according as that position is filled by the women we now meet as school girls will be the higher life of this portion of the Republic through long years to come. And far more powerful than any influence from the outside world is the steady, quiet, persistent pressure of this group of the true " upper class," the best women who are shaping the coming order of social affairs through a school life they superintend.

XXXIV.

Fourth. Already can be seen the tendency of this broadening out of the ideal of education in the best of these seminaries for young women, in the growth of higher literary and esthetic ideals. There can be no question of the native capabilities of the Southern mind, especially of Southern womanhood, for high achievements in the coming literary and artistic life of the nation. Already are we gathering the first fruits of this interesting development in the shape of a new Southern American literature, no longer shut up in narrow, provincial limits, but, while the outgrowth of the history and conditions of Southern life, truly American in spirit, in vital connection with the highest literary ideals of the present. It is possible that, for the coming generation, the most original literary production will be in this portion of the country. Certainly, nowhere in Christendom are the materials so rich and abundant for a fresh outbirth of poetry and romance or so suggestive in the broad realm of social and civic investigation. We mark with great interest the growth of artistic and musical culture in all these States. The foremost architects of the East and the West, Richardson and 19 Root, were of Southern birth. Many of our rising young people in all departments of esthetics hail from this portion of the country. Hitherto these young people have been compelled to seek the Northern centers of instruction or go abroad for their training or patronage. But now Baltimore, Washington, St. Louis, and New Orleans are becoming notable centers of literary activity and high achievement in music, architecture, industrial and ornamental art. The younger cities are moving in the same direction.

The new opera house, now built in almost every considerable Southern town, is one of the most significant indications of the growing demand for a better style of public amusement. In that people's temple of culture, good music, superior dramatic performance, a higher class of popular lecturing, conventions and assemblies of every sort that bring the leading people of the adjacent country together, are for the first time possible. The closing exercises of the best public and private schools are improving in good taste, being truthful illustrations of what the school life proposes to do, rather than a sham exhibition, made up for the occasion—a grotesque picture of what has not been done.

The South is destined in a near future to become the seat of great wealth and a brilliant society. Whether that wealth and that society shall be at the disposal of a genuine refinement, wielded in the interest of the higher culture, or bring in a new era of demoralizing luxury, social pretension and political corruption, will depend largely on the outcome of this movement inaugurated in the foremost institutions for the training of Southern girls.

XXXV.

Fifth. The reformation and reconstruction of the ordinary primary school of the South has been one of the most important educational achievements of these past years. The venerable humbug inherited from motherland, the old-time " infant school," has been for generations one of the most hopeless weights upon American educational life. The training by a good mother in the life of a well-ordered Christian family is doubtless God's own university for the little child. But when the little one first leaves this natural method of instruction it is of supreme importance that it should be taken up by a school fashioned on the plan of a large family, where the acquisitions of the home life shall be utilized and expanded into a broader training for the larger companion. ship of society and the sterner occupations of practical life. If, at this critical age, the child is cast into the regulation infant school ; a crowd of small children, too often huddled around an incompetent woman, " keeping school " to keep herself alive or to while away the lonely years of a barren widowhood or maidenhood, indulged in all the little caprices, tyrannies, and selfish freaks of ungoverned childhood, taught in the stupid and soul-stifling ways only possible to such a place, with the ever-present degrading spectacle of favoritism and flunkeyism which is so often the moving spirit of success, it is easy to predict the result.

If the competent teachers would tell the tale of their own bitter and almost hopeless experience with the multitudes unfitted for orderly or thorough school work in this paradise of spoiled childhood, we should better understand the failure of even the best public and private schools with pupils of larger growth. Add to this the almost criminal stupidity of foolish parents who permit a child to run wild through the precious years when the foundations of a good education should be laid, a terror at home, a curse to himself, and a nuisance to the community, till he is launched into school a young savage, and we shall have a key to the situation in many a family. The demoralization of the great revolutionary epoch is doubtless responsible for much of this neglect and perversion of youth. The physical conditions of life in the open Southern country are still very unfavorable for the schooling of young children. The toils and sorrows of good teachers, all the way up, to repair the ravages of this neglect and perversion of children through their first eight years, are only known to themselves and God.

We are happy to chronicle the beginnings of a great reform in this matter. The new graded schools in the cities and larger towns have been of inestimable value, especially in the department of primary instruction. It has been demonstrated to thousands of good people since the establishment of this system that young children can be governed, educated, and led through " ways of pleasantness and paths of peace" up to a successful youth and manhood without the chronic peril of the old-time notion of Plato, "a boy is the wildest of all wild beasts." In the new education, as in the true Christian family, we first realize the ideal of the Master, " Suffer little children to come unto me, and forbid them not, for of such is the kingdom of heaven."

This reform has taken a firm hold on the superior schools for girls in its most attractive development. Under the leadership of educators like Miss Blow, Miss Conway, Miss Kelly, Mrs. Seaman, and numbers of like-minded experts of the new education, the primary department in many of these schools is now the most beautiful illustration of the true philosophy of culture in an expansion of a good family, with methods of instruction drawn from the ideal of a true motherhood—the divine method by which the Father of all educates the children of men. The Kindergarten, so often only a name, is coming to a better organization; not a noisy nursery, trampling out the life of a long-suffering "kindergartner," but the method of training best adapted, in our civilization, for use in a good home; elsewhere a vital element of the natural system of primary instruction and discipline upon which all good schooling depends. Here, far more than in the multiplying of facilities for the higher education, will be found the way out of the maze in which the school life of the South has so long wandered in aimless confusion, almost hopeless of good results.

XXXVI.

Sixth. " The building of God, the house not made with hands," we call Education, is one compact structure from foundation stone to ridgepole, and only by the process now outlined can it be honestly and permanently lifted to " nearer commerce with the skies." The natural method of lifting the roof is to place a mighty lever under the mudsills. Then, as the ground floor rises, every story above is raised and the whole house exalted. The reckless and pretentious use of the time-worn maxim, " Education descends from the university," has nowhere borne such bitter fruit as in our own land. It should be said in praise of New England that the fathers of its educational system never fell into the conceit of baptizing common schools with uncommon names. The common school, the high school, the academy, the preparatory school, the college, the university, from the first rose in well ordered gradation. Each department honestly attempted its proper work, and however imperfectly it was done, it did not pretend to be the work of the story above. The one mistake of admitting boys to college on an imperfect preparation, into which some of these minor institutions fell, was atoned for at the expense of the unhappy student thus favored. Of the thirty freshmen in our own alma mater, in the class of 1847, a dozen came from the superior preparatory schools of New England, while the remainder were admitted in various stages of incompetence. But the scheme of instruction was pitched on the highest keynote; with the result that half the class fell out, with wrecked health or from discouragement, before graduation day. But, unfortunately, the new States of the West built up the majority of their higher schools on the false system of calling small things by large names; with the result that, west of the Hudson River, outside half a dozen of the older foundations, the country swarmed with " colleges" which for the first half century of their existence had no standing in educational centers; although good academic and occasionally fair college training was found in their classes and many celebrated public men obtained their only schooling therein. But the better sort of youth must always use the best means of education at hand; whether George Washington, making his own school books at thirteen; Abraham Lincoln, splitting rails to earn the money to pay for the loss of a borrowed volume; or more favored men, graduating from a country academy with an imposing college diploma.

The evil of this system is not seen in the student of unusual natural ability and phenomenal persistence, but in the average scholar, who honestly believes what he is told, and goes forth with college airs, lifted up with the conceit of possessing the higher education, to face the inevitable humiliations of after-life. It is only within the last thirty years that the great Northwest, which has wrought with such prodigious energy in the building of the common school, has begun to place her system of higher education on the solid foundation of genuine college and university work. The great State of Ohio still permits a group of pretentious academies to so obscure the public vision that it seems to remain unable to establish a State Normal School.

XXXVII.

Nowhere has this bad habit wrought such mischievous results as in the Southern States, especially during the recent educational movement of the secondary and higher education. The one false note in the broad

educational scheme of Thomas Jefferson was his imitation of the European organization of the secondary and higher instruction, illustrating
the chronic habit of our Europe-smitten class, which has well been
styled, "adopting half of an European arrangement, with no regard to
fundamental differences in society." When Jefferson fastened the name
"college," on a preparatory village academy and established a "University of Virginia" which, for many years, continued to be a great
crowd of boys admitted to an elaborate elective system of study, often
with the most meager preparation even for a good secondary school, he
sowed the seeds of a crop of institutions that have covered the Southland with splendid educational titles, which are only advertising circulars for students.

Every bad fashion declines to a grotesque imitation at the lower
end of society. The negro girl of fifteen whom I saw with the wreck
of a crimson opera hat tilted on her saucy head, the remnant of an
embroidered sacque tied about her bare and dingy waist, a tattered
cheap calico skirt dangling about her knees, while her bare feet and
legs were half buried in the red mud of the highway, was a fit comment
on the style of young ladyhood that paraded the sidewalk in full dress.
So a thousand little schools, often of small claim to any notice, by their
flashy catalogues and absurd pretensions, caricature the original mistake of giving the name of students of high degree to crude school
boys and girls.

The foremost university and college men of the West and South are
now fully awake to the evils of this educational blunder. Doubtless,
in the majority of these establishments, there is good teaching, often
commendable scholarship, and much that claims the sympathy, even
challenges the admiration, of the fair-minded observer. But there can
be no permanent good and nothing but ultimate evil in educating a
generation of youth into a false estimate of themselves. Calling a
second-rate school a "college" or a great building full of boys and girls
in all sorts of elementary and secondary school work a "university"
is a sham, however valuable may be the institution of its kind thus
developed. But this mischievous practice vitiates all the work done
in this class of schools. It fills their managers with a conceit of superiority that confounds all limitations of good scholarship. It prevents
thousands of boys and girls who need a solid foundation in the elements
from getting even that, while their years are wasted in vain wrestling
with matters above their comprehension. It blinds the eyes even of
intelligent people to the condition of educational affairs in their own
States and communities, and postpones the inevitable waking up of
whole sections of the country to their real condition.

Here, as will be seen further on, we bear cheerful testimony to the
incalculable good wrought in many of these schools. We recognize
the devotion, ability, self-sacrifice of their teachers, and the inspiring
example of the better class of their students. The mistake has not

been so much the fault of the former as the mischievous management of the whole realm of secondary school life; and it is more charitable to understand and more grateful to apologize for it than to hold it up to the reprobation of the educational public.

XXXVIII.

Of all schools, those which undertake the education of American women should be grounded on truth and honesty and drive from their precincts as with a scourge of small cords every form of pretense and sham. For the American woman of the coming generation, whatever may be the theory with which she enters upon her career, will be brought face to face with a condition that will test every faculty and expose every flaw in her preparation for life. And, of all others, the Southern American girl, who in ten years will be found struggling with the most complex and difficult social problems that now confront any people, may well claim that her schooling shall rest on foundations of truth, practical efficiency, genuine character, wholesome physical habits, and healthy aspirations that can not be moved.

Here is the place where the sham we now deplore is especially mischievous, in too many institutions in the South. The boy, however misdirected at school, if endowed with ordinary capacity and push, finds his level among his fellows and in due time is forced to put off his student conceit and put on the most effective manhood at his command. But the girl thus trifled with at school goes out into a hotbed of perilous flattery. From the hour when she receives her lying diploma, in a cloud of " illusion," amid the rain of flowers and the " thundering applause" of the ordinary commencement crowd ; on through the sickening atmosphere of village incense, represented in the local press ; the idol of fond, worshiping friends; lifted on the tide of inflated masculine rhetoric that flows through the disgusting " society column " in the metropolitan journal; her life wavers in a mirage of self-delusion. Out of that realm of falsehood she emerges, often too late, at thirty, with broken health, bowed under the cares of a family she is incompetent to rear, sinking down into the American slough of female invalidism or, worse yet, swelling the throng of foolish wives and mothers who perpetuate their own misfortunes and " glory in their infirmities." And the most melancholy feature of the case is that the girl is not to blame for all this, but is the victim of a system of miseducation which would ruin any generation of youth less fortified by native ability and generous aspirations than the better sort of the young women of our country.

It should be said, in justice, that we find in a majority of the private and denominational schools for Southern girls a growing concern to elevate the work and reduce the pretensions of this class of establishments. But the difficulties in the way of reform are so formidable that it is not strange that they are so gradually overcome. The popular ideal of the secondary and higher education in many localities compels the most faithful teachers to a reluctant conformity. The majority of girls that enter the boarding schools have come up with insufficient primary instruction and are in no condition to begin the work of a sound academic training. They are at an age when the desire to break out of girlhood into the dazzling region of young ladyhood is strongest. Too old to go back to the three R's, they often demand a number and quality of studies utterly beyond their capacity. Along with these "solid branches" they expect to become proficient in music and art. Unless their demands are complied with they are disappointed and inclined to go where the largest pretensions invite them to the indulgence of their wildest expectations.

The faithful student, limited in time and aware of her own deficiencies, too often destroys health and breaks down the educational faculty by overwork. The careless and frivolous push on, in the way best understood by their teachers, who, with one hand strive to implant some good elements of mental discipline, and with the other are compelled to uphold the faltering steps of the pupil on the slippery slope she essays to climb. Many of the girls are spending their last years in this seminary. There is no evidence that another would do more for their real education. There is rarely any endowment of the school, and its corporation or religious denomination insists on the success of numbers sufficient to keep it above debt and expand its facilities. All these things press hardly on the faithful group of men and women who bear the strain of the entire management.

Another evil result of the situation is the growth of the class of sham educational establishments that flood the country with their lying circulars and boastful catalogues; vexing anxious parents with the solicitations of an army of educational "drummers," "bulling" their own and "bearing" rival institutions. That, amid such an environment, bending beneath the load of pecuniary disability, these schools should not often make rapid progress out of their present condition is not remarkable. Rather is it an evidence of the steady progress of vital and honest ideas that so many of the schools for Southern girls should have become so excellent, and their teachers and their work better appreciated in all portions of the country. It is significant that the most reliable of these institutions do not sport the name "college," although many of them have facilities for a good training through the earliest years of college life. It would be invidious and needless to print the names of these admirable seminaries; for their excellence is known of all who are looking for the superior schooling of their daughters, and they are, by all odds, the most successful in the number and quality of their pupils. Nowhere could a generous endowment of money be more useful than in enabling this class of institutions to enlarge their faculty to meet the increasing popular demand for a genuine higher education. No class of worthy American teachers is doing so much good work, for a compensation so small, under so many discouragements, as the teachers of these schools.

XXXIX.

This pressure has at last brought the Southern people to look with partial favor on coeducation, in the higher seminaries of learning. The State universities of Arkansas, Kentucky, Missouri, Texas, and Mississippi, possibly others, now admit girls to all the opportunities and honors of college life. The majority of the new State normal schools are coeducational; some of the most flourishing academies are of the same sort. Unless some of the denominational colleges can obtain the means to occupy the place of Vassar, Smith, Bryn Mawr, Wellesley, and other similar foundations, an increasing number of students will be sent northward every year. It is impossible to state the number of Southern girls now being educated in the academical, normal, artistic, and professional departments of these or similar institutions. It probably reaches several thousand, besides the throng that crowds the northern Chatauquas and summer schools. It will be useless to resist this hegira by a loud and arrogant proclamation of the equal or superior merit of home educational establishments, or to fall back on the exploded notion of a system of Southern school books. The leading educational public of the South is no longer provincial, but National, and proposes to push the effort for the superiority of its own section on the lines of a generous appreciation and emulation of the best everywhere, rather than retreat into a dark corner and blow a brazen trumpet.

In our view it is now only a question of money that hinders the establishment of a genuine Southern woman's university, good as the broadest and best, at some central locality on the border between the lower and upper region of these States. The millions required for such a foundation, acceptable to every girl who can get her hand on two hundred dollars a year, are in somebody's bank account, and the prayers of the faithful will, in due time, transfer them to their own place, a genuine benediction to a people so deserving of friendly aid and so filled with a mighty hunger for the bread and water of the soul.

XL.

Seventh. The secondary school for girls in all portions of our country is now confronted with the necessity of establishing a department of pedagogics. The assumption that has descended from the college and university to the academy, for now these many years, that good scholarship is an all-sufficient preparation for the work of the teacher, is now boldly challenged by the vast majority of competent educators, backed by the protest of sensible parents and public-school men. That the successful student of such an institution is somewhat qualified to imitate the pedagogic work of his own teachers, including their blunders, in the same type of school of which he is a graduate, is not disputed. But the radical changes in methods of instruction in the most conservative colleges and seminaries, including the girls' academy, demand a special training, to be had at present only in a few of the more advanced institutions. It is almost incredible that so few of these important foundations for the higher education of woman, established during the past twenty years, have a satisfactory arrangement for the training of the large proportion of their graduates who intend to teach without the reading of an educational treatise, the hearing of a lecture, or an intelligent conception that there is a science, a history, and a great literature of pedagogics, possibly with an occasional disparaging reference to the entire scheme of instruction known as the New Education. Thousands of these young graduates are sent forth to occupy the most responsible positions, often over the heads of the skilled teachers who are considered indispensable to the primary and grammar grades of the best public schools.

The failure of the free high school to meet the intelligent demand of the educational public is largely owing to the fact that the pupils coming from the excellent lower departments find themselves often in the hands of graduates who never taught school a day and never read or studied an educational book, in profound ignorance of the beautiful ways by which these pupils have come up to them, often contemptuous of everything save the regulation drill of the college whose diploma they hold. A term of this mechanical teaching is enough to quench the ardor and exasperate the soul of the unhappy student, who falls out in disgust or plods on in a realm of dull routine. Our college men, who "have no use for normal methods," meaning the natural methods of instruction wrought out by the highest experience of four thousand years, are hardly aware how these schools of the higher education are depopulated and deprived of multitudes of youth who are thus chilled, wearied, and turned back from a liberal education by this experience in the secondary school. The coming question in all these higher and leading secondary seminaries is the establishment of a department that shall at least put their graduates in touch with their professional work. Some of the State and a few of the denominational colleges and universities have now established a professorship of pedagogics, and the necessity of making a special provision for the multitude of young women who are looking to this profession is forcing itself upon the attention of the managers of the academy.

Nowhere is this necessity so apparent and so imperative as in the South. The public normal school, State and city, has only begun to do its work, and the summer institute is still in its incipient stage. A State like Texas requires an annual supply of 3,000 teachers for its public schools alone, and not 500 are graduated or brought into the State who have received professional training. There is no such waste of public money in these sixteen States as in the employment of thousands of these teachers, who so often come to the most serious professional occupation not only with very inferior scholarship, but almost wholly without special preparation. Without some decisive movement on this line, the voting of additional supplies for public education only means the support of a larger number of educational incompetents for longer terms, fumbling with the children in inferior schools.

There is no surplus of teachers in the North from which to draw a supply even of specialists for the South; and there is no good reason why the thousands of bright and capable girls in these sixteen States should not be able to obtain the preparation for this work. When we consider how easy it would be to establish a department of pedagogics in any of the numerous public seminaries for girls in the South, the wonder grows that it is not attempted. The Peabody educational fund has done its best work in the establishment of the Peabody Normal School at Nashville, Tenn., and in its contributions to the State and city normals and institutes receiving its aid. But the small sum it is able to disburse, less than one hundred thousand a year for the whole South, is but a suggestion of the great need. It is one of the hopeful symptoms of progress that several of these great seminaries for women in the South are now seriously contemplating this demand and we believe the coming decade will see a decided movement in this direction.

XLI.

Eighth. This rehabilitation of the secondary and higher education for Southern girls, not only by the revival of old but the establishment of many new institutions, is all the more significant, since it is almost entirely the work of the educational public at home. Outside of a few hundred thousand dollars contributed to a small number of schools by private benevolence, this great expenditure has been met by the Southern people. And the impetus has largely come from the superior women of the South, who have often pushed on a reluctant community or inspired a lagging church to furnish improved facilities for the education of their daughters. The introduction of the new methods of instruction, the kindergarten and industrial training, have been often due to the zeal of the foremost women of this department of the new educational life of the South. The State of Mississippi owes the foundation of its peculiar institution, the Normal and Industrial College for white girls, to the persistent efforts of a few noble women who persuaded the legislature to its establishment, organized societies in many counties for assisting deserving young women to attend it, stood in its defense through all its trials, and will make it a wise and effective southern arrangement, to be adopted by other States. We hear of organizations for loaning money to needy girls whose success is the promise of the further development of such a beneficent agency for student aid.

XLII.

Ninth. The importance of industrial training, especially in the science of home-making and the various occupations of women, is now a burden on the hearts of many of the thoughtful women of the South. Several organizations have sprung up, in different cities, to further this end. So far these enterprises are confined to the larger cities like Baltimore, Washington, Louisville, St. Louis, Nashville, New Orleans, Atlanta, and Charleston. All good things grow fast among a people so appreciative and enthusiastic as the foremost class of Southern women interested in the education of Southern girls. It will not be surprising if this movement reaches a development in the coming decade that will attract the attention of the whole country. The public school, for many years, outside the leading cities and larger towns, can not do the work of the secondary education. One of the most important considerations therefore is to adjust the work of these denominational and private academies to supplement the best common schools. In this way, with no violent changes, the South may hope to build up a system of good instruction which will offer to all her children and youth the young woman's great chance in life—a fit training for the world's greatest opportunities for good American citizenship.

In the appendix to this circular of information will be found a list of the principal schools of the secondary and higher education for Southern girls accessible to the National Bureau of Education. Special effort has been made to obtain information bearing upon this portion of the present essay. All that has been said in this connection is the result of personal observation for the past twelve years through all the Southern States, including personal visitation to and acquaintance with many of these schools and their leading teachers.

PART II.

NORTHERN AND SOUTHERN WOMEN IN THE EDUCATION OF THE NEGRO IN THE SOUTH.

XLIII.

No experiment in school life within the memory of man is so full of interest and instruction to the educational public of all civilized countries as the attempt at teaching and training the enfranchised Negro for American citizenship during the past thirty years in the Southern States of this Republic. The notable European educational experiments of the past half century have dealt with the lower classes of their native peoples, differing from the ruling orders mainly by their long and obstinate isolation in an inferior position in society. This persistent exclusion from the higher opportunities of life had resulted in a fearful development in all these countries of the weakness and wickedness peculiar to lower-class humanity; including all the constituents of illiteracy; ignorance, superstition, shiftlessness, vulgarity, and vice. But it has still been held by a class of social theorists that the Negro is so fatally separated from the superior races of the world that he is an exception to the laws that govern educational development. Yet it has been demonstrated that his besetting infirmities and vices are in no essential respect different from those of the European races under similar conditions. Indeed, in the most dangerous of them, the sexual infirmity, he does not surpass the lower orders of several European nations, after a thousand years of such personal freedom as has been possible in European society. It was reserved for the American people to deal with this, as with many another social problem declared insolvable or closed to further experiment elsewhere, under conditions so peculiar and on a scale so vast that the result can not be ignored. What, in the opinion of the writer, this result has been, at the close of one generation of this interesting experiment, will appear in this portion of the present circular of information. And it will also be even more evident that, for the most favorable results in this experiment thus far, the country is especially indebted to the consecrated and practical work of American women.

71

Here, as nowhere else in the troubled realm of our later American life, has the effort to develop the best possibilities of a newly emancipated race been somewhat isolated from the fiercer complications of its political and social environment. Neither in the great schools for the Negro established by the Nation and the Northern Christian people in the South, nor in the common-school system for the Negro supported by the Southern people, has there been any exasperating attempt to solve the vexed question of the present or future social relations of the two races. Since the complete restoration of the revolted States to their autonomy in the reconstructed Union, the political element in the education of the colored folk has not assumed special importance. The problem has been to ascertain if the children and youth of 7,000,000 people, of a different race, three hundred years ago a group of pagan savage tribes in Africa, until the year 1865 really held in chattel slavery, practically emancipated only twenty-five years, are capable of that instruction of the head, the heart, and the hand which is the basis of good American citizenship. These favorable conditions have largely been due to the fact that, while many excellent and some very able men have been distinguished figures in this experiment, yet even they have been indebted far more than they are aware to the industry, p tience, tact, practical faculty, and obstinate devotion of the women who have borne the burden of the real instruction and discipline in these schools. The time has not come to unfold the full significance of this advent of American womanhood in the civilization of a body of people now twice as numerous as the entire population of the United States during the presidency of Washington, destined perhaps to an increase as large as the present census of the Union. There are yet so many obstacles in the bitter heritage of the past, the embarrassments of to-day; the malignant strife of sectional politics, especially the lamentable separation of several great American churches on sectional lines, that the historian may well postpone the theme to the cooler and more impartial audience of the future.

But no estimate of woman's work in the recent educational movement of the South will be complete without an honest effort to chronicle this deeply interesting phase of a mighty educational enterprise; to give, as far as possible, an impartial account of the way in which it came up and has gone on during the brief and hurried generation since 1860; to gather out of conflicting opinions and confused experiments some general and reliable facts concerning the results; especially to emphasize the most interesting fact of all, that here is a new and notable demonstration of woman's beneficent influence in our American civilization. And not the least important consideration in this great movement is the fact that here, as nowhere else, have the best things been accomplished by the "working together for good" of the people of both sections, divers churches, and the leading political organizations. For, while the women of the South even yet, on the one hand, do not fully comprehend the profound significance of this mission wrought in their midst by their sisters of the North, or on the other hand recognize what a service has already been rendered to the welfare of Southern society by the young Negro men and women in the common schools; while different classes in both sections are sometimes pushing this work in a narrow spirit of sectarian proselytism and mutual distrust; and while the lower strata of politicians, by their miserable jealousies and malignant misrepresentations, have arrested the wise and benevolent scheme of national aid for the overcoming of Southern illiteracy; and the so-called upper strata of whole sections of the country proclaim a boycott of the New Testament law of love by drawing the social line at a white woman teacher in a negro school; yet the good Providence that has waited on our national development from the first has been calmly superintending and directing all beneficent endeavors for the ultimate good of the children and youth, bringing nearer the time when all these conflicting parties will confess, with wondering gratitude, that they have been the instruments of a higher power.

It is not strange that a work so difficult, gigantic, and original, begun amid the receding waves of a prodigious civil war, should, for a time, have separated its best workers into hostile camps, apparently striving for irreconcilable ends. As a noble fleet caught by a tempest in mid-ocean may be threatened with wreck by collision or blown apart by raging hurricanes, only to find itself together in some far distant haven on another slope of the globe, so the powerful rival forces engaged in educating the Negro for American citizenship, even yet almost incapable of mutual understanding, are destined, even in our day, to a great awakening, when all shall cry out with joyful amazement, " Stand still and see the salvation of God."

XLIV.

The fit appreciation of this educational work depends on some knowledge of its origin and growth. With this view we invite the reader to a brief sketch of the beginning and progress of the effort to educate the Southern Negro successively as " contraband of war," " freedman," and " citizen of the United States," during the past thirty years. With no attempt at detail, the account of this interesting experiment is offered from authentic sources.

Negro slavery was not established in the British American Colonies as a missionary institution, but never in human history was a transformation so vast and rapid effected in the life of any great body of people as in the condition of the ancestors of the seven millions of our Negro American citizens. During the past two hundred and seventy years these people have been transported from a condition of absolute barbarism and paganism in the dark continent, 3,000 miles away, to the only country that had ever been in fit condition to attempt their emancipation and elevation to republican citizenship. For, in spite of the romantic legends which captivate the imagination of some of the historians of this people, our British and colonial fathers, three centuries ago, only knew the Negro as an African savage and pagan, gathered at home into contentious tribes and nationalities, "easy to be entreated" to sell his own flesh and blood to supply the greed of servile labor for a new country. From 1620 to 1808 a steady current of these people was pouring across the Atlantic into our Southern States, how many can only be guessed. The legal suppression of the slave trade, in 1808, only checked the current. The traffic lingered in New England till 1820 and was never entirely suppressed in the Gulf region of the South until the final abolition of slavery. Whatever may have been the horror and waste of life in the transfer, the African slave "increased and multiplied," until in 1860 there were hardly less than five millions of servile and a quarter of a million of free Negro population in the country, all but 200,000 of whom were to be found south of Mason and Dixon's line.

With such a people, so circumstanced, education through books and schools could have little to do. The majority of the Northern States, up to 1860, were shamefully negligent of their duty to their colored people, and schooling was an impossibility for the slaves. In the earlier periods there seems to have been less public opposition to the teaching of the Negroes in the South, perhaps from general indifference to education. But after the first great political division over slavery extension in 1820, with the growth of the abolition sentiment in the North, the lines were more closely drawn. The leading Southern States enacted severe laws against the instruction of the slaves, and, in the absence of law, public opinion forbade it in them all. Later, the free blacks found the slave States no place for comfortable living.

Yet, by the nature of the case, such laws were liable to frequent evasion. The slaves were owned by the cultivated and ruling class of the South. Probably at no time were more than 2,000,000 of its white people directly concerned with the institution. These 2,000,000 largely monopolized the educational, social, religious, financial, and civic forces of fifteen States. With the 5,000,000 or 6,000,000 of nonslaveholding whites, the Negroes had little to do. Thus it was practically impossible to prevent any slaveholder, especially of those who lived in the open country, from giving to favorite servants such instruction as his good nature or sense of religious duty might demand. A considerable number of superior house servants, in this way, picked up a good deal of instruction, and the schooling of free Negroes was not absolutely neglected in the 21 larger cities.

In Washington, for thirty years before the war, there had been persistent and successful efforts to establish schools for the free Negroes. The result of this schooling was a body of remarkable colored people in the District who took up the work with the advent of freedom. The present excellent colored schools of Washington are supervised by the

the son of one of these old schoolmasters, assisted by two young men who were born in freedom in Louisiana. The heroic effort of Myrtilla Miner to establish a normal school for colored girls in Washington was for several years represented by the training school for teachers, built up by an excellent woman of that race, Miss Briggs, born and educated in Massachusetts. The Catholic Church had also done something in this direction in Washington, Baltimore, and Louisiana.

But the chief educational training of the southern Negro before 1860 was in the severe university of slave life. It could not be otherwise than that a savage people thus distributed through the superior class of fifteen republican States should greatly profit by the contact. Apart from occasional exceptions, the condition of these people was not one of special hardship; indeed, it was favorable to the growth of the strongest attachments in the more favored household servants. For more than two centuries the American Negro received the most effective drill ever given to a savage people in the three fundamental conditions of civilized life: First, regular and systematic work; second, the language; and, third, the religion of a civilized country. During the same period the American Indian, in the exercise of a haughty independence, rejected all these conditions and, with exceptions that emphasize the rule, remains a savage to-day.

It was a prodigious step towards civilization when these Africans were put to steady labor and trained even to the slow and unskilled type of agricultural industry developed in the South. Their abler workmen became mechanics, and at present the leading builders in some of the Southern communities are of the same class. The plantation of the Davis families was once owned and well managed by a man who before 1860 is said to have become the commercial agent for the sale of the plantation products in New Orleans. It was another step towards civilization to learn the English language, the great language of freedom. It was imperfectly learned by the masses, but the upper class learned and used it with better effect than a considerable portion of the present inhabitants of the British Islands, and along with this came a marked cultivation from the conversation and social life of the superior sort of white people. The better-off Negro was really the humbler member of the family in thousands of the best homes of the South, and with his great natural aptitude for language and manners his education went on apace.

The most important element in his training was his reception of the Christian religion at the hands of the ruling Southern people. It is easy to ridicule the mixture of pagan and Christian faith which is the actual religion of multitudes of our colored citizens, and they have fallen too easily into the crowning heresy of white Christianity, the separation of religion and morality; but no man except a professional enemy of Christianity can doubt the prodigious influence for good of the religious training of the Negroes in their estate of slavery. The Christian master and mistress, and a large portion, often the most distinguished of the clergy, wrought faithfully on this line; and never was a more genial soil for profound religious impression than the tropical nature, intense imagination, and kindly social aptitude of this child of the sun.

XLV.

So when the ruling class of the South made war for the disruption of the Union and the establishment of a new confederacy, they were not only able to bring in a majority of the nonslaveholding whites, but to control the valuable services of an equal number of slaves for the conduct of things at home. It was not because the Negro was cowardly and stupid that he stood by the South everywhere until liberated by the advancing armies of the North. As fast as the Nation set him free he worked and fought, 200,000 strong in the Union Army, for freedom. But he stood by " the old folks at home," till he saw the Stars and Stripes, as the best thing to do. He loved the women and children, served them with beautiful fidelity, and loves them to-day best of all on earth. Bishop Haygood, the foremost educational observer in the South, declares that the conduct of the Negroes during the war was largely owing to their sense of religious duty. But they were wise enough to know that this " white man's war " was all for them. No body of people, 5,000,000 strong, so circumstanced could have gone through that awful period as they bore themselves, without a most effective schooling in the fundamentals of civilized life, the result of their training in the university of Southern society through two hundred and fifty years.

By one stroke of the pen slavery was abolished, on paper, and by the fall of the Confederate armies, in fact, in 1865. Within the subsequent five years these 5,000,000 emancipated freedmen found themselves citizens of the world's chief Republic, voters, members of legislatures, filling every office but the highest in State and Nation. And, as by a dramatic change of scene, a plantation of the Confederate presidential family became t he property of a family slave, and the immediate successor of Mr. Jefferson Davis, of Mississippi, in the Senate of the United States was Mr. Revels, the first colored member of that body. The fact that this prodigious revolution, apparently the wildest experiment in human affairs, did not swamp the Southern States in hopeless anarchy and destroy the Nation, we owe, first, to the training of the Northern people in republican institutions and the rapid development of the Americani idea of self government which, in 1876, practically forbade the persistence in the insane attempt to govern 15,000,000 of people by their own emancipated slaves. We owe it also to the republican training of the Southern white people, who, through a good deal of violence, did place their State governments right side up and compelled the Northern people to stand by the rule of the upper strata of society.

But now comes in another element in the problem, even yet half developed, *the education of the freedmen for reliable American citizenship*, and this is the last word concerning Southern affairs. If the Southern Negro, within half a century, can be reasonably trained in the education of the heart, the head, and the hand, he will find his own place, and an honorable place at that, in the great brotherhood of our new republican life. Otherwise, the most thoughtful man has the most profound concern for the woes that will befall that devoted portion of our land. The education of the freedmen now involves the whole question of republican civilization in our Southland, not only the success of free labor and free government, but the higher question of the social, mental, and religious progress of the white population of these States; for the grandest work given to any people to-day is the duty and privilege offered to the Southern people to educate the Negro citizen for the Republic that is to come. The effectual doing of this work, with the help of the North and the Nation and the sympathy of all civilized peoples, will lift it into the highest place in the confidence and love of Christendom.

XLVI.

In the stormy years of the past centuries we read of the priesthood of the Catholic church following the conquering armies of the European powers on two hemispheres to convert the conquered peoples to the Gospel of Christ. But in the history of the human race there is no record like that of our great civil war; when, in the very midst of the conflict, the Christian people of the North and the National Government sent forth an army of teachers and poured forth money without stint to carry the knowledge of letters into the very heart of a hostile country, among a population in revolt against the existence of the Union itself.

It was inevitable that, at first, the helping hand thus offered should be taken by the colored people that were thrown across the track of the advancing Union armies. Very early in the war, the Government forces came in possession of large districts along the Southern Atlantic coast, of the city of New Orleans, the valley of the Mississippi as far as Vicksburg, and a good portion of Tennessee. At the same time, multitudes of vagrant freedmen and destitute whites were thrown across the border, often a serious incumbrance to military operations at critical points. With an instinct that seemed to behold the outcome of this great conflict the friends of Christian education in the North pressed in wherever there was an open door.

As early as September, 1861, the American Missionary Association, representing the evangelical Congregational church, opened its first school for "the contrabands," at Hampton, Va. In the following January schools were opened at Hilton Head and Beaufort, S. C. In March, 1862, 60 teachers were sent to the eastern Atlantic coast from Boston and New York and in June, 1862, 86 teachers were at work at various points between Hampton Roads and Hilton Head. The great influx of destitute colored people along this shore compelled the military authorities to appoint Gen. Rufus Saxton to the superintendency of these people in the Carolinas and the work grew apace. In March, 1862, the American Tract Society gathered 50 destitute contrabands in a building near the Capitol at Washington, D. C., with Dr. Johnson for instructor. Under the encouragement of Gen. Wadsworth this school increased and multiplied until more than 2,000 pupils of all ages were being instructed in 1864, partly by act of Congress appropriating a portion of the taxes of the District, but largely by the free gift of the people from the North.

Early in 1862 teachers were sent to Tennessee, who began the work of instruction in the same way. In 1863 the gathering of vast crowds of colored people threatened the most serious embarrassment to the armies of Gen. Grant advancing upon Vicksburg. With the remarkable power of laying his hand upon the right man for important military duty, characteristic of this great commander, Gen. Grant called to his office in Holly Springs, Miss., the young chaplain of an Ohio regiment, the Rev. John Eaton, a native of New Hampshire, teacher in Cleveland, and superintendent of public schools in Toledo, Ohio, and placed in his charge perhaps the most distracting task given to any man in those days: the duty of superintending the colored people through the entire region included in the Army operations. This meant, first, the separation of these people from the active Army, the employment of their effective men and women in various kinds of labor, the support of the myriads of their poor, with an indefinite military authority to do all things possible for their welfare. Gen. Grant had not mistaken his man, and to John Eaton the country owes the largest and most effective system of educational operation in any one district of the Southern States between 1863 and 1865.

Without definite instructions the military authorities in the Valley of the Mississippi began to encourage the teachers from the Northwest. They gave them transportation, rations, opportunities to gather their schools; turned over vacant buildings to their use, and, in various ways, assisted in their work. The desire of the freedmen to learn was something marvelous. In their ignorance they associated knowledge with power, and multitudes of their adult people flocked to these schools. When enlisted in the army, their white chaplains became schoolmasters, and 20,000 of the 80,000 enrolled in the armies of the Southwest were thus taught to read.

The work assumed vast proportions, and in 1866 Col. Eaton had 770,000 of these people under his superintendency, with several subordinate officers in charge, and a vast system of instruction in four States. In Memphis nearly all the colored children of school age were gathered in schools, and multitudes of adults were willing to pay from 25 cents to $1.25 per month for tuition. Within six months the freedmen paid $87,000 for schooling and perhaps a quarter of a million dollars was first and last gathered from their scanty earnings for the instruction of themselves and their children in school. Industrial schools were also opened for women, and orphans were gathered in temporary asylums. The teachers who thronged to this work were an excellent representative of the best mind and heart of the North. Many of the men who went in at that time have become the presidents and principals of important seminaries for both races, and hundreds of the choicest women from Eastern and Western homes gave their time and often their life to this beneficent work.

The poor white people were not neglected whenever it was possible to include them in this dispensation of letters. Indeed, there was never in the history of Christendom a movement that had in it less of any base alloy, more thoroughly born out of the heart of Christian good will, than this spontaneous advance to the educational front by the Christian people of the North.

The churches of every denomination engaged at once in this most Christian endeavor to give the Negro that mental and moral training without which his new-found freedom would be only a curse to himself and a peril to the country. Foremost in this effort was the American Missionary Association, for many years the most thorough, intelligent, and successful of all our Christian agencies for the schooling of the colored race. This association had its central support from the Congregational churches, though, at first, assisted by people of all creeds and assisting wherever its means would permit. The Freedman's Education Commission, including all churches, was established, with branches in the New England, the Middle and the Western States. Large sums of money and vast stores of provisions and clothing were disbursed through these channels. One book-publishing house in Cincinnati, Ohio, sent $15,000 worth of school books to the front for free distribution at the occupation of Nashville, Tenn. The beginnings of the colored school which has since grown to Fisk University were laid in the barracks of that city; and Nashville, which had already gained an enviable reputation for its public and private schools for white people, before 1860, rapidly grew into the great educational center for the Southwest which it has now become.

XLVII.

But already the educational work was outgrowing the ability of the military authorities to control it, while the zeal of rival organizations in the North threatened complications at every point. In 1865 the Government of the United States appeared upon the field in the organization of the Freedman's Bureau. For seven years, under the superintendence of Gen. O. O. Howard, this organization besides doing a great deal of other work was the central agency through which the Government and various organizations among the people of the North and

foreign lands contributed to this great work of education. All funds
in the hands of the military superintendents of freedmen, rents,
licenses, fees from abandoned plantations, and properties of various
sorts thrown into the hands of the Government during the war, were
consolidated into the "refugees and freedmen's fund." The sale and
rents of property belonging to the Confederate States were, by act of
Congress in 1866, turned over to the Freedman's Bureau for the support of schools. Another large source of income was the direct appropriation of money by Congress. From these three sources, beginning
with the moderate sum of $27,000 in 1865, the income of the Freed-
man's Bureau reached nearly a million dollars ($976,853.89) in August,
1870. Between January 1, 1865, and August 31, 1871, when the Freedman's Bureau ceased to exist, the sum of $3,700,000 in money passed
through its hands, which, added to $1,500,000 worth of other than cash
appropriations, amounted to more than $5,000,000 expended under the
direction of the Government of the United States for the education of
the Negro in seven years.

At the close of its labors not less than a quarter of a million of pupils
were receiving instruction in the various schools under its supervision.
Normal schools for the instruction of teachers and the foundations of
academical, collegiate, and professional schools were then laid, which
have since risen to commanding importance in the various Southern
States. There is no record more intensely interesting to every friend
of humanity or more deeply instructive to the student of pedagogy
than the enormous literature which grew up around this work between
the years 1861 and 1871. In the reports of Supt. John Eaton and
others in the early period, and in the subsequent voluminous docu-
25 ments issued by Secretary Alvord, of the Freedman's Bureau, and the
various agents in all the Southern States; in the records of a score of
Christian and other educational associations that vied with each other
and with the Government in this great enterprise, and in the enormous amount of writing in the newspaper and periodical press, Congressional debates, political and educational addresses of the period,
will be found the materials for a volume of thrilling incident and instructive history in the record of that eventful time.

In 1864 Gen. N. P. Banks, in command in Louisiana, made the first
regular attempt to tax the Southern people for the support of a system
of free schooling, and for a time the scheme had as much success as
could be expected under such circumstances, 50,000 colored people having learned to read. During the existence of the provisional governments the national authority was invoked for the protection of these
systems of popular education established in several of these States.

While much can doubtless be said in disparagement of this early effort
to plant the common school in these conquered Commonwealths without the consent of their leading classes of people who were still disfranchised, there is no doubt that much was accomplished in the way of

awakening an interest in popular education among the humbler classes of the people. The men from the North in official position during this period were not veteran schoolmasters, but young soldiers. Their Southern associates in office, of both races, were largely untrained, either in civic or educational affairs. It was a hazardous experiment to impose a complete school system, like that in the North, upon a people who never had enjoyed and were largely distrustful of it, and to support it by a taxation often absurdly beyond the means of the country. In some quarters the attempt was made to force the coeducation of the races. In others dishonesty and ignorance made a wreck of the enterprise. It was well that this great effort to push the cause of popular education finally gave place to the proper activity of the Southern people, restored to their civic duties. Yet this effort, revolutionary as it might be, was largely instrumental in preparing the ground for the work of coming years.

XLVIII.

Meanwhile, it may be well to follow out the work of the National Government incidental to the Freedman's Bureau, and show how far the South is indebted to national interest in education to-day. From 1861 till the present year Congress has given a great deal of incidental aid to education in all these States. In many cases, as at Harpers Ferry, Hampton, and other points, it gave valuable Government property and facilities for both races. At Charleston, S. C., it passed over to the hands of Dr. Porter a valuable property, the United States Barracks, to be used in his admirable school for white boys, the sons of reduced people in that State. Every session of Congress has witnessed more than one grant of this sort for the encouragement of education in the South. Some of the more recent of these appropriations are the gifts of valuable military properties in Fort Smith, Ark., and Baton Rouge, La., also Government swamp lands in Louisiana, and a rich mineral tract in Alabama. All these have been donated outright by Congress for the common school, secondary, and university, and, in one instance, denominational education of white youth.

In 1862 Congress paused amid the tumult of war to make a new appropriation of public lands for the establishment of agricultural and mechanical colleges in all the States, and the sixteen Commonwealths of the former slaveholding region have received 3,420,000 acres of land from this munificent donation. Every State has made some use and several a valuable use of this fund both for its white and colored people. In 1890 Congress supplemented this gift of public lands by voting a sum of money to the agricultural and mechanical colleges of all the States— $15,000 a year at first, increasing in ten years to $25,000, with a proviso that the colored citizens should be fairly considered in the distribution. Every Southern State is now supporting or preparing to support industrial education for the Negro under this form of national aid.

The National Government has also established and contributes largely to the support of the admirable system of public schools for white and colored children in the city of Washington. These schools for colored pupils are a model for all similar communities in the States southwest of the national capital. The system includes all grades, with a high school and training school for teachers of both races, which are attended by many children of the most distinguished officials of the Government, and are, beyond question, the best schools in the city. The Government also laid the foundation of and still subsidizes Howard University, Washington, which offers the most ample opportunity for collegiate, legal, medical, and normal training at moderate cost to colored youth of both sexes from the whole country.

XLIX.

With the close of the Freedman's Bureau, in 1870, the direct action of the National Government upon the growing education of the South came to an end. One by one the Southern States were organizing a system of elementary common-school instruction for both races, which, although painfully inadequate to grapple with the fearful illiteracy of the poorer classes and not entirely in favor with the leaders of public opinion, was yet gaining ground and promised to become the same permanent agency of Southern society as it had long been in the North. The various private and church movements that had been largely occupied with elementary education now gradually withdrew, and for the past ten years there has been no general habit of aiding in the schooling of Southern children below the age of twelve, either by the contributions of money or the supply of teachers from the North. But it soon became evident that, for many years to come, the impoverished Southern people would not be able to offer to the freedmen any general system of secondary or higher education, or even the normal training of teachers to take charge of the common schools for the colored race. And upon this point especially has the Northern private and church work for the freedmen been concentrated since 1870.

The great mass of work now done by the North for the colored people is concentrated in a score of associations, representing the different religious bodies, acting without interference, in a field so vast that there is room enough for all. The Catholic Church has not forgotten its old habit of bringing instruction to the colored people, and is represented in several useful establishments, latterly by the munificent gift of Miss Drexel, for the training of the superior children which are the upper grade of its system of parochial schools. The Episcopal Church seems waking up to the same obligation, and at Raleigh, N. C., supports a flourishing seminary for the training of colored clergymen, besides efforts in various localities through these States. The Friends, in proportion to their numbers and means, for the past thirty years, have done a great deal for both the colored and white children of the South, and still are supporting a considerable number of schools. It is not unlikely that this small religious body has contributed near half a million dollars to these efforts since 1860. The Presbyterian Church, North, now supports 58 schools, with 6,000 pupils, white and colored. Of these, the most important are of the higher sort for the freedmen. The Baptist Missionary Society has several large and flourishing colleges for the freedmen, and its labors and expenditures for the last twenty years must be estimated at many hundred thousand dollars. Several of the smaller denominations, both of the evangelical and liberal churches, have contributed with great generosity; the latter chiefly through the constant donations of their wealthy people to institutions like Miss Bradley's school for whites at Wilmington, N. C., the Hampton, Va., Normal and Industrial Institute for Negro and Indian students, and the excellent Normal Institute at Tuskegee, Ala.

L.

But the most prominent of these agencies has been the Freedmen's Aid Society, representing the Northern Methodist and the American Missionary Associations, chiefly supported by the Congregational churches of the country.

At present the Freedmen's Aid Society supports 21 schools for colored pupils, at an annual expense of $220,000. During the past twelve years $1,577,917 have been expended in its colored and white institutions of learning in the South. Its 21 schools for colored pupils employ 233 teachers and contain 4,971 students. Several hundred thousand children are now being taught by the colored teachers trained in its seminaries. Several of these larger schools have valuable departments for educating ministers, for housework for girls and farming and carpentry for boys, and support an excellent school of medicine. This organization also is establishing schools of superior grade for white pupils, and seems on the point of a prodigious effort to which its present achievement is only the introduction.

But perhaps the most notable success in the secondary, normal, and higher training of colored youth has been achieved by the American Missionary Association. Since the day, in 1861, when it set up its first 29 little school for "the contrabands" in sight of the beach vexed by the first slave ship that landed at Hampton, Va., this association has been indefatigable in developing that peculiar type of academical and collegiate education among the freedmen which has made the Congregational body of Christians so famous in the higher educational life, first of New England, and afterwards of the northern portion of the West. The American common school was established in New England when this denomination was in the ascendant, and it is only justice to say that no body of Christians has, on the whole, been so firm in its allegiance to the common school. At present its labors in the South are largely directed to training superior colored youth of both sexes for the work of teaching in the new public schools. It now supports six institutions called colleges and universities, in which not only the ordinary English studies are pursued, but opportunity is offered for the few who desire a moderate college course. In each, special attention is given to training common-school teachers and in most of them a valuable department of education for boys and girls is under way. There are besides, 73 schools of a less pretentious type, being practically high schools, for the colored people in the larger cities of the South. Last year this association disbursed $287,000 for 13,395 pupils of various grades. During the past thirty years, $10,000,000 has thus been wisely and economically admiministered for the colored people of a dozen States, and probably more than a million children have been taught by its graduates.

LI.

Nearly all these institutions educate young men and women together, and the majority, theoretically, are open to white pupils; but only at Berea, Ky., and a few smaller schools, is there a noticeable mingling of the races. Their school buildings are uniformly the most striking and modern of any in the South, occupying conspicuous positions, often surrounded by spacious grounds, and in many cases including a well-cultivated farm and workshops. Their teachers are almost entirely white people from the North, although colored and white Southern teachers are being introduced. They all require tuition fees, and the larger schools furnish board, in spacious dormitories, where the young women are instructed in domestic pursuits. The ordinary expense is usually within $100 a year, and a considerable proportion of their pupils are able, by work at the schools and teaching at vacations, to raise that sum, although the majority are more or less supported by student aid from the North. The presidents, professors, and teachers in all these schools are an excellent representative of American schoolkeeping, the men and many of the women being graduates of leading colleges, normal schools, and higher institutions. Through all these schools is constantly passing a throng of distinguished visitors from North and South, who contribute valuable addresses and sometimes courses of lectures. Several years ago the Congregational and Baptist schools were placed under the able supervision of superintendents of instruction, and all are rapidly improving as educational institutions. They are all under the most pronounced Christian influence, each with its church affiliation, and the moral, religious and social training is perhaps the most valuable part of the work.

It is impossible to estimate the widespread influence of this group of 22 colleges and 100 normal and academical schools, dispersed from Harper's Ferry to Texas, with 25,000 of the superior young colored people under instruction. No less than $15,000,000 have, first and last, been put into this special work. Already the leading people of the South are thoroughly awake to the great value of these establishments. Each of them includes distinguished Southern men on its board of trustees and the States of Virginia, West Virginia, South Carolina, and Mississippi make an annual appropriation for the industrial and normal departments of several of them.

At present the chief support of this class of schools comes from the North. Within the past few years large sums have been contributed for new buildings and facilities, Mrs. Valeria Stone of Massachusetts being one of the largest contributors. Mr. John F. Slater, of Connecticut, made a bequest of $1,000,000 for the education of colored youth, and a corporation similar to the Peabody education fund, with ex-President R. B. Hayes for president and Bishop Atticus Haygood, of Georgia, and Dr. J. L. M. Curry, of Washington, as secretaries, has been formed for the distribution of its income. Mrs. Mary Hemenway, 30 of Boston, has been conspicuous among the large number of Northern women who have been known as generous contributors to these institutions. Mr. Rockerfeller has largely aided Spelman Seminary, in Atlanta, Ga., and United States Senator McMillan, of Michigan, has 31 made a generous contribution to the Mary Allen school for colored girls in Texas. The most conspicuous of these recent gifts is the great donation of $1,000,000 by Mr. Daniel Hand, of Connecticut, to the American Missionary Association, to be used largely for student aid. Indeed, it would be impossible to do justice to the wise and persistent benevolence of the Northern churches and individuals, moved by the Christian and patriotic impulse of training these 2,000,000 of colored children and youth for American citizenship. The present policy of all these associations seems to be the development of these great colored seminaries for the permanent use of the South, encouraging the Southern people to unite in their management and support, until they shall become the future universities for the higher professional and industrial education of the superior class of the colored race.

In this way have the North and the Nation extended the helping hand to the South in giving, first, to the freedman the elements of knowledge, and, of late, that higher training which has raised up a body of many thousand colored teachers, clergymen, and enlightened young people, who are now the most powerful agency in the new leadership of the race.

When it is objected that all this schooling, above the primary grade, has been of little value to the Negro, the objector forgets that no people can get on without a head; a genuine aristocracy of character, intelligence, and executive power. The head that the great body of our colored citizenship will ultimately follow is not found on the shoulders of any class of white men. The American white man can do, just now, but one radical thing for the colored man, outside respect for his equality before the law, and that is to help him to that education which shall develop a genuine upper class which will lead him to his own place in American affairs.

LII.

With the information afforded by this brief sketch of the rise and
progress of this vast adventure of educating the American Negro for
his new American citizenship, I now proceed to record my own experience in a twelve years' careful observation of that portion of the work
especially in charge of the Christian churches and people of the Northern States. In a subsequent chapter of this circular I will treat of
the corresponding effort of the Southern people, in the establishment
and support of a system of free common schools for the Negro in every
State, now supplemented by normal and industrial training for the same
race.

In the winter of 1880, after a previous summer tour of observation in
Virginia and North Carolina, I finally entered upon the "ministry of
education," which for the past twelve years has engrossed my entire
energies and carried me into all the sixteen States once known as the
South. I came up to this deeply interesting ministry through many
years of observation, study, journalism, lecturing, and service on educational boards of all departments of school life that occupied the leisure of a crowded ministry in the Universalist and Unitarian churches
in the Eastern, Middle, and Northwestern States. For the past twelve
years the Southern work in the field has occupied two-thirds of each
year, the remaining months having been spent in the equally important
service, through speech, the press and private communication, of giving
to the Northern educational public a truthful account of Southern life,
as far as it is involved in the great educational movement for the last
twenty years; the most interesting and characteristic feature in what is
sometimes called the New South. The work done in the Southern States
has almost entirely been "a labor of love," including the visitation and
careful observation of all varieties of educational institutions, constant
school talks to children and students of every age, courses of lectures
to teachers in all classes of seminaries, common schools, normal schools,
and institutes, with frequent public addresses and preaching and constant intercourse with all classes of people of both races. For six years
this work was combined with an important position as chief editorial
writer in the New England and National Journal of Education, and the
press of all sections has been with great unanimity opened for my use.
A small library of pamphlets has also been written and distributed containing the results of my observation; two of these published by the
National Bureau of Education. Several of these pamphlets, now out
of print, by the suggestion of the United States Commissioner of Education, are included in this circular, as throwing additional light on the
subject and further illustrating the work of Southern and Northern
women in this department.

It should be said, in justice to my own religious denomination, that,
for the past twelve years, this ministry of education has been supported

by the American Unitarian Association and benevolent men and women, chiefly with a view to its operations in behalf of the common-school system and the education of the colored people. It should be understood, in this connection, that, outside its own theological schools and a somewhat indefinite connection for a time with Harvard University, Antioch College, Ohio, and an occasional undenominational academy, the Unitarian is the only Christian church in the country that has never seriously attempted the work of what is called denominational Christian education. Its distinguished representatives in the educational field, following the leadership of Horace Mann, in every State, have been foremost in the support of the people's common school and every phase of popular education. It is, therefore, perfectly in the line of this educational policy that the present representative of this ministry of education has been probably the only educational missionary supported by the people of one religious denomination for a work through the Southern States entirely disconnected with theological or ecclesiastical obligations, the primary object of which is the development of the American system of common schools, in their best practical methods of operation, in every community of these sixteen States. The universal approbation with which this ministry has been received by all classes of the Southern people, with full understanding of its meaning, is one of the most significant indications of the steady growth of public confidence through all these great Commonwealths in the people's common school; a warning that may well be taken to heart by every class of the opponents of this, the most radical, essential, and indestructible of the foundations of republican government and American society.

LIII.

Under these circumstances, I have regarded it a subject of personal congratulation and an evidence of a growing liberality in the religious public that, through the past twelve years, almost every religious denomination—Christain, Hebrew, or Ethical—has cheerfully afforded me the most ample opportunities for my work, with constant invitations for public addresses on every day in the week. But the most valuable of these opportunities have been found in the universal invitation to visit every class of educational establishment, with the most thorough opportunity for observation of their work; with friendly and even confidential communication with their teachers and managers. The first invitation of this kind, and one of the most important in its results, was the proposition in the year 1880, the first year of my continuous work, by the American Missionary Association (Congregational) and the Freedmen's Aid Society (Methodist) to visit all their mission schools for the Negro in the Southern States, deliver courses of lectures to their students and teachers on the art of instruction, meanwhile carefully inspecting their entire educational management. These schools were established in every Southern State at the most vital centers, and in no way could such correct information be obtained concerning the entire status of the Negro population of the South as by this familiar communication with their students, drawn from every portion of this vast area. For two years this engagement held, only suspended because the special work contemplated was accomplished. It involved a residence in these institutions during a considerable portion of these years, with every opportunity for close observation. It was soon apparent that, without official invitation, I was expected to visit the similar schools of all the religious denominations of the North on my line of operations, with substantially the same opportunities.

The intimate connection with this class of schools was no bar to the most friendly reception by every class of educational institutions through these sixteen States. Armed with the best testimonials, I placed myself at once in connection with the public-school authorities, State, municipal, and local. I also found the "latchstring out" of every important private and Protestant denominational and collegiate school for white students in every Southern State, with opportunities for observation and work only limited by personal ability. I was constantly among the new Southern common schools for the Negroes, and in constant and friendly relations with the educational public of the section. In this way I was saved from the chronic temptation to a partial view, enabled to compass the entire circle of life in which the question of Negro education is involved. Meanwhile I have never lost my hold on this body of Northern Mission Schools, which still remains practically the citadel of the whole system of the schooling of the seven millions of these people, furnishing a large majority of their superior teachers and professional leaders.

I regard it a peculiar advantage in the just estimate of this department of Southern education that I have been able to study it from a point of view singularly favorable. I have traversed all the Southern States as an educational observer, fully committed to the most advanced ideas of universal education, with no question concerning the essentials of American civilization; with as little partisan, sectarian, or sectional prejudice as is consistent with a devout belief in the religion of Jesus Christ and an immovable faith in American republican civilization; with a sincere and growing appreciation of and affection for all classes and both races of the Southern people.

My first impression of Negro education at Hampton, Nashville, Memphis, New Orleans, Austin, Montgomery, Talladega, Atlanta, and other important centers of the secondary and higher instruction was a profound astonishment at the intelligence, mental vivacity, teachableness, remarkable subordination to discipline, and general good conduct of the pupils in all these great schools. During these first two years I probably saw in them 10,000 colored students in all the Southern States east of the Mississippi, besides Texas. I found in them all an audience for my familiar lectures, not alone on school work, but ranging through the whole theme of their new American citizenship, which gratified me by its intelligent and responsive appreciation, and let me into many of the secrets of effective public speech. Since those years I have rarely prepared an educational address, even for a Northern university, which has not been "tried on" as a familiar extemporaneous talk before a colored audience; and the talks that most deeply interested them have proved to be, with due elaboration, the most acceptable to the critical student crowd in the college chapel or the great assembly on commencement day.

LIV.

I was constantly asking myself and everybody I met, how this condition was to be explained? These students were generally from the superior class of colored people, at least the class which had the greatest desire for good schooling. But, as late as 1880, they were chiefly the children of parents who had once been enslaved, with small opportunity for scholastic treatment at home and receiving little advantage in the poor country schools from which they came. They had not been so long under the influence of their present discipline as to be essentially changed in these particulars. It was the first of the numerous puzzles in Negro education which I encountered, and I doubt if I should so soon have begun to unravel this tangled skein had I not all this time been among the people who, in some respects, know more of the general capabilities of the Negro ; certainly have been more intimately connected with him, than the people of the North. I found the more zealous of the workers in these schools quite carried off their feet by this phenomenon which, along with the mysterious "magnetic" quality of the race, often seemed to involve the whole life of their teachers in a mental and spiritual mirage, in which all things were magnified, and these children of nature loomed up as a new-found superior race. Not only was it claimed by many of these teachers, especially the religious workers, that the Negro student was as capable as his brother in white of every grade of mental training, but in religious capacity was actually the superior of the American white child and youth of European descent. Many of the Northern churches and communities were lifted to a strange and powerful enthusiasm by the fervid reports of this class of workers, enforced by the interesting platform exercises and pathetic singing of the troups of traveling students that usually accompanied the missionary. It was certainly a temptation to the young college graduates, often soldiers, who were appointed to the supervision of these great schools, to believe the testimony of their enthusiastic subordinates concerning their new constituency. They honestly enough assumed the titles—president and professor—in institutions christened by the most venerable educational names—college and university—and governed essentially on the same plan as Harvard, Yale, and Princeton. It was no disparagement of these teachers, often gathered from the best schools of the North, always drawn from a good social class, frequently representing the most distinguished society, that in the mental and moral intoxication of this singular environment, possessed by a consecration in which religious and patriotic considerations were intimately blended, they should be swept along the swift " tide of successful experiment." Successful it was, in a striking degree, in the enthusiastic desire for education and the sacrifice it inspired in thousands of these young people, their parents and friends ; successful in the devoted and exhausting toils of their faithful teachers—living under the same roof, bound with a tie almost as close as the family relation to this palpitating crowd of dependent, affectionate and exacting boys and girls ; uniformly successful in the glorified reports of the work before excited congregations of Northern Christian people, trained by fifty years of missionary support in foreign lands, elated by the still recent triumph of the national arms, emancipation and reconstruction in the South, ready to put forth more money and receive with distinguished honors their own children and friends returning from the Southern field for the usual summer campaign at home.

LV.

But I could not fail to see what an advantage it would have been at the early stage of this great enterprise, could these workers have been brought into friendly relations with the superior class of the Southern people, who within twenty years had been the masters and mistresses of this enslaved race, and who had periled and lost their all in an honest and heroic defense of Southern society as it existed up to 1860. It would have given these new comers the inside view, without which the most vital facts concerning a people so circumstanced can not be correctly known. It would have somewhat cooled the ardor of the early enthusiasm, dimmed the rainbow hues of many a splendid prophecy, but also have saved many a noble man and woman from the reaction into a disappointment and disgust as misleading as the mount of exaltation from which they had descended. Still, only in this way could the marvelous fact of this wonderful liveliness and eagerness of mind and undeniable capacity for many sorts of information find an intelligent explanation.

But, unhappily, this intimate communion even with the Christian people of the South had not then become possible, and even to-day is very imperfectly established. I found a group of admirable Southern men, as often laymen as clergymen, in all these educational centers, with a remarkable appreciation of the service rendered to the South by these schools ; ready to welcome all the sensible teachers and workers to a personal acquaintance that often ripened to friendship ; in all practicable ways standing between the schools and the majority of the community. And there were " noble women not a few " who, in spite of the disparagement of society and the indifference or hostility of the churches, persisted in a close communion with the corresponding class of these workers, always ready to aid to the uttermost of their power.

But the work was so exacting in itself, the situation of the majority of the schools so remote from the residence of the better sort of people in the towns, and the home and outdoor duties of their Southern friends so overwhelming, that less came from this acquaintance than could be hoped. And it must be remembered that some of these workers were neither qualified by previous culture nor breadth of view to appreciate anything beyond the immediate task at hand. This class regarded themselves, honestly enough, as persecuted apostles in heathendom; often interpreting as slights, neglect, and malignant opposition what had no such real intent. At all events this was the situation in 1880. And such, in a modified degree, it remains, after the growing mutual understanding of the past ten years.

But meanwhile the more thoughtful educational and religious public at the North has learned to put a more sober estimate on the accounts of this work by its immediate workers; while direct opposition and unfriendly feeling in the South has gradually subsided, with a decided movement in State and church among the Southern people for building up institutions of the same grade for the same object. Indeed, several of the more important of these great seminaries are already under a mixed management of Northern and Southern trustees, or subsidized by the States or communities in which they are established.

LVI.

But the radical problem still remained unsolved. How should I account for the condition in which the better sort of these students presented themselves at these schools, or even for the singular aptitude of considerable numbers who came up from the most unpromising surroundings? One reasonable explanation could only be found; the previous training of the colored people through their generations of servitude, especially by the Southern women and the clergy.

Whatever may have been the original aptitudes or disabilities of the native African, three centuries ago in his home beyond the sea, and whatever of truth there may be in the enthusiastic estimate of his capabilities for all sorts of excellence by some of his new teachers, this factor must come, as a large element of the situation, as I first observed it, in the year 1880. Any race, in circumstances similar to the colored people previous to 1860, finds a way of concealing its higher aspirations and develops the habits essential to making a comfortable estate of an inevitable system of bondage. The friendly Northern and European man, especially the woman, does understand the upper side of the Negro nature as it can hardly be divined, even by the most faithful worker for his uplifting of Southern birth and association. Still, the lower side of this people is best known through long and troublesome experience in the communities of which they are a vital part. Unhappily, the average Southern white man and woman have become so accustomed to the "often infirmities" of the "brother in black" that the suggestion of a common human nature is somewhat of a strain upon the imagination and the story of his actual advancement, under the educational discipline of freedom, is apt to be rejected as a delusion or resented as an affront upon the superior race. On the other hand it is almost impossible for the Northern man of British descent to conceive the possibility of any growth toward the higher estate of manhood in such a condition of chattel bondage as enveloped the colored race previous to the civil war.

But a little exercise of the reason and that interpretative imagination, without which logic is the champion liar and even experience the chronic misleader in human affairs, should long ere this have opened the eyes of fair-minded people to the indebtedness of the American Negro to this element in the schooling of his house of bondage. And when, as in my own case, an exceptional opportunity was offered for years to observe and work, in the confidence of all sides of Southern society, save an occasional jealous, conceited, or grumbling schoolmaster or a small editor spoiling for a Northern "head to hit," I should be unfaithful to our American civilization in all its varied constituents did I not bear hearty testimony to the great work of preparation on the old Southern plantation for the new schoolhouse imported from the North.

LVII.

Here is a great estate in the heart of a wide country, connected with others, great and small, by broad spaces of partially occupied lands. The family in possession stands to its working class in a relation more nearly resembling the patriachal family of the Oriental world than is elsewhere possible. If of the superior class, it is a group of people educated by the usual methods of the secondary and higher academical and college training of half a century ago, possibly one or two members improved by travel and graduation from Northern or European schools. But, whatever may be the attraction abroad, the home life offers the one quality that appeals most strongly to the educated man and woman ; the opportunity for the exercise of an almost absolute power and an influence practically irresistable. The men of the household, if ambitious and able, represent at home and abroad the most powerful aristocratic class in Christendom. The women of similar qualifications are received at the National Capital as social magnates and pass for their full worth as guests, even in portions of the country in a growing political hostility to their own.

But the mass of good women in any country are not magnates of fashion ; rather home-keepers, careful mothers of children, good managers of the domestic environment. And here is the center of the marvelous power exerted by the Southern woman of the better sort through long generations. Powerless to change the social organization into which she was born, early schooled to turn away from more than one pit of perdition, along the slippery edge of which she moved in her daily round, she turned to the genial social life of a new country in a Southern clime for entertainment. But her best womanly energies were concentrated on the few points in her home life, where her own will was law. We have seen how her influence prevailed in the home and family education of the Southern girl, often compensating for the serious defects of the old academic school system of the South. But even more exacting was her relation to her husband's slaves. This whole area of mental and moral destitution lay open beneath her gaze. Whatever may have been the fidelity to the higher duties of mastership in the masculine side of that old plantation life (and I am disposed to credit the master with a good deal of good service, especially in the arrangement of outward affairs and the administration of practical justice between man and man), still the peculiar relation of almost irreponsible power sustained by the white man to the slave woman was a temptation at once to self-forgetfulness and the capricious overindulgence of his favorites that no quality of saintship yet developed this side the water has been able to resist. With full comprehension of the perils amid which she walked, the wise Christian woman was forced to become a missionary at every point. All that woman's power could accomplish was done by her. Even the woman of the world, if not hopelessly demoralized by vanity and childishness, instinctively acquired some of the most valuable elements of the religious character in such a " strait between two " as her life must be.

LVIII.

The most promising of the young slaves in such a place come especially under the eye of the mistress and are promoted to household service. And that youth must be a "fool and blind" who does not profit, in a score of ways, by the university of the old-time planter's home, with its attractive habits of confidential life and outspoken sentiment and opinion, abiding in an atmosphere of genial social intermingling, with its everlasting "talk by the way" with every eligible guest that could be allured to its boundless hospitality. So the "old-plantation home" became the best possible training school for the general enlightenment and discipline of a people whose fathers, perhaps—certainly whose grandfathers—had been captured, brought across 3,000 miles of ocean, and landed, a crowd of pagan savages, upon a foreign shore.

And it was the most natural thing in the world for this woman to call in her clergyman as adviser and colaborer, especially the Protestant minister, whose power is sheathed in an elastic theology of influence, representing, chiefly, the great dissenting bodies of Christians, schooled in the conflicts of British ecclesiasticism. The better the pastor the more readily does he coöperate with the mistress of the little kingdom for the réligious and moral uplifting of the people. Bishop Haygood is probably not far-from right when he declares that the wonderful behavior of the slave population during the war was largely the result of its previous religious training. It is true that on the great plantations of the lower South, multitudes of these people would hardly feel the touch of this double relation of the church and the woman side of the planter's mansion. But, in the border States, and along the vast Piedmont region, the association of servant and master was closer and the influence from above more widely diffused.

The four years of the war intensified this peculiar training of the women of the household. On thousands of lonely estates, indeed everywhere in the country, the woman came to the front. Left with the children, the infirm men, and the slaves, she toiled on, under a strain of mind, heart, and circumstances almost inconceivable. The abler of the negro youth learned the lesson of the hour apace and took on something of responsible manhood and womanhood impossible before. No wonder that the personal attachments between the races, especially the generation that went through the war, are still the most characteristic and beautiful manifestations of our Southern life. Indeed, the love of the Negro, especially for the white woman and the child side of the home, still abides in a depth far below his gratitude, confidence, and attachment for his Northern friends, to whom he owes freedom and citizenship. This persistent affection of the ordinary Negro, especially for the "old folk at home," the women and children, is one of the most precious possessions of the South; far more important to the future of these States than the wealth of material resources so loudly heralded to the nations. This confide nce once gone, the Southland, with all its magnificent opportunities, becomes a social pandemonium. That preserved, all good things are possible through the might of time, the reconciler of all discords here below. All the more abhorrent is the attitude too often assumed by a class of Southern politicians who pander to the lower element of race prejudice by an insolence and injustice of speech and behavior, to which the old-time relation of master and servant in respectable classes is a stern rebuke.

LIX.

I found among the more thoughtful class of the teachers and workers in these great schools a growing appreciation of all this, and a gratitude to God for what had been done by the Southern women and the clergy of the old time to make their own work a possibility. And here I put in my earnest protest against the too common habit of a portion of the Southern political and religious leaders, of charging on these teachers a studied and systematic depreciation, even defamation, of the better class of the Southern people. Of course, these men and women are in their places to represent the American idea of to-day ; to prepare their pupils for the full citizenship guaranteed to them by the National Constitution and laws; to do what every fair-minded and broad-hearted Southern man believes is the only way to escape perils that can not be magnified. There has been and still remains a good deal of misinformation concerning the actual conditions of Southern life before and since the war. Doubtless there is still undue credulity in listening to the representations of their pupils and their friends, who naturally can see only their own side of a realm so vast as the complex life of the Republic. And it would be strange if among the many thousands of workers who have drifted through these schools during the past thirty years there had not been some whose influence was mischievous and who deserved the displeasure of all sensible Christian people.

But with the qualifications that must always go along with the fair estimate of any great moral enterprise, worked amid especial complications and perils, I pronounce this general charge of unfriendliness to the Southern people by the respectable class of these teachers groundless and, as sometimes pressed in high quarters, simply malignant. I have visited every one of the great, and many of these secondary schools, in all the Southern States during the past twelve years, and known, in the confidential way that belongs to such relations, the habitual influence of these leading institutions. And I unhesitatingly declare that influence thoroughly friendly to the South, according to the ideals of its own superior class. I find everywhere the influence of these schools most resolutely opposed to all the results so often imputed to the education of the Negro by its opponents. Whatever failure there may be, and there must be a considerable margin of failure, is not due so much to the schooling as to the prodigious difficulties surrounding the enterprise of developing the offspring of a slave population into responsible American citizenship, with its varied mental, moral, social, and industrial constituents.

Especially have I known that the longing desire of these good women instructors is not for what is called "social recognition." They are all socially respectable and many of them represent families of distinguished position. Their time is so occupied that social life, in its ordinary acceptation, is almost as impossible as to the inmates of a Catholic convent. But what they are longing and praying for is the sympathy, confidence, and communion with the Christian women of the South for aid in their difficult work. Such a coöperation is perfectly practicable, and nothing prevents it but a chronic habit of elevating a provincial social law to the rank of a Christian principle. As it is, I believe no body of people, especially of superior women, ever wrought in any good work, in this or any land, with a more single eye to the welfare of their constituency and a more delicate consideration for the people amid whom their lot has been cast than these teachers and missionaries.

LX.

There is no compromise with a true spirit of Christian freedom and patriotism in claiming what has been now asserted for the educating influence of the old order of Southern society in preparing the freed- man for his new American citizenship. It only confirms the fact that there is a God-side to a great deal that is only temporary and often largely opposed to human development in this world. It is this which keeps our human life, with all its follies and diabolisms, after all, worth living, and at last comes in, at the downfall of every great institution outgrown by humanity, as a saving grace in the reconstruction for a higher estate. Certainly there can be no excuse for one situated as I have been to remain insensible to the prodigious work done by the women of the old South and the Southern clergy, in the mitigation of the hardships of slavery and the invaluable preparation for the "good time coming," by their faithful labors in the long years before the flood. And it should be remembered that in comparison with the toils, trials, and sorrows of this life on the old plantation, the most devoted mis- sionary of education and religion in the Southland to-day has no cause for spiritual pride or special discouragement. And here, in a future not far away, will be woven a bond of sympathy between the Christian women of the North and South, all the stronger because its recogni- tion and expression have been so long delayed by circumstances beyond their control.

LXI.

In studying the mental aptitudes of these students, I was impressed anew with the fundamental truth of what is called "The New Educa- tion." Its ground principle is the fact that the mental, moral, and in- dustrial training of the child and youth must proceed along the path drawn by the instinctive mother-sense. When Pestalozzi, in his famous book, "Leonard and Gertrude," set forth the divine law of education in the two propositions that the mother is the inspired teacher of the gener- ations and that the natural methods of instruction and discipline in a good home must be followed in every grade of school, he spoke also the reconciling word concerning the training of the Negro for American citizenship. These students, even of the better class, were the children of nature, with no heritage of school culture, educated solely in the university of life, in the environment of their narrow lot. The next step should have been far more apparent than it was to many of these new teachers: to place these children in a school, organized, disciplined, and instructed according to the most rational handling of these natural methods which make the school an enlarged and glorified home. Where- ever these beautiful and effective methods were adopted, I saw the most gratifying results. The young Negro, born and reared in the country, had already developed a sense-faculty and habit of observation that furnished the greatest opportunity for the skilled teacher. I have repeatedly seen, in primary schools for colored children under eight years of age, evidences of ability in this direction full of encouragement to every friend of the race.

It was one of the inevitable educational disabilities of this Southern work that it proceeded so exclusively from the church as hardly at first to recognize the school side of the North. What is called, in theological parlance, "Christian education," includes that department of parochial, academic, and collegiate training under the special charge of the clergy of the different denominations of Christians. In respect to methods of instruction, it is usually half a century behind the so-called "secular education" in the better sort of the common schools. Even in the realm of moral discipline, where its asserted superiority exists, its methods of operation are often, in comparison with the discipline and moral training of the New Education, narrow and ineffective. The managers of these great seminaries for colored youth were chiefly clergymen or young graduates from colleges where the reformation of the past quarter of a century in educational methods wrought by the common schools had not been duly appreciated, often disparaged, in the double interest of sectarian theology and scholastic pedantry. A great amount of devoted labor was thus being wasted in the vain effort to school these children by reversing all the methods of nature; forcing the school-book between the learner and the thing to be learned; endeavoring to demonstrate the capacity of the race for the higher culture of the university; wrestling with problems that still divide the greatest educators in the most eminent seats of learning. I attributed a good deal of the failure of these graduates, especially of the mass of pupils who only linger a few months or a brief year within college limits, to these erroneous methods of instruction. A better system at first would have greatly helped along the movement and taken out of the mouths of objectors the most telling arguments against its influence on the pupils.

But, within the past twelve years of my acquaintance with these institutions, this defect has been gradually modified. A better class of teachers has been enlisted. Skilled supervision has been called in. Some of the ablest school men and women of the country have been brought into this work. The Hampton Normal and Industrial Institute is now one of the best models of a great school for this class of pupils in America; and all the leading seminaries have, more or less, profited in this respect. The majority of them now recognize the imperative need of special instruction and practice in pedagogy for the large number of their graduates who go forth to teach in the common schools. Their buildings are often occupied during the summer vacation by normal institutes, conducted by distinguished experts from all portions of the country. A great original treatise on the natural methods of education is yet to be written in our country, and its writer may possibly be a teacher schooled in this instructive and suggestive realm where the young colored citizens of the South are trained for the American manhood and womanhood that make for good American citizenship.

LXII.

The influence of the ante-bellum plantation training already described still lingered among these students in a constitutional habit of submission to the authority of their white teachers, especially when reënforced by kindness and confidence. No pupils are so easily governed by a skilled disciplinarian, working on the lines of moral development, as these. They are still the childlike children of the Republic, not yet demoralized by our wretched American heresy of child-spoiling which initiates into a precocious manhood and womanhood in their tenderest years. This docile dependence on their beloved teacher, this openness to reasonable suggestions for their own improvement, this spirit of heroic self-sacrifice and endurance of hardship in their school life, were an irresistible fascination, especially to the devoted women who were most intimately connected even with the deeper moral and spiritual training of the boys.

But it was the uniform experience of these instructors that underneath this docile exterior, often near the surface, lingered the elements of the original character still untrained in the severe school of responsible life. The Negro slave did learn and learned remarkably well the passive virtues possible in his lot. He also learned to work, and he learned the language and the religion of a civilized people. This was the "saving clause" in his emancipation, which prevented his sudden elevation from swamping the South in anarchy. But, unlike the European races, he had not endured the awful schooling of "sword, pestilence, and famine" through centuries of upward struggle out of the hell which the lower side of European civilization remained for a thousand years. Thus he still greatly lacks the peculiar qualifications of effective American citizenship; self-control and the habit of dealing with justice, firmness, and kindly tact with men.

Here was seen the most formidable obstacle to his rapid advancement. Every great school seemed to me like a floating tropical island, liable at any hour to be swept by an irresistible tempest of destructive excitement, "the wind blowing as it listed," often lashed to a cyclone at the slightest apparent provocation.

The most experienced teachers confessed themselves often powerless before such demonstrations, standing appalled by the opening of these yawning deeps of primitive nature, as by the abyss of an earthquake. Herein is displayed the superior tact and disciplinary skill of the better class of the Southern people, who know these liabilities and guard at once against the martinet system of restraint and the powerful excitements which so often react into dangerous excesses. But it is a strong proof of the radical stamina of the Negro chai acter that he has survived the terrific strain imposed upon him by the ignorance of the North at the close of the war, too often intensified by the reckless hostility of the people in contact with his new citizenship. That out of such a test of a full generation he has emerged, on the whole, a better, more intelligent, industrious, and hopeful citizen, is " greatly to his credit" and full of hope to the patriot and Christain.

LXIII.

I was now led to examine the very positive conviction of an influential class of his teachers, that there is little difference in the capacity of white and colored youth for schooling of the ordinary sort. I also noted the equally positive opinion of many Southern people, not un- friendly to the elementary training of the Negro, that, while the young children, possibly to the age of twelve, were remarkably bright and teachable, there was little to be expected beyond that age; a fatal race limitation of intellectual power coming in to baffle the effort for the secondary or higher education. It seemed to me, after long and careful examination of these schools, that both these theories left out the very important consideration of heredity in estimating the capacity of this class of children and youth. It is not necessary to regard hered- ity as the implacable fate of the materialist, or to ascribe to it any inor- dinate influence, to hold that the ability to gather knowledge through books and the ordinary processes of school training is prodigiously increased thereby. A people who never enjoyed the opportunity of this sort of training may be all the time gaining in many important phases of mental capability. The senses may be stimulated to the last degree, and the mental habits essential to success in common life, war, or the form of society amid which it abides, will acquire a remarkable vigor. If, as in the case of the American Negro, this race has lived in the most intimate contact with a powerful and educated people that is its master and director, it will, in addition, appropriate a great deal of information, and even form, by unconscious imitation, habits of men- tal activity similar to the superior class.

But meanwhile that special training of the will in connection with mental effort which enables the youth not only to observe, but to classify, arrange and adjust information, proceed from facts to their fit disposi- tion, learning to convey to its own place whatever is acquired and forming the habit of rapidly assigning any mental acquisition to its proper department; that power which, in the depths of the mind, appears like a pair of mental pincers, seizing upon and disposing of whatever comes in range, is wanting. This condition of prolonged childishness, of dependence on a commanding will, had hindered the formation of the mysterious faculty which distinguishes the descendants of a long line of well-schooled people, like the native population of Scotland and New England, from all other " sorts and conditions " of pupils.

I found the vast majority of these students, however bright and eager for knowledge, greatly deficient in this staying power. It was easy to excite interest and lift up these classes on a high wave of enthusiasm, and in studies which require chiefly an exercise of the memory in dealing with disconnected facts there was often brilliant progress. Here came in that wonderful capacity for civilization so often misjudged as a sort of animal aptitude for "imitation," whereby the Negro in two hundred and fifty years of slave life has made greater progress out of barbarism than any previous race in history. But the best teachers were least misled by this facility, and realized more and more the difficulty of establishing in these shifting mental sands a solid basis for steady growth and accurate judgment. It seemed as if the task of the thoughtful teacher in this work was twofold; on the one hand to judge discreetly how much to offer and how great a pressure to impose on the power of acquisition, and on the other to carefully build up in the deep places of the intellect the beginnings of the power which insures scholarship as distinguished from the random appropriation of facts; a power that would tell on another generation and go on increasing as the opportunities and experiences of a genuine educational training were established. Such a task indeed demands the wisdom of a Pestalozzi or a Froebel, and was far beyond the ability of the majority of the workers in these schools, though even there appreciated by the more skillful.

33

LXIV.

This consideration would have greatly modified the courses of study I found existing in many of these schools. I was surprised to note how much was often attempted with children and youth just out of the simplest life of the country; coming up to this high place to acquire even the common habits of decent living; with a range of ideas and a vocabulary so limited; confused and overwhelmed by a life as strange and exacting as if the children of an ordinary American common school were suddenly shot into the society of Windsor Castle, or stranded in the academic groves of Oxford or Cambridge. I wondered why the preoccupation of mind inevitable to such a change; the absorbing, as through the pores of the skin, of a strange new environment; the oppressive change from the wildest freedom to the strictest discipline; did not suggest the absolute necessity of a very elementary, simple introduction to real school life; an adaption of the kindergarten, natural methods, and industrial training to a condition so peculiar.

But I found, in the majority of these schools, a fixed course of study, in no essential way different from the ordinary graded school of our most cultivated communities. It seemed to me a sheer impossibility that the average student could successfully grapple with this style of persistent mental labor, in addition to all he was compelled to see and think and feel and do by the necessities of his new position. And I marveled at the delusion that these pupils were acquiring a correct and fruitful impression of these branches of study, so rapidly gone over, where a review or examination only added new confusion to the mind.

I could understand the reasons, or rather the excuses, for this course of proceeding, so evidently unprofitable and sure to bring this whole system of instruction into disrepute. These pupils were in great poverty; could often take only snatches of school life; were frequently supported by the gifts of churches and benevolent people, who required constant encouragement by favorable accounts of progress. They were wild to study great things and a great many of them, and often fractious and unmanageable if restrained within their proper capacity. Beside, the sharp rivalry between the different sects by which these colleges and universities are supported is a grievous temptation to attract students by cheapening education, admitting incompetents, and grading by lower tests. All the evils of this sort of competition, so destructive in every department of our American school life, I found aggravated here.

So I early came to the conclusion, not that there is a fatal race limitation to the capacity for acquisition at the age of twelve to fifteen, or that the higher education is an impossibility to an increasing number of these students; but that there has been, and still is, in many quarters, a great lack of pedagogic skill in laying the foundations of the Negro school life, in helping these children not only to fix the habit of acquiring and retaining knowledge, but especially in developing the power of assimilation and of imparting it in turn to others. It is no special reflection on the managers of these excellent institutions that this mistake was made. They were working in an untried field, where the experts might well pause. Their failures were no greater, all things considered, than the blunders in the schooling of the children of the white race that everywhere confronted me; and I respected the earnest desire of the higher class of these workers to learn from their failures. Indeed, soon after these early visits in 1880 all these missionary associations established a more careful supervision of their school work, which in some form now exists in them all. The splendid gifts of the Slater and Hand funds, and the marvelous persistence in generous giving by the Northern people, have enabled these bodies to add a proper industrial and, sometimes, a genuine normal department to the purely academic system that at first so largely prevailed.

LXV.

But here comes in an important consideration in estimating the results of the education of the Negro during the past twenty-five years. It is true that a great many of these pupils have been a sad disappointment to their teachers and friends, as far as the development of mental power and even moderate scholarship goes. It is also true that a considerable number of the attendants in these high places have returned home in a lamentable state of " big head," which has made their "little learning " a mischievous and sometimes a " dangerous thing." And if this was the result in the upper regions of culture, among the superior class, what could have been expected in the common schools, where the vast majority were gathered, under such conditions, in charge of such teachers; in all ways so weighted with burdens that there is no wonder that the meager three months a year, in a country school house, with all its interruptions and disabilities, was often a demoralization rather than an education? Nobody whose opinion is worthy of respect will maintain that such schooling as half the colored children of the sixteen Southern States even now obtain is much more than a name. It is simply the best these people can obtain under the circumstances. In several of the Southern cities, in 1880, I found the colored public schools in charge of Southern white teachers; in some cases of superior character, good attainments, and respectable social standing. Their success was no better than that of the Northern teachers already described; although their acquaintance with the peculiarities of the race was an advantage. But the vast majority of the teachers in the Southern colored common schools are of their own race; largely graduates of the schools in which they are now employed. But, even with all these drawbacks, I saw enough to confirm me in my faith of the capacity of the average colored boy and girl for the acquirement of the schooling essential to good American citizenship and of the abler youth for a respectable, sometimes a remarkable degree of scholarship. The methods of instruction are slowly improving; the demand for better teachers increases. In short, with half a century of the work inaugurated during the past twenty-five years, the Republic will not be ashamed of its ten millions of new-made citizens or disappointed in the heavy outlay of money, time, and toil in the building up of the colored people's university; the common school, supported by the South, in connection with the secondary and higher seminary, so far largely the contribution of the North, to this truly national work.

LXVI.

But, meanwhile, it does become these great institutions that must retain the leadership of the school life of the race for another generation, educating the higher grade of teachers and the upper class for the guidance of their people, to ponder well the responsibility for the fit mental training of their 50,000 students. No pressure of sectarian propagandism or " boom " of heedless benevolence or any other unworthy motive should come in to swerve their policy from the strict line of truth. " Christian education " is education according to the divine law of human development implanted in the soul of man, interpreted by the growing educational experience of the ages, and no violation of these immutable laws and methods can be atoned for by the utmost zeal in the realm of special religious or moral cultivation. In several directions there was a speedy and encouraging response to good teaching in all these schools. The Negro has a genius for language. In the two hundred years of his American bondage he made a greater stride towards the speaking of intelligible English than entire districts of English-born people have achieved in the two thousand years since the Roman occupation of the British Islands. He has even been able to impress his own dialect upon his master class to the extent that a full generation of correct language-teaching will hardly bring several millions of white Southern people up to the condition of the more intelligent pupils in these mission schools. Nowhere do the beautiful methods of language instruction, now a part of our progressive school work, bear more abundant fruit than among the children of this susceptible and talkative people; and nowhere are the stupefying and unscientific old-time ways of teaching "the three R's" so convicted of absurdity and inefficiency as in the Negro schools. The progress in writing and drawing, when properly taught, has been remarkable. The handwriting of large numbers of these students showed great natural aptitude and, in free-hand drawing and design they are often superior to the white pupils of similar grade and class. The aptitude for ornamentation appeared in the good taste displayed in dress, the arrangement of flowers and adornment of rooms, wherever the fit opportunity was offered. I have overlooked a score of colored girls who, two years before, had never slept in a bed and were strangers to many of the common habits of decent living, waiting at table, arrayed in gowns of their own making, in manners and appearance challenging admiration. The work of classes in physics, in the construction of apparatus and excellent manipulation in electrical experimenting and ingenious devices in general, proves the mechanical faculty stored up in what is to become one of the most valuable operative classes in the country.

If the present senseless no-method of teaching history could be changed to the free oral story-telling method for little children and the introduction to the notable characters and stirring incidents of our national life, no body of young people in the United States would more eagerly and intelligently deal with it, especially when connected with a teaching of geography which makes it in truth a "description of the earth." In the higher mathematics and philosophy, all studies demanding maturity of mental habit, poise of mind, accurate analysis, and good judgment, I find these pupils generally deficient. But it is quite too early to pronounce on their incapacity, much less to jump to the reckless conclusion that the Negro mind stops growing at fifteen years of age. When a reasonable method of teaching arithmetic, elementary algebra, and geometry is domesticated in the common schools of the South; when the charming natural methods of imparting nature-knowledge are tried upon these children of nature; when philosophy changes from the drumming a cast-iron theory of things human and divine into the heads of children and youth who are yet only half conscious of a soul; in short, when the exploded methods of instruction that still hold in the majority of Southern schoolrooms give place to the New Education and a vigorous system of moral instruction wakes up the fine material in both races for an excellent teaching force, we shall behold results in all these seminaries that will be a new revelation to the educational public. It is a great misfortune that these institutions, built up with such consecration of money, time, and precious life, could not at once reflect the best methods of instruction in vogue in the centers of Northern public-school life. For lack of this there has been a fearful waste of energy and often a failure of satisfactory results, and the prejudice of the enemies of Negro education has been confirmed by the people supporting many of the students therein.

LXVII.

It has been a prodigious advantage that in the industrial training that has gradually been introduced into these schools the methods have been good and the success almost uniformly gratifying. The bad habit of associating scholarship with idleness and contempt for manual labor was certainly not brought to the South by the managers of these institutions, although it has, in some cases, been intensified and prolonged by their reluctance to adopt natural methods of instruction and industrial training. Nowhere has there been a more remarkable display of native ability for mechanical, operative, and even decorative work than among the trained students at Hampton, Claflin, Clark, Spelman, Tuskegee, and others of these great seats of the new instruction for the children of the freedmen. The stolid prejudice against the employment of the Negro in any capacity save as a field hand is giving way in the face of the excellent work done by many of these young people. If the wicked Negro-hatred of the great labor organizations and the ignorant immigrant workmen that now degrades labor and misrepresents the better sentiment of the North, can be arrested on the border, the South in due time will possess in its colored people one of the most satisfactory industrial classes in the world; not best because it now works cheaply, perhaps receiving all its style of unskilled work is worth, but because there is in this people a capability for both intelligent and skilled workmanship that will yet surprise the country.

The root of much of the misunderstanding and injustice from which the Negro everywhere is the sufferer is the constitutional sense of general white superiority coupled with the pagan notion that superiority of class, race, or culture implies a perfect and divine right to a control of all inferior classes that amounts to a virtual slavery. It is yet to be decided in the future development of man what is the limit of this vaunted Anglo-Saxon superiority. In an era when martial skill and superiority in general executive power is at the front, he remains the topmost man of the modern world. But, in more than one department of life, especially in the realm of the spiritual and artistic culture of the race, he is notably second best; the Oriental and the Southern European leaving him far in the rear. There will never be a lack of sufficient Anglo-Saxon manhood and womanhood in our country to assure the preservation of constitutional Republican institutions and the vigor and enterprise that are the propelling forces of our civilization. But just what the fierce, overbearing, and often brutal Anglo-Saxon man needs most of all, especially in these States, is the modifying and mollifying influence of a people possessing the very qualities which at first made it a serving class, but in the " good time coming," will lubricate, soften, humanize, and broaden the whole structure of American society. If there is no God in the world, no Providence in history, and no place for the humbler peoples of the earth, then a war of races will be the close of the intolerant semi-barbarism that can not live alongside a depend-ent class without subjecting it to perpetual servitude. But if there is anything in what we all prophesy, that the kingdom of God is on its way, and, as it comes, superiority everywhere will be another name for an overwhelming obligation to follow the Master in "seeking and saving that which was lost," then the " ways of God to man" will be "vindicated" most of all in the relation of the Anglo-Saxon Amer-ican to the peoples intrusted to his charge in this, the world's normal school of Republican society, "coming from the East and the West, the North and the South," to sit down, each "under his own vine and fig tree, with none to molest or make afraid."

LXVIII.

But I soon freed myself in my observation of these seminaries from the narrow pedagogic crotchet of testing their general success by their immediate achievement in scholarship. About 80 per cent of the people of southern Italy, 48 of Central Europe and a smaller per cent of Great Britain, are still unable to read. Each Southern American State has a body of native white illiteracy, great enough in some possible division of political parties, to rule the commonwealth. So I could not, like some eminent critics, dismiss this great work of Negro education as a failure, on a simple estimate of its mental results. The basis of education is char-acter training, without which all sharpening of the mind, discipline of the executive, or development of the artistic faculty only intensify and confirm the most intense barbarism. Here must we look for the ful-crum over which the lever of the Northern schools for the Negro in the South should pry. So my attention, though never distracted from the mental instruction and discipline going on in these schools, was more and more directed to the observation of the methods by which the children of these millions of newly emancipated adult slaves should be led out from the religion and morality of the plantation to the type of morality and religion which is the solid foundation of American citizen-ship.

I soon found that the imperious demands of the situation had wrought their inevitable results on this entire body of teachers. For two hundred years the American church has fitly glorified the hemisphere of the Christian religion turned towards God; while the corresponding obligation to "love thy neighbor as thyself," has largely been determined by a secular gospel of "the life that now is." But if, in this work, there came down to the Southland a minister or layman, man or woman, who had felt moved at home to depreciate "mere morality" in the interest of "spiritual religion," his conversion to the whole gospel of Christ was speedy and complete. For this worker, if sincere and practical, was at once confronted with a people who had been chiefly trained to one side of the vast globe of Christianity, often without a suspicion that there was another slope that looked off on the wide domain of a personal character based on the common Christian morality. It was impossible to give to the Negro slave much more than the side of Christianity which touched on his peculiar lot. All consideration of the nature of man as a free citizen of this Republic; his natural right to himself; the use of his own mind; the development of his special order of manhood and womanhood; all that questioned the absolute divine right of the system of society of which he was the underpinning, was necessarily left out. The most evident result was the development of a type of religious character which came up, as, indeed, three-fourths of the Christian people in the world now remain, with no practical faith in the Christian doctrine of the native divine childhood of man as man, or, that the Christian religion demands an essential modification of the old pagan heresy that, in this world, things rightly go by the might of the strongest. But the side of religion that consoles and comforts amid the trials of a hard mortal lot, making this life tolerable to the most and bearable to the least favored of the earth, offering the glories of heaven to the converted as a compensation for the diabolism even of Christian civilization, was so faithfully instilled into the slave population that, with its natural affectionateness and emotional susceptibility, it wrought most powerfully. Doubtless, as Bishop Haygood declares, this was a vital factor in the submission of this people to the conditions of the old life, and largely explains the wonderful devotion of the Negro to the Southern women and children during the war.

LXIX.

But, unfortunately, the outcome of this partial training here, as in all Christian lands, was the failure to connect the moralities of common life with the upper realm of the so-called "Christian experience." So these new teachers came to a work which sometimes first opened their eyes to this defect of the popular religion, and enforced the practical mandates of the Gospel as never before. They found in this student a child-man, or woman, not a "fallen" creature, only half conscious of the claims of the two most essential moralities, chastity and truthfulness, and all the minor morals that cluster about these central pillars of Christian manhood and womanhood. They found a perilous habit in their pupils of confounding the demand for common morality with the arbitrary law of a master enforcing his own whim. The ready definition of freedom I heard in a class: "A free country is a country where a man can do what he pleases," was the practical notion of too many of these youth. No wonder that for years in all these schools the one imperious necessity was not so much " school discipline,"—for the Negro youth inherits a habit of unquestioning obedience which can be easily developed into a remarkable order by a moderate effort—as the grounding the child and youth in the fundamental moralities, without which his entire educational structure would be " a house built on the sand."

It was soon discovered that a good deal beside the ordinary "word of command," or the commonplace of reward and penalty, is essential to this. First, it appeared that the whole notion of religion as a wild half-pagan orgy of the passions and senses should be gradually eliminated. The revival, in some form a necessity of the Christian school, was utilized ; but shorn of its excessively emotional characteristics and made a season for the imparting of solid instruction on the duties of a Christian life. The lazy boy who, converted in one of these seasons, got out of bed at 5 o'clock on a winter morning, split a big pile of wood, built a fire and welcomed his astonished mother to a breakfast well on the way, saying, " Mother, they have got a new kind of religion up at the mission school that tells me to get up in the morning and help you get breakfast," was one of the first fruits of this new dispensation.

I have visited all the great and many of the smaller schools of this sort in the South, and am confident that in no church in America, with the most intelligent membership, are the implacable demands of the Christian moralities more persistently, clearly, and effectively presented, through organization, discipline, home life and outdoor relations, with greater profit to the hearers than in them all. The labors of this devoted band of Christian teachers and workers for the moral and social uplifting of their disciples has added a new chapter to the record of Christianity in America, and, in due time, will be acknowledged in South and North. As Julius Cæsar went off into Gaul and Germany and Britain to learn how to return as Emperor of Rome, so the church of Christ, North and South, is indebted to this body of missionaries to the freedmen, largely to the woman side of this working corps, for such a refreshment of power in the union of practical morality and the popular religion as will give it a new and commanding force in dealing with the awful problems of our new American life.

LXX.

Here has been displayed as never before the " power and potency " of a wise Christian womanhood in lifting her own sex out of the slough of unchastity, the bottomless pit of ancient and modern life. The most discouraging feature in "the race question" in the South is the widespread belief among the superior class that this and the corresponding vice of untruthfulness are especial race characteristics, permanent and ineradicable, in the Negro. This profound skepticism concerning the possible virtue of the Negro woman is an important element in the violent resistance, especially of Southern women, to social contact. It is honestly believed by multitudes of good Southern people that no cultivation of the mind, no training of the industrial faculty, no religious experience, will essentially change this characteristic. While this conviction prevails, the popular Christianity of the South will stand behind the absolute denial of all social opportunity to the Negro, irrespective of his apparent advancement in the more superficial traits of civilization.

This opinion is, of course, the heritage of the "old estate," and is still too well confirmed by the actual condition of great numbers of the Negro population. But, outside one State, the Southern people have not been brought in close contact with any prominent lower class save the colored man or woman. Their own white "low-down folk," often as immoral and far more dangerous than their former slaves, are already "in the swim" of reformation, often ready to seize on the new opportunities of American life. So it is not recognized that what is regarded as normal race characteristics of the Negro are simply the infirmities of our common human nature, always and everywhere under similar conditions. The sexual weakness of the Southern Negro is no greater than of vast populations of the Old World—the people of southern Italy, of southeastern Europe, of South America, of myriads in the Orient. Wherever the lower orders of mankind have been held under the iron discipline of despotic power, coupled with the only dispensation of religion possible in such a state of society, the masses have been left in childish unconsciousness of the sanctity of home life and the obligation of the common moralities. The ordinary unchaste Negro woman is not the "fallen woman" of the old civilization, but a half-animal creature, on her way up from the lower realm of human existence to a family life in accord with the fundamental virtues of a Christian civilization. Truth is uniformly the latest comer of the virtues even in a highly civilized state. Even yet in the great practical affairs of this world it is a virtue "more honored in the breach than in the observance." The hopeful feature in the moral instruction of the Negro is that he is a moral child, first learning the character-side of the Christian religion, not the "degenerate son of noble sires."

I appreciated the skill with which the admirable women I everywhere met in these schools adjusted their machinery of reformation to the conditions; illustrating the old saying of Col. Davy Crockett, in the comic almanac—"to shoot the Mexicans in their crooked intrenchments, I used crooked artillery." A great use was made of industrial training, and it was inevitable that the mental instruction of the average pupil must often be made to give way to the more radical moral discipline. The one thing essential to success was found to be constant occupation of the mind and hands. The great majority of these schools were coeducational, for the good reason that the training of the sexes together in the radical virtues of chastity and truthfulness was the only assurance that the graduate would not be dragged down by marriage with an unfit companion on going out into life. "How do you keep your boys virtuous in this great school?" I asked a celebrated leader in this work. "I get them out of bed at 5 o'clock in the morning, give them a smart military drill, put them through their paces in study and work till 9 o'clock at night: and I will answer for all the damage they will do after that hour."

LXXI.

Nobody save one who has the inside look at these large assemblies of youth can realize the intense and ceaseless drain upon the mind and heart of the devoted women who are educating these leaders of the new race into the common virtues which must be the corner stone of all their success. "Beset behind and before," as every attractive colored girl in our America is, by temptation, she has found her providential protec- tress, the defense that no American church has hitherto been able to give, in this body of devoted apostles of womanhood. I am convinced from the most careful observation that the per cent of sexual failure among these young women graduates, after fair trial in these schools, is not greater than in modern "polite society" and far less than among the women of several of our immigrant peoples from abroad. There is a steadily growing respect for the moralities of life among the better sort of colored people in the South. The regulation scapegrace Negro preacher, generally a liar, often a boor, a thief, and a caucus politician, the champion blatherskite, is being supplanted by a class of respectable, often educated, and effective young clergymen, trained in these schools. And when Southern housekeepers tell me that edu- cation has spoiled the servant class of the home, I marvel why they for- get that the descendants of their old faithful "mammies" and "aunties" are generally now "set in families," often successful housekeepers on their own account, as thousands of comfortable homes of colored people in town and country demonstrate. The present class of young women servants is now largely drawn from the old set that were occupied in field or menial drudgery. With no home opportunity for training, com- ing from the undesirable life in which they are reared, even if treated with as much consideration as the ordinary servant girl elsewhere, they can not reasonably be expected to have what the American woman ex- pects, as Dr. Johnson said: "All the Christian virtues for three and six- pence a week." The time is at hand, under the lead of these great schools and the people trained therein, when the still divided churches of the North and South will unite in the greatest mission work now open to the religious people of America; the moral and social uplifting of the illiterate classes of the sixteen Southern States; a work now of more importance to a Christian civilization than the effort to bring the masses of the pagan world into the acceptance of Christian truth.

LXXII.

It is everywhere asserted that the fundamenta. educational necessity of the Southern Negro is industrial training. In the large sense this subject now assumes to the thoughtful educational public, the assertion is correct. In the narrow, reactionary sense in which it is pushed by people who only see the little environment amid which they are living, it means what never can or will happen.

If the Negro has only stepped out from his old estate of chattel slavery into the permanent condition of a European peasantry, with a wall of iron and granite about him and his occupation, with no civil, industrial, or social outlook beyond the present condition of the majority of his kind, then the entire system of education now pursued at the South is a fatal blunder. The free common school, however poor, is a ladder up which every child is invited to climb to every place that beckons the American boy or girl for the service of American citizenship. The secondary and higher education, supported from abroad or, as now, by every Southern State, is only the upper section of that ladder. No man or party, however positive, intolerant, or effective at present, can resist the logic of the training now given by the Southern people to the colored folk. The only limitation to the upward climb is in the capacity of the climber. The superior will prevail when he has demonstrated his superiority, and no man can change this law. Similar states of character, intelligence, and usefulness to the community will, in the outcome, assure to every man's children all the rights guaranteed by law to every citizen, leaving social and personal relations in charge of the unwritten law that nobody enacted and nobody can repeal, being the measure of the average civilization and Christianity of the community in which it prevails.

Thus the loud call for industrial education for the Negro will be answered in the same way as a similar demand in any portion of the country. The Negro, outside the vagrant and criminal class of the Southern cities and villages, for which the local authorities are largely responsible, is not the champion lazybones he is published. He does his full share of the work in the country, although his reward is not always in proportion to his services. His defects as a laborer are the same as of all classes of ignorant workers, toiling by the old-time methods of muscular effort, unchanged by mental, moral, or social improvement. The curse of the South to-day is just this sort of labor in every department of her industrial life. In figures the cheapest, in reality it is the dearest labor in any civilized land, and out of it can never come the development of this great country, so prophesied, lauded, and longed for by its progressive people. It is not capital or intelligent white immigration that is half so much needed by States like Georgia, Mississippi, Alabama, by all the essentially Southern Commonwealths, as that thorough training of the head, heart, and hand that will lift up the entire working class of both races in range of the corresponding class elsewhere in the Republic. That done, each State will move forward by the aid of its own citizenship and be in a condition to invite, welcome, and utilize all that may come to it. There will be no large response by any considerable class of desirable people to come to the South to aid the politicians and the reactionary set they so largely represent in their effort to reduce the Negro to a perpetual peasant and essentially reëstablish the old order of affairs. There should be investment, immigration, and aid that reënforce no party or class save that portion of the Southern people, the true educational public, who are bravely struggling against prodigious odds to place their communities on the highway of a genuine American civilization, by lifting their own people out of the bonds of provincial and narrow civil and industrial habits.

The valuable industrial training for the Negro is what he is getting in these great schools now under consideration. First. It will enforce the dignity of labor upon a class who will be called to lead a less favored constituency in the near future. Second. It will put the thinking brain into the working hand; making the masses intelligent and their leaders skilled workmen, capable of meeting the growing demand of the South for all varieties of industrial effort. Third. It will put the conscience into the hand and lift the mass of common workmen above their wretched habits of shirking, cheating, and generally unsatisfactory work that now make life hardly worth living for all dependent on this class. Fourth. It will put the soul into the hand and teach the youth of both races and all classes the fit use of money, by laying up " treasure in heaven;" learning to save on the lower side in order to spend on the upper side of life. The Negro has enough now, if he has this art, to place himself far above his present estate and give him opportunities enjoyed by no laboring class in this country a century ago.

This type of Industrial Education, of course, must be a vital department of all schools. Manual training, sewing, cooking, all are a useful part of it. But whatever ignores the mental, moral, and spiritual element in the training of American youth will only confirm the awful greed for money-getting, with no regard to man or concern for the law of God, which is becoming to-day one of the most serious perils of the South. No man from abroad has the moral right to go to these States with the sole idea of " business." His supreme obligation is to cast in his lot with the really superior class who are working, as no other set of American people are, to bring in the kingdom of God in the Southland.

Here, once more, we bear testimony to the spirit in which the majority of these Northern teachers have wrought in the Southern educational field.   While a portion of them, very naturally, have had "an eye to the main chance" and have not left the South poor or wrought without pay, these good women have "borne the burden and heat of the day," amid such disadvantages of schooling, often with such over-pressure of work and deprivation of all that makes the outward life of an educated American woman a blessing, that nothing but an unselfish service of the Master can account for the persistence in their mission.   And it should not be forgotten that, whatever may have been the attitude of Southern society, these women who have really sought it with the same diligence and tact essential anywhere, have often found among the Christian women of the South the reliable support of personal friendship, generous sympathy, and appreciation which has been to them a great comfort and the prophecy of the coming day when we shall all "see eye to eye" in the glorious union of churches and peoples for the common good.

LXXIII.

And, now, if the question is again forced, What has all this work of the Northern Christian people really accomplished for the Negro and, through him, for the South and the Nation?—I answer: Just what education, in its just estimate, is now doing for all children and youth in American schools.   A mischievous heresy of the time is the pedantic notion of making the American common school an arrangement to secure "scholarship" for the masses.   Honest instruction in anything on the lines of truth, that scorns the shallow and shabby habit of calling common things by uncommon names, filling the child with a conceit of what he is not, is essential to all successful schooling.   But "scholarship" in any genuine sense is a virtual impossibility to the mass of mankind.   The common school of the American people is an institution for the training and development to manhood and womanhood of American youth through a scheme of instruction and discipline which blends the moral, mental and executive elements in due proportion.   If it sends out its graduate at the end of five or ten years well started on that line of life, with an eager desire for mental improvement added to a solid standing on good character and the ability to use his mental and moral acquirements in his everyday work in life, this is all we have the right to ask.

Tried by this test no body of youth in this country can give a better "account of their stewardship" than the majority of those who have been under the influence of these mission schools long enough to be really affected thereby.   Even the rough plantation boy or simple girl who drifts through Atlanta or Fisk, or lodges for a time in one of the minor seminaries, generally goes home more inclined to do something better.   But it requires a genuine course of some years—perhaps better if varied with occasional teaching or home life—to bring out the best result. Whatever may be said of the superficial scholarship of the majority of their pupils, or of the occasional over-elation of some of the weaker heads, the general effect of their training is good and helpful, not only to themselves but to their people. I know of what I affirm. I have lived for twelve years past in constant contact with and careful observation of these young people. There are now thousands of them scattered through the South. Many of them have married their school companions; indeed, the coeducational feature of the system is one of its most valuable elements, tending to bring together, on a higher plane of Christian friendship and marriage, where such object lessons are most important. I find these people at work in all the superior avenues open to their race; in the church, as pastors and workers of an improved style, physicians, mechanics; the women good mothers and housekeepers, bringing up their children " in the fear of the Lord;" the life of the common school as teachers; blessing the churches and communities in which they live; in short, acting well their part of leadership in every realm of life among their people.

When it is said that their education unfits them for work, the assertion simply means that intelligent, ambitious, self-respecting American youth, of every race, class or "previous condition" will not and ought not to become workers of the old-time sort; servants under the despotic control of a selfish and exacting mistress; laborers in a life little above the old conditions of slavery; humble, cringing, or reckless and "striking" operatives, enlisted and maneuvered by demagogues in the bitter war of labor against capital. These educated young people are doing what the children of every respectable family in any part of our country are doing; working according to the improved industrial methods, in modern style, moved by the new ambitions of the day and time. Already have the communities of the South had reason to be grateful for what has been done in this way. The system of common schools for the colored folk would be impossible without their work in the schoolroom. The Negro church would be sloughed in a half-pagan superstition without their ministry in the pulpit, and the Sunday school. They are leading the way as honestly, effectively, and successfully as any people, all things considered, to a better time coming for the States which must remain the permanent home of the race.

In another place, in my observations on the common school and woman's work therein, I shall write of the great service of the colored young women therein. Suffice it here to repeat what has all along been repeated, that in this blessed ministry of education the women of the North, by what they have contributed and what they have done, have not only laid the sixteen Southern States and the American people under a weight of obligation that only time will reveal; but which, also, time, the all-reconciling force in human affairs will be certain to bring to the remembrance, appreciation, and grateful acknowledgment of the Republic.

LXXIV.

Of course the question must be met and answered, What is to be the final status of this class of schools? It will be decided by each religious body on grounds satisfactory to itself. But certain tendencies are already apparent, all pointing in the same direction.

First. It has been for some time apparent that the elementary schooling of colored children should be left to the local public schools as fast as they are competent to do the work. Probably, in a large majority of cases, this would be feasible, especially as in these communities the common-school teachers are largely drawn from these institutions. It will be impossible to gather the funds in the North for the support of a great system of elementary education in the South. No State in the Union, not even Massachusetts or California, now pays so much per capita for the most complete system of public schooling as it costs these institutions for the training of their graduates, over and above what is received for tuition fees and student work. There has been too much of the tendency in all these Northern churches to push their Southern educational work on the lines of the parochial and "Christian education" scheme, against which the Northern Protestant people are almost a unit in opposing the Catholic programme in their own States.

The Southern colored people can not educate their children in their own parochial schools without such incessant demands upon Northern benevolence as will not much longer be met. If the colored people can be aroused to their own responsibility and lifted above a present dangerous dependence on Northern charity, they can, in different ways, supplement the public school and make it in time adequate to their needs. Whether they do it will depend largely on the cheerful coöperation of these great institutions with local boards of instruction. There is no doubt that all these seminaries, called colleges and universities, would be far more effective if their number of students were decreased by a third, carefully sifted, and the work of the institution concentrated on a class of pupils who, by age, capacity, and character will repay the labor and money expended upon them. At present every incompetent, half-trained, unreliable scholar sent forth feeds a popular prejudice against negro education, perpetuates the reign of poor teachers and useless schools, and works unfavorably in the reaction at the base of supplies. For a generation yet this class of academies will virtually have in its hands the fixing of the standard of teaching ability and general professional character among the colored people of the South. Every institution established by State or local home effort will be compelled to follow these models. It would be far better could 25,000 students, sifted from the mass that is rushing upon these institutions, be selected, assisted, if need be, to remain until well trained and then graduated, than to expend thousands on children who can as well be schooled in the ordinary way.

LXXV.

Second. This will involve the necessity of a general effort to endow the best of these schools until they are raised above their present neces sity of "living from hand to mouth."

The result of this would be a superior class of teachers, better paid and more permanent, three most desirable elements of success. The schools themselves would then be lifted above their precarious dependence on annual contributions by churches, Sunday schools, and personal gifts. They would also be fortified against the two home perils : a raid by ambitious colored churches and interested leaders to capture and manage them in their own way, and the occasional upheaval from the lower regions of Southern life, which is still to be guarded against in every State.

LXXVI.

Third. Thus defended and concentrated it will be perfectly safe to call to these boards of management and instruction friendly and competent Southern men and women of both races, anticipating the time when all these schools can be handed over to the Southern people, the grandest educational gift ever yet conferred upon any people, by the combined philanthropy and Christian patriotism of the North and the Nation.

These suggestions are in no way original with the writer. They are all strongly confirmed by the growing conviction of the most experienced managers and workers in this field. Indeed more than one of these colleges is now virtually planted on this platform and others are looking that way. It is high time that the indiscriminate and often thoughtless giving of our Northern people for the education of the Negro should give place to a concentrated effort to secure and thoroughly establish the positions already gained. Through the entire summer the streets of our Northern cities are swarming and our churches besieged by a host of solicitors, of both races, often wholly unknown or commended in the reckless way in which people can be sent from any community anywhere to beg for "a good cause." As an old railroad president growled out to one of these petitioners, " You can't educate 20,000,000 people by passing round a hat." Our Southern friends mistake in their goodnatured indorsement of many of these solicitors, and provoke reaction by favoring this incessant application.

While there has probably been no more questionable or incompetent management of such funds than could be expected, there has been the usual result of spreading great sums of money in a miscellaneous way over vast spaces, often to be handled by workers incompetent or visionary. Many a church pays an annual tax for the support of a good brother or sister " missionary down south," when the same money applied to build a colored schoolhouse, place in it a better teacher, and extend its term would help ten times the number of children, besides forging one more link in the chain of union and good feeling between the people of both sections. But we aré aware that all this depends largely on the final union of the still disrupted churches of the three great religious denominations that contain nine-tenths of the Southern people. This final triumph of American patriotism and the Christian religion once achieved, all good things would seem possible.

PART III.

SOUTHERN WOMEN IN THE SOUTHERN COMMON SCHOOL.

LXXVII.

On a midsummer day in August, 1880, I was first introduced to the university life of our Southern States. Dr. Ruffner, State superintendent of education in Virginia, had summoned the first gathering of the teachers of that State in a midsummer institute, and the University of Virginia had tendered the use of its buildings, with all their facilities, while the foremost of the professors and their families gave their vacation to the instruction and entertainment of their guests. Several hundred of the white teachers of the State assembled, representing every portion of its territory and almost every family of eminence in its history. Indeed, as one overlooked this remarkable gathering of teachers it almost seemed like a rally of the descendants of the noblest people of the Old Dominion to celebrate the illustrious marriage of which Thomas Jefferson published the bans sixty years before, and which, after a stormy courtship of more than half a century, was concluded in those midsummer weeks.

For a whole generation Thomas Jefferson and the group of like-minded public men of old Virginia had labored with the people of that State to establish a thorough system of education. Jefferson's plan originally included the emancipation and industrial training of the Negroes; a free common school for all white children; a system of high schools, partially free; and a State university. During his life he only accomplished the founding of the State University, which, with several denominational colleges and a number of secondary schools, in connection with private instruction, was relied upon to educate the respectable classes. A system of free instruction for the poorer white people was repeatedly attempted, but never attained the dignity of a common school that any large number even of that class in Virginia cared to use.

Who will say that times have not changed, when the same class that rejected Jefferson's school in 1820, in fifty years, as the conservative party in the State government, struck hands with Massachusetts in the management at Hampton; adopted the Richmond free-school system, begun by Boston women; established a system of public instruction for both races, essentially the same as in all the States; in the free high

117

schools and State normal school for white and colored pupils indorsed
the support of the secondary education by the State; resumed the work
of subsidizing the university, and crowned the whole by calling to the
leadership the son of an old Virginia college president, Dr. Ruffner, the
Horace Mann in the public school revival in the new South? For ten
years this work had gone on, of course amid the opposition and hindrance of a revolutionary epoch. And I count it one of the chief opportunities of my life, as it was the dedication service of my new ministry
of education, that I should be included as one of the corps of lecturers
that were drawn from every section to aid in this memorable session
of six summer weeks.

34   The conductor at the university was Dr. Newell, the eminent State
superintendent of schools in Maryland. The institute was opened by
imposing ceremonies, including an address from the governor, who came
out of the war with only a left arm. Distinguished gentlemen and
ladies from different portions of the Union supplemented the daily instruction by addresses and entertainments. In the audience, even
among the teachers, was represented almost every Virginia family of
eminence, from Patrick Henry, the brother of Washington, Jefferson,
down to the recent military and civil dignitaries. There was no holding back by the university people, in whose person the higher education in Virginia at last struck hands with the common school. The aged
librarian of the university was there, showing his first commission,
signed by Jefferson, and it almost seemed as if the silent marble statue
of the great President might be awakened to life in visible thanksgiv-
ing for the coming of this memorable day. For, as the day when Jefferson's educational plan was rejected was the precursor of woes innumerable to the Old Dominion, so was that summer gathering of
teachers at Charlottesville and of colored teachers at Lynchburg on
subsequent weeks the herald of the new epoch of glory which awaits
the new Virginia in the new Republic.

LXXVIII.

Every Southern State had followed the example of the Old Dominion previous to 1860. In several of the great cities the common school
for white children and youth had been established. Two or three of the
States had, perhaps, done better than Virginia in their attempts at a
free common school for the masses. But, practically, the Southern system of education up to 1860 was as close an imitation of the English
methods of half a century ago as could be expected in a new country.
The result was a vast amount of white illiteracy, of which there is
very little accurate record in the statistics, while the slave population,
of course, was almost wholly untaught. Even this system in 1865 was
involved in the same ruin that overwhelmed all, save a few of the
border States.

But, although this was the only consistent and persistent educational effort of the South up to the year 1860, yet we shall do the Southern people great injustice if we suppose there had not been through its entire history great and partially successful efforts looking towards the education of the white masses, at one time even contemplating the emancipation and instruction of the slaves.

We repeat that Thomas Jefferson, the author of the Declaration of Independence, was also the broadest-minded American school man on the ground at the beginning of our national existence. New England had already established the free district school, the academy, and the college, encouraged and partially supported by the State, and in 1776 was the only part of the country which had a complete system of popular education. But New England had not yet wrought out that interdependence among its schools which now prevails, and had not contemplated our modern State university, unsectarian in religion and elective in curriculum, which is now found in every Southern and Western State.

This was the crown of the grand temple of American education seen in vision by Jefferson a hundred years ago. His scheme, as before stated, included the emancipation and industrial training of the slaves, the free district school for the white masses, the county academy for the secondary, and a State university, including opportunity for training in letters, professions, arts, and arms, for the higher culture of boys. In greater or less degree the main features of this system were accepted by the leading statesmen of Virginia and were largely indorsed by the most eminent publicists and scholars of the Southern colonies, even men of the people, like Gen Marion, of South Carolina, giving a hearty assent. In every Southern colony, especially Virginia, an honest effort was made to provide for the education of the entire white population, and few probably contemplated the perpetuity of negro slavery. But these efforts failed entirely, because the Southern colonies were poor and had been overrun and greatly demoralized by the war; because the nonslaveholding whites were ignorant, unorganized, and indifferent; but chiefly because the average planter and slave-owner did not believe in this theory with sufficient vigor to consent to be taxed for schools to which he did not care to send his own children. But the leading statesmen of the South in the First Congress did heartily unite with the North in persuading the southern Atlantic States to give up their claim on the vast western wilderness and to enact that great statute which, at once, dedicated the mighty Northwest to free labor, offered to every settler a home, and set apart a generous portion of every township for the support of schools, with ample provision for the higher education of the superior few.

For seventy-five years, until the breaking out of the civil war, this vision of popular education seen by the fathers was never absent from the heart of any State of the South. When the history of Southern education shall be fairly written the wonder will be, why, with such a constant and growing desire among a portion of its influential white people and such brilliant and earnest advocacy from great numbers of its leading minds, so little had really been accomplished. Very early, in Virginia, South Carolina, Kentucky, and Louisiana, the matter of free public education had been broached and discussed in legisla. tures, in some cases incorporated ˙in the words of the fundamental law. These efforts culminated in every Southern State, at different periods, in schemes which, however ineffectual, really committed the State to the theory of the education of the people.

In Maryland a system of county academies was endowed by the State. In Virginia the university of Jefferson was established in 1820 and an arrangement, by which some $50,000 annually was appropriated for the schooling of poor children, either in free schools or by paying tuition to private academies, prevailed up to the breaking out of the war. With even more intense earnestness did South Carolina wrestle with the same problem of overcoming the ignorance of large masses of her poorer white class. More than one of her eminent governors repeatedly enforced the subject upon the legislature. Educators like Dr. Thornwell and a brilliant group of schoolmen, extending up to the last decade of slavery, had endeavored to reconstruct the ineffectual system of free schools for the poor, then in vogue. The cities of Baltimore, Wilmington, Del., and Charleston, S. C., had built up the free school, essentially on the Northern basis, before 1860, and Savannah and Augusta, Ga., and Mobile, Ala., had followed on the same road. Great efforts were also made in Louisiana to establish schools for the white masses and considerable sums of money were expended for many years, with very questionable results. New Orleans had built up a double-headed system of English and French public instruction, of which the city was very proud. A remarkable series of men in that city attempted to endow education and charity. Chief among these was John McDonogh, a native of Maryland, who went to New Orleans in 1809 and died in 1850, leaving what he supposed a property of $2,000,000, to be distributed for industrial and popular education in New Orleans and Baltimore, with further outlook for Northern cities and towns. Had the scheme carried and the property been faithfully nursed this would have been, perhaps, considering the time, the grandest benefaction up to that date for education in the country. If a brilliant array of great men and splendid women had been sufficient to insure the education of the people, the city of New Orleans, a generation ago, would have led the South and challenged the most favored Northern metropolis in varied and abundant opportunities for the entire white population. Money was given with profusion, and brilliant examples, lofty oratory, and a sincere effort backed the outlay. It was only another. illustration of the fact that no people was ever yet educated, in this Republic, by anybody but itself. Here, especially, popular indifference and ecclesiastical hostility have prolonged the struggle even to the present day.

The most interesting contest during this period was in the State of Kentucky. The State laid the foundations of a common school fund and earnestly began the experiment of educating its white children. Then broke out the famous educational war to suppress this generous movement, engineered by hostile church influences in combination with a narrow political policy and social intolerance. That the people's common school was saved, the Commonwealth owes largely to the prodigious efforts of the famous divine, Dr. Robert Breckenridge, who, through a series of years, threw himself with all the resources of his powerful manhood into the heart of the contest, saved the school fund of the State, and kept alive the purpose to educate the people. Yet in this "holy war" the common school of Kentucky was wounded nearly to the death, and is not yet out of hospital, though making steady advances.

The State of North Carolina, on the whole, had scored the greatest success of any of the original Southern States, and under the zealous superintendency of Dr. Calvin H. Wiley, at a short period previous to the war, seemed on the way to the establishment of a vigorous system of public instruction for the white masses, large numbers of children being gathered together for several months in the year, and $268,000 appropriated—the largest sum expended by any Southern State for free education.

The new State of Missouri before 1860 had already attempted the western system of schools with partial success, and St. Louis, by the help of magnificent land grants from the Government, had laid the foundation of her present eminence in education.

The republic and afterwards the State of Texas began, with splendid intentions, in setting apart public lands as extensive as all New England for education, but up to 1860 there had been no great result. Arkansas and Florida were but feebly stirred with educational ambition. Outside its large cities, Georgia was firmly wedded to the academical and collegiate idea. Mississippi was, perhaps, the educational laggard of the Southwest. Alabama in 1854 had attempted a scheme of public schools which one of her enthusiastic superintendents compared favorably with those of "boastful Massachusetts."

LXXIX.

But the radical cause of failure was not far to seek, and the history of popular education in the South before 1860 points one way. Always we find a desire easily waked up among the poorer masses of white people for better schools; always a noble brotherhood of eminent men pleading their cause, but always the average man of wealth, the country planter, indifferent, obstructive, or hostile to the idea, even to the extent of nullifying any system on the ground. This class owned the property, made the laws, and shaped the educational policy of the country in all these States. Living an isolated life, absorbed in their own interests, with no desire to bring their children in contact with their inferiors in school, they could never be held up to the large taxation and vigilant administration essential to success. The schools established for the poorer classes, with few exceptions, were poor schools. A strain of complaint at careless administration of funds, unwillingness or forgetfulness to keep records or report to authorities, the poor quality of teachers and the indifference of the people themselves to the scanty supply of schooling, runs through these reports in all the States. Whatever may be true in Europe, any system of churching or schooling in the United States of America that fences off a lower class for a special work will be at once neglected by those who give it and despised by those to whom it is offered. In many cases the superior children of this sort were educated in private schools, and it was possible for an energetic youth of obscure parentage to get at the elements of knowledge. But the numerous difficulties in the way were too much for great multitudes of the poor, who subsided into an ignorance that filled every thoughtful man with alarm. In two or three of these States--Missouri and North Carolina especially, in lesser degree Kentucky and Tennessee—the more democratic idea prevailed and greater results were achieved. But at the date of the breaking out of the civil war, outside a few of the larger cities, the American idea of schooling the mass of white children for the honorable and difficult obligation of American citizenship had either not been adopted or in any effective way enforced in these fifteen States, while the 5,000,000 of their slave population, with individual exceptions, were abiding in absolute ignorance of letters.

LXXX.

The time will come when the Southern ex-Confederate States will do full justice to the efforts made to build up the American system of common school instruction for the entire population during the troubled years of the "reconstruction period." This period held on in some of the States for ten years after the close of the war. While it continued, the State governments were mainly in the hands of that portion of the white people in sympathy with the newly enfranchised freedmen, while for a time their political opponents were disfranchised, or, even when rehabilitated, held aloof from political action. Of course these governments were upheld by the military power of the nation. It was a period of intense and implacable political conflict; indeed, for all practical purposes of reconciliation, a continuance of the civil war, with even more distracting results in the States thus governed.

But undoubtedly the best thing done in this turbulent era for all these States was the honest attempt by their State governments, for the first time in their history, to put on the ground the full American system of common school instruction. In each of the eleven restored Commonwealths a common school system was established, sufficient, could it have been thoroughly enforced, to well begin the immense

labor of educating the whole people. It was a movement destined
to partial failure by the circumstances of the case. The old well-
to-do class was in poverty, for a time disfranchised, and in a state of
obstinate resistance to the whole order of affairs. There was no money
to support the large expense, no suitable outfit of buildings, no body
of competent teachers, and, more than all, no belief in the system itself
by the large majority of educated and professsional people. The Northern officials were not veteran educators, but young soldiers and politicians, profoundly ignorant of Southern society, even when honestly
attempting to establish in South Carolina and Mississippi the common
school system of Massachusetts and Ohio. There was also the usual
amount of plunder, rascality, and general diabolism that inevitably follows the attempt to govern an American State by the military and
centralizing methods of old-world administration. No wonder that,
under these conditions, the new system of Southern common schools
established and generally put in operation during these years should
have failed to realize the enthusiastic expectations of the North, and
should generally have been largely modified as soon as the majority of
the Southern white population were restored to their political status
and once more resumed control of public affairs.

Yet, it will remain a perpetual wonder that so much was really done,
even under these unpromising circumstances. Large sums of money
were contributed by the National Government, through the Freedman's
Bureau, and by private contributors at the North ; great numbers of
teachers from the same States, and even from the Canadas and abroad,
pressed into the work, and occupation was given to many Southern people ; many thousands of children in all these States were gathered
in schools, and more was accomplished than can be described through
the clumsy vocabulary of educational statistics. In the school reports
a thousand children are but a thousand " figureheads." But the fifty
good heads in that motley crowd, destined to " figure " in the rising
educational work of their State for a generation, can only be known
through the widespread influence for good of their magnetic manhood
and womanhood. Several important points were made during these ten
stormy years in which, like a child born on shipboard in a tempest,
the present southern American common school saw the light ; its cradle
rocked by high winds ; its very existence in perpetual peril ; yet, by
the help of a protecting Providence, coming into port at last with a
sturdy pair of legs of its own, prepared to run the children's race through
coming years.

LXXXI.

The first great point was that the large number of Southern people
of the poorer white and colored sort who, for years had been longing
for educational opportunities, found in this movement their first chance
of securing for their own children, often for themselves and the whole

population they represented, the inestimable blessing of free education. To them must be added the considerable number of the ruling class who had always been in sympathy with these views, and, even in face of the displeasure of their own friends, had joined with more or less vigor in the work.

Second. A large number of persons of competent education, many of them old teachers, were either persuaded to resume work or forced by pecuniary necessity to teach. Besides them, an opportunity was offered for occupation to a considerable class of educated men and women in re- duced circumstances to earn a living in the schoolroom. What with the revival of the colleges, academies, and private in addition to the public schools, the demand for teachers was never so great. Indeed, it was almost the only place where an educated woman could earn her bread. So, at once there began that movement of superior Southern womanhood upon this profession which has become the most character- istic feature of the new education in the South. A part, and a most important part it has already become, of this movement was the intro- duction of colored men and women as teachers in the common schools of their race. It is impossible to measure by any Anglo-Saxon stand- ard the mighty import of the fact that even an hundred young men and women, born in slavery, within twenty years were standing, with the support of public authority in the State of their birth, on the teacher's platform, instructing the first generation of the five millions of their people ever invited to come in at the open door of the people's common school.

Third. For the first time in these years these States seriously en- tered on the critical experiment of public taxation for universal educa- tion. No Southern State before this had taken the position that the schooling of the whole people is a just and legitimate claim upon the property of the Commonwealth. Whole classes of the Southern peo- ple still do not accept this, the fundamental theory of the American com- mon school, as is shown by the constant complaint of the injustice of edu- cating the Negro at the expense largely of the white property holders, as if this were not the corner stone of the system—that in consideration of the contribution of labor in the creation of wealth, wealth should be freely taxed for that enlightenment of the masses which makes labor more profitable, property more secure, and works generally for the com- mon good; and that this assessment shall be made by the vote of the whole people, since the whole people contribute to the prosperity of the State. In this case there was injustice, in that the superior class had little voice in legislation and the ignorant masses were in the hands of political "rings." But the great principle was so effectively driven into the average Southern mind that no reaction has dislodged it to the pres- ent day.

Fourth. A great many schoolhouses were built and school property purchased by national or Northern funds during this period. Some of the colleges, for a time, were used by the public authorities.

LXXXII.

On the whole this ten years work can not be justly called the imposition of the Northern public school system upon the conquered South, as is even now asserted by unreconciled opponents. It was rather the one department of the provisional or "carpetbag" State governments that met a long felt and deeply-seated necessity of Southern society. For this reason it was hailed by thousands of good people in political opposition to their government and welcomed with unspeakable joy and gladness by the entire population whose educational needs had been neglected under the old régime. And how large that portion of the white people was, none of the recent Southern historians of the old-time school system seems to know or cares to tell. The positive assertion of a class of Southern educators, that the present illiteracy of Southern white people is one of the results of the war, is pure assertion, unsupported by fact. There was no system of educational statistics in any of these States before 1860. But enough can be gathered from the most authentic sources to show the absurdity of this claim. There was, doubtless, during this period as during the war, a suspension of school life to large numbers of the children of the more favored class, and this accounts in a measure for the coöperation of many of these people even then with the movement for the only schools which, in their impoverished condition, they could use. But the slaveholding class, all told, never included one-third the white population of the South. Thus, to multitudes of the remaining white people, this establishment of the free common school came as the first fruits of their own emancipation into that intelligent and independent citizenship which, in the brief period of twenty-five years, has made the "third estate of the South" virtually the controlling political power in the majority of these States.

Outside of the eleven ex-Confederate were the four old border States, Maryland, Delaware, Kentucky, and Missouri, in which this peculiar system spoken of did not prevail, besides the new State of West Virginia. In all these Commonwealths, especially Maryland, West Virginia, and Missouri, the work of popular education was at once taken up, and under the eminent leadership of educators like Dr. Newell, Dr. Harris, and a brilliant corps of teachers great results were achieved. 35 In the Central States also, notably in Virginia and Tennessee, the work began soon after the close of the war, and under the superintendency of John Eaton, Dr. Ruffner, Superintendent Binford, the 36/37 Peabody Normal School, at Nashville, and the remarkable body of public school men and women that have always kept Virginia and Tennessee the most hopeful of the ex-Confederate Southern States in popular education, decisive results were obtained, while several of the Gulf States had not yet overcome their enforced political apprenticeship.

LXXXIII.

But through all these troubled years, up to 1880, one steady beam of light penetrated the confused twilight, and one calm, penetrating voice of encouragement cheered the heart of every patriot educator through these sixteen heavily burdened and sorely stricken Commonwealths.

Never was the good providence of God more signally manifested than in the inspiration of George Peabody, a New England boy, for the establishment of the great educational fund called by his name. The organization and administration of this magnificent charity seem to have been, even to the present day, under the same protection. In its presidency, Hon. Robert C. Winthrop, of Massachusetts, has richly earned the title to a statesmanship of education that will abide when myriads of great political names have floated down the tide of time.

No man in the United States was so fitted for the delicate, almost perilous office of first secretary of this board as Dr. Barnas Sears, of New England. For thirteen years this strong, wise, and sweet scholar and divine traversed all these States, rocking amid the earthquakes and volcanic eruptions of reconstruction politics, "bearing gifts," of which the least were the moderate sums of money at his disposal, the best, those words of sympathy, friendly encouragement, common sense, and manly defense of education prophetic of the present coming together of the better souls of both sections. I remember the story told me in a city of Texas, that one night at a public meeting held for the consideration of the imperative educational needs of the town, when nobody seemed to know the way out of the tangle, a quiet stranger from the audience came to the platform, asked permission to speak, and, in a voice scarcely above a whisper, said : "I am Dr. Sears, agent of the Peabody educational fund. I have heard your debates and appreciate your situation. I will give you as much as you will raise to establish your new common schools." The same brief message established the common school at almost every educational center in these States. In a journeying of twelve years through all the Southland, I have heard only blessings for the memory of this great and good man and unstinted praise of the wisdom of this fund. No other two millions of dollars invested in education have wrought such wide-spread beneficence as this.

Dr. Eben Stearns, a veteran of normal school and academical instruction in the North, was spared for the last and best years of his life to organize the Peabody Normal School at Nashville, Tenn., which under the administration of his devoted successor, Chancellor William H. Payne, of Michigan, is growing into the preparation for the final endowment which will probably make it the first real normal university of the Union.

The later administration of Dr. J. L. M. Curry, of Alabama, most thoroughly furnished and most courageous of all advocates of universal education in the South, who, after thirty years of brilliant service as member of the National and Confederate Congresses, professor, clergyman, minister of the United States to Spain, and author, has finally returned to the agency of the Peabody and assumed the additional control of the Slater educational fund, has only broadened and deepened the obligation of the South and spread abroad, through all lands, the admiration for the wisdom of this model educational trust. It only remains that the new industrial South, the sound and splendor of whose rising importance are filling the Nation and arresting the attention of the world, should, through a group of its new wealthy men, build the southern monument to this group of heroes, in the shape of an addition of $10,000,000 to the Peabody educational fund.

LXXXIV.

It was at the close of this the first effort of the Southern people to establish their own system of public instruction, in accordance with their own estimate of financial ability, only four years after South Carolina, Louisiana, Mississippi, and Florida had come into the management of their own political affairs, that my first visit to Virginia, already referred to, took place. In that most eventful month of my educational experience I spent three weeks in attendance on the State institute for white teachers at the University of Virginia, in Albemarle County. The fourth week was given to the institute for colored teachers, at Lynchburg. Here, for the first time, I was introduced to a gathering of several hundred young people of this race, already engaged in teaching in the common schools of the State, who had come, often at great sacrifice, to meet Dr. Ruffner and his corps of instructors. One resolute group of these young men had walked 100 miles through the stifling heat of August to be present. The most effective teachers of the school were the brothers Montgomery, two young men, born in freedom, taken in 38 childhood from New Orleans, educated by a friend of my own boyhood in Vermont, now supervisors of the excellent public schools for colored youth in Washington. That visit to Virginia in August, 1880, struck the keynote of the ministry of education which has engrossed my entire attention during the past twelve years, leading me through every Southern State, to every important educational center, with a wide opportunity for observation of every description of educational establishment or arrangement, in contact with the foremost educators and representatives of the educational public in these sixteen States.

It is because of this unusual opportunity for personal acquaintance with the whole field of Southern education during the past twelve years that this circular of information is so largely a record of personal experience. These years, from 1880 to 1892, cover what may be called the second period of the recent educational movement in the South, especially as concerns the establishment, by State and local effort, of its new public schools.

LXXXV.

Previous to this date the work had been largely experimental, in
the face of a constant sense of inability by the people to shoulder the
expense; a sharp and obstinate resistance by a portion of the university, college, and academical men, who looked upon the common-school
movement as hostile to their own establishments; the denunciation of
the ecclesiastical enemies of State education, except as a subsidizing
annex to the old European system of sectarian "Christian education";
and the half-hearted support of the average politician, ready to crush
the schools in the interest of reaction, or, if that were impossible, to
capture and manage them in the interest of partisan politics. The
teachers, with the exception of the men who had come down from a past
generation, were largely women, often of the most distinguished families, compelled by circumstances to this work at first, but often remaining in it from the highest motives. Almost every city of 20,000 people
and upwards in these sixteen States in 1880 had already established a
system of graded schools for both races; in Baltimore, Louisville, St.
Louis, Charleston, Nashville, New Orleans, Savannah, Augusta, and
Mobile, the original schools, revived and largely improved, for the first
time taking the colored children and youth in charge. A secondary class
of cities, like Lynchburg, Petersburg, Raleigh, Montgomery, Atlanta,
Jackson, Memphis, Little Rock, and a few others, had, for the first time,
established public schools by local taxation, of every grade. Besides
these, in the twelve States below the border, there were, in 1880, probably not fifty villages (cities as they are called) of from 2,000 to 5,000
people with a similar arrangement. Indeed, in Texas (the State perhaps best able at that time) there were not half a dozen, and only two
of its five leading cities had established a reliable school system.

In the open country the common school had everywhere been set up
by legal enactment, after the feeble fashion of the day. Almost every
locality sufficiently populous had its school for white and colored children, but seldom housed in a suitable building, lasting rarely more than
three and often only two months in the year, with such teaching as
might be expected under these conditions. The cities of secondary importance and villages were chiefly getting on in the old way, with a
swarm of little private schools, one town of 8,000 white people, as I
remember, having thirty of these establishments. There were not half
a dozen good circulating libraries, and I do not recall one large free
library south of Washington. There were no reliable educational statistics, and nobody seemed to have any clear understanding of the number of children and youth in any school, of the length of the terms, or
efficiency of the teachers. An eminent judge of the supreme court of a
Gulf State deplored the fact that there was but one place, the State
university, where a boy could be sent with any expectation of reputa-
ble schooling, and that institution was a crowd of boys chiefly in need
of the most elementary education. The schools of the city of New Or-

leans were in a state of siege, their teachers working like a heroic band of missionaries, without pay, under the lead of good Supt. Rogers, whose patient and cheerful courage at this juncture saved the system from wreck. The old University of South Carolina, at Columbia, had just struggled up to a new life, supported by the agricultural and mechanical education fund voted by Congress in 1862. The University of Texas had not been established, and the University of Kentucky was enjoying one of its brief periods of convalescence from the series of ups and downs through which it had fought its way to its present estate. National aid for common school education was advocated and voted for in Congress by all but 3 of the 22 Senators of the eleven ex-Confederate States.

LXXXVI.

But from this year on began the new era, which, in the years from 1876-'77 to 1889, has shown the brilliant result recorded in the annexed table, compiled by the present United States Commissioner of Education. By reference to this statement it will be seen that, during these thirteen years, the sixteen Southern States have nearly doubled their common-school enrollment of white and nearly trebled that of colored pupils. The enrollment in all classes of schools for the colored people for 1889 was 1,238,622. The whole expenditure in 1888-'89 for common schools in the South was $23,226,982. The total amount expended for the Southern common school in thirteen years is $216,644,699. The average school session varied, in 1889, from the South Atlantic division, eight States, ninety-five days, to the Southern Central division, seven States, eighty-eight days in the year.

TABLE NO. 1.

Table of common school enrollment, expenditures, etc., for sixteen Southern States for thirteen years.

[Prepared by Hon. W. T. Harris, U. S. Commissioner of Education.]

Year.	Common-school enrollment.		Colored schools.		Total colored enrollment.	Expenditures, both races.
	White.	Colored	Normal.	Other secondary and higher.		
1876-'77	1,827,139	571,506	3,785	4,726	580,017	$11,231.073
1877-'78	2,034,948	675,150	5,236	7,735	688,181	11,760,251
1878-'79	2,013,584	685,942	6,171	8,253	700,366	12,181,602
1879-'80	2,215.674	784,709	7,408	7,996	800,113	12,475,044
1880-'81	2,234,877	802,374	7,621	8,372	802,372	13,359,784
1881-'82	2,249,263	802,982	8,509	9,889	821,380	14,820,972
1882-'83	2,370,110	817,240	8,509	9,889	833,638	14,324,925
1883-'84	2,546,448	1,002,313	10,771	13,035	1,026,119	17,053,467
1884-'85	2,676,911	1,030,463	8,390	15,110	1,053,963	17,227,373
1885-'86	2,773,445	1,048,653	6,297	16,831	1,071,697	18,439,891
1886-'87	2,975,773	1,118,556	1,771	11,577	1,131,904	20,821,999
1887-'88	3,110,603	1,140,405	5,439	12,254	1,158,098	21,810,158
1888-'89	3,197,830	1,213,092	7,462	18,063	1,238,622	23,226,982
Total amount expended in 13 years..						216,644,699

AVERAGE SCHOOL SEASON.	Days.
North Atlantic division (9 States)	157
North Central division (11 States)	137
South Atlantic division (8 States)	95
South Central division (7 States)	88

LXXXVII.

The following tables, compiled from the last and forthcoming reports of the National Bureau of Education, in connection with Table 1, furnish an overlook of the present condition of the common-school system in fifteen Southern States. In this estimate, Missouri, although a former slave State, and the District of Columbia are omitted, as properly belonging to the Western and national system of education. Table No. 2 gives the actual condition of school attendance by the children between the ages of 6 and 14, the real American school age. Table No. 3 gives the sum per capita expended by each Southern State for common schooling, with the amount expended in mills per dollar of assessed valuation.

TABLE No. 2.

Table giving the whole number of pupils enrolled in the common schools of fifteen Southern States, with the number in average daily attendance in 1888–'89.

State.	Whole number of pupils enrolled in the common schools.	Average daily attendance.	State.	Whole number of pupils enrolled in the common schools.	Average daily attendance.
Delaware	32, 552	21, 271	Tennessee	436, 524	308, 969
Maryland	179, 460	99, 220	Alabama	270, 204	172, 101
Virginia	336, 948	195, 525	Mississippi	319, 711	193, 119
West Virginia	187, 528	119, 990	Louisiana	125, 573	90, 551
North Carolina	337, 382	208, 657	Texas	440, 467	340, 000
South Carolina	194, 264	136, 358	Arkansas	216. 152	141, 500
Georgia	321, 176	217, 896			
Florida	86, 008	63, 652	Total	3, 814, 935	2, 531, 363
Kentucky	330, 986	222, 554			

TABLE No. 3.

Table giving the sum per capita expended by each Southern State for common schooling, with the amount expended in mills per dollar of assessed valuation.

State.	Sum per capita expended for common schooling on basis of average attendance.	Mills per dollar expended on assessed valuation	State.	Sum per capita expended for common schooling on basis of average attendance.	Mills per dollar expended on assessed valuation.
Delaware	$11. 60	....	Alabama	4. 36	3. 01
Maryland	18. 67	3. 7	Mississippi	5. 78	7. 01
Virginia	8. 29	4. 7	Louisiana	6. 01	2. 06
West Virginia	10. 90	7. 6	Texas	10. 24	4. 08
North Carolina	3. 36	3. 4	Arkansas	6. 84	5. 08
South Carolina	3. 30	3. 03	North Atlantic division.	21. 67	4. 04
Georgia	3. 99	2. 05	South Atlantic division.	7. 80	4. 03
Florida	7. 68	5. 06	South Central division..	6. 93	4. 04
Kentucky	9. 67	4. 03	North Central division .	19. 37	7. 09
Tennessee	3. 75	3. 09	Western division	29. 99	5. 02

LXXXVIII.

My report of the common-school upbuilding during the twelve years since that memorable summer visit to Monticello, the home of Jefferson, the earliest educational statesman of the South, is not concerned with the stormy period of reconstruction, when the North and the nation were laboring to plant the American common school, for the first time, in the reluctant soil of the former slave States. Neither does it concern, save by comparison, the initial period of home effort, between 1870 and 1880, when the people of every Southern State made their first great movement which in twenty years has wrought such remarkable results. My personal observation covers the second period, during which it may be said the American common school has become a vital part of the life of every Southern Commonwealth, and has been permanently lodged in all the Territories that will henceforth increase the number of the distinctively Southern members of the Union. I have now to chronicle the deeply interesting story of the steady growth of the Southern common school as I have watched it by personal journeying, observation, and labor in eight months of annual field work and four months of annual study during this period.

And I repeat, that I call attention to my own observations, from a growing conviction that only by such testimony can the educational public of the South, to say nothing of the North, obtain any reliable notion even of the superficial facts of the case; and only by such careful study of the common school movement, in connection with the past history and industrial, social, educational, and religious condition and present status of affairs in the South, can any reliable estimate be formed of the real significance of the movement, not only to this section but to the Republic and, indirectly, to Christendom. It will thus be seen what far-reaching issues are involved in this great experiment.

Indeed, the American common school is now, by all odds, the most potent agency by which the Southern section of this Republic is passing over from an aristocratic to a democratic republican American form of society. In comparison with it, all other influences now at work in the new South are comparatively superficial or, at best, indecisive. There is still a powerful party in this section laboring for the restoration of " the old South " on its original aristocratic foundations of the immutable distinction of race and class. This is a possibility, and no present developement in its political, ecclesiastical, social, and industrial affairs, with one exception, is strong enough to resist it. That one exception is the portentous political uprising of its third estate, in which great masses of the plain white people in all these States, under the name of the Farmers' Alliance, have practically, for the time, obtained the political control of them all. At present this movement is so involved in the conflicts of local and State politics, and so confused by the personal ambition and crude political theories of some of its prominent leaders, that " it does not yet appear what it shall be." But it may be safely predicted that it signifies in the immediate future the reign of the white people instead of the domination of a class, and in a later future the elevation of the colored citizen to his fair and rightful participation in public affairs.

But even this deeply significant movement is entirely dependent for its complete success upon the fundamental agency of republican civilization, the Southern common school. Only as the masses of the white population, who occupy the open country, can obtain suitable advantages for schooling their children, and be persuaded to local effort for the better training of the colored folk, in many portions the majority, will this movement be able to slough off the crowd of demagogues now rushing to its leadership; free itself from crude and suicidal theories of government that would scuttle any American State; rise superior to the destructive prejudice of the race above and the degrading jealousy of the classes below; arrest the drift of intelligent young people from the country districts, and generally refresh, broaden, and elevate the entire public policy of the section in its relations to the national life. And the most hopeful feature of the movement is that it has everywhere been accompanied by an imperative demand for better common school facilities, and in every State, save one, a decided step forward in the improvement of the country schools has been made.

The remainder of this portion of the present circular will deal chiefly with my own observation of the Southern common school in its large and profound relation to the present drift of Southern society. And as the most significant feature of all, especial attention will be given to the work of Southern women in its development and in the regions of Southern life adjacent thereto.

LXXXIX.

But it can not be too often repeated that only the most general and superficial idea of the common-school system of a country, in the present condition of these fifteen Southern States, can be obtained from reading tables of statistics. Everywhere unsatisfactory, the science of educational statistics is the latest departure in the new South. Even for the rough purposes of the local distribution of school moneys it is by no means satisfactory to the people of these States, and, at best, has but an approximate value for the common necessities of administration. The whole vocabulary of common-school life has a different meaning in the open country, even in the cities, of States not yet with twenty years' experience of universal education, and a region like New England, where the system was established two hundred and fifty years ago. As well compare one of the great "universities" for the colored people—a crowd of children and youth, nine-tenths of whom would be unable to enter the upper grades of a good graded grammar school and the majority would be found in the elementary department— with Harvard, Columbia, and Ann Arbor, or the average "female college" of these States with Vassar, Smith, and the Harvard Annex, as the average country school, in which the vast majority of Southern children are still compelled to receive their training in letters, with the "country district school" of the Northern and Western States. The persistent complaints of eminent Northern school authorities over the defects of the Northern district school come from the sharp contrast between the great educational progress in cities and villages and the slower movement in the open country, also from the constantly stimulated ideal of common-school instruction, which bids fair to provoke a reaction in the educational public.

The city and an increasing number of the graded village schools of the South are organized, disciplined, and, in many cases, taught, by the prevailing methods of "the new education." Their superintendents, often men of large ability and admirable zeal, with an increasing number of their teachers, are laboring earnestly to keep themselves in elbow touch and hearty sympathy with their professional friends in other portions of the country. But, outside certain favored districts and occasional schools, the entire country-school system of the South is in no condition to institute a fair comparison with that of any Northern State, either in the ability of the people for its support, the character of its school buildings, the quality of its teachers and the facilities for instruction, the length of its term and regularity of attendance, the number of years given to school life, the social and educational environment, the facilities for reading, the character of the occupations of the children out of school, and the home life of multitudes of the humbler classes. A good country district school in Massachusetts or Indiana is the outgrowth of the entire history and civilization of the locality and the Commonwealth, the spiritual thermometer which, better than any other test, reveals the status of that neighborhood and its relation to the present condition of Christendom. The three or four months' white or colored Southern country school, especially in the vast lowland regions where illiteracy most prevails, even if the best that the people can afford, established and supported with a zeal and sacrifice often pathetic and worthy of all admiration, is another sort of institution, of which the best that can be said is that its intelligent friends are "forgetting the things that are behind and pressing forward to the things that are before." Many of the village graded schools are in the midst of a desperate struggle out of the jungle of embarrassments and difficulties in which they were born and cradled into the "cleared land" where education can "have free course, run, and be glorified." And more than one of the larger Southern cities is, to-day, in the hands of the vilest of all rings, an educational political clique, with only hope from the political dynamite that will blow open the eyes of the people to the rights of the children.

XC.

All this is no special disparagement to Southern schoolkeeping. The common school everywhere is a slow growth and, like the child, is destined to pass through the whole circle of childrens' diseases before it finds itself on a pair of legs strong and swift enough to run the race.

First comes the effort of the sectarian churches to capture the new school, pack it with their own members as teachers, and use it as a proselyting machine. Next the local politicians jump upon it and endeavor to make it a tender to the political engine. Then comes in the insidious and all-pervading social influence in which every little group of families endeavors to get possession of the reins, adjust the whole arrangement to their own notions, and, through their own sisters, cousins, and aunts, as teachers, virtually educate the town. Not less mischievous is the reign of pedantry; when a narrow schoolman at the head of the system switches off a public school upon the side track of a petty, fruitless, and obstinate effort to change it to an imitation college or academy of the old-time sort. Besides these, there are morbid tendencies innumerable—as numerous and as mischievous as the enemies that fight the life of a child from the cradle to manhood—that keep the public school in " a state of siege ;" so that only by the eternal vigilance of an intelligent and resolute educational public can it be kept to its own work till safely landed in that central position where every class can be relied upon to become its defender in any hour of peril.

The common school has fought its way up to its present vantage ground of power in every Northern State through generations of conflict. Even yet it is " under arms " against the assault of its eclesiastical and political foes, often in combination, that would change the American to the European and Canadian type of public education. So powerful are these influences that there are not a score of cities of 100,000 people in the North where the people are able to command the services of an educator of the first class as superintendent of schools; and even the important office of State commissioner of education too often comes in at the end of a political " deal," bestowed with no good will to the children. It is not, then, remarkable that the Southern common school, not yet a generation old, born and cradled in a revolutionary epoch, environed with peculiar and obstinate difficulties of its own, should be still beset almost to the death by all these hostile influences, often in their most aggravated form. That such is the case is, however, the hard fact that must modify the estimate and reveal the absurdity of the prodigious praise of its reckless and boastful " boomers, " North and South. That it has survived and, at the end of twenty years, come out victor in this " holy war " is another stubborn fact that challenges the admiration and demands the sympathy of the true educational public at home and abroad.

XCI.

These words of caution are especially in order in view of a twofold style of misapprehension of the present condition of Southern public-school affairs, which not only affects the proper judgment through the North, but is in great danger of confusing the educational public at home.

The first is the inevitable American habit of inordinate exaggeration
and a boastfulness that borders on insolence in pushing the claims of
any portion of the country to public consideration. There is just now
a real danger that the Northern educational public will be filled with a
thoroughly misleading notion of the real status of the Southern common school. The more reliable educators, the real statesmen, and the
genuine educational public of that section are not responsible for this
exaggeration. In the South it is the work largely of the local press
and the great army of all sorts which in every community makes a
religion of the indiscriminate laudation of its own locality, its people
and institutions, its essential superiority to every other people and
society at home or abroad. But an especial cause of this tendency is
found in the highly colored representation of the numerous companies
of influential persons engaged in the industrial development of the
mining, manufacturing, transportation, and immigration interests of
these States. More than one of these State official departments is publishing to the world, as an attraction to " respectable immigration" to
the South, a thoroughly unreliable account of the common-school facilities of vast regions of country, doubtless with advantages of a sort,
but so poorly supplied with educational furnishings that their own
" respectable people " are steadily emigrating to the towns and cities,
largely to the Northwest, in search of the same advantages. The
Northern press is largely in the hands of the vast combinations of capital that are moving upon the South in an industrial invasion second
only in power to the armed host of a generation ago, and easily lends
itself to the highly-colored publication of anything that will move an
emigrating army in its train.

XCII.

These influences are not peculiar to Southern life, and their exaggerations are easily understood by the more intelligent portion of the people everywhere. But within the past five years there has been a special and systematic misrepresentation of Southern educational affairs,
originating in the peculiar combination of hostile forces which has tem-
porarily defeated the movement for national aid to education in Congress. The most effective instrumentality employed by this combination has been the systematic falsification, misrepresentation, and
misreading of the facts relating to the educational status of the South
by an influential section of the Northern metropolitan press. By a
dishonest manipulation of statistics, the skillful casting of false lights,
exaggerating the positive and suppressing the negative side of educational progress, wilfully misinterpreting the just and natural praise of
the best-informed educators and bringing to the front the absurd over-
statements of people of no local reputation for educational ability; by
persistent malignant assaults upon the foremost friends of national aid
in the North, and the studied concealment of its almost universal in-

dorsement by the weight of educational opinion in the South ; by adroit playing upon sectional, political, and ecclesiastical prejudices, the lead-ing press of the Northern cities has been made the vehicle to dissemi-nate a view of the progress, prospects, and general efficiency of the common school that fills its best-informed friends everywhere with amazement and indignation. As a result, the scheme for national aid was finally defeated in the Senate by New England senatorial votes, cast under a thorough misapprehension of the present condition of Southern education, the necessities of the masses of Southern children, and the improbability of any effectual change that will meet the de-mands of the present generation.

A moment's examination even of the tables appended to this circular will demonstrate the absurdity of this wholesale misrepresentation. There are to-day not less than 6,000,000 children and youth in the six-teen Southern States in imperative need of a good elementary education, only possible from several years attendance on a good school, at least six months in a year. Of these some four and one-fourth millions are represented by the vague educational mirage denominated " enroll-ment." Some two-thirds of this drifting multitude are reported in " average daily attendance " in schools kept from eighty-eight to ninety-five days in the year. Fifteen Southern States and the District of Columbia will pay this year less than $25,000,000 for common schools for all these children, not three times as much as the State of Massa-chusetts for her 400,000 ; only one-third more than the State of New York for her 650,000 school children. From the most reliable estimates of the National Bureau of Education the South Atlantic and South Central Division, including fifteen Southern States and the District of Columbia, had in 1888, respectively, 57.25 and 54.08 per cent of their population from 6 to 14 in common schools of this short annual dura-tion, with all the chances of a brief term of school life. Meanwhile the North Atlantic and North Central Divisions had respectively 73.99 and 77.53 and even the new Western Division 66.93 per cent of the same age in average attendance on schools nearly twice as long in session each year, with a much larger habit of prolonged schooling. The two southern divisions are able to expend annually per capita, on this " average at-tendance," including little more than one-half the real school population, but $7.80 and $6.93, while the North Atlantic, North Central, and Western Divisions expend, respectively, $21.67, $19.37, and $29.99 on an " average attendance," nearly twice as large as the South. The result is that the North Atlantic Division, including the six New England States, with New York, New Jersey, and Pennsylvania, the most wealthy and cultivated portion of the Union, schools 73.99 per cent of its population between 6 and 14 by an expenditure of 4.04 mills per dollar on its assessed valua-tion. Meanwhile the South Atlantic Division, the original portion of the Union that helped win national independence and establish the Republic and give to its earlier years the great company of statesmen grouped about Washington, without national aid, which has been poured like a river through the whole Republic west of the Alleghénies, *is to-day expending 4.03 mills per dollar on its valuation, only 1 mill per dollar less than the rich and powerful Northeast, to educate 57.25 per cent, little more than half its children between 6 and 14, from 88 to 95 days in the year.*

This brief statement of "figures that don't lie" casts an electric light upon the delusion whereby five Senators from Maine, Rhode Island, and Connecticut—States where 99.99, 69.90, and 76.42 of each 100 children are in daily average attendance on schools of longer duration and better quality, with greatly superior facilities for private school instruction—were persuaded to defeat the national educational bill in the Senate on the plea that, in the words of the great popular scientific journal of the country, "The South is doing very well now." This plain statement of facts dissolves the whole realm of cloudland and sectional fog in which the Northern educational public has been set adrift during the past five years, piloted by the "cultivated" leadership of metropolitan journalism, in humble imitation of the present attitude of upper-class England, until the present year in Parliament, resisting to the death every movement to give an effective free school system to the masses.

XCIII.

But, on the other hand, great injustice is done to the Southern common school and the educational public responsible for it, by a class of critics who have insisted upon judging it by the severe test of the natural methods of schoolkeeping which only within the past twenty years have been heartily accepted in the most favored seats of popular education in the country. Even tried by this standard, before which the major half even of New England schoolkeeping would go to the wall, there is no excuse for the wholesale depreciation of the movement to which we have been treated by this class of hypercritical experts. Our northern Chautauquas, summer institutes, and normal and professional seminaries of all kinds are thronged with the young teachers, especially young women, from all these States. A rising flood of Southern visitors is pouring through the most celebrated schools of the great Northern cities, intent on the observation and capture of the best things. An increasing number of young men from Southern colléges is going abroad for advanced study, and were it not that so many of them, on their return, are caught up by Northern institutions, the whole region of Southern education would be more largely refreshed thereby than at present. But, as it is, there is already a great deal going on in the graded schools of all the Southern States that need not fear comparison with anything done under similar conditions in the East or West. Especially are many of these schools rich in the quality of their women teachers, numbers of whom represent the best families and bring to their work the social culture and personal enthusiasm peculiar to the foremost society of the region. For the past ten years the most eminent educators of the North, men like Harris, Soldan, Dickinson, Parker, Dunton, Walton, Hancock, Newell, and scores of women of corresponding reputation, have made their annual summer pilgrimage to the South to superintend the State and local institutes, that, by the encouragement of the Peabody Education Fund, have been held in every State, for teachers of both races. These visiting experts uniformly return enthusiastic in their praise of the fine spirit and hard work, often reaching the pitch of consecration, with which they have been greeted. No school of pedagogy in the country reaches so broad a field and exerts an influence so radical as the Peabody Normal School at Nashville, in which 114 students, elected by competitive examination from ten States, are trained, for two years, partly at the expense of the Peabody Education Fund, with another division of 245 largely from the State of Tennessee. Every Southern State has established its normal schools for teachers of both races, or is on the eve of doing the same.

But the most powerful influence for good in the Southern common school is the great desire for learning among a large number of its pupils and the enthusiasm and devotion of a growing number of its teachers. Our Northern people have been told this by their own teachers working in the great schools for colored youth, and the pathetic story of the labors and sacrifices of these young pupils and their families has drawn both tears and liberal checks from thousands of churches through the length and breadth of the Northland. But too often the other side of the story, when rightly viewed even more inspiring, has either been left out, "damned with faint praise," or systematically misrepresented—the story of the upbuilding of the new Southern common school, so far almost at the expense and by the persistent efforts of the class overwhelmed with ruin in the great civil war.

XCIV.

The historian of the Republic in the near future will fill his broadest page with illuminated type to record the fact that in the closing decade of the first generation after the war this people, as the first offering of its reviving prosperity, expended $216,000,000 in the support of their new free common schools, $50,000,000 of which were given for the first experiment in human history in the universal education of 5,000,000 of slaves, emancipated by a military chief, without compensation, involving the absolute destruction of the only industrial system ever known in fifteen American commonwealths.

And it should be remembered by the fastidious educational expert that, after all has been said in praise of the natural methods of instruction, the South during the past twenty years, at the best, has only "kept school" according to the same ideas by which the North, before 1860, was developed into that mighty industrial civilization that, in five years, trained the "Grand Army of the Republic." that saved the Union and launched the reconstructed United States on its present career of unexampled national prosperity. The bottom educational factor in this country is an American boy or girl, inspired with the hopes and ambitions of republican society, with a boundless horizon in front, working for the education, more or less, that will become the tools of manhood or womanhood, the one element so persistently ignored by a large class of our educational critics in their unfavorable contrast between the school training of the United States and Continental Europe. The knowledge gained in a school, whether primary or university, is valuable in proportion as it is fused, absorbed, incorporated into the lifeblood by a strong motive power in the scholar. The poorest old-fashioned Yankee gristmill, with a swift mountain stream behind it, will grind more grain than the splendid group of flouring palaces of Minneapolis in a drought with no reinforcement from steam. In thousands of crude country schools, ex-tempore academies, and "shingle palaces" with the sign "college" above the front door, the children of the sixteen great Northern States east of the Mississippi were educated into the generation that, in saving the American Union, did more for the uplift of mankind than all the universities of Europe for the last century. To-day the best thing that can be said for Southern education is that it is "fighting it out on that line," with the advantage of national sympathy, experience, and "material aid," and the near prospect of an industrial prosperity which will enable it in time to develop every realm of instruction according to the best modern ideals.

The one thing that everywhere forces itself upon my attention, in passing through these Southern schools of every grade, is that I am again living over the educational life of the New England of fifty years ago. The same crowd of brave boys, with their lively sisters, pretty cousins, and youngish maiden aunts, are pushing on, through the same difficulties, to the same end, as in the old district schools of Franklin County, Mass., New Salem and Deerfield academies, and the Amherst, Williams, Mount Holyoke, and Harvard of half a century ago. There is no general educational stagnation in these sixteen Southern States. Through them all pours a steady onflowing tide, bearing 6,000,000 of young Americans and all belonging thereto towards the "good time coming." As in the Father of Waters there are eddies, bayous, great inland lakes, marshes, snags, and sandbars, and periodical overflows that threaten to bury civilization under a new deluge; but in spite of all these things the mighty torrent pours on, always flowing the same way, towards the open sea,—thus, while there is sore need of improvement in every good way, a loud call for more money, better teachers, more effective methods of school-keeping, longer terms, more years in school, and especially more children brought on the school grounds and more and better schoolhouses to contain them, yet below all this the great river flows on, pouring from the hills of the Lord toward the boundless ocean. The 20,000,000 of the Southland are afloat on its irresistible tide. And, while all sorts of discussion are going on, in regard to schooling, in general—the training of different classes and races, the limit of the common and the rights of the private and denominational school, the character of schoolbooks, all of which is duly reported to the country by the critical schoolman of the average type, whom we "ever have with us;"—yet all this is a grand debate on the deck of a craft steadily borne onward by an inland sea that no man can resist, and even the great Republic has, so far, been powerless to tame. And even while the eager disputants are wrangling over the present critical situation, the man on the outlook calls a new landing, and the old situation is forever left behind.

This is the "conclusion of the whole matter," as I see it. There is no excuse for magnifying the results already gained, especially in the interest of a general upbuilding, which is more dependent on the progress of true education than upon all things else. Much less is there excuse for that most unscientific and useless criticism which leaves out of the account the motive power of American institutions propelled by the irresistible forces of our new American life. Nowhere is that motive power more evident than in the new educational movement of the New South; and all prophets of despair, wherever they may prophesy, will be left behind, stranded each on the little sand-bar of his own pessimistic "fad," while the children of the South will move onward to their own place in the glorious confederation of American life.

XCV.

It has been my intention through the investigations of the past twelve years to do ample justice to all the positive successes achieved in the Southern common school. But below this, of far greater interest, a class of more significant facts at once attracted my attention.

The first and most radical of all was the fact itself of this effort of the Southern people to establish the American common school for "all sorts and conditions" of its population. Here was the decisive "new departure," which more than all things else struck the keynote of the New South. The Old South, or the Southern confederacy, if successful, could have achieved many of the results now loosely ascribed to the new order of affairs. It could have attracted a large and superior population from classes sympathetic with its social order in our own or foreign countries. It could have developed manufactures; flourished in literature and art; rebuilt and enlarged its old system of education; grown in wealth; given new proofs of the charm of its social life, and made new demonstration of splendid military and political ability—all the outcome of a republicanized aristocracy, the flower of the classic ideal of the Republic.

But the pivotal point amid the confusion of the past generation is the establishment in this section of the Republic of the American common school for the whole people. It is not established according to the European fashion, an elaborate system of class education, nowhere quite free, controlled by a central government to train the different strata of subjects each for its own place in the empire. It is everywhere the American system, proceeding from the people, supported by taxation imposed upon the people by themselves, supervised by officials elected by and responsible to the people, open through all its departments to the humblest, free to all who come, proceeding on the idea that nothing in this world is too good for the common training of American children and youth for their common life on the windy uplands of American citizenship. I saw at once that this step was not taken by the educational public, that from 1870 has laid out the road for the children and youth, under any misapprehension. It was taken deliberately, once for all, and during the past twenty years, although at times the column has wavered and the usual number have fallen by the way, deserted or gone over to the enemy, yet in no State has there been more than a delay on the march, never a permanent check or an enforced retreat.

It was a most interesting study to learn who was responsible for this radical new departure. Not the North, save by example; for the Northern common-school system had been for generations a political scarecrow in the South, and the attempt to force it upon these States in the reconstruction period had bred disaffection and resistance almost like the breaking forth of a new conflict. Not the nation; for the support of this educational experiment by the National Government had seemed an intolerable grievance. If I looked at any entire class, even of respectable people at home, I might decide that the system had been sprung upon these States and could not endure. If I considered the actual poverty of the masses, even of the old superior class, during this decade, 1870–80; their reluctance to taxation; the endless demands upon the community, and the perpetual wrangles and protests against this new imposition, I might be discouraged. All these things I saw. But underneath this surface current I was soon aware of the prodigious undertow of which all these demonstrations were only the signs; all, in one way or another, dependent thereon. The long suppressed desire of multitudes of the better sort of all classes and both races had at last found expression. The blind impulse of two centuries on the Atlantic coast, even more intensified in the new Southwest, liberated by the overturnings of a revolutionary epoch, had now become a force like one of the forces of nature, not to be resisted. A resolute and intelligent common-school public had been developed; nobody knew how; hardly conscious of itself; often unrecognized as a party; while the movement went on, diffused abroad, but always felt like a rock of resistance or, if provoked, like a devastating hurricane of wrath at any serious organized attempt to abolish, restrain, or essentially change the character of the people's common school. The wiser politicians and real statesmen recognized the people's will through the subtle political sense that makes even the ablest and best-furnished man a real statesman or politician, and took their stand upon this as the "corner stone not to be broken." The great debate in the Senate of the United States on national aid to education, in 1884, revealed to the country an educational ability and a recognition of the American idea of universal education among the Senators of these States that, for the first time, informed the Northern people of the imperative need and mighty longing of their Southern neighbors. Only five of the twenty-two Senators representing the eleven ex-Confederate States then voted against the Blair bill, and at least two of these were committed to the opposition of the free school for all classes of American children and youth. It was indeed a momentous and most hopeful revelation to all who had the eyes to see it; this planting of its feet by the new South on the hard pan of American republican civilization, in this indorsement, by every State, of the American common school; the one institution at which every enemy of the American Republic, at home or abroad, is driving to-day with all its might.

XCVI.

Second. Another most significant fact was, that in these common schools for the first time all classes of the dominant race of the South had been brought together with mutual recognition of each other's rightful claims and respect to the deliberate verdict of all in a great public concern. Doubtless the war period had greatly strengthened this feeling by the sharp experiences of military life and the sympathies awakened by the mutual endurance of a great public calamity involving a whole people in a common ruin. The isolated and sharply divided character of the old Southern life bore its fruit of a division of the white population into obstinate cliques, classes, and religious parties, with the inevitable friction and misunderstanding of this order of society. But here in the new common school for the first time the children of the men who had fought and the women who had suffered together during the terrible years of conflict were brought together for a common interest. The result was not only an uplift of the lower orders, but a great awakening in the superior class of honest pride in a population hitherto not fairly understood. The neighborhood jealousies left by an unsuccessful and ruinous war were thus overcome by mutual labors and sacrifices in the most reconciling of all works, the "working together for good" of the children. The clergy learned to appreciate the prodigious force of moral instruction by the whole people in a people's school established not only for instruction in the elements of knowledge, but mainly for the training of that worthy manhood and womanhood that makes for good citizenship. And even the least approachable of all classes, the intellectual exclusive, revolving in his little circle of narrow university life, was compelled to come forth from his hiding place and in some way, often painfully blundering and unappreciative, contribute his quota to a common schooling in which he only half believed.

And here, for the first time, did the Southern people of the dominant race really begin to learn their new relation to their own colored folk, who within ten years had passed through the distinct conditions of "slave," "contraband," "freedman," and "citizen of the United States and of the several States." More than in any other relation has the South been taught by the Southern common school for its colored children and youth the radical distinction between their old and new time relations. The one was the relation of a parental order of society to a vast population destined to permanent inferiority of rights, condition, and culture by the dictates of nature enforced by the relentless benevolence of irresistible law. The other is the relation of a superior class, in a Christian republic, to the same population—the last people that has stepped over the threshold of civilization; by the act of Providence, indorsed by the will of the nation, confirmed in all the rights and obligations of republican citizenship. This relation, not yet fully understood and only gradually becoming apparent to either race, is nowhere so clearly set forth as in the people's common school. For here the State recognizes the fundamental principle that the public wealth shall be fairly taxed to educate all the children. And since the public wealth is more than half the product of the labor of the masses, the class whose power of organization, direction, and forecast changes the crude result of the labor of millions to the "valuation" of a State, should rightly pay from their abundance for the common education, which is the only assurance of the permanent prosperity of the whole. And, over and above the duty of a superior class in a republic to educate every child as far as possible up to the capacity of independent and self-relying citizenship, towers the grander obligation of a common Christian brotherhood, without which democracy and freedom itself are only new and hopeless arrangements of individuals and classes, doomed by pagan selfishness to a national ruin which is only a question of time.

XCVII.

Third. Another important element in the indirect influence of the common school in these States is the stimulus given to local activity in public affairs. A hundred years ago Thomas Jefferson proclaimed the great advantage of the New England township system of local government as a training school of citizenship. In fact, although the political theories of the South from the beginning have all been in the direction of the decentralization of government and the diffusion of political

activity through local points of administration, the only portion of the
country where this theory has been consistently applied has been, from
the first, the conduct of public affairs by the whole body of voters,
assembled periodically in the town meeting of New England. Neither
in the Middle nor Western States has the "town" assumed anything
like this importance as an original center of administration, while the
county has been exalted beyond anything known in the past or present
of the old Northeast. It was one of the many plans of Jefferson in
his early manhood to introduce this New England system into Virginia.
The plan failed for reasons connected with the whole organization of
Southern society. Recently the subject of local government in the
South has attracted attention, and investigations and interesting contributions have been made to the subject, especially by the group of
young men in Johns Hopkins University, Baltimore, Md., to whom the
South is indebted for valuable essays in the direction of the educational
40 history of the section. In fact, the most practical and vital beginning
of local administration in these States has been the establishment of
the school district and the appointment of local trustees for its management. These officials, white or colored, are appointed in various
ways : by popular election, nomination by the county school board, or
the courts, and act under the supervision of the county superintendent,
himself under the general supervision of the State board, represented
by the State commissioner of education. Here is an excellent opening
for local activity in the most important matter of public concern, which
should be disconnected with partisan politics, and will be lifted above
disturbing influences in proportion as the district board of management is competent and zealous in the performance of its duties ; and,
although the local school officials in many portions of the South are too
often painfully incompetent or negligent, yet enough is done to demonstrate the great importance of these thousands of new centers of political activity in the sixteen Southern States.

The Southern county, unless exceptionally populous, is the weak
side of its public system of administration. The people living in it
are dispersed through the lonely areas, with small opportunity of
communication with the county town. Hundreds of these divisions
contain less than 10,000 people ; many of them 5,000 ; often the majority
of the people colored laborers or renters of land. The boundless embargo of mud in winter; the unspeakable condition of country roads
at all times; the confinement of home work through the busy season ;
the poverty of multitudes, make any influential relation with county
affairs practically impossible save to the favored few. The county
court-house is the little "hub" of this domain, often strangely isolated
even from neighboring counties. It is easy to be seen how naturally
the most concentrated form of human government—a county court-
house ring—controls local affairs, and by its well-known methods
wheels about the majority, obedient to its will. The county officials

are the hardest worked and poorest paid men of ability in the Republic. The county judge in Texas, under the law, not only sits on the bench, but performs the duties of county superintendent of schools and two or three minor offices, which in a New England county would be assigned to separate officers, each probably receiving a salary as large as this unfortunate functionary, oppressed by a sort of roving commission to do everything for everybody in an all-outdoor region often half as large as a New England State. Faithful as he may be, of course something must be neglected, and that "something" is too often the superintendence of the public schools, by all odds the most important work to be done. In this situation it can readily be seen what possibilities of usefulness are latent in the school district, polarizing the people around their most precious interest, the schooling of their children; calling to the front the superior men and women of the community (for in some of these States women are competent to hold these offices), and bringing a score of active neighborhoods thus organized in constant communication with the chief town.

XCVIII.

Fourth. Of corresponding value is the graded school for both races, already established in large numbers of these county towns, not only to its own patrons, but to the educational affairs of the whole county. Before the war the Southern States were dotted by these local educational centers, created by the establishment of an academy, locally styled "college," on which sometimes an extensive region depended for education. This institution naturally hugged the court-house, though sometimes located, like the higher college, in the open country, gathering about it the little community built up by itself. But, valuable as were these schools, they only could reach a limited number even of the white population, the remainder of the children gathered in little private groups, sometimes in the poor man's "free school," or under tutorship in the rich man's family. But the establishment of a thorough system of graded public schools in a leading Southern town marks the dawn of a new educational era for the whole region round about. If successful (and the majority of them are reasonably good and many of them beyond comparison the best schools the country has ever known), they make the place at once an educational center of commanding importance. The majority of the children, in time, become its pupils. Either free or with a small tuition fee an upper class is developed, in which the families desiring to send their children to college can oversee their preparation while living at home. The better sort of superintendents are in the habit of attending summer schools in the North or conducting institute work at home, besides making visits of observation to the great school centers. In this way the best methods of instruction are introduced and the teachers instructed

8819——10

therein by weekly meetings. In some cases a teacher's class for pupils in the higher grades of the school is established. A school library is founded and often becomes an invaluable annex to the school. The more intelligent people of the whole county visit in the rooms, sometimes thronging the schoolhouse, and go home with new ideas of education. A steady current of good families from the country sets in upon the town, often waking up a good-sized real-estate "boom" to meet the demand for new houses. The country teachers visit the school are often brought in, once a month, at the session of a county association, where they meet the city teachers, form new acquaintances, and go home instructed and encouraged. Many young people, especially young women, attend these schools from outside as the best academy in reach, and especially for learning the superior methods of school instruction, discipline, and organization. In this way the country district school may be supplied with good teachers from the families of its own locality, while it would not be able otherwise to call to its brief term and small salary a competent schoolmaster or mistress.

All these advantages are shared by the colored people. For, although their children are educated in separate schools, they are able, if vigilant, to secure a fair proportion of the public education and stand in the same relation to their own people through the county as I have described. And sometimes the colored folk are more zealous and persistent in the support of their schools than their white neighbors are of their own. And whatever may be said to the contrary, I have rarely visited a Southern county, with an average negro population, where these people, by suppressing their church, neighborhood, and family jealousies, working together under the lead of their own best people, combining to build schoolhouses, insisting on competent teachers, saving money to add to their salaries and extend the school term, and, generally, standing by a good school when they have it, could not greatly improve the public facilities for their own children, win to their cause the most substantial white people, and make their district a valuable "object lesson" for the neighboring country.

XCIX.

It is almost impossible that even an expert schoolman from any country outside these sixteen American Southern States should be able to appreciate the significance of the movement by which a Southern village, especially a "county town," slowly disentangles itself from the confusion of educational arrangements in which it was left twenty years ago, and, under the lead of a few resolute and influential citizens, is brought to the critical point of local taxation for the support of a system of graded schools for both races and all classes, free to all, in session nine months in the year, demanding either the remodeling and enlarging of old buildings for temporary occupation or the "bonding" of the town to build schoolhouses suitable for the new experiment. A Western community that, for half a century, has been working out this system, brought from the old States, subsidized by national gifts of public lands, refreshed by a constant reenforcement of the most vigorous life in the world, with no opposition, save from the clergy of two or three churches wedded to the parochial system; or a New England town that, for two hundred years has been so familiar with the American system that even the ghost of Horace Mann, advertised to lecture in the town hall on education, would not persuade the Browning Club or the Chautauqua Circle to adjourn, have no measures by which to test the profound significance of this movement in a community in South Carolina, the heart of Virginia, or the "Teche country" in Louisiana.

Could I transfer to these pages a full representation of what I have seen and lived with in hundreds of these communities through the past dozen years I might hope to convey a picture of the school itself, more or less faithful and easy enough to be understood. But when, proceeding below the surface, I attempted to convey to an average Northern community a fair impression of the whole state of society out of which this school has fought its way to even its present estate; what that long effort signifies to the whole community, its peculiar, often pathetic meaning to every respectable family of the white population and its prodigious importance to the colored contingent; by what misgivings and apprehensions in the elder and through what strange uplifts of hope, longing, splendid ambitions, and exultations of pride in scores of eager boys and girls, it is environed, as by the semitropical atmosphere of a changeful Southern summer day; how the new " superintendent," often a college graduate of twenty-five, after a vacation tour among the summer " normals " of the North, with a month's glance over the schools of Boston, Washington, or St. Louis, finds himself, on the first day of October, the virtual sovereign of the little city, with a task of teaching a thousand children to live and work together; holds the entire community " at arms' length " while the new experiment is being tried; trains a score of young people who never taught, or old village "schoolmistresses " who know it all, to teach and discipline according to the methods of the new education, as he imparts them in his weekly drill; while the whole county is looking on and all the curious and idle people are making a picnic of his schoolroom; here is a situation so peculiar that it needs either a new sense or a power of " putting one's self in the place" of his neighbor only given by the special grace of God to appreciate it in the fullness of its meaning, not only to that town, county, and State, but to the future of the Republic. But let me describe a characteristic visit to one of these places, such as I have spent eight months in the year for the last twelve years in making. And if the picture includes the separate features of different localities, it will be all the more realistic from the blending of the many local peculiarities which combine wherever one of these old Southern inland towns

for the first time in its history "girds up its loins" to the supreme
effort of educating its entire body of children and youth in the American common school.

C.

I have decided to accept the hearty invitation of "his honor the
mayor," the board of aldermen, school trustees, and graded school superintendent to visit the county seat of ——, in the heart of an old historic realm, in one of the Southern Atlantic States, with the assurance
of a welcome from the good people, of "every sort and condition," and
the promise of genuine Southern hospitality during the week of my
sojourn. The city editor puts in a postscript, "Dear sir, you will find
there is nothing mean about us here. You can lecture every hour in
the day if you want to, with always plenty of people to hear." The
superintendent of schools adds a confidential letter, sketching the
situation, with great hope that the coming of somebody from abroad,
supposed to know the situation, fully indorsed, will strengthen his
hands, confirm the wavering, shut the mouth of opponents, and perhaps checkmate the scheme of a little squad of local politicians to capture the new school and reduce expenses, or, in other words, to starve it
into a little annex to the county political ring.

Fully impressed with all this ceremony of preparation, as by the
overture of an opera, I arrive, if possible, on the great day of the week,
Saturday, for a general overlook of the situation. The little burg is
crammed through all its main streets with the visiting Saturday crowd
from the county, a mingling of races, classes, and folk of all sorts, representing Southern life from its lowest to its highest estate, in half an
hour's observation giving a more vital impression of local affairs than
a library of the new Southern novels.

The Northern man who, for fifty years, has been thinking of Southern black and white humanity, massed in hostile columns, rubs his eyes
at this first spectacle of such an universal mingling of a thousand people in a whole day of good-natured half-business, half-excursion, if
the place happens to be "dry," thoroughly kindly association that
would be impossible at home, a sight that gives the first rough jolt to
all his preconceived theories of life in the South. He notices the respectable dress, good behavior, and general intelligence of a considerable portion of the colored crowd and the free and easy manners of all
classes, the way in which everybody seems to manage to get a little
"fun" out of everything, and says to himself: "If a New England
community could once import this wonderful social spirit, this hopeful,
childlike obstinacy in getting the best out of everything, what a paradise might we have, with everything else in the world at our command."
If the town is still "wet," as the day goes on the little hot liquor sa-
loons are loaded to the muzzle, and as social distinctions disappear in
the gutter and "low-down" black and white are mixed in all the devil's
doings, it is probable that a dozen fights and possibly a murder will

figure in the startling headlines of a great Northern metropolitan journal as "Another Southern outrage," "Outbreak of a race war," etc. My own conclusion, at the end of a dozen years' careful observation, is that bad whisky and ignorance are at the bottom of 75 per cent of the "outrages" and "race collisions," and that a campaign of one generation of a good common school, backed by a sensible church administration, and the Women's Christian Temperance Union would make the South certainly not the most turbulent end of the United States.

I am greeted at the railroad station by half a dozen of the city dignitaries and by choice established for the week in comfortable quarters in one of the pleasant hotels that are now found in almost every growing town in the South. And here let me touch my hat to the noble army of "drummers," the splendid cavalry corps of the industrial army of the Republic. Not their least important office is their prodigious influence in the improvement of the hotel service in hundreds of Southern towns. They are the best customers of the landlord in these places, expect the best rooms, demand fair accommodations, boycott an obstinately "mean" hotel, gather on Saturday where the best company can be found, dance on Saturday night with the prettiest girls, the better sort seen Sunday morning in church, and generally take a hand in anything wide-awake going on. Not the least among them is the popular school-book agent, often a thorough schoolman, competent to superintend the education of a first-class city, conduct an institute, deliver a lecture, talk to a Sunday school, sing in the church choir, make himself agreeable, especially to the "lady teachers," and go about, the educational "man of all work" of this portion of the country.

Every squad of reactionary school men that raises the periodical cry of "Southern school books for the South," and every prophet of dismay in the North who bewails the danger that Southern children are being educated for a new war of rebellion, "reckons without his host." As far as this thing goes, "the Union is safe," while this splendid army of educational "critter soldiers," Hampton, Wheeler, Custer, Phil Sheridan, and Stonewall Jackson fused into one, goes careering on its annual raid from New York to Mexico, brandishing its invincible improved "small arms," the superb modern schoolbooks, with pictures to match; "supplementary reading," kindergarten gifts, plans for school libraries, flag-raising on the schoolhouses, etc. The people of the United States may as well make up their minds at once that young America down South neither dresses in the sackcloth nor dines on the ashes of the past, but is rapidly becoming the most ambitious and exacting set of youngsters in America. They demand the best things, schoolbooks included, as any set of solemn professors, ambitious local publishers, or reactionary politicians will find out to their confusion.

Nobody but a madman attempts to deliver a lecture on education in a Southern town on Saturday night, unless he chooses to mount the horse-block in front of the court house and " try titles " with everything going on in the public square. But an early caller at my hotel is probably one of the clergymen, to invite me to what turns out to be " a union service" of the leading churches of the place on Sunday night to listen to the first address of the new visitor, a sermon on children, or some topic paving the way for the work of the coming week. A Southern Sunday in a county seat is no " day of rest" for anybody who can be brought into church work. The graded-school superintendent is usually superintendent of a Sunday school and as many other things as one man can be, and his teachers are the foremost workers in the woman's end of the churches, charitable and temperance organizations. The male colored teachers are often ministers, and, if graduates of one of the great colored universities, whether men or women, leaders of their people in all good things. I shall probably be invited to address two or three Sunday schools, sit in the pulpit with one of the ministers in the forenoon, speak to 500 colored people in the afternoon on " How to make an American citizen," with a double row of old " uncles" and " aunties" in the front seats, especially in the passage where I picture the " big-head" graduate of the colored university educated beyond the point of hard work, responding in a loud chorus of "amens." In many of these towns the morning services in the churches are not well attended. Indeed there seems quite too much dependence on the periodical coming of the " evangelist" to wake up " the valley of dry bones" that religious affairs, through the mud, rain; and despondency of a Southern winter in these remote towns, are apt to become. But the Sunday night must be forbidding that doesn't bring out a crowd at the union service of the " ministry of education," conducted by the assembled clergy, with all the heartiness and warmth of appreciation of a down-South audience. In a twelve years' wandering through all these States, not a dozen clergymen or churches have openly raised the question of my own religious connection with the Unitarian Church, and almost every Sunday, generally in the largest Protestant house of worship, sometimes in the Hebrew tabernacle, I find the best opportunity of the week.

The press of the town is open to ample notice of my visit and often to long reports of my public addresses. Monday begins with a regular visitation of the public school. The graded school for white children, especially in an inland town, is often gathered in the building and grounds of an old-time academy. Here I find perhaps 500 scholars, the majority of the white school population, hard at work trying the new experiment of schooling the children of every class together. The young superintendent has general charge of the educational affairs of the place, with perhaps an hour or two of teaching in the higher class, assisted by a young man. The remaining teachers, who bear the burden of the work, are women. They are a very interesting group, perhaps including the widow of the governor or the general of the Confederate era or a " relict" of the first family of the place in the old time, the two or three best private school-teachers displaced by the new arrangement, often an expert primary teacher from the North, and half a dozen girls, more or less educated, in their first year's work. This body of instructors is expected to receive a Saturday's drill, alternating with the colored teachers in the organization, discipline, and methods of instruction of the new education. I find a collection of educational periodicals and books in their hands, and a school library in process of gathering for the pupils, the first free library ever known in the place outside the Sunday school.

The school work, under such conditions, goes on with the peculiar "vim" characteristic of everything heartily done in a Southern community. A judicious mixture of military drill, marching to the beat of the drum, and promotions with military titles take the place of the ancient ineffable disorder and "studying aloud" alternated by the savage thrashing of uproarious boys. Indeed, the discipline in large numbers of these graded schools is almost ideal, the enthusiasm and constitutional following of popular leadership in the white and the hereditary habit of obedience in the colored children doing the work.

Of course the scholastic results of all this must be for the time uncertain. These children have been gathered in from a score of private schools, often with no real preparation, unaccustomed to the whole life they are now living. A great deal of their energy is absorbed in learning lessons in the art of living together; working to a common end; waking up to the meaning of education, more important than anything in the books. Probably I find the beginnings of industrial work in the schools of both races. In each is a class being fitted for college. The superintendent is training his half dozen brightest girls to fill the vacancies or new positions in his teaching force, perhaps a dozen spirited young men and women from the county among them. I am expected to talk to every grade of the children, often to give a lecture each day to both divisions of teachers. Sometimes a general holiday is granted for a grand gathering of young America in the biggest audience room in town, or I am present at a tree-planting or commencement exercise. These, with an occasional educational barbecue or county association of teachers, fill out the crowded week.

At least once, sometimes twice, during the visit, a public free lecture is expected, in which, with perfect freedom and pungency of application, the whole subject of the new education in all its bearings, is discussed. Meetings with the school board, invitations to private hospitality, and the mighty talk of the South, that "goes on forever," fill out the days with a medley of public, private, social, often the most delightfully confidential, and friendly intercourse, that stamps the occasion as another vital experience of a busy life.

Everybody wants to talk on everything, with a freedom and, generally, a courtesy and ready sympathy which tempt to giving the best at hand. The bright side of the Southern character, its longing for a just and kindly understanding, gratitude for honest appreciation, the

growing pride in the grandeur of the new national life, especially the
enthusiastic response of the children and young folk to the uplifting
ambitions and opportunities symbolized by the old flag, all bear wit-
ness to the mighty forces of native American energy in these States,
biding their time of full development. If there be an academy in the
place, I am expected to visit that and make the usual address; if a
college, to do likewise. Indeed, this ministry of education becomes
every year, in my case, more and more a ministry of American ideas
and the superior American civilization to thousands of Southern children of both races and all classes, who, with the teachers, young
parents, and natural leaders in church and society, make up the educational public of the South.

CI.

This is but a poor outline of week on week of similar visitation, of
course more or less successful, with the usual " ups and downs " of field
work in any good cause. Doubtless in every place there is an un-
sympathetic crowd that keeps out of the way. There are churches and
clergymen who "have no use" for me; teachers that want nobody
about from abroad because they have nothing to learn ; local and county
boards of education that do not educate, and who are too busy even to
see or hear; sometimes schools so crude or entertainment so primitive
as to discourage work at all. But I never spent a day in any place
that did not contain the " ten righteous " that would save any Sodom.
And the picture I have drawn is one so common that it is fair to judge
the upper side of the new Southern schoolkeeping by it, according to
the golden rule of criticism, that he who does not appreciate the best
has no capacity to judge of the worst in anything.

But the one indescribable element in all this is the flush of spring-
time in every community blessed by a successful movement for the
graded school. It becomes at once the center of public interest; the
great, new, blessed thing that has come in to untangle old snarls,
reconcile chronic neighborhood quarrels, inspire fresh hopes, show a
way out of the dark race problem, polarize a thousand families, all
looking to the great schoolhouse, and generally make life again worth
living, in the new experience of the young, in communities for thirty years
past slowly emerging from the sorrows, sacrifices, losses, and humiliations of a revolutionary epoch. If our good Northern people who are
now crowding the great winter routes of travel through all the Southland really desire to get at the heart of the New South, let them stop
off at one of these little cities, waking to a new life in the old plantation country, walk into the graded schoolhouse, introduce themselves
to the teachers, hear and see and, if they are able, talk to the children,
leaving a gift for the library " to be remembered by," and they will not
only return with such an inside view as they never had before, but will
have left behind them an investment of loving kindness, patriotic sym-

pathy, and a benediction of peace and good will, compared with which the millions of Northern gold flowing Southward are but dross. For the Union that is to be is, more than all else, the union of heads and hearts and hands now being wrought out among the twenty millions of young Americans—more than in all places else wrought out in the laboratory of American patriotism, the American common school.

CII.

In due time this graded school, planted in the leading town of such a district, finds its natural environment. Everything pertaining to education, the general culture and moral uplift of the adjacent country, gets into vital relations with it. If the county board and commissioner of education are worthy of their place, an association of teachers is formed, which meets at stated periods and utilizes the superior faculty of instruction for the general good. The summer school for teachers is held in the graded schoolhouse; often presided over by the town superintendent. Every year, several of the more ambitious of these young people, especially women, go northward to one of the numerous centers of summer instruction; or encamp in the cities, the jolliest and most indefatigable crowd of sight-seers and students that one meets on the pavements of Boston, New York, or St. Louis. The Chautauqua reading circle, the book club, all the new methods for the extension of good learning and the forwarding of mental companionship among the active-minded people of North and South, go on apace.

Meanwhile, the town itself steadily grows by the influx of good families from the country, brought there to school their children. In many cases the first movement in real estate since the depression of the war comes in this way. I remember how an entire region of an old Southern city was still littered by the black ruin of the fire caused by the Federal occupation until one of the earliest years of the '80's found it covered with a score of new houses, built to accommodate these families from the surrounding country, brought there by the new graded school. And the term "educational center," has a peculiar meaning when applied to one of these numerous old towns—before the war known as the residence of a few superior families—with its whole network of traditions dating back to the colonial days. The new educational movement brings it again to the front in a way most attractive to the best people. The graded schools draw thither from the upper, not the lower strata, of the open country; and the old village that has been sleeping under its great trees, its historical houses decaying amid their neglected grounds, wakes up like the sleeping beauty at the touch of the prince, puts on new life, and renews its youth.

The most attractive places in the South, at present, are this class of historic communities, aroused to a new life by an educational revival which brings the young element of society to the front. Many of them have established the new opera house, which becomes the mental "clearing-house" of the county, bringing a better class of lectures, concerts, and dramatic entertainments, attracting conventions and public meetings, and, best of all, giving the good people of the town and vicinity frequent opportunities of meeting each other and thus break-out from the narrowness of social and sectarian church exclusiveness.

If in addition, as is now often the case, one of these old family mansions is fitted up as a comfortable winter boarding house, or a nice new hotel is built, there can be no more sensible and delightful way of spending a Southern winter for a cultivated Northern family really desirous of knowing how good people down South live. Such a family would easily find plenty of agreeable company; and, if they showed a genuine interest in the place, would learn more of Southern affairs in a month, with infinitely more comfort and rational enjoyment for themselves, than by a ten years' touring over the great routes of travel, with annual "roosting" amid the crowds that swarm the piazza of a "palatial hotel" with palatial prices; looking off into a desolate pine forest or a pestilent jungle; with the idea that the black and white tramps and "riff raff" of the neighborhood are a fair representative of "Southern society."

I rarely lay down a Northern newspaper or magazine in which some "ready writer" has not for the thousandth time "sized up" the Southern situation on the strength of a pocketful of excursion tickets, a month at Jacksonville, St. Augustine, Thomasville, or any of the great resorts; an hour in a negro school and a stroll among the slums of the village, without asking "Whom did these people see and through what colored glasses did they look upon the country, that they seem to know more of it than I, after living a dozen years in the heart of this civilization, with eyes wide open to its shortcomings, with no letting down of my old New England ideals; but with an honest intention to see things for myself, give theories the go-by, and gather what new hope I can for the new South in the new Republic in the momentous years of the coming national life."

CIII.

Of course, the graded school, with its cluster of academical, professional, and collegiate institutions, is a somewhat different affair in one of the prosperous cities of the South, especially in a great town like Atlanta, Birmingham, Nashville, Chattanooga, or the new cities of Texas. Here the educational plant was generally made at an early date; the school system has been often generously supported, has grown rapidly, become a leading interest, and is in no special way differentiated from the public schools of the Western cities of similar character that have come up since the war. In several of them the schools were supervised, really built up, like those of New Orleans and Charleston at an earlier date, by able schoolmen from the North. At present, with the exception of Texas, whose rapid educational growth still makes her dependent on the Northwest for superior teachers, the schools of the cities east of the Mississippi are managed and largely taught by their own people. The States of Tennessee and North Carolina have furnished a group of men and women of remarkable ability in the higher grades of common-school work, as the colleges and universities of Virginia and Maryland are still the greatest source of supply for instructors in the higher education through all the South.

But even in the most active of these new cities, where material interests appear to run riot and dwarf the higher life, the common school is a perennial fountain of the better influences that in due time will control the new wealth and dictate the final social status of the place. The students drawn to cities like Nashville, Atlanta, and others of similar importance are, in themselves, with their friends and families that often follow them, an important element in the population. There are probably 2,000 students of this sort in Atlanta, twice as many in Nashville (which still remains the most important educational city of the South), large numbers in New Orleans, and hundreds in any one of fifty smaller educational centers like Staunton, Macon, Austin, Springfield, and Memphis. There are probably 10,000 of the better population of several of these new cities that have been brought there by the educational opportunities of the place.

Sitting one day in the office of the superintendent of schools of Atlanta, that good-natured functionary was suddenly called to face a cyclone in the shape of a breezy, bouncing woman who burst upon him with the leading question, "When can my Jane get into school?" With as much calmness as possible in this high wind of indignation the good "major" pointed to a long list of names hanging on the wall and said, "There's Jane, and as soon as we get to her she shall have a seat; but you see that there are hundreds waiting outside, while the city is building schoolhouses every year." "Well," stormed the good lady, "I think such a woman as I has rights in these schools. Didn't I make my husband move to Atlanta, invest $10,000 in his business, and both of us are working like dogs to educate the children, and now Jane can't get in!" "Well, well, good woman, we'll take Jane's case into consideration and she shall have a seat at the beginning of next term," and the cyclone was deflected without further peril, to the pavement. "That woman," said the major "has ten children. Eight of them are already disposed of, and Jane came of school age only a week ago."

That is the kind of family that is storming the gates of every Southern city and town that has established a successful system of common schools, often to the damage of the open country, whole divisions of which are losing their most substantial people for lack of good educational facilities, their places being taken by "renters," or colored occupants of the old plantations, generally an inferior class. This movement from the open country can only be arrested by making every village of a thousand people an educational point, and the more favored country folk leading a revival for local taxation and the private assistance of public schools. The national educational bill, in this way, would have given the outdoor South, where three-fourths of its children live, a great lift; doubled the school term; especially encouraged the people who still are compelled to shoulder the burden of support for schools which they often can not use; and, in arresting this "break" for the cities, in many ways have conferred a blessing upon every State.

At present the larger cities, like Washington, are swarmed by thousands of negro families, often a charge upon the community, drawn there to put their children in the schools. They can not be kept out; and nowhere could money be better invested than in a gift to these public school authorities to enable them to establish a thorough industrial department, compulsory for every child, as is already partially established in the Washington, D. C., schools by a grant from Congress. There is already in many of these larger towns a body of graduates of their public schools, the most hopeful of the younger population, ready for all good work in the growing life of the community; a most hopeful contrast to another crowd of ignorant, "loud," mischievous young men and foolish girls that still misrepresent the best life of the South, the curse of the smaller villages and open country by their brutal Negro hatred and absurd provincialism; "powder and ball for the political demagogue;" the "lynch-law" fraternity; the heaviest burden of the South, which all good men deplore. And the most painful fact of the matter is, that a good system of country and village schooling with all that goes therewith would have saved thousands of them for good citizenship, leaving the mischievous class in a permanent minority, and relieving their localities from the bad repute in which they are so often involved by their semibarbarism.

CIV.

It could be wished that in that great national jargon, known as the tariff debate, in which the country will be involved for the coming two years, some of our Southern statesmen would be moved to tell the country the honest truth concerning their growing manufacturing towns, especially of the smaller sort, considered as agencies of civilization in their respective neighborhoods. A generation ago an enterprising merchant of Columbia, S. C., a Scotchman by birth, conceived the idea of establishing cotton mills in a deserted region in the west of the State; a great "piney woods" country, largely inhabitated by the most deplorable of native American white folk, known as the lower sort of "crackers;" despised even by the old-time slaves as "poor white trash." The idea was to gather these people in as mill operatives and, for the first time in their lives, give them steady occupation, decent homes, and bring around them generally the agencies of civilization. Five years ago I spent one of the most interesting days of my ministry in Graniteville, the present name of the town that has grown up around this cluster of mills. As a financial venture I learned that the experiment had been a success, holding on through the war and steadily growing since. I found what might be called without exaggeration a model village, with churches and schools, no liquor sold, comfortable homes for the working people, and no visible remains of the old barbarism in the adjoining country. The portrait of " The Georgia cracker in the mills," drawn by Miss Graffenreid, a Southern woman, in the Century Magazine, which has " fired the heart" of the Georgia editor, is correct enough as far as it describes the condition of these people in their original barbarism and squalor. It may be true in some little manufacturing villages or city factories managed in the interest of a greater barbarism to make money, whatever becomes of the people who do the work. But it certainly is not true in communities like Graniteville, S. C., Columbus, Ga., Anniston, Ala., Wilmington, N. C., where Amy Bradley, a down-east school ma'am, with great-hearted Mary Hemmenway, the educational Lady Bountiful of Boston, twenty years ago set up the Tileston Free School for the children of "dry pond," the " poor white trash " end of the town. She has not only dried up the moral marsh and changed these people to a respectable laboring class, with a fair proportion of the better sort, including teachers, artists, and professional people, but has now resigned leaving her institution one of the model schools of the State.

There is another side to American manufacturing industry than the possible increase of prices for some articles of home consumption, and that is the development of manufacturing centers as agencies of the higher civilization. The first lift out of the unspeakable degradation of the class referred to, that portion too shiftless to emigrate in the old time to " Egypt," or later to Texas, has come from the establishment of manufacturing centers that have given them employment, often at the expense of the corporation, which has, as at Anniston, Ala., and numerous other towns, built schoolhouses and churches, decent homes, and, in ways so familiar in hundreds of our great Northern industrial communities, made the "factory village " a genuine people's university. This is all the more important in the South; while the operatives in all its new industries are chiefly its own white and colored people of the humbler classes. It is already demonstrated that there is no " white trash" so trashy that a manufacturing town, managed on Christian principles, will not redeem it to civilization.

And it is coming to be understood by Southern economists, who steer by the headlands of demonstrated facts rather than cruise through the drifting fogs of theory, that these sixteen States have, in their 7,000,000 colored population, the most reliable and valuable material for a great operative and mechanical industrial class in America. The yearly exhibition of the industrial department in all the great schools of these

people, including the public schools of Washington, D. C., has already
given the go-by to the notion that the Negro who, in three hundred years,
has made greater strides out of African barbarism towards modern civilization than was ever made in Europe in a thousand years is doomed by
a mysterious race infirmity to be a perpetual "peasant" of the old-time
European sort. If the South and its financial friends who are coming
to its aid can have the wisdom for the next twenty years, to put in an
effective six months' common school in the country and nine months in
town, with manual training, housekeeping, and as much of general industrial instruction as is possible, and meanwhile discourage and in all legal
ways discountenance the most intolerable despotism that threatens this
Republic, the gigantic combination of European immigrants in trades
unions, that practically crowd American-born labor to the wall, elbow off
the Negro, and place the whole field of mechanical and operative industry in the hands of a self-elected congress of labor demagogues, it may
realize its present dream of development into a wealth and power unknown and impossible in its original estate.

CV.

Some five years ago I was invited by the enterprising mayor of Asheville, N. C., to visit that little city of the mountains, then rapidly coming into notice as a charming sanitarium and pleasure resort, with
eight months of practical summer and four months of a mild, mountain winter. I found myself, even in May, in an almost ideal realm, a
great bowl in the hills watered by pleasant rivers, a garden of floral
beauty, with numerous sightly outlooks, rimmed around with an encir-
clement of mountains from 3,000 to 6,000 feet above tidewater; the
village itself at an altitude of 2,200 feet above the sea. Here was evidently the mountain resort of the future for the whole country east of
the Mississippi. Situated midway of the great southern Appalachian
upland realm, 600 miles in length and 200 in breadth, extending from
Harper's Ferry, W. Va., to Birmingham, Ala., including a portion of
nine Southern States, crowded with mineral wealth, burdened with
mighty forests, its pastures capable of grazing "the cattle on a thousand
hills," and, when the dog pest is exterminated, the favored home of the
sheep, with a milder climate and a more fertile soil than the famous
old States of northern New England, within the past ten years for the
first time brought in vital connection even with the lowland portion of
its own States, destined in half a century to be one of the most attractive portions of the eastern United States, Asheville can not fail to
become in time the most noted and cosmopolitan of our mountain
cities.

But my errand was of another sort—at the suggestion of the new city
government to wake up an interest in the establishment of the Southern system of graded schools. At that date it is doubtful if outside of
the two Virginias, Tennessee, northern Georgia, and Alabama, there

was a graded school in this vast country of eastern Kentucky and western North Carolina, including wide corresponding regions in the other States. Small public schools, generally little better than nothing, were scattered about through these vast and lonely areas, and, with such private instruction as was available and an occasional academy, were the dependence of the majority of more than a million of this mountain white population. Every year its upper strata slid off in an immigration to Texas and the new Southwest. A portion of its more enterprising youth, especially in Tennessee, made their way to the low-land schools, becoming as I saw them there generally, a hard-working, hopeful, and occasionally a very successful student material. The idea was that Asheville should establish a good public-school system which would be an educational beacon for the whole hill country.

At present Asheville is becoming the true educational capital of this mountain world. Its public schools are said to be among the best in the State. The famous Bingham Academy for boys is to be transferred to its suburbs. Other valuable institutions of learning and charity are coming up, and, with the magnificent estate of the Vanderbilt family and other attractive places, its cluster of grand hotels and new industries, it is steadily increasing in importance. There is no more valuable native population in the country than the better sort of these mountain people, and, even its lower estate, with its chronic habit of poverty, shiftlessness, ignorance, and gross superstition, in which some undeniable primitive virtues strike hand with a savage ferocity, is probably more approachable, through the agencies of American civilization, than the majority of the humbler European immigration that is now tasking to its uttermost the mental and moral agencies of the whole North.

Already the movement has begun which is planting in the wildest regions of this mighty wilderness centers of mining, manufacturing, and lumber industries. In every one of these new settlements the old battle between the Archangel and the Prince of Darkness is in full blast. Everything takes passage on the new railroad. The place can easily become a "Hell Town," astonishing the most violent of the native tribes with its new varieties of diabolism; or, by the early planting of a good graded common school, it may catch the children early, arrest the demoralization, and make each new city in the wilderness virtually a missionary station of civilization to the region round about. The people of this entire region were largely loyal to the Union during the civil war, and, with the colored contingent of the lowlands, put into the field for the preservation of the Republic 300,000 soldiers, a larger army than was ever commanded by Washington in the old Revolution. Surely the North and West, through whose capital and enterprise this great and interesting region is now so largely being developed, will rise to the opportunity of putting in, at every available point, those potent agencies of American civilization that, in due time, will work a peaceful revolution and reclaim this so long neglected portion of the country.

CVI.

The clergy of all sects, North and South, need a thorough stirring up and conversion from the old-time theory, still the song at every great gathering of the churches, that only by what is called "Christian education," meaning thereby the establishment of expensive academies and colleges, a perpetual drain upon these already overtaxed denominations, demoralized by sectarian rivalries, rarely able to secure the best teachers and slow to adopt superior methods of instruction, at best impossible of attendance by seven-eighths of the white people of this mountain country and nine-tenths of the lowland colored folk, is there any hope for building up these waste places of the South. A judicious number of academical and collegiate schools, well endowed, taught according to modern methods, with an industrial annex after the type of the splendid Miller Manual-Labor School of Albemarle County, Va., with as little of the sectarian and as much of the "common Christianity" as is possible, and the organization of the Christian moralities into their lifeblood, would be an invaluable aid, especially in this "land of the sky," corresponding to the better class of mission schools for the negroes in the South. But the sooner the whole American church gets out of this medieval heresy that the American people's common school is "godless," "secular," "unmoral," "immoral," or is rightly described by any of these theological nicknames, and with a more concentrated organization of its own legitimate educational realm goes in heartily to bring the great masses of "low-down" America into the people's university, as it can easily be made, the better for the republic, better for the millions of children and youth that now abide in darkness, and, best of all for the Church of Christ, by this great movement emancipated from an ecclesiastical conceit that more than all its theological heresies impairs its usefulness and postpones the coming of the Kingdom of God in America. If Christianity is what it is proclaimed, the light of the world, it has long ere this so permeated the civilization of our own land, set its type of morals and shaped its ideals of civilization, that the whole American people, instructed by the church, is competent to take up, support, and superintend the only agency that can redeem the lower story of the Nation, the improved people's common school, without this constant impeachment of practical atheism by the leaders of the great contentious sects that, in two thousand years, have not learned the meaning of the Master's prayer "that they all may be one." However this may be, there is no hope for the reclamation and uplift, either of the white illiteracy or colored barbarism of our Southland, save by the same institution to which the North, more than to any other cause, owes its present potency and power, the improved and modernized common school, through all its grades, from the plantation primary to the university of the State.

CVII.

If, now, the question be asked "to what must be ascribed the re-markable development of the American common school through these sixteen Southern States during the twenty years from 1870 to 1890?" as far as my own observation extends, I unhesitatingly reply, very largely to the direct and indirect influence, especially among the white population, of Southern women. My own observation of the Southern common school began midway of these years, at the close of what might be called its early formative, experimental period, and has continued through its remarkable growth of the past decade, when it may be said to have become a vital part of the civilization of all these States. I am not disposed to do injustice to the masculine side of the educa-tional public of the South during this momentous period, when its most important interest—the future education of the children—has really been nearest the heart of all thoughtful people. Without the educa-tional statesmanship of the great common school leaders of the South, men like Drs. Ruffner, Curry, Haygood, Newell, Joynes, Baldwin, Gov. Thompson, Armstrong of Alabama, Trousdale and Smith of Tennessee, Rogers of Louisiana, Binford of Virginia, Finger of North Carolina, Cooper of Texas, Mallon of Georgia, and of others like minded, espe-cially the brilliant corps of young superintendents of graded schools, like Moses, Tomlinson, Johnson, Woolwine, Branson, and a steadily in-creasing number of such as they; the powerful influence of the Pea-body Normal School at Nashville, Tenn., in its earlier days under the masterly administration of Dr. Stearns, and in its enlarged sphere of usefulness under President Payne; fairly including the services of the more celebrated educators in the great colored mission schools, like Armstrong, Ware, Steele Alexander Wilcox, Cravath, Pope, Burnstead, Hitchcock, Patten, King, and others only less eminent than they; be-sides the large number of Northern schoolmen, from Dr. Sears through a growing list always ready to respond to a call for any reasonable work over the border, it would have been impossible to organize and officer the Southern common school and hold it up against the perpetual as-saults of its enemies and the chronic discouragement and inefficiency of its half-hearted friends.

And less known in educational circles, but no less essential to the success of the movement, has been the work of the city boards of education and the county boards and superintendents that, with all their failures, have certainly gone through a great deal of difficult and valuable work. With occasional exceptions, where the new graded school had been captured by the local political "ring" or muddled by the quarrels of rival sectarian or social cliques, I have found the city boards of education composed of the most reliable men in their re-spective communities. Such men are the most valuable friends of the schools in the South. Their knowledge of business, experience in pub-

8819——11

lic affairs, close touch of popular opinion, and wise foresight of public necessities, especially their desire to learn the mystery of the new gospel of popular education, make them often a bulwark of defense against the obstinacy, narrowness, and irritable inefficiency of teachers and the social friction and ecclesiastical " offishness " that are among the most formidable obstacles to success. And all honor should be paid to the noble brotherhood of public men who, with a courage and tact beyond all praise, have piloted the educational ship through all the perils of its earlier voyaging out into the open sea, where it now rides the waves with flying colors, confident that every wind will waft it to the haven of success.

And in the case of the colored people, beyond question, more is due to the young men who have gone forth from the numerous mission schools as teachers for the upbuilding of that division of popular education than to any other influence.

CVIII.

But, when all this is cheerfully conceded, the greater fact has been impressed upon me through the entire years of my ministry, that the most effective of all the forces that wrought this great advance in Southern popular education has been from the first the persistent influence of the higher Southern womanhood. There has been and still continues to be, especially in the older Southern States, a powerful class of influential men distinctly opposed to any thorough development of the American common school, even for the white, and obstinate in their opposition to it for the colored people. There are statesmen and politicians of whom Gen. Grant, in the White House, said: "There's too much reading and writing now to suit a good many great men up in the Capitol." A respectable division of the clergy of every church is still in the bonds of what they choose to call "Christian," but what really means the intensely sectarian type of denominational, academical, and collegiate schooling that makes an educational institution an annex to a church. A considerable class of socially exclusive heads of families even in their own decay hold stoutly to the faith that the ancient social régime was the grandest on earth and in its revival is the only hope of social upbuilding in the South of the future. A portion of the faculties, sometimes even of the State universities and of the sectarian academical colleges and academies for both sexes of the white population, still in their hearts believe that all schooling beyond the three R's and a little industrial training is the prerogative of the few who can make their way to the class of schools they represent and be content with the style of educational manipulation that prevails in their institutions. This latter class is perhaps more obstructive than all; for, in addition to its honest opinion that the old time Southern education was better than anything to-day, and its obstinate adherence to the classical type and mechanical methods of the secondary and higher instruction everywhere in vogue half a century ago, they are tempted by their personal interest to oppose the establishment of the graded school, which robs them of the majority of their elementary department and threatens even the upper story with the rivalry of the free high school. In several States this special influence is largely responsible for the slow progress of universal education, and through the whole South, as in England, it is to-day largely arrayed in opposition to the secondary, higher, and even normal professional education as a part of the public system.

All these hostile forces, working together, greatly impede the satisfactory development of the common school. The "religious press," too, often raises the old war-cry of "Godless," "secular," "immoral," in its treatment of this great public interest. The legislatures are besieged by a lobby that works against generous appropriations even for the elementary, and often succeeds in defeating the just treatment of the State university and similar claimants. It was the persistent opposition of this class that finally turned the tide in the South against the national aid which would have placed the Southern common school, in ten years, high and dry above the wash or even the overflow of hostile public sentiment in every Southern State.

And to this must be added one of the most serious hindrances to the success of the common school, both in country and town: the presence, often as superintendents and teachers in the higher classes of the graded schools, of a class of men, either old and incapable of understanding the nature and demands of the work they are doing, or young graduates of colleges thoroughly out of sympathy with common-school work. Again and again have I seen a public movement, generously inaugurated and for a time heartily supported by the leading people of a community, so mismanaged by the persistent conceit and half-hearted faith of its leading teachers of this sort that it finally fell into disrepute and was brought under the fire of the class that everywhere believes in that system of public economy which knocks out the brains of things to save money. In more than one of the larger Southern cities the common school to-day is in the hands of a little educational ring of masculine teachers and school officials of this sort, with steady loss of confidence in the substantial classes on whose support public education must depend.

So widely extended and effective was the opposition of these classes from the first, that, in connection with the undeniable financial inability of whole States, and the chronic Southern popular hostility to taxation for any purpose, some influence more vital, irresistible, and persistent than the "good fight" of the good men composing the more visible school public must be found to account for the decisive victory already won in this holy children's war.

CIX.

That influence, I repeat, can only be found in the revival of the old and the awakening of a new and powerful impulse for education among

the superior sort of all classes and conditions of Southern women. Elsewhere we have told the story of the Southern woman of the more
favored class, in the long years before the war, and have shown the great
indebtedness of the Southern people to the efforts of the same class,
amid the wreck and discouragement after 1865, in restoring, even in
better condition, the old-time arrangements for the education of girls.
But it must be remembered that, during the remaining school years of
the children who, in 1865, were from 6 to 10 years of age, especially in
the eleven ex-Confederate States, the large majority of the former well-
to-do people were in no condition to send either girls or boys to the
only class of schools they had ever supported. Private tuition was
equally impossible, according to the former methods. A great deal of
temporary work was done in these years by home instruction. A distinguished Senator of the United States informed me that, in a political
campaign through a large portion of his own State, he found himself
endowed with a new office, school examiner; in almost every house
being requested to "examine" the children in their home lessons. There
was also a prodigious eruption of private schools, chiefly established by
the better-educated ladies of good families, who, in their own homes or
such buildings as were available, gathered little groups of their neighbors' children for such instruction as was possible under the circumstances.

When we consider the past educational history of this class of Southern women we can easily realize the great desire for the schooling of
their children at the close of the war. Through vast regions the schools
had been closed, or, when open, disturbed by frequent alarms and
excitements during those fearful years. The pent-up educational spirit,
now released by the coming of peace, rushed forth and filled every
channel open for its reception. Thousands of children received all
their school training, previous to 1880, in this class of schools, with
such instruction in the home and the church as was available.

The brilliant and successful lady principal of one of the most celebrated schools for Southern girls tells the story of the beginning of her
own education in a little private school where everybody "studied
aloud." She finally hit upon a way to get her Latin lesson in the midst
of the confusion, by pounding her bench with her fist, " beating her
music out" amid the jargon of her noisy environment. Nobody can tell
what a community of resolute, intelligent, American women can accomplish until the experiment is tried. Some of the most entertaining
volumes of the new Southern literature are the picturing of neighborhood life in the more quiet Southern retreats, where families "refugeed"
during the great conflict, with the marvellous " ways and means" by
which they not only lived but made life very well worth living under
the circumstances. The Southern woman who can sketch a vivid and
naturalistic portrait of child life during the period now considered,
with the schooling of all kinds through which the more ambitious of
them pushed their way up to scholarship, would be sure of an audience

of 20,000,000 American boys and girls, with probability of translation into half a dozen European and Oriental languages. The accomplished president of one of the Western State universities, a boy at the close of the war, living on the old Ball estate, where Mary Washington was born, felt the spirit of that vigorous old lady in the air, and chopped trees in the "piney woods" to earn the money that sent him to the university. Of course, the men of the period had their share in this first movement for the children. But during those years of trial the South turned to its foremost women for hope and cheer in all things. And especially in everything relating to the education of the children the voice of the woman was supreme.

CX.

But this temporary makeshift for the education of several millions of white children and youth could not permanently satisfy a people so ambitious as the mothers, "sisters, cousins, and aunts" of eleven American States. So thousands of families that had never before thought of the common school in any other relation than as the "low-down free school" for poor white folk, before the war, found in it the only hope of educating their own children and satisfying the rising demand of the classes below them in the social scale. In all the old-time cities, like Nashville, New Orleans, Mobile, Savannah, Memphis, Charleston, where the graded school was in operation in 1860, it was taken in hand at once, put on its feet, and supervised and taught often in a more effective way than before. In my first visit to New Orleans in 1869, I found the free high school for girls in operation, with earnest and commendable work going on. The best of their former teachers who were living were at work and many women of the leading families and education had joined the teachers' corps. The Peabody educational fund enabled an increasing number of towns for the first time to establish the free common school, by dividing the expense with the people, and in this way the movement towards free instruction for all captured the most commanding educational centers of the South, in the graded school planting the citadel of the people's new hope.

But here came in a mighty reënforcement to the old school public of these States, in the multitudes of families of the "plain white people," in town and country, who, now for the first time, asserted the right to their place at the educational feast, however meager it might be. And this demand came, to a great extent, from the more vigorous and intelligent mothers and ambitious daughters of these classes. While it was possible under the old academical and collegiate systems, that a bright boy could make his way up from the humblest surroundings and, often by the aid of a more prosperous neighbor, reach the university, there was small chance for the girl of the family, perhaps with a better mind, and with longings she was compelled to suppress.

It should always be remembered that, in 1860, the slave-holding families of the entire South, with their professional environment, did not include one-fourth the white population of fifteen States. There has never been any reliable account of the opportunity for even elementary education enjoyed by several millions of the "third estate;" the off-hand assertion of late Southern writers that in States like Georgia, Tennessee, and Virginia there was no real lack of such facilities, having no reliable foundation, indeed, being disproved by overwhelming proofs, the declarations of the most eminent Southern authorities and the frequent appeals of conventions held in the interest of public education up to the very year of secession. In any general dearth of opportunities the girl is always left out. Anybody who knows this section of the Southern people can understand the prodigious awakening of ambition and hope through all its classes at the close of the war. These men had formed the almost invincible soldiery of the Confederate armies, until the dwindling prospects and terrible privations of the cause, with the emancipation proclamation, had wrought a steady discontent in the ranks during the closing years of the conflict. As a class, the coming of peace found these people, in some respects, in a better condition to face the world than their old neighbors. At once began that upward march of "the plain people of the South," which in a short generation has turned the face of that section to the rising sun, placed it foremost in the great iron industry, created thousands of new landholders, built up flourishing cities by the energy of these new workers, and to-day has placed the "Farmers' Alliance" in virtual possession of political power in every Southern Commonwealth.

The educational record of this portion of the Southern people is largely to be read in the history of the new common school of the villages and open country. Even to-day only a small minority of their young people are found in the academies and colleges, although they are entering in larger numbers everywhere. Some of the most promising girls I have met in my wanderings have been of this class. I remember one little woman, from the hills of Western Virginia, whose prize essay on one of Shakespeare's plays brought also a testimonial from the new Shakespeare Society of London, educated by money borrowed of a younger brother, with obligation to pay by teaching, that he might take his turn at school. The first real movement for the schooling of this class, after the war, was through the public-school system for the country, established by the temporary governments, lasting in some of the States till 1876. Whatever may have been the sins justly chargeable to these ten years of "carpet bag" administration, the masses of the Southern white people should be forever grateful for this honest attempt, for the first time, to educate all the children. Imperfect as were these schools, they were better than three-fourths of the Southern people had enjoyed before. Thousands of children spent their only school years in them, and gained that love of knowledge and ambition for further progress which has wrought so powerfully in the upward striving of the "third estate" even to this day.

CXI.

One of the most significant features in this new order of affairs was the calling to the front for the first time of great numbers of young women as teachers in these new schools. Before 1860 the somewhat limited opportunity of the "lady teacher" in the South had been, by the very necessities of the case, the vocation of the lady of good family. There was no considerable number of women, from the class now spoken of, whose acquirements were up to the work of instructing even their own neighbors. But now came in a new régime, in which the competent women of all orders and conditions were summoned to the front to meet the greatly increased demand for teachers. Of course, the large majority of the workers in the new schools were men. Even in 1889, in fifteen Southern States and the District of Columbia, the ratio of male to female teachers was, in the South Atlantic 52.3, in the South Central Division 60 per cent; while in the North Atlantic it was 20.3, North Central 32.8, and Western Division 31.2 per cent. The smallest percentage of male teachers is found in the New England States, in only one of which does the percentage of male teachers reach 18 per cent; while Massachusetts, with perhaps the best general educational facilities in Christendom, has only 8.9 per cent of men in its public-school teaching corps. The proportion of male and female teachers to the whole number in the respective States once known as the South, with the District of Columbia, will be found in the following table:

TABLE NO. 4.

Whole number of different teachers employed in 1888–'89 in fifteen Southern States, and the United States and its five divisions, classified by sex. Proportion of teachers who are males.

United States, Divisions, and fifteen States.	Whole number of—			Ratio of male teachers to whole number.
	Male teachers.	Female teachers.	Both sexes.	
				Per cent.
United States	124,929	227,302	352,231	35.05
North Atlantic Division	18,324	71,838	90,162	20.03
South Atlantic Division	20,241	18,462	38,703	52.03
South Central Division	29,203	19,512	48,715	60.00
North Central Division	53,127	108,603	161,730	32.08
Western Division	4,034	8,887	12,921	31.02
Delaware	203	454	657	36.09
Maryland	1,084	2,644	3,728	29.01
Virginia	3,258	4,165	7,423	43.09
West Virginia	3,444	1,897	5,341	64.05
North Carolina	4,450	2,657	7,107	62.06
South Carolina	2,210	2,040	4,250	52.00
Georgia	4,095	2,829	6,924	59.01
Florida	1,419	1,174	2,593	54.07
Kentucky	4,508	4,383	8,891	50.07
Tennessee	5.146	2,572	7,718	66.07
Alabama	3,791	2,125	5,916	64.01
Mississippi	3,557	3,558	7,115	50.00
Louisiana	1,169	1,347	2,516	46.05
Texas	6,660	3,957	10,614	62.07
Arkansas	4,372	1,573	5,945	73.06

CXII.

It is not easy, certainly in New England, to appreciate the prodigious significance of this movement which, in one generation, has brought the Southern woman to the front as teacher in the new Southern school until she now, in one division, is within 2, and in another within 10 per cent of equality in numbers. The large majority of teachers in the colored schools of the South are still men, so that it is not improbable that the women teachers are in a small majority in the schools for white children and youth. At first, twenty years ago, in the early stages of this woman's movement, an observation especially of the common schools revealed a condition of affairs perhaps never before seen in the annals of education. On the one hand, great numbers of the better educated ladies of the best families were taking up school-teaching often as a matter of necessity. The widows and daughters, often the wives of living Confederate officers and public men, some times of the highest rank, were given these positions in preference. While the academies for girls absorbed perhaps the larger number of the better qualified of these persons, many were still found in the common schools both of the city and country, not only teaching white, but in 1880, in some of the larger cities, at work in the colored, schools.

The United States Commissioner of Labor reports that, whereas sixty years ago there were but 7 paying industrial occupations for American women, there are now 346. But even now there are not forty-six ways, possibly not twenty-five, outside a few localities, where a Southern girl at home can make a respectable living in any way and, twenty years ago, school-teaching was certainly, even with its small compensation, the most attractive and reliable of the dozen uncertain methods of keeping the wolf from the door. In the earlier years of my own Southern visitation I was constantly meeting ladies of fine presence and good acquirements teaching in the graded schools of the towns and cities and in the country districts where their old family home was located. Of course, many of the more elderly of these persons had no considerable professional gift. A more than usual number of them were enfeebled and discouraged by the experiences of the past. Many of the younger class were very young, compelled to begin the work of life with little scholastic preparation and nothing of the period of enjoyment and freedom everywhere dear to the heart of the girl. But, acquainted as I have been with all classes of the women teachers of the North for many years, I can truly say that I believe these women, during the first ten years of the Southern common school, did more valuable work, for smaller compensation, under more discouraging circumstances, than I have ever seen elsewhere. And, best of all, I found among them less of discontent, less complaining of the hardships of the teacher's lot, a greater willingness to be instructed, with an equal zeal and energy for self-improvement, than I have found elsewhere.

Along with these representatives of the old-time prosperous families, I also was greatly interested by the increasing number of energetic young women, pushing up from social surroundings where school-teaching for the first time was becoming a recognized profession. These girls, often with only the poor advantages of the country or village common school, would begin in a small way, in the three months' term of the country, use their money for a season at the academy; next year teach a larger school, perhaps in town; push up to a good summer institute or Chautauqua assembly in the North at vacation, and, in the way so familiar to the women of the North, pull up the younger children of the family, sometimes bearing the heaviest burden of the household.

CXIII.

There is all the difference in the world between the sort of influence exerted upon children in school by a mechanical, routine style of working even " improved methods," under ordinary circumstances, and the vitality garnered up and perpetually going forth from this army of Southern women in the new educational movement of the past generation. Multitudes of these teachers for the first time were brought outside their old exclusive family life into the most familiar relations with the children, and necessarily with the parents, of people of whom they had known little, often in the humblest walks of life. Perhaps never in the history of civilization has the superior culture and worth of the women in any country been brought so largely into the work of instructing the unlettered classes. And these children thus taught were not a European peasantry, receiving " with meekness " the gifts of the Lady Bountiful with perpetual reminder of an impassable social separation. They were the children of the majority of the people who, for the first time, had realized their commanding position in affairs, forcing to the front, filled with the new ambitions and the inevitable jealousies of the new Southern life. And alongside of this strata of upper-class teachers was working the new contingent of girls coming up from the ranks, often displaying a capacity beyond their more cultivated and favored sisterhood. And all these women were bearing their own burdens, almost too great sometimes to be endured. Here was a combination of circumstances of all others calculated, especially in the religious women, to develop original power, awaken new views of duty, broaden the horizon, and blend the earnest workers of every class in a noble sisterhood, consecrated to the great uplifting of the masses. And here, every hour of the day, were being woven those bonds of sympathy and appreciation, the intense love of the faithful teacher even for the foolish and erring child, through the whole blessed realm of labor and love in the common school. Just what the Christian minister or the metropolitan religious journal means by its flippant and cruel stigmatizing of such a realm of consecrated labor and Christian endeavor as " Godless," " secular," only "imparting mental shrewdness" to American children, is what I, whose privilege it has been for twelve years past to live among these people and mark the beneficent outcome of their work in every way, can not pretend to understand.

CXIV.

I everywhere took note of the superior intensity, fidelity, teachableness, and zeal for improvement, especially among the younger teachers of this sisterhood of instruction, in all Southern schools. The great opportunities for success in business life and all industrial occupations in the South are still monopolized by young men. Outside the operative class and the half dozen ordinary occupations, like dressmaking, boarding-house keeping, the indefinite region of " fancy needle work," and a limited employment in clerkships of various kinds, there is yet no rapid development of opportunity for profitable labor for young white women in the South. The realm of household service, the higher operative labor and a great deal that, in the North, employs thousands in respectable and well-paid woman's work, will more and more be cared for by the more intelligent and enterprising young women of the colored race. This will compel the white girl, seeking employment, to push towards those occupations dependent on general intelligence and expert training. The rapid development of the school system, more marked every year, with the rising demand for better teachers, the corresponding increase of wages, length of school terms, improved buildings, etc., will stimulate the educated young women of the South to redoubled efforts to capture this profession. Already is it becoming difficult to hold young men of competent ability to the teacher's work even in the most responsible and best paid positions in the common schools. In Texas, the most enterprising of the public-school States, I found the whole region of superintendence and higher-class teaching "a dissolving view," with changes so frequent as to seriously impair the efficiency and almost destroy continuity of work in the larger towns, already the people of one of the most cultivated of the larger cities having elected a woman as superintendent.

The same state of affairs that persuaded Supt. A. J. Rickoff, in Cleveland, Ohio, twenty years ago to "dust out" his entire crowd of schoolmasters, chiefly young men, teaching in view of business or professional life, and place at the head of all, except the high and normal schools, the best women that could be obtained by the salary of a man, whereby the schools of that city were pronounced by eminent European visitors the best in the Union ; that gives to the young women of Massachusetts 90 per cent of the positions in the common schools, and to women every position in the public schools for white children in Memphis, Tenn., is steadily moving to the same result through the South. The Southern young white man of to-day no longer worships his own State, but like the American "smart boy" everywhere, goes where he can get or do the most good. Even the Southern young woman is beginning to follow his footsteps. She has an honorable place in the schoolroom in every border city from Baltimore to St. Louis. She is making herself felt in the higher occupations—artistic, professional, journalistic, literary—in all the States. Probably several thousand of these young women are now in the best schools of the border cities, and the Northern colleges for women.

CXV.

But the home field of education is becoming their proper preserve. Many of the more successful common-school teachers of the earlier period—like Misses Haygood, Conway, Kelly, and Rutherford—are now 43 at the head of the most important seminaries for girls. Every Southern State seems to have now accepted the situation and is giving higher educational opportunities at public expense to its young women. The three Southwestern States—Missouri, Arkansas, and Texas—now admit women to the State University, and two of them have excellent normal schools with a vigorous development of the normal institute. Several of the States east of the Alleghenies have opened the State University to women, and all of them have either established or are about to provide normal instruction for teachers. In six of the Southern States modified woman's suffrage in school affairs and the right to hold official position in school administrations are granted to women. In New Orleans, Tulane University has made the new departure of the woman's annex, in the Sophia Newcomb College for girls. A few influential women in Mississippi rightly claim the honor of inaugurating the movement which persuaded the legislature five years ago to establish the free Normal and Industrial College for Girls, an institution where a young woman with free tuition and small expenditure can obtain a good academical education with normal professional training, and with some industrial, bread-earning occupation a compulsory feature. Georgia has already established a similar school and South Carolina is preparing to do the same.

And this great movement, including the people's common school, of which it is the outcome, is, to far greater extent than is understood, the work of the women of the South. The old-time prejudice against all save the social leadership of woman still hinders the progress of the common school and is felt more strongly in the academical and collegiate establishments, largely sectarian and still greatly controlled by the clergy. I find numbers of important towns that still "linger shivering on the brink;" held fast by the superstition of masculine superiority in education, whoever the man may be; and "fear to launch away" by placing their public instruction in the hands of a splendid woman, to whom the heart of the community gravitates with a prophetic instinct that can not be forever suppressed.

For the most notable outcome of the great war of redemption in the South has been the emancipation of woman from the European to the American relation to society. During the four years of conflict she garnered up her powers and trained herself to a new leadership in practical life. She was the moving spirit in the revival of education in its secondary and higher departments for girls. During the ten troubled years that followed the coming of peace, in the home, the private, and the new common schools, she blazed a way out of the woods towards the open country of universal education. To-day she is in possession of, probably, the majority of positions, and does three-fourths of the valuable teaching in the common schools for white people. Everywhere, at home and in the neighboring States, she is pushing in at every open opportunity; ringing the bell and banging " the knocker on the big front door" locked on the inside. The coming ten years will record her victory. In placing in her hands, to as great an extent as even in New England, the affairs of administration and instruction in the people's common school, and in opening to her, as freely as in the West, admission to every realm of the higher education, the men of the South will give the best proof of the reality of that chivalric estimation of their own womanhood which is their boast. Chivalry, in its American acceptation, is simply the Master's golden rule everywhere applied in life. To-day the country awaits, with " great expectations," the final demonstration of the higher civilization by the New South, by placing in the hands of its good women the education of its younger children, with equal opportunity for study and service through the whole upper story of the secondary and higher culture, from the plantation primary to the University of Virginia.

CXVI.

No feature of the new Southern common school is more burdened with far-reaching consequences than the department established and supported for the benefit of more than 1,000,000 children and youth of the colored people. It would greatly clear up the Southern situation if two sets of people, both doubtless honest in their convictions, would take themselves outside of preconceived theories, in which they are wandering as in a Florida everglade, with no practical outcome, and the only possible result new complications in the future.

The first class is a considerable portion of the Southern white people, especially in the rural districts, who either question the value of education to the Negro laborer or protest against the "injustice" of educating him in free schools supported, as they are very largely, by the taxation of the white race. While no Southern State save two, we believe, has been persuaded by this party to refuse to be taxed for the support of at least the elementary common school for all children, yet in more than one State a movement has been inaugurated to return to the system abandoned by Kentucky, of setting apart the whole taxation of these people for their own use, or in some way withdrawing the aid of the white people. In one State a law of this kind was defeated by the decision of the courts. In every State there is enough of this agitation to alarm and exasperate the colored folk and at once play into the hands of the colored churches, many of whose clergy are trying to establish the parochial sectarian school system, and stimulate the sectional spirit which all good people in the country deplore.

For in the first place if anything is demonstrated amid the confusion of tongues that rages around "the labor question," it is that intelligent labor in the masses, organized and guided by the skilled labor of experts, is the only method by which any American State can develop its resources and build itself up into the varied type of industry characteristic of Republican institutions. The most serious burden upon labor to-day in our country is the illiteracy, incompetence, and general hand-to-mouth style of working and living in which millions of our countrymen still flounder. The man who asserts that the seven millions of our colored citizens are worse off for their education for the past twenty-five years, either does not know what he is talking about, or does know exactly that the logic of his contention leads back to slavery, or a condition so little removed therefrom that any State in which it prevails may as well make its "last will and testament," and prepare to disappear from the fellowship of civilized communities within the coming generation. The only cure of the present defects of negro education is more schooling of a better kind, solid elementary instruction six months in the year, with industrial training by a class of teachers reliable as moral guides no less than competent as instructors in letters. The secondary and higher education of these people, outside what the State can afford, is now well cared for in the great mission schools. In proportion as the Southern people do their duty the North may be relied upon to help, and Congress will respond to any practicable system of national aid acceptable to the educational public of the South.

The "injustice" complained of is a part of the American common. school system whereby the State of Massachusetts, perhaps by a third of her population, taxes itself $8,000,000 yearly, paying $20 a head to educate her 400,000 school children, 90 per cent of whom are given the advantages of a free high school, with unlimited years for attendance, beside a score of good normal schools with free tuition for teachers, and such facilities for good reading as are enjoyed nowhere else. The American idea is that the property of the State shall educate its children, and the denial of this fundamental principle would precipitate a "labor agitation" compared with which the disturbance of to-day is a summer's breeze to a cyclone. Not only justice, but every consideration, industrial, social, political, and religious, points to universal education as the bottom question in every American State, the neglect of which unsettles everything, the wise handling of which will settle all things aright, with persistence, patience, patriotism, and God's providence as irresistible allies.

CXVII.

On the other hand, a portion of the educated colored people and their Northern friends do great injustice to the Southern educational public, which, in establishing and supporting the common school for the Negro now these twenty years, defending it against its enemies and making it somewhat better every year, deserves the approbation of the Republic and especially the hearty coöperation of the colored citizens and their sensible friends. The separation of colored from white children in schooling is simply inevitable, and, like all inevitable conditions, has great advantages in the present condition of the race. Only in separate schools can the children of these people acquire the entire circle of personal qualities which make the self-reliant citizen, be protected from unfavorable associations, and be schooled in the ways best adapted to the first generation of a race that has received education through the medium of letters. Besides, the coeducation of the races in the South would practically deprive the superior class of young colored people of their most valuable opportunity at present— their leadership in the common-school training of 1,000,000 colored children—by all odds the most important professional work now open to them, including, as it so often does, the building up of an intelligent and reliable ministry, and the improvement of the Sunday school in the colored churches.

I am often discouraged by what seems to me a failure to appreciate the present opportunities of the younger third of the Negro people by a considerable portion of their educated class who persist in looking at the general situation through the clouded spectacles of their own peculiar disabilities. Every wise and good man deplores these disabilities, and labors for their gradual removal. But too many of this class fail to appreciate the fact that to-day no set of educated young people in Christendom has such an opportunity as themselves in the mental, moral, religious, and social leadership of 7,000,000 people—a nation within a nation—so intimately inwrought into the very texture of civilization in one third our American States that not only their welfare but that of the Republic is largely dependent upon the outcome. Every consideration, not only the highest, but wise expediency, personal concern, and common sense, now implores the more favored class of this people to put out of mind everything that will conflict with the practical work on hand. That work is, within a generation, to bring the younger third of this great population to such an industrial, mental, moral, and social state of fitness for full American citizenship that no State will either dare or desire to withhold from it all legal protection in the common civil rights accorded to the whole. While national legislation may do somewhat, Northern sympathy more, and a growing conviction of both civic and Christian obligation among the Southern people most of all, it should be understood plainly that this result depends more on the consecrated labor and the intelligent, firm, and conciliatory attitude of perhaps a hundred thousand educated and able men and women of that race than upon all other influences combined.

CXVIII.

And no division of this leading class now occupies such a post of vantage as the teachers in the common schools for the colored people. There are now 23,000 of them, and their number is constantly increasing, through the enlarging opportunities of the great mission schools and the system of normal instruction now supported in every Southern State. It only needs a larger body of competent people to open every public colored schoolhouse door in the South to teachers of this race, with increasing opportunity in the seminaries for higher instruction established by the North. At present the men are in a considerable majority in this work, partly because a larger proportion of young men are competent and because the superior class of the younger colored clergy often combine teaching with the ministry. The more intelligent young men too often are making the serious mistake of crowding the few professions open to them, or thronging the cities and the National Capital for office work, instead of following the example of great numbers of educated white men in looking to the various mechanical trades and industrial openings where they are especially needed, and where there still remains large opportunity for success. Many of these men are now invaluable, not only as teachers and preachers, but as general workers and leading citizens among their people.

We here enforce again what has already been said—the unique opportunity and commanding position of the colored teacher in the Southern common school. There is no more pestilent nuisance in America than an ignorant, vicious, mischief making man or woman in this position, unless it be the "big-head" graduate of a colored university, contemptuous of labor, inflated with the "little brief authority" of the schoolroom, a social "masher," a political wire-puller, and a general intermeddler and disturber of good feeling between the better classes of the community. But nowhere, in this or any other country, can a more valuable work be accomplished than by "the right man" from Hampton, Fisk, Atlanta, or Tuskegee, "in the right place," his schoolroom, an office where he, the man of all good work, is building up his people in all good things.

CXIX.

And especially is the colored woman teacher—competent in acquirements, character, professional ability, religious consecration, womanly tact, and practical and patient industry—such a benediction to her people as nobody can understand, unless, like myself, he has seen, year after year, the development of this class of the colored teaching-body in the border cities and through all the Southern States. There are now probably 8,000 colored women teaching school, the great majority of them in the common schools. Of course, too many of them are every way incompetent and too few thoroughly qualified for this greatest of all sorts of American woman's work. But a larger number every year are doing better service, and a considerable class are so good that I never spend an hour in the schoolroom with one of them without feeling that the colored woman has a natural aptitude for teaching not yet half understood by her own people, but certain to make her a most pow-erful influence in the future of both races in the South.

For two hundred years the Negro woman has been the servant, nurse, "mammy" and "aunty" of the foremost Southern people, and with all her shortcomings, past and present, is still beloved by the children as no class in similar condition has ever been in our country. The most stubborn "Bourbon" statesman melts and talks like a Christian gentle-man in praise of the good old sister in black who was more to his boy-hood than even his profuse rhetoric can set forth. Here is the provi-dential furnishing, in this native loving-kindness, unselfishness, end-less patience, overflowing humor and sympathetic insight into child nature, for the office of the teacher, with the added qualifications of suitable education, moral stamina and the social refinement that come so easily to the educated colored woman. It is useless to argue this point with one who does not know what is now going on in the school-rooms of the South ; and there is no necessity for argument with any competent observer, after suitable observation.

CXX.

44   Thirty years ago, Myrtilla Miner, a northern schoolmistress, began the seemingly hopeless work of establishing a high school for free col-ored girls in the city of Washington, D. C. Her biography, now written, tells the pathetic and inspiring tale of her career in that city. At her death, she left a small property dedicated to the higher instruction of colored girls. A dozen years ago I first visited the Miner Normal School, then under the control of the directors of this fund, taught in a large building owned by the corporation, in connection with the public schools furnishing trained teachers for their use. The principal,
45   Miss Briggs, a colored woman, born and educated in Massachusetts, was one of the most competent experts in this work I have ever known and, under her admirable management, the school made good progress. Her later years were passed in Howard University as professor of peda-gogics, where she died in 1890, regretted by all who knew of her great work. By what seems to me an unwise and visionary policy, this fund was detached from the normal school and is now involved in an attempt at mission and industrial work in the city. But the normal school, thus established, is now supported as a part of the common-school sys-

tem, and, under the principalship of Miss Lucy Moten, a remarkable young woman, educated in the Salem (Mass.) Normal School, sustains its high reputation and supplies the colored schools of the city with their teachers.

The Magruder school building is used largely as the practice department for this school, and I have rarely seen better primary work anywhere, with more suggestive and satisfactory results in scholarship, deportment, drawing, and the industrial work usually attempted by children of these years, than can be seen there at any time by any visitor. In these Washington schools, by their payment of good wages and favorable conditions, has been gathered a group of excellent colored teachers and admirable women. Many of them have been educated in the normal schools of the North as well as at home. They are not only good teachers, but women of high character and personal refinement, known and esteemed at home and abroad.

The great mission colleges, especially the Hampton Normal Institute and similar institutions established by the Southern States, are rapidly increasing this class of excellent colored women teachers. As the young educated men of the race improve their opening industrial opportunities, the call for young women will increase until they will become the majority, as in the schools for white children and youth. As it is, their work is even more radical and essential to the future of their people than that of any other class. As teachers in the common and the Sunday school, leaders of the women in the churches, wives of the clergymen and other educated men, influential through their knowledge of industrial matters, especially valuable in the reform and uplifting in the home life of their people, their work and worth can not be overestimated. For only as the home of the Southern Negro is built on the solid foundations of chastity, temperance, intelligent industry, and all the qualities that make for Christian womanhood, is there any rational hope for the permanent advancement of the race. What this sisterhood of noble young women should now have is the sympathy, wise coöperation, and material aid of the Christian women of the South, for the results of what they are doing are already felt, and more and more will prevail in every Southern home.

CXXI.

Thus have I attempted, of necessity in a manner sketchy and bounded a good deal by my own personal observation as the interpreter of all I have read and heard of Southern education, to give the outlines of my own estimate of the educational situation of the South, as concerns especially the elementary and secondary schooling of its children and youth, and, as the title of my essay indicates, with particular reference to the heart of the matter : the direct and indirect influence of " Southern women in the recent educational movement of the South." I anticipate that in laying such emphasis upon the woman-side of the matter

I go beyond the estimate of the more conservative view of many of the most esteemed educators of these States. But I can see no reason for believing that the trend of educational thought and development is essentially different in this from the other portions of the Union. There, as everywhere in our country, I find the nobler class of young women moved by the common desire for a broader culture and a more intimate acquaintance with the class of studies that touch on the conduct of life, with an irrepressible ambition to do their part in the new industrial and professional openings to their sex. And above all do I mark the zeal, energy, and ability with which they have responded to the call of their people for service in the schoolroom. Great numbers of them, far greater than is understood at home, are now domiciled in our Northern cities, doing what is not called for, perhaps not heartily approved in their own neighborhoods. But the time is rapidly passing when any capable and worthy Southern girl will be compelled to leave her own section to find a sphere for any honorable pursuit, either for bread-winning or the higher dispensation of the bread of life to hungry souls. There is not an important educational position in the South to-day that is not somewhere well filled by a woman. And her success makes her not only an " object lesson " for thousands of ambitious girls, but the pride of the community. The leading women teachers of the South are already a conspicuous figure in Southern society, as seen from outside; and, with their literary and artistic sisterhood, they are coming to occupy the place of the Southern woman of society of a generation ago.

CXXII.

It was my original intention to follow out these suggestive lines of development in the recent educational movement in the South by a sketch of their logical bearing upon much that I see in the industrial, literary, artistic, social, moral reform, and religious life of these States. Happily for the permanent civilization of this section, the Southern woman of to-day, by her intense and pathetic reminders of the past and the prodigious power of public opinion, is held to a more gradual and conservative evolution of her coming estate than her sister either in the new and limitless West or the free and cultured East. But she is moving on the same lines as the great influential superior class of women in the North, who are not always represented by the leaders of the radical so-called " woman's movement," though ready to secure every right, fill every position, and use every opportunity that the " sober second thought" and Christian common sense of American womanhood will demand. As fast as that demand becomes articulate and fairly representative of the foremost American womanhood it will be received and granted by the American people, as it has been during the past half century. Neither a reluctant Southern manhood, local theories, nor the exigencies of Southern society will do more than retard the corresponding woman's movement in these sixteen States.

It is not necessary, just now, to explore these widely diverging lines, which, like the railroad tracks of a great prairie city, spread themselves onward and outward, till they dwindle and fail in a far-off horizon. There is far too much obstinate theorizing, vague prophecy, and loud and boastful proclamation now for the good of the Southern people. What the peculiar type (as Mr. Breckinridge says, "the provincial flavor") of the coming Southern manhood and womanhood is to be; how far even the best characteristics of the old aristocratic order are to be reproduced, exalted, and glorified in the democratic order which is now so rapidly materializing; whether the approaching wealth, as in the North, is to be educated and directed into that large and beneficent giving, for the upper side of life, which is the glory of American civilization, the coarse and brutal insensibility to which fact declares the majority of the leaders of the so-called "labor movement" not only incompetents in business and "shriekers" in politics, but vulgar and second-rate in their general estimate of human society; or whether, for a generation, the lower and more hateful results of new accumulation are to inflict on these communities a dispensation of shoddy, selfishness, and dishonesty, provoking, as even now seems to be threatened, an uprising of the "plain people" to overthrow all established laws of financial development, with down-rushing political chaos beyond—it is not profitable here to inquire. The noblest heart and mind of the South is to-day laboring with these problems. Such a deliverance as that which comes to us in the commencement address of President William Preston Johnston, of Tulane University, New Orleans, before the University of Alabama, in July, 1891, is a landmark toward the future in which all true Americans may unite.

CXXIII.

But one duty appears to me, above all others, imperative upon the educational public of these Southern States—in every way possible in their present circumstances, by the acceptance of every honorable gift, by the coöperation of the home, the church, and the State, to give to the present generation of Southern girls the full educational opportunity of our present American life. No enlightened man certainly will disparage the importance of all that is being done for the higher training of Southern boys. The only regret is that the insanity of materialism and the supposed necessities of common life are driving so many of them away from the opportunities now at hand. In the higher grades of the excellent public grammar schools of Atlanta, Ga., a representative industrial Southern city, I found room after room with a little group of a dozen boys or less to a swarm of girls, and the boys' high school, not one-third as large as the girls' high school, established by Supt. Mallon and presided over for years by the queenly grace and culture of Laura Haygood. In another more populous city I found but 2 boys and 200 girls in its coeducational high school. Indeed, up to the actual college age the girls, from the age of 10 to 18, are already in overwhelming majority in the Southern schoolroom wherever I go. But even here a great deal more should be done, and can be done, for the betterment of the education of these girls.

It is of the first importance that a more thorough system of training teachers, especially for elementary school work, should be at once established. I do not know of half a dozen genuine city training schools for teachers south of Washington. It is simply a blunder, almost " an outrage," to thrust a young girl, even a high school or "female college" graduate, with no knowledge even that there is a science and art of education, perhaps not a month's experience in caring for children, into one of these swarming primary schoolrooms in the cities, or into the jungle that the average ungraded country school must be. The conceit of certain "great educators," male or female, that the girl graduate, even from Vassar, is competent without training to teach school, is fast becoming the champion educational heresy of the time. And of all countries in the world the South is the place where a thorough system of normal training in the natural methods of school keeping is most important. A few thousand dollars extra in any one of twenty Southern cities thus wisely expended would increase the value of their schools beyond measure, and only thus can a permanent class of reliable teachers be developed. The State normal schools are too few to supply the demand, and the brief summer institutes only deal with teachers often confirmed in bad habits. Every important school for girls in the South and every graded school should make this a prominent department and work it with all the vigor possible.

CXXIV.

Outside of Washington and two or three special State schools I am not aware of any important movement in the South to make industrial training, even of an elementary type, a prominent element in the schooling of white girls. This important department of modern school-keeping is far better organized and more liberally dispensed to the colored than to the white girls of the South. Nobody disputes the necessity of doing all things possible to qualify the average colored school-girl for the inevitable duties of her lot, and everybody knows the melancholy failure of that dangerous "little learning" which leaves her a victim to laziness and a candidate for ruin. But there are hundreds of thousands of young white women in the South looking with a mighty longing for that training in some one of the 346 bread-winning occupations now in the busy hands of their Northern sisters. It is little less than sheer cruelty and heartless selfishness, though veneered with eloquent sentimentality, to keep these good girls adrift outside the pale, beating about in unskilled work, till forced by public sentiment into a hasty, early marriage, in its outcome an evil more fatal even than the free divorce of the North. The Southern woman of to-day, outside the frivolous class, desires to work. But she also desires and has the right to demand that she shall be taught those improved methods of work which, perhaps, more than anything fix the character of society and the estimate of genuine refinement. The "conservatism" that denies this is simply a back-water slough of reactionary despond, in which no progressive Southern community will long be content.

CXXV.

We repeat, what has been said before, that the time has come in the South, as elsewhere, when the silly American habit of calling even second-rate common things by uncommon names should be discountenanced, nowhere more sternly than in the higher education of young women. The showy, expensive, and misleading parade of young girl graduates of high and academic schools, trained to enact a gorgeous spectacle which is an educational sham if not a farce, amid the hurrahs of crowded opera houses, the adulation of friends, and the sickening glorification of the local press, is the most discouraging element in the movement for the higher education of young women. It makes one even respect the obstinate command of tough old Gen. Hill that the girls in the University of Arkansas should dress in checked gowns and sunbonnets. The very name and catalogue of many of these academies for girls is, in itself, the most forcible argument for a severe and relentless "new departure" towards the upper story of an education that is of the higher sort in something beside a "thundering in the index" and an overgrown printed course of study. At various points in the South, as we have before indicated, this reform is stirring in the minds of the real leaders of education, making sensible people disgusted with the boastful comparison of poor and superficial with genuine schools, every year bringing to the front a larger number of resolute girls who will either get what they want at home or find it elsewhere, and giving a pathetic force to the appeals, almost heartbreaking in their intensity, of the noblest teachers for the means of establishing the real woman's college and university as it is now understood in the great educational centers of every country.

And these things must be given, and given as speedily as may be, to furnish the young women of the South for the imperative demands of the present. They must be given with the expectation of meeting the logical result of "the woman's movement" for higher culture as the years go on. Surely the men of the South, who have filled the world with the praise of their womankind in the past, and to-day insist, sometimes even with heat and violence, that the society made by her in the old time was the best upon earth, will not bely their own faith by the unmanly fear that the broadest and loftiest education approved by the consensus of Christendom will in any way dwarf her capacity or pervert her womanhood. Rather will they rejoice to consecrate their new wealth to its noblest use, the training of the young womanhood of the South for the enlarging duties and thronging opportunities of "the grand and awful time," even now at hand, blending with the swift-advancing splendors and solemnities of the years to come.

CXXVI.

TABLE No. 5.

Table containing a list of the institutions for the superior instruction of women in fifteen Southern States.

[This table is copied from the reports of the National Bureau of Education for 1887, 1888–1889, and gives information concerning all institutions for the superior education of women in fifteen Southern States at that time in the possession of the Bureau. A circular addressed to and widely distributed among this class of schools has brought a large number of catalogues to the department, and from this collection additions have been made to the list. The personal observation of the author of this circular of information has brought him in connection with a large number of private schools for girls of which the Bureau of Education has no knowledge. It is hoped that every school in the South will henceforth send its catalogue every year to the Bureau for preservation in the library.]

ALABAMA.

Location.	Name.	Religious denomination.	Professors and instructors.	Students.
Athens	Athens Female College	M. E. So	5	90
Eufala	Union Female College	Nonsect	4	68
Huntsville	Huntsville Female College	M. E. So	15	235
Do	Huntsville Female Seminary	Presb	5	50
Marion	Judson Female Institute	Baptist	15	134
Do	Marion Female Seminary	Nonsect	11	105
Talladega	Synodical Female Institute	Presb	6	146
Tuskaloosa	Central Female College	Baptist	12	215
Do	Tuskaloosa Female College	Nonsect	15	235
Tuskegee	Alabama Conference Female College	Meth	9	156
Springville	Springville Institute		4	138
Demopolis	Marengo Female Institute	Nonsect	9	115
Greensboro	Southern University *	M. E. So		

ARKANSAS.

Whitman	Whitman College*	M. E. So	10	252
Arkadelphia	Ouachita Baptist College *	Baptist	20	309
Batesville	Arkansas College *	Presb		†25
Boonsboro	Cane Hill College	do		†63
Fayetteville	Arkansas Industrial University *	Nonsect		†164

DELAWARE.

Dover	Wilmington Conference Academy	M. E. So	8	139

FLORIDA.

Winter Park	Rollins College*	Cong	16	100
De Land	John B. Stetson University	Baptist	9	111
Orange City	St. Johns River Conference*	Meth. Epis		†45
Leesburg	Florida Conference College	M. E. So		†49

* Coeducational.   † Women students.

TABLE No. 5—Continued.

Table containing list of institutions for the superior instruction of women, etc.—Continued.

GEORGIA.

Location.	Name.	Religious denomination.	Professors and instructors.	Students.
Athens	Lucy Cobb Institute	Nonsect	19	130
Covington	Georgia Methodist Female College	Meth	7	137
Cuthbert	Andrew Female College	...do	8	
Dalton	Dalton Female College	M. E. So	9	181
Forsyth	Monroe Female College	Baptist	7	116
Gainesville	Georgia Baptist Seminary for Young Ladies.	...do	5	80
Griffin	Griffin Female College		4	80
La Grange	La Grange Female College	M. E. So	11	175
Do	Southern Female College	Baptist	21	217
Macon	Wesleyan Female College	M. E. So	19	326
Newnan	College Temple	Nonsect	10	130
Rome	Shorter College	Baptist	15	163
Thomasville	Young Female College	Nonsect	5	181
Lawrenceville	Lawrenceville Seminary *	...do	4	100
Marietta	Harwood Seminary	M. E. So	7	147
Bowden	Bowden College *	Nonsect		52
Macon	Mercer University *	Baptist		

KENTUCKY.

Location.	Name.	Religious denomination.	Professors and instructors.	Students.
Clinton	Clinton College	Baptist	9	212
Danville	Caldwell College	Presb	13	133
Georgetown	Georgetown Female Seminary	Baptist	10	123
Glasgow	Liberty Female College	...do	9	113
Harrodsburg	Daughters' College	Nonsect	9	140
Hopkinsville	Bethel Female College	Baptist	6	75
Lexington	Hamilton Female College	Christian	15	154
Do	Sayre Female Institute	Presb	12	100
Louisville	Hampton College	Nonsect	14	
Do	Louisville Female College		10	50
Millersburg	Millersburg Female College	M. E. So	16	197
Mount Sterling	Mount Sterling Female College	Nonsect	4	47
Nicholasville	Jessamine Female Institute	...do	9	131
Pewee Valley	Kentucky College for Young Ladies	...do	6	41
Russellville	Logan Female College	Meth. So	9	140
Shelbyville	Science Hill School	M. E. So	12	152
Do	Stuart's Female College	Presb	7	91
Stanford	Stanford Female College	Nonsect	10	90
Woodburn	Cedar Bluff Female College	...do	9	80
Glendale	Lynnland Female College	Baptist	8	54
Maysville	Hayswood Female Seminary	Nonsect	8	60
Louisville	Louisville Female Seminary	...do	11	100
Lexington	State Agricultural and Mechanical College.*		26	625
Eminence	Eminence College *	Christian		†71
Hopkinsville	South Kentucky College*	...do		†60
Murray	Murray Male and Female Institute*..	Nonsect		†81
New Liberty	Concord College*			
Bowling Green	Pleasant J. Potter College*			
Cedar Bluff	Female College			

LOUISIANA.

Location.	Name.	Religious denomination.	Professors and instructors.	Students.
Clinton	Silliman Female Collegiate Institute	Presb	8	111
Mansfield	Mansfield Female College	M. E. So	8	90
Minden	Minden Female College	Nonsect	4	80
New Orleans	H. Sophia Newcomb Memorial College of Tulane University.	...do	14	175
Keachie	Keachie College	Baptist		†84
New Orleans	Tulane University*	Nonsect		†282

* Coeducational.   † Women students.

TABLE No. 5—Continued.

Table containing list of institutions for the superior instruction of women, etc.—Continued.

MARYLAND.

Location.	Name.	Religious denomination.	Professors and instructors.	Students.
Baltimore	The Woman's College of Baltimore	Meth. Epis	18	140
Baltimore (Park Place.)	Baltimore Female College	Nonsect	8	57
Cambridge	Cambridge Female Seminary	do	4	52
Frederick	Frederick Female Seminary	do	10	125
Lutherville	Lutherville Seminary	Lutheran	10	96
Westminster	Western Maryland College*	Meth. Prot.		†7J

MISSISSIPPI.

Location.	Name.	Religious denomination.	Professors and instructors.	Students.
Blue Mountain	Blue Mountain Female College	Nonsect	21	220
Brookhaven	Whitworth Female College	M. E. So	14	179
Clinton	Central Female Institute	Baptist	9	120
Columbus	Industrial Institute and College for Education of White Girls of Mississippi.	Nonsect	22	382
Corinth	Corinth Female College		4	110
Holly Springs	Franklin Female College	Nonsect	5	100
Meridian	East Mississippi Female College	M. E. So	8	
Oxford	Union Female College	Cumb. Presb	10	75
Pentotoc	Chickasaw Female College	Presb	4	
Port Gibson	Port Gibson Female College	M. E. So	6	100
Shuqualak	Shuqualak Female College	Baptist	9	94
Starkville	Starkville Female Institute	do	10	214
Summit	Lea Female College	do	8	60
Fayette	Fayette Academy	Nonsect	4	50
Holmesville	Kavanaugh College*	Nonsect		†57
Oxford	University of Mississippi*	Nonsect		†11

NORTH CAROLINA.

Location.	Name.	Religious denomination.	Professors and instructors.	Students.
Asheville	Asheville Female College	Meth	8	160
Charlotte	Charlotte Female Institute	Presb	15	168
Greensboro	Greensboro Female College	Meth	15	170
Lenoir	Davenport Female College	Nonsect	8	84
Murfreesboro	Chowan Baptist Female Institute	Baptist	8	72
Do	Wesleyan Female College	Meth	6	51
Oxford	Oxford Female Seminary	Presb	9	117
Raleigh	Estey Seminary	Baptist		172
Raleigh	Peace Institute	Presb	17	169
Do	St. Mary's School	Prot. Epis	14	140
Statesville	Statesville Female College	Nonsect	10	104
Thomasville	Thomasville Female College	Baptist	8	87
Dallas	Gaston College	Luth	5	89
Hickory	Claremont Female College	Nonsect	9	87
Louisburg	Louisburg Female College	M. E. So	8	82
Salem	Salem Female Academy	Moravian	32	311
Wilson	Wilson Collegiate Institute	Nonsect	5	108
Littleton	Littleton Female College		10	67
Oak Ridge	Oak Ridge Institute*	Nonsect	9	274
Conover	Concordia College*	Christian	6	137
Wilmington	Tileston Normal School*	Nonsect	8	200
Cedar Grove	Cedar Grove Academy*	do	2	87
Rutherford	Rutherford College*	do		†53

* Coeducational.   † Women students.

TABLE No. 5—Continued.

Table containing list of institutions for the superior instruction of women, etc.—Continued.

SOUTH CAROLINA.

Location.	Name.	Religious denomination.	Professors and instructors.	Students.
Columbia..........	Columbia Female College	M. E. So	13	140
Due West	Due West Female College.............	Nonsect	10	146
Greenville.........	Greenville Female College.............	Baptist	14	227
Walhalla..........	Walhalla Female College	Nonsect	5	80
Gaffney City	Cooper Limestone Institute	Baptist............	8	105
Sumter	Sumter Institute	Presb	10	140
Spartanburg.......	Columbia Female College..............	M. E. So ....,	12	100
Williamston	Williamston Female College	Nonsect	12	176
Columbia..........	Winthrop Training School	....do	5	54
Clinton	Presbyterian College of South Carolina.*	Presb..............	....	†40
Anderson..........	Female College........................	....	....	....

TENNESSEE.

Location.	Name.	Religious denomination.	Professors and instructors.	Students.
Brownsville	Brownsville Female College	Baptist	9	99
Do..............	Wesleyan Female College	Meth ....,	4	56
Columbia..........	Columbia Athenæum	Nonsect	17	162
Jackson ....:	Memphis Conference Female Institute.	M. E. So	10	160
McMinnville	Cumberland Female College	Cumb. Presb	5	150
Murfreesboro......	Soulé Female College	M. E. So	7	89
Nashville, 108 Vauxhall street.	Nashville College for Young Ladies ..	....do	18	407
Nashville..........	Ward's Seminary for Young Ladies...	Nonsect	19	314
Pulaski...........	Martin Female College	...do	13	184
Rogersville	Synodical Female College	...do	12	94
Shelbyville	Shelbyville Female College	...do	6	100
Winchester........	Mary Sharp College	Baptist............	7	182
Gallatin	Howard Female College	Nonsect	9	124
Nashville	Belmont College	...do	14	....
Athens .... ⎱ Chattanooga ..... ⎰	U S. Grant University.................	Meth	40 ⎱⎰	330 183
Memphis	Clara Conway Institute	Nonsect	30	700
McKenzie	Bethel College*......................	Cumb. Presb......	....	†134
Maryville..........	Maryville College*...................	Presb	....	†109
Milligan	Milligan College*	Christian	....	†41
Mossy Creek	Carson and Newman College*	Baptist	....	†147
Tusculum	Greenville and Tusculum College* ...	Presb..............	....	†46

TEXAS.

Location.	Name.	Religious denomination.	Professors and instructors.	Students.
Georgetown	Ladies' Annex, Southwestern University.	M. E. So ....:.....	14	122
Belton	Baylor Female College		18	250
Waco..............	Waco Female College	Meth	14	186
Chapel Hill	Chapel Hill Female College	M. E. So	8	113
Austin	Commercial School and German English Academy.*	Nonsect	5	80
Walnut Springs ...	Central College.......................	....do	8	276
Sherman	Sherman Institute.....................	....do	15	440
Sulphur Springs...	Central College.......................	M. E. So	9	213
Whiteright........	Grayson College	Nonsect	12	532
Sherman...........	North Texas Female College	M. E. So	19	260
Austin	University of Texas*..................	Nonsect...........	....	†40
Fort Worth	Fort Worth University*	Meth. Epis........	....	†125
Georgetown	Southwestern University*	M. E. So	....	†138
Italy	Hope Institute	Christian	....	†67
Salado	Salado College........................	Nonsect............	....	†44
Tehuacana	Trinity University	Cumb. Presb......	....	†112
Waco..............	Baylor University*....................	Baptist	....	†267

* Coeducational.	† Women students.

TABLE No. 5—Continued.

Table containing list of institutions for the superior instruction of women, etc.—Continued.

VIRGINIA.

Location	Name.	Religious denomination.	Professors and instructors.	Students.
Abingdon	Stonewall Jackson Female Institute..	Presb	5	63
Do	Martha Washington College	Nonsect	20	161
Charlottesville	Albemarle Female Institute	Baptist	8	60
Christiansburg	Montgomery Female College	Nonsect	9	118
Danville	Danville College for Young Ladies	M. E. So	9	118
Do	Roanoke Female College	Baptist	6	90
Hollins	Hollins Institute	...do	17	160
Marion	Marion Female College	Luth	12	116
Norfolk	Norfolk College for Young Ladies	Nonsect	11	214
Petersburg	Southern Female College	...do	10	65
Staunton	Staunton Female Seminary	Luth	9	80
Glade Spring	Southwest Female Institute	Baptist	11	137
Gordonsville	Central Female Institute	Nonsect	9	82
Richmond	Richmond Female Institute	Baptist	12	124
Staunton	Augusta Female Seminary	Presb	21	225
Do	Sherwood Female Seminary	Baptist	10	30
Do	Virginia Female Institute	Prot. Epis	21	99
Keswick Depot, Albemarle County.	Miss Randolph's Edge Hill School for Young Ladies.			
Dayton	Shenandoah Institute		8	122
Bristol	Sullin's College	Christian	11	220
Warrenton	Fauquier Institute	Prot. Epis	8	70
Winchester	Episcopal Female Institute	Prot. Epis	9	80

WEST VIRGINIA.

Location	Name.	Religious denomination.	Professors and instructors.	Students.
Clarksburg	Broaddus College	Baptist	7	59
Parkersburg	Parkersburg Female Seminary	Nonsect	3	40
Wheeling	Wheeling Female College	...do	9	52
Bethany	Bethany College *	Christian		†32
Flemington	West Virginia College *	Free Will Baptist.		†12
Mountain Lake Park	Briarbend Seminary	Nonsect		40

* Coeducational.   †Women students.

CXXVII.

TABLE No. 6.

[Copied from Report of United States Bureau of Education for 1888-'89.]

This table, though very incomplete, may be useful for the purpose of comparison, and, like all the tables here published, may enforce the importance of a thorough system of educational reporting to the national Bureau of Education by every variety of schools in the country.

Summary of statistics of institutions for the higher instruction of women for 1888-'89.

States.	Number of schools.	Number of instructors.			Students.			Number of graduates in 1889.	Number of volumes in libraries.	Value of scientific apparatus.	Value of grounds and buildings.	Amount of productive funds.	Income from productive funds.	Receipts from tuition fees.	Total income.	Benefactions.
		Male.	Female.	Total.	Number in preparatory department.	Number in collegiate department.	Total number.									
1	2	3	4	5	6	7	8	9	10	11	12	13	14	15	16	17
NORTH ATLANTIC DIVISION.																
Maine	2	15	11	26	30	70	493	61	9,100	$8,500	$205,000	$146,000	$7,200	$8,340	$19,000	$1,500
New Hampshire	3	7	19	26	96	315	441	32	2,400	2,305	225,000	32,000	1,920	3,270	5,190	
Massachusetts	9	103	181	284	29	1,756	2,099	231	75,437	46,000	3,094,000	1,062,925	68,235	331,506	424,970	41,719
New York	13	40	243	283	808	1,121	2,806	149	46,165	133,997	2,330,128	693,127	36,507	212,357	253,397	44,708
New Jersey	2	3	18	21	21	35	144	19		1,550	120,500			18,900	18,900	
Pennsylvania	12	56	128	184	275	866	1,334	142	31,180	15,000	960,000	713,000	41,180	22,500	77,300	3,100
SOUTH ATLANTIC DIVISION.																
Maryland	6	17	55	72	249	344	669	53	9,645	14,800	421,000	175,000	4,250	13,000	20,350	210,000
Virginia	19	56	132	188	444	1,402	1,944	113	10,520	5,500	651,000	2,500	150	60,331	64,481	5,000
West Virginia	3	2	17	19	19	85	159	11			26,000			1,200	1,200	
North Carolina	15	37	117	154	462	958	1,753	139	23,150	8,650	463,500	1,000	80	80,200	92,512	5,000
South Carolina	5	10	49	50	199	507	722	73	2,100	1,300	110,000	1,000	80	15,000	15,700	
Georgia	9	30	71	101	350	1,019	1,569	141	8,580	5,200	392,000	40,000	2,000	8,750	20,125	
SOUTH CENTRAL DIVISION.																
Kentucky	19	34	138	172	864	1,200	2,278	153	13,180	5,450	489,000			63,985	76,535	5,750
Tennessee	11	21	112	133	220	740	1,677	121	21,550	8,500	426,000			32,386	42,542	
Alabama	9	11	72	83	246	511	1,251	103	10,153	7,500	395,000			49,860	49,860	16,000
Mississippi	11	16	88	104	578	843	1,517	67	6,650	2,425	283,000			22,650	46,204	
Louisiana	2	3	11	14	56	104	160	4	1,100	300	40,000			3,000	5,600	
Texas	3	11	26	37	114	273	510	15	2,000	675	138,000	28,000	2,600	42,000	42,200	2,000

TABLE No. 6—Continued.

Summary of statistics of institutions for the higher instruction of women for 1888-'89—Continued.

States	Number of schools	Instructors: Male	Female	Total	Students: No. in preparatory dept.	No. in collegiate dept.	Total number	No. of graduates in 1889	No. of volumes in libraries	Value of scientific apparatus	Value of grounds and buildings	Amount of productive funds	Income from productive funds	Receipts from tuition fees	Total income	Benefactions
NORTH CENTRAL DIVISION.																
Ohio	10	44	113	157	145	735	1,059	106	15,091	$4,000	$884,633	$185,000	$9,490	$47,742	$67,228	$95,700
Indiana	1	6	3	9	76	37	146	10	500	500	50,000			2,124	2,492	
Illinois	8	24	90	114	198	355	950	63	11,500	6,300	519,100	23,000	1,300	29,242	29,454	5,000
Michigan	1		7	7	175	50	50		1,530	1,500	50,000			3,000	4,300	500
Wisconsin	3	2	44	46	66	101	328	14	5,750	3,400	125,000	45,000	2,500	8,790	11,290	1,000
Minnesota	3	4	29	33	370	82	273	28	4,850	600	215,000			41,450	47,200	6,500
Missouri	13	31	108	139	154	1,048	1,720	81	8,250	5,400	530,000	70,000	4,200	72,565	83,165	4,200
Kansas	2	6	30	36		74	363	4	1,600	850	474,000			18,172	18,172	
WESTERN DIVISION.																
Oregon	1	1	10	11	30	123	153	2	1,000							
California	3	12	33	45	133	163	377	17	4,600	200	340,000	50,000	3,500	12,500	16,000	
SUMMARY.																
North Atlantic Division	41	224	600	824	1,259	4,163	7,317	634	164,582	207,352	6,937,628	1,647,052	155,042	596,873	798,757	91,027
South Atlantic Division	57	152	432	584	1,223	4,315	6,816	530	54,545	35,950	2,063,500	219,500	6,560	178,481	214,368	220,000
South Central Division	55	96	447	543	2,078	3,671	7,393	463	54,633	24,850	1,771,000	28,000	2,600	213,881	262,941	23,750
North Central Division	41	117	424	541	1,184	2,482	4,889	306	49,071	22,550	2,847,733	323,000	17,490	223,085	263,301	112,900
Western Division	4	13	43	56	163	286	530	19	5,600	200	340,000	50,000	3,500	12,500	16,000	
Total	198	602	1,946	2,548	6,407	14,917	26,945	1,952	328,431	290,902	13,959,861	2,267,552	185,192	1,224,320	1,555,367	447,677

Statistics of institutions for the higher instruction of women for 1888-'89.—PART I.

	Location.	Name.	President.	Date of charter.	Year of first opening.	Religious denomination.	Professors and instructors.			Students.					
							Male.	Female.	Total.	Number in preparatory department.	Number in collegiate department.	Number of resident graduates.	Number in other departments.	Total number.	Number of graduates at commencement of 1888-'89.
	1	2	3	4	5	6	7	8	9	10	11	12	13	14	15
1	Cambridge, Mass	Society for the Collegiate Instruction of Women.	Arthur Gilman, A. M., secretary.	1882	1879	Nonsect	55	0	55	0	115	0	0	115	5
2	Northampton, Mass	Smith College	Rev. L. Clark Seelye, D. D.	1871	1875	Nonsect	14	15	29	0	355	10	......	437	49
3	South Hadley, Mass	Mount Holyoke Seminary and College	Miss Elizabeth Blanchard, acting president.	1836	1837	Nonsect	5	36	41	0	304	12	......	306	49
4	Wellesley, Mass	Wellesley College	Helen A. Shaffer, M. A.	1870	1875	Nonsect	6	67	73	0	675	10	......	685	76
5	Aurora, N. Y	Wells College	Edward S. Frisbee, M. A.	1867	1868	Nonsect	4	8	12	5	46	0	......	53	7
6	Le Roy, N. Y	Ingham University	Rev. Wm. W. Totheroh, D. D.	1857	1837	Nonsect	1	17	18	70	25	3	65	127	8
7	Poughkeepsie, N. Y	Vassar College	James M. Taylor, D. D.	1861	1865	Nonsect	9	28	37	0	243	2	......	311	49
8	Bryn Mawr, Pa	Bryn Mawr College	James E. Rhoads	1880	1885	Nonsect	16	6	22	0	99	17	0	116	24

Statistics of institutions for the superior instruction of women for 1888-'89.—PART II.

Name.	Number of years in college course.	Number of State scholarships.	Number of other scholarships.	Annual charge for tuition.	Average cost of board and lodging per annum.	Number of volumes in library.	Value of scientific apparatus.	Value of grounds and buildings.	Amount of productive funds.	Income from productive funds.	Receipts from tuition fees.	Total income.	Benefactions.
2	**16**	**17**	**18**	**19**	**20**	**21**	**22**	**23**	**24**	**25**	**26**	**27**	**28**
1 Society for the Collegiate Instruction of Women	4	0	0	$200	$300	2,500	$1,000	$30,000	$75,000	$3,500	$15,800	$19,310	
2 Smith College	4		78	100	250	6,000	30,000	500,000	470,000	27,500	30,725	68,225	$15,000
3 Mount Holyoke Seminary and College	4			*200		14,765		319,000	205,000	13,500	†56,265	69,765	6,500
4 Wellesley College	4			150	200	34,272	10,000	2,000,000	242,000	20,000	†184,250	204,250	
5 Wells College	4			100	300	2,000	9,000	45,000	200,000	9,000	6,750	15,750	
6 Ingham University	4			30	200		400	88,000			9,077	9,077	0
7 Vassar College	4	0	†8	100	300	18,300	96,591	532,628	483,127	26,729	†116,201	142,930	1,000
8 Bryn Mawr College	4	0	†12	100	275	6,280	8,000	420,000	700,000	40,000	11,300	52,000	1,100

* Includes board.   † Includes receipts for board, etc.   ‡ And 6 fellowships.

CXXVIII.

According to late authority there are now in 15 Southern States some 150 schools for the superior instruction of women, of which 50 for the white race are coeducational. Nearly all the superior schools for the colored race are coeducational. The State universities of Arkansas, Mississippi, Texas, and Kentucky admit women. Tulane University, Louisiana; Rutherford College, North Carolina; U. S. Grant University, Maryville; Carson, Newman, and other colleges in Tennessee; Fort Worth, Southwestern and Baylor universities, Texas; and Bethany College, West Virginia, are coeducational. Of this number 44 are reported as nonsectarian, the remainder divided among 10 religious denominations. Eight thousand young women are reported in the collegiate department of these institutions, beside large numbers now attending schools of similar grades in the Northern States. Nearly a hundred schools admitting women in the South are authorized by law to confer degrees. One hundred and twenty-seven of these schools report an income of $335,000. It is reported that in 41 public schools giving secondary instruction to girls, in 14 Southern States and the District of Columbia, there were in 1886–'87, 4,800 female students, with 300 preparing for college. In 82 schools, classed as partly public, there were 4,300 girls receiving secondary instruction, of whom 220 were preparing for college. In 288 private schools, 14,500 girls were receiving secondary instruction, of whom 100 were preparing for college.

It should, however, be remembered that all statistics relating to the number of Southern girls receiving the secondary and higher instruction in the South fail to give a complete estimate; indeed, fall largely below the true number. The reasons for this are,

First. The neglect of this class of schools to report to the United States Bureau of Education, the one reliable agency for obtaining educational statistics, and fairly representing the educational condition of the country to itself and foreign nations. Under the present efficient administration of the Bureau a persistent effort is being made to obtain a report from every school of sufficient importance to attract public attention in the country. The forthcoming Columbian Exhibition at Chicago offers a notable opportunity to the private and denominational schools of the South, for the first time, to give to the country a satisfactory account of themselves.

Second. Many of the best schools for girls in the South are of a semiprivate character, in charge of superior teachers, with a limited number of pupils, publishing no catalogue and making no special effort at public report. These schools represent what is left of the old-time system of instruction by tutors in the wealthy families of the South, and mark a decided improvement in that type of instruction.

Third. It would be very desirable if the Catholic Church authorities

would give to the country a reliable account, not only of their institu
tions for the education of girls, but of their general methods of instruc
tion, discipline, moral, religious, and social training ; also the movement
of the Church in educational work among the Negroes. Many of these
schools are understood to have introduced industrial training with
excellent results.

Fourth. It is especially important that the great central American
agency for the education and training American children for good
American citizenship, the common shool, should have the benefit of all
successful experiments in every department of school life. The entire
realm outside the common school is in one sense, in our country, the
realm of liberty.

Many suggestions for the general improvement of educational affairs—
moral, religious, industrial, and social—can there be tested and, when
their value is fully demonstrated, adopted by the common school as
far as possible. In this direction alone must we look for the final
solution of the present conflict between public, private, denominational,
and collegiate systems of education, and to this end all good schools
may " work together for good."

CXXIX.

Fifth. But perhaps the most serious obstacle to a just estimate of the
extent and value of the educational opportunities now offered to young
women of the white race in the Southern States is the confusion arising
from the habit, originally formed in the States west of the Hudson
River, of bestowing the highest educational titles upon schools of secondary and often merely elementary character. Whatever may have
been the defects of the original system of education in the New England States, the name of the school from the beginning to the present
time has been a correct exponent of its grade and character. The district, high, and normal divisions of the common school; the academy,
institute, and seminary ; the college, and later the university and school
of technology, mark the fixed departments of educational work as understood and administered at different periods. But with the great movement of population westward came in the mischievous, confusing, and
untruthful practice of nailing a sign with an imposing name over the
door, especially of the private and denominational schoolhouse. From
the Berkshire hills to the Pacific these great States have thus been
filled with educational establishments whose names were no correct indication of their quality. The common-school system alone has been
free from this vicious habit, preserving the legitimate names: District
school for the ungraded collections of children in the rural districts;
with kindergarten, primary, intermediate, high, city training and State
normal, and university, to indicate the established divisions of educational work.

The same excellent habit adheres to the new common-school system of the South, the term "graded" being used to distinguish village and city systems from the district school of the open country, and high, normal, and university being fitly applied to the upper story of the public-school structure. But the entire region of the private and denominational system of education through these sixteen States, at present and for years to come perhaps destined to even a greater relative importance than in the North, is so involved in this confusing and unreliable nomenclature, itself largely implicated in personal, sectarian, and local pretensions, that it is simply impossible, even for the most careful and fair-minded observer, to convey to the educational public abroad a reliable impression of the actual value of the schooling imparted under these various names.

This, however, can honestly be affirmed—that the foremost educators and the leading educational public of the South are following the heroic movement of the Central and Western States out of this jungle of unveracity up to the high ground of a substantial and truthful basis for all grades, especially of the private and denominational systems of instruction. In this laudable effort the United States Bureau of Education is now in condition to coöperate, and each of its forthcoming reports will be more satisfactory than ever, not only as a reliable source of information concerning the actual condition of public education, and a catalogue, as complete as possible, of private and denominational schools of every character, but, what is equally desirable, will be able to furnish a reliable educational map, in which the different grades of schooling will be accurately represented in the educational landscape.

CXXX.

TABLE No. 7.

List of Catholic schools for girls, with number of parochial schools, and whole number of pupils in fifteen Southern States and District of Columbia and Territories.

[Copied from Sadlier's Catholic Directory for 1891.]

ARCHDIOCESE OF BALTIMORE, MD.

Female literary institutions.	Where situated.	Number of pupils.
Academy of the Visitation	Georgetown, D. C	90
Do	Park avenue, Baltimore, Md	187
Do	Mount De Sales, Baltimore County, Md.	100
Do	Frederick City, Md	84
Do	Washington, D. C	90
St. Mary's Institute	Annapolis, Md	40
St. Joseph's Academy of Sisters of Charity (mother house) in United States.	Emmitsburg, Md	100
Notre Dame of Maryland (mother house)	Govanstown, Md	160
Convent of Notre Dame	Baltimore, Md	30
Notre Dame Collegiate Institute for young ladies	Govanstown, Md	136
Institute of Notre Dame, young ladies and kindergarten	Baltimore, Md	134
St. Peter's Academy of Sisters of Mercy	do	50
St. Catherine's Normal Institute	do	170
Convent of Notre Dame	Annapolis, Md	
Academy of the Holy Cross	Baltimore, Md	80

TABLE No. 7—Continued.

List of Catholic schools for girls, with number of parochial schools, etc.—Continued.

ARCHDIOCESE OF BALTIMORE, MD.—Continued.

Female literary institutions.	Where situated.	Number of pupils.
Academy of Mount St. Agnes	Mount Washington, Baltimore County	30
St. Edwards Academy	Cumberland, Md	50
Holy Cross Academy	Washington, D. C	160
Academy of the Sacred Heart of Mary	Washington, D. C	
St. Cecilia's Academy	do	142
St. Francis Academy, for colored girls	Baltimore, Md	70
St. Mary's Academy	Leonardstown, Md	50
Convent and Academy of Notre Dame	Hagerstown, Md	125
St. Thomas Academy	Charles County, Md	10
Mission House	Towsontown, Md	60

Parochial schools, 88; pupils 18,000; also many private Catholic schools.

ARCHDIOCESE OF NEW ORLEANS, LA.

Sacred Heart Convent School	New Orleans	100
Sisters of Mercy (industrial night schools for young women)	do	
Sisters of Notre Dame (German convent, asylum, and schools.)	do	
Sisters of Mount Carmel (asylum and schools)	do	
Sisters of Christian Charity (German, two institutions, convent and schools.)	do	
Sisters of the Holy Family (asylum and schools)	do	
Sisters of the Immaculate Conception (convents and schools.	New Orleans, Labadieville and Lockport.	
Sisters of Our Lady of Lourdes	New Orleans	
Ursuline Academy and Boarding School	do	75
Sacred Heart Convent	Convent post-office, La	100
Colored School	do	60
Sacred Heart Convent	Grand Coteau, La	50
Colored School	do	30
Academy of the Holy Angels	New Orleans	111
Academy of Our Lady of the Sacred Heart	do	60
St. Joseph's Academy	do	200
Dominican Convent	do	75
Select school connected therewith	do	100
St. Simeon's Select School	do	160
St. Vincent's School	do	120
St. Agnes Academy	do	126
St. Alphonsus Convent of Mercy	do	150
Sisters of the Holy Family (school for colored girls)	do	120

Parochial schools, 70; whole number of pupils in religious schools: white, 10,951; colored, 1,499; private Catholic schools in each and every parish.

ARCHDIOCESE OF SANTA FÉ, N. MEX.

Academy of Our Lady of Light	Santa Fé	100
St. Vincent Academy and Boarding School	Albuquerque	150
Academy and Public School for Girls	Las Vegas	150
Sacred Heart Academy (boarding school and public school for girls.)	San Miguel	140
Sisters of Loretto School (for Indian girls)	Bernalillo	75

Parochial schools, 10; scholars, 1,200. Private schools in almost every parish.

DIOCESE OF CHARLESTON, S. C.

Sisters' Academy	Charleston	85
Ursuline Academy	Columbia	
Roarding and Day Academy	Sumter	

Parochial schools, 8; scholars: white, 500; colored, 130.

TABLE No. 7—Continued.

List of Catholic schools for girls, with number of parochial schools, etc.—Continued.

DIOCESE OF COVINGTON, KY.

Female literary institutions.	Where situated.	Number of pupils.
La Talette Academy	Covington	130
Academy of Notre Dame	do	80
St. Walburg's Academy and Boarding School	do	52
St. Catherine's Academy and Boarding School	Lexington	86
Visitation Academy, Boarding, and Day School	Maysville	50
Academy of the Immaculate Conception	Newport	91
Academy of St. Joseph	Paris	40
Academy Mount Admirabilis	White Sulphur, Scott County.	63
Mount St. Martin's Academy	Newport	

Parochial schools, 30; scholars, 6,458.

DIOCESE OF GALVESTON, TEX.

Ursuline Convent	Galveston	125
Do	Dallas	75
St. Mary's Academy	Austin	225
Academy of Sisters of St. Mary	Denison	250
St. Mary's Academy	Marshall	110
Academy of the Sisters of Providence	Palestine	100
Academy of the Sisters of St. Mary	Sherman	250
Academy of St. Agnes	Texarkana	150
Academy of the Sacred Heart	Waco	150

Parochial schools: White, 13; colored, 4; scholars, 4,148.

DIOCESE OF LITTLE ROCK, ARK.

St. Mary's Convent Schools	Little Rock	430
St. Ann s Convent School	Fort Smith	130
St. Mary's Convent	Helena	98
St. Joseph's School for Colored Children	Morrilton	100
Do	Conway	60
Sisters of St. Joseph School	Marienstein	
Sisters of St. Benedict	St. Scholastica	
Sisters of Mercy (for colored children)	Hot Springs	50
St. Augustine's (for colored)	Little Rock	30
Sisters of St. Benedict (for colored)	Pocahontas	35
Sisters of Charity (for colored children)	Pine Bluff	170

Parochial schools and academies, 34. Scholars: white, 1,400; colored, 400.

DIOCESE OF LOUISVILLE, KY.

Academy of the Holy Rosary	Louisville	50
St. Catherine's Academy of Sisters of Mercy (with night school).	do	125
Mount St. Benedict's Academy	Portland	82
Presentation Academy of Sisters of Charity	Louisville	90
Ursuline Academy	do	30
Academy of the Sacred Heart	Crescent Hill, Jefferson County	35
Bethlehem School	Bardstown	74
St. Columba's Academy (Sisters of Charity)	Bowling Green	182
Calvary Academy	Calvary Post-office	35
St. Clare's Academy (Franciscan Sisters)	Chicago	95
St. Teresa's Academy	Concordia	37
St. Mary's Academy (Sisters of Loretto)	Elizabethtown	51
St. Augustine's Academy (Sisters of Loretto)	Lebanon	75
Loretto Academy	Loretto	
Nazareth Academy (Sisters of Charity)	Nazareth	120
St. Frances Academy (Sisters of Charity)	Owensboro	140
St. Mary's Academy (Sisters of Charity)	Paducah	125
St. Catharine's Academy (Dominican Sisters)	Springfield	
St. Vincent's Academy (Sisters of Charity)	St. Vincent, Harding County	98
Bethlehem Academy (Sisters of Loretto)	St. Johns, Harding County	30
Mount St. Joseph's Academy (Ursuline Sisters)	West Louisville	40

Parochial schools: white, 40; colored, 7; total number of scholars, 10,616,

TABLE No. 7—Continued.

List of Catholic schools for girls, with number of parochial schools, etc.—Continued.

DIOCESE OF MOBILE, ALA.

Female literary institutions.	Where situated.	Number of pupils.
Academy of the Sacred Heart	Selma	....
Academy of the Visitation	Summerville	50

Parochial schools, 19; number attending, 1,627.

DIOCESE OF NASHVILLE, TENN.

St. Cecilia's Academy	Nashville	....
St. Bernard's Academy	Nashville	....
Notre Dame de Lourdes Academy	Chattanooga	....
Select School	Jackson	....
Select School	Knoxville	....
St. Agnes Academy	Memphis	....
Notre Dame de la Salette Academy	......do	....
St. Patrick's Select School	......do	....
St. Bridget's Select School	......do	....
St. Joseph's Select School	......do	....

Parochial schools, 17; scholars: white, 2,600; colored, 150.

DIOCESE OF NATCHEZ, MISS.

St. Joseph's Boarding School	Bay St. Louis	47
Mary Teresa's Institute	Chatawa	26
Academy of our Lady of Perpetual Help	......do	....
Bethlehem Boarding Schools	Holly Springs	26
Holy Angels' Academy	Scranton	88

Parochial schools: white, 20; colored, 6; Indians, 2; whole number scholars, 2,307.

DIOCESE OF NATCHITOCHES, LA.

St. Vincent's Academy	Shreveport	30
Colored school	Fairfield, near Shreveport	60
St. Francis' Convent	Mansura, Avoyelles Parish	36
Presentation Convent	Marksville, Avoyelles Parish	60
St. Mary's Convent	Shreveport	70
St. Hyacinth's Convent	Monroe	57
Convent of Divine Providence	Natchitoches	80
Colored School	......do	45
Alexandria Convent	Alexandria	90
Pineville Convent	Pineville	35
Cloutierville Convent	Cloutierville	50
Colored School	......do	30
Ilebreville Convent (colored)		40

TABLE No. 7—Continued.

List of Catholic schools for girls, with number of parochial schools, etc.—Continued.

DIOCESE OF RICHMOND, VA.

Female literary institutions.	Where situated.	Number of pupils.
St. Joseph's Academy	Richmond, Va	165
Academy of the Visitation	do	90
St. Mary's Female Academy (German)	do	85
St. Patrick's Academy	do	110
St. Mary's Academy	Alexandria	85
St. Mary's Academy (school for colored children)	do	68
St. Mary's Academy	Norfolk	40

Parochial schools, 32; scholars, 2,000.

DIOCESE OF SAN ANTONIO, TEX.

Ursuline Convent	San Antonio	330
Nazareth Convent	Victoria	230
Sacred Heart Academy	Halletsville	73

Parochial schools, 26.

DIOCESE OF SAVANNAH, GA.

Convent of the Sisters of our Lady of Mercy (with day and free school).	Atlanta	
Academy of St. Vincent de Paul	Savannah	107
St. Mary's Academy	Augusta	280
St. Joseph's Academy	Columbus	65
School for colored children	Sharon	25
Do	Washington	30
St. Joseph's Academy	do	40

Parochial schools, 5.

DIOCESE OF ST. AUGUSTINE, FLA.

Sisters of St. Joseph's	St. Augustine	
Do	Jacksonville	
Do	Mandarin	
Do	Fernandina	
Do	Palatka	
Do	Moccasin Branch	
Sister of the Holy Names of Jesus and Mary (white and colored schools).	Key West	
	Tampa	
Holy Name Academy	San Antonia	

Parochial schools, 20; scholars, 1480.

DIOCESE OF WHEELING, W. VA.

St. Joseph's Female Academy	Wheeling	130
Academy of the Visitation	Abingdon	40
St. Mary's Academy	Charleston	96
St. Joseph's Academy	Clarksburg	50
Academy of the Visitation	Parkersburg	125

Parochial schools, 14; scholars, 1,800.

DIOCESE OF WILMINGTON, DEL.

Academy of the Visitation	Wilmington	
Convent and Academy of St. Gertrude	Ridgely	

Parochial schools, 7; scholars, about 1,500.

TABLE No. 7—Continued.

List of Catholic schools for girls, with number of parochial schools, etc.—Continued.

VICARIATE-APOSTOLIC OF ARIZONA.

Female literary institutions.	Where situated.	Number of pupils.
Sisters of St. Joseph	Tucson	90
Sisters of Mercy	Florence	110
Sisters of St. Joseph	Yuma	75
Do	Prescott	80
Sisters of Mercy	Silver City	70
Sisters of Loretto	Las Cruces	130
Sisters of Mercy	Las Mesilla	95
Do	El Paso	80
Sisters of Loretto	San Elzeario	70

All the above institutions combine academical and parochial schools.

VICARIATE-APOSTOLIC OF BROWNSVILLE, TEX.

Convent of the Incarnate Word	Brownsville	134
Do	Corpus Christi	65
Ursuline Convent	Laredo	84
Convent of Sisters of Mercy	Refugio	65

Parochial schools, 8.

VICARIATE-APOSTOLIC OF NORTH CAROLINA.

Academy of Incarnation	Wilmington	50
St. Mary's Academy	Charlotte	30
Sisters of Mercy	......do	70
Sisters of Mercy { white	New Berne	35
{ colored	......do	81
Do { white	Wilmington	74
{ colored	......do	212

Parochial schools: white, 8; colored, 3; scholars: white, 379; colored, 325.

Catholic mission schools for negroes in Southern States.

Name of place.	Schools.	Pupils.	Name of place.	Schools.	Pupils.
Baltimore, Md	10	1, 100	Natchitoches, La	2	115
Charleston, S. C	1	512	New Orleans, La	26	1, 330
Covington, Ky	1	200	North Carolina	3	335
Little Rock, Ark	4	217	Richmond, Va	8	401
Louisville, Ky	6	540	St. Augustine, Fla	5	350
Mobile, Ala	4	135	San Antonio, Tex	2	115
Nashville, Tenn	1	200	Savannah, Ga	7	375
Natchez, Miss	6	294	Wilmington, Del	1	....

The above table has been compiled from Sadlier's Catholic Directory for 1891. The author of this circular of information was very desirous of giving a complete account of the Catholic system of education for women in the Southern States, but having never been invited, during his twelve years' ministry of education in the South, to visit any of these institutions, and having received but few and unimportant responses to circulars sent from the Bureau of Education, it has been impossible to give any idea of the relative importance of these institutions, their educational methods and plan of organization. A request to Chancellor Rev. T. J. Donahue, L. T. D., Baltimore, Md., that, under the central oversight of his eminence, Cardinal Gibbons, a chapter of this circular should be prepared, giving reliable information on these points, was declined, on the ground of preoccupation, with the suggestion from his eminence that application should be made to the different bishops of the Catholic Church in the Southern States. As this would involve the request that these officials should each prepare a similar document, with the strong probability of a similar response, the author of the circular regrets that it seemed impracticable to take this advice. The pages of this circular, however, in any subsequent edition, will be held open for a full statement of the Catholic system of education in the South, as far as relates to the education of girls, the coöperation of women, and the educational and mission work among the colored people.   46

CXXXI.

EDUCATION OF THE COLORED RACE IN THE SOUTH.

Under this division, by permission of Dr. W. T. Harris, United States Commissioner of Education, we republish the following set of tables containing the most complete account of the condition of education among the colored people of the sixteen former slave States and District of Columbia yet given to the public. As this record is still two years behind the present date, the situation in 1891–'92 is everywhere somewhat better than shown by these figures.

The same unfavorable criticism must attach to this as to every great mass of Southern educational statistics. And the remarks already made concerning the nomenclature of schools apply with even greater force to the entire scheme of private and denominational instruction for the colored than the white race and with far more significance to the former. But the responsibility for the latter defect rests largely with the denominational mission boards that established the more important schools at the close of the war; giving the name "college" and "university" to these great collections of several hundred colored children, while their proper college students could be counted sometimes on the fingers of one hand.

But it must be allowed that these mission schools, in several important respects, have led in the entire Southern educational movement of the past twenty years.

First. Preëminently in what has now become so largely the American practice; the coeducation of the sexes in every department of instruction. With few exceptions the largest and best of these seminaries are coeducational, and this feature is one of immense value in the training in letters and proper school discipline of the first generation following the emancipation of the race.

Second. Until recently there has been more valuable instruction in pedagogics in the superior schools for the colored than for the white race in the South. Every "college" and "university" has contained superior teachers, trained in the best normal schools of the North and Canada, and at present, through the aid of the Slater fund, this is becoming a marked feature in all of them. As a consequence, the natural methods of instruction have been introduced more largely every year to the colored public schools of the South by their graduates. The same remark applies to the normal schools for colored students established by the Southern States, all of which are giving fair instruction in the art of teaching.

Third. These schools have anticipated the feature of Industrial Training, now so highly valued, in its introduction to Southern education. Indeed, Gen. S. C. Armstrong may be called the father of industrial training in the South, for his great normal and industrial institute for colored youth and Indians at Hampton, Va., had become famous before any movement of similar importance had been inaugurated below the line of the border States in the South. And still, in the dozen Southern States where industrial education is most needed for both races, the colored people are receiving the larger proportion and are making excellent use of this great advantage.

Fourth. Another important practice in our American education, mentioned with great praise by Richard Cobden thirty years ago, on a visit to this country, the employment of women teachers for boys from the age of 12 to manhood has been notably illustrated in these great mission schools for colored youth. As before stated, the great burden of actual teaching and the moral, religious, and social training of the many thousand boys and young men of this race in these institutions has been sustained by the superior women of the North, enrolled as teachers, and to their beneficent influence must be ascribed the remarkable advance in personal purity, "good morals, and gentle manners" among this class of students, with the general commendable behavior of these young men and their growing influence in the uplift of their people. In this respect the common school of the South is falling into the American custom; and many of the secondary schools for boys would be greatly improved in manners and morals by a judicious mingling of able and influential women in their corps of teachers.

Fifth. Although we strongly deprecate the giving of unsuitable names to schools of the secondary and elementary instruction, yet in the organization of the more important of these mission schools for the colored folks, the broad idea of the university and college as outlined by Milton and Jefferson, a great seminary for the complete development of the student into an intelligent, moral, industrious, effective, and patriotic citizenship, has been more fully borne in mind than in the similar institutions for the white race in any part of the country. There are not half a dozen colleges or universities in the Union so safe as a residence for a growing boy or girl, where so many good things are proposed, so much careful personal attention bestowed upon the students, with so large a proportion of the instructors at once practical and consecrated guides of youth as in this class of establishments. If administered on this line, another generation will see them among the most unique and important educational communities in Christendom, realizing more fully than has been deemed possible before the noblest ideals of the foremost educators of the past and present age.

PUBLIC SCHOOLS.

The three tables following (Tables 8, 9, and 10) exhibit the statistics of the colored schools of the former slave States placed in juxtaposition with those of the white.

TABLE 8.—*Colored school population and colored population 6 to 14 years of age in the former slave States compared with the white, mainly for* 1889.

State.	Age of children enumerated.	Number enumerated.		Estimated population 6 to 14.		Per cent of total.	
		Colored.	White.	Colored.	White.	Colored.	White.
1	**2**	**3**	**4**	**5**	**6**	**7**	**8**
Alabama	7–21	226, 925	295, 766	164, 410	214, 330	43. 4	56. 6
Arkansas	6–21	106, 300	297, 665	78, 220	219, 080	26. 3	73. 7
Delaware	6–21	*7, 070	⁴36, 468	†5, 485	†28, 293	⁻16. 2	*83. 8
District of Columbia	6–17	†18, 200	†33, 300	13, 720	25, 100	35. 3	64. 7
Florida	6–21	†52. 865	†60, 782	41, 860	48, 130	46. 5	53. 5
Georgia †	6–18	267, 657	292, 624	186, 031	203, 381	47. 8	52. 2
Kentucky	6–20	†109, 158	†555, 809	70, 150	357, 229	19. 4	83. 6
Louisiana †	6–18	‡176, 097	‡160, 040	132, 134	120, 085	52. 4	47. 6
Maryland	5–20	§68, 400	§226, 806	47, 540	157, 560	23. 2	76. 8
Mississippi	5–21	‖273, 528	‖190, 436	179, 233	124, 753	‖59. 0	‖41. 0
Missouri	6–20	48, 478	816, 886	30, 600	515, 600	5. 6	94. 4
North Carolina†	6–16	216, 837	363, 982	142, 600	239, 150	37. 4	62. 6
South Carolina	6–21	§180, 475	§101, 189	165, 933	93, 029	§64. 1	§35. 9
Tennessee†	6–21	162, 836	489, 674	102, 600	308, 400	25. 0	75. 0
Texas	8–16	139, 939	405, 677	157, 400	456, 300	25. 6	74. 4
Virginia	5–21	¶265, 347	¶345, 024	167, 367	217, 703	¶43. 5	¶56. 5
West Virginia	6–21	10, 497	248, 437	6, 840	161, 790	4. 1	95. 9
Total				1, 692, 123	3, 489, 904	32. 7	67. 3

* In 1886.	† Estimated.	‖ In 1887.
† In 1888.	§ U. S. Census of 1880.	¶ In 1885.

TABLE 9.—*Enrollment and average attendance in colored public schools, compared with white, mainly for 1888-'89.*

State.	Number of pupils enrolled.		Per cent of total enrollment.		Number of pupils enrolled to every 100 children 6 to 14.		Average daily attendance.		Ratio of average attendance to enrollment.	
	Colored.	White.	Colored.	White.	Colored.	White.	Colored.	White.	Colored.	White
1	**2**	**3**	**4**	**5**	**6**	**7**	**8**	**9**	**10**	**11**
									Per ct.	Per ct.
Alabama............	105, 106	165, 098	38. 9	61. 1	64	77	69, 273	102, 828	65. 9	62. 3
Arkansas...........	56, 382	159, 770	26. 1	73. 9	72	73	....	....	....	....
Delaware*.........	4, 587	27, 965	14. 1	85. 9	84	99	2, 017	19, 254	44. 0	68. 9
District of Columbia	13, 004	22, 760	36. 3	63. 7	95	91	8, 597	19, 022	77. 0	77. 3
Florida.............	34, 008	52, 000	39. 5	60. 5	81	108	....	....	....	....
Georgia †...........	120, 390	200, 786	37. 5	62. 5	65	99	....	....	....	....
Kentucky	42, 526	288, 460	12. 8	87. 2	61	81	28, 833	193, 721	67. 8	67. 2
Louisiana †.........	51, 539	74, 034	41. 0	59. 0	39	62	37, 656	52, 895	73. 1	71. 5
Maryland...........	34, 072	145, 388	19. 0	81. 0	72	92	15, 227	83, 993	44. 7	57. 8
Mississippi.........	172, 338	147, 373	53. 9	46. 1	96	118	102, 708	90, 411	59. 6	61. 3
Missouri...........	32, 168	579, 873	5. 3	94. 7	105	112	....	....	....	....
North Carolina*....	125, 844	211, 498	37. 3	62. 7	88	88	75, 230	133, 427	59. 8	63. 1
South Carolina......	104, 503	89, 761	53. 8	46. 2	63	96	†69, 892	‡59, 357	66. 9	66. 1
Tennessee*.........	94, 435	342, 089	21. 6	78. 4	92	111	64, 711	244, 258	68. 5	71. 4
Texas §............	96, 809	281, 958	25. 6	74. 4	63	62	....	....	....	....
Virginia	119, 172	217, 776	35. 4	64. 6	71	100	65, 618	129, 907	55. 0	59. 6
West Virginia......	6, 209	181, 319	3. 3	96. 7	91	112	3, 589	116, 401	57. 8	64. 2
Total	1, 213, 092	3, 187, 408	27. 6	72. 4	72	91	....	....	‖62. 3	‖65. 0

* In 1887-'88.
† In 1888.
‡ There were also 7,109 not classified according to race.
§ A few counties not reporting are estimated.
‖ Includes only the States tabulated in the same column above.

TABLE 10.—*Length of school term, and number of teachers, with their monthly salaries, in colored and white schools, mainly for 1888-'89.*

State.	Average number of days the public schools were kept.		Number of teachers in colored schools.	Average monthly salaries of teachers.	
	Colored.	White.		Colored.	White.
1	**2**	**3**	**4**	**5**	**6**
Alabama........................	75¾	75¾	1, 968	$22. 33	$23. 15
Arkansas.......................	....	....	*1, 500	38. 00	46. 25
Delaware †......................	117	168	84	....	....
District of Columbia	179	182	202	....	....
Florida........................	150	150	700	....	....
Georgia ‡.......................	....	....	§1, 987	....	....
Kentucky	93	94	1, 200	38. 78	34. 58
Louisiana ‡.....................	91	95	730	33. 00	27. 50
Maryland	172	190	590	....	....
Mississippi.....................	‖91	‖91	3, 097	24. 28	34. 93
Missouri	....	....	686	....	....
North Carolina †................	61. 5	64	2, 617	21. 84	24. 62
South Carolina..................	....	....	1, 622	....	....
Tennessee †.....................	....	....	1, 564	....	....
Texas	....	....	2, 278	....	....
Virginia	....	....	1, 951	....	....
West Virginia..................	....	....	180	....	....
Total........................	¶86. 2	¶98. 6	22, 956	¶27. 35	¶32. 74

*Approximately.
† In 1887-'88.
‡ In 1888.
§ Number of colored schools, excluding those in cities under local laws.
‖ County schools only.
¶ Includes only the States tabulated in the same column above.

Remarks upon the tables.

Number of colored children in the schools.—It will be seen that, taking all the above States together, the colored children form 32.7 per cent, or a trifle less than one-third of the total school population 6 to 14 years of age, while the colored pupils form only 27.6 per cent, or little more than one-fourth of the total enrollment; *i. e.*, the colored population supplies considerably less than its due proportion of pupils to the public schools. This is the case in each of the States individually, with the exception of North Carolina and Texas, where the proportion of children and of school enrollment is about the same, and the District of Columbia, where the proportion of colored children is 35.3 per cent and of colored pupils 36.3 per cent.

Looking at the actual number of pupils enrolled for each 100 children of 6 to 14 years of age (columns 6 and 7, Table 9) it is found to be 72 for the colored population and 91 for the white, a decided difference; and if the number of white children receiving an education outside of the public schools could be taken into consideration a still greater discrepancy would appear.

Regularity of attendance.—Not only are there fewer colored pupils than white enrolled in proportion to the number of children, but the regularity of attendance of colored pupils is less than the white. The summaries of columns 10 and 11, Table 9, show that out of every 100 colored pupils enrolled 62.3 on an average attend each day; and out of a like number of white pupils 65 attend each day on an average. This is not a very great difference, however, and under all the circumstances may be considered a satisfactory relative showing. In Alabama, Kentucky, Louisiana, and South Carolina the regularity of the colored pupils exceeds that of the white.

Length of school term.—The colored schools are kept an average of 89.2 days in the nine States which furnish the necessary data for determining this item, and the white schools an average of 98.6 days (columns 2 and 3, Table 10). Delaware furnishes a large part of this difference, due to the colored people being left mainly to their own resources in that State. In Maryland, also, there is a considerable difference in the length of the school terms. Outside of these two States the difference is trifling.

Teachers' wages.—The average of the monthly wages of colored teachers in six States reporting this item is $27.35; of white teachers, $32.74 (columns 5 and 6, Table 10). This difference may be considered to proceed in part from the circumstance that among the white teachers there are a greater proportional number of the higher and better-paid grades than among the colored, thus raising their average.

In Kentucky the average wages of the colored teachers exceed those of the white. This results from the colored districts being larger than the white districts, containing more children, and therefore drawing more of the State money, which is applied exclusively to the payment of the district teacher.

TABLE 11.—*Amount and disposition of the sums disbursed from the Slater fund from 1883 to 1889, inclusive.*

	1883.	1884.	1885.	1886.	1887.	1888.	1889.	Total.
Alabama	$2,100	$2,450	$5,000	$3,800	$4,400	$4,600	$3,600	$25,950
Arkansas					600	800	800	2,200
Florida						1,000	800	1,800
Georgia	6,200	500	6,814	5,100	6,200	6,850	9,700	41,364
Kentucky		1,000	1,000	700	700	700		4,100
Louisiana		592	1,400	1,000	3,100	3,500	4,100	13,692
Mississippi	1,000	2,600	2,000	2,000	4,450	4,800	4,400	21,250
North Carolina	2,000	740	4,400	3,600	4,200	5,300	5,100	25,340
South Carolina	2,000	750	3,500	2,700	3,660	4,300	4,000	20,910
Tennessee	950	4,325	7,600	5,800	6,500	6,500	6,800	38,475
Texas		600	600	600	900	1,360	1,360	5,420
Virginia	2,000	2,000	3,000	3,650	4,190	4,190	3,150	22,180
District of Columbia		1,000	1,000	600	600	600		3,800
Special		550	450	450	500	500	500	2,950
Total	16,250	17,107	36,764	30,000	40,000	45,000	44,310	*229,431

* The sum of $45,000 has been appropriated for the year 1889-'90.

TABLE 12.—*Expenditure of moneys derived from Peabody Fund, classified by race.*

ALABAMA, 1888-'89.

White:

Thirteen scholarships at Nashville	$2,600	
Normal schools	2,250	
Birmingham Training School	500	
		$5,350

Colored:

Normal schools		800

Unclassified:

Teachers' institutes (13 white, 9 colored)	1,250	
Public schools	1,000	
		2,250
		8,400

ARKANSAS, 1888.

White:

Ten scholarships		2,000

Unclassified:

Public schools	2,200	
Teacher's institutes	1,608	
		3,808
		5,808

GEORGIA, 1888.

White:

Fourteen scholarships		2,800

Unclassified:

Newnan public schools	500	
Teachers' institute	1,042	
		1,542
		4,342

LOUISIANA, 1887-'88.

White:

Eight scholarships	1,600	
State Normal School	2,000	
		3,600

Unclassified:

Public schools	1,000	
Teachers' institutes	1,000	
		2,000
		5,600

TABLE 12.—*Expenditure of moneys derived from Peabody Fund, etc.*—Continued.

NORTH CAROLINA, 1887–'88.

White:
Fourteen scholarships $2, 800
Normal schools 2, 013
                                                    $4, 815
Colored:
Public schools 200
Normal schools 180
                                              380
Unclassified:
Public schools 2, 105
                                              7, 300

SOUTH CAROLINA, 1888–'89.

White:
Ten scholarships 2, 000
Normal school 2, 000
                                              4, 000
Colored:
Normal school 1, 000
Unclassified:
Teachers' institutes 167
Public schools 4, 450
                                              4, 617
                                            9, 617

TENNESSEE, 1886–'87.

White:
Fourteen scholarships 2, 800
Peabody Normal College 10, 000
                                           12, 800
Unclassified:
Teachers' institutes (6 white, 3 colored, in 1888–'89) 1, 200
                                           14, 000

TEXAS, 1887–'88.

White:
Nine scholarships 1, 800
Normal school 2, 000
                                           3, 800

VIRGINIA, 1887–'88.

White:
Fourteen scholarships 2, 800
Normal school 2, 000
Teachers' institutes 1, 691
                                           6, 491
Colored:
Normal school 500
Teachers' institutes 380
                                           880
                                           7, 371

WEST VIRGINIA, 1886–'87.

White:
Eight scholarships 1, 600
Unclassified:
Normal schools 1, 000
Institutes 1, 500
                                           2, 500
                                           4, 100

TABLE 13.—*Statistics of institutions for the instruction of the colored race, for 1888-'89.*

Location.	Name.	Religious denomination.	Instructors.	Students.
	NORMAL SCHOOLS.			
Huntsville, Ala........ ...	Central Alabama Academy.........................	M. E........	5	140
Do	State Colored Normal and Industrial School	Non-sect....	10	257
Mobile, Ala	Emerson Institute......................	Cong	10	289
Montgomery, Ala......	State Normal School for Colored Students........	Non-sect....	19	325
Talladega, Ala........	Normal Department of Talladega College	Cong	....	35
Tuskegee, Ala	Tuskegee Normal and Industrial Institute.......	Non-sect....	27	399
Helena, Ark	Southland College and Normal Institute *.......	....	5	61
Pine Bluff, Ark.......	Branch Normal College of Arkansas Industrial University.	Non-sect...	7	200
Washington, D. C.....	Miner Normal School	... do	7	40
Do...............	Normal Department of Howard University	...do	6	163
Tallahassee, Fla	State Normal College for Colored Teachers	...do	3	54
Atlanta, Ga..........	Normal Department of Atlanta University.......	...do		110
Augusta, Ga	The Paine Institute	M. E., So....	8	129
Cuthbert, Ga..........	Howard Normal School *	Non-sect....	2	124
Thomasville, Ga	Normal and Industrial School *	....	7	367
New Orleans, La......	Normal Department of New Orleans University	M. E........	....	17
Do............	Normal Department of Straight University	Non-sect....	....	40
Holly Springs, Miss....	Mississippi State Colored Normal School..........	... do	3	168
Jackson, Miss	Jackson College........................	Baptist	8	220
Tongaloo, Miss	Normal Department of Tougaloo University	Cong	3	25
Jefferson City, Mo	Lincoln Institute *............................	Non-sect....	7	168
Ashborough, N. C......	Ashborough Normal School......................	Friends.....	2	75
Fayetteville, N. C.....	State Colored Normal School	Non-sect....	3	153
Goldsboro, N. C	......do	... do	3	89
Plymouth, N. C........	......do	...do	3	106
Raleigh, N. C	St. Augustine Normal School and Collegiate Institute.*	P. E	9	155
Salisbury, N. C........	State Colored Normal School *...................	Non-sect....	3	129
Aiken, S. C.............	Schofield Normal and Industrial School	....	8	302
Charleston, S. C.......	Avery Normal Institute........................	Cong	6	250
Greenwood, S. C	Brewer Normal School *.......................	...do	3	186
Knoxville, Tenn	Slater Training School	....	5	239
Memphis, Tenn	Le Moyne Normal Institute.....................	Cong	12	176
Morristown, Tenn	Morristown Normal Academy....................	M. E........	6	269
Nashville, Tenn.......	Normal Department of Central Tennessee College	... do	....	188
Do...............	Normal Department of Fisk University	Cong	6	48
Do.......	Normal Department of Roger Williams University	Bapt........	6	221
Austin, Tex...........	Tillotson Collegiate and Normal Institute........	Cong	13	234
Hempstead, Tex	Prairie View State Normal School................	Non-sect....	8	140
Hampton, Va	Hampton Normal and Agricultural Institute....	Cong	61	651
Petersburg, Va	Virginia Normal and Collegiate Institute	Non-sect....	13	326
Harper's Ferry, W. Va.	Storer College...............................	...do	9	194
Total		....	316	7,462
	INSTITUTIONS FOR SECONDARY INSTRUCTION.†			
Athens, Ala	Trinity School	Cong	5	186
Marion, Ala...........	Colored Academy...........................	...do.		....
Prattville, Ala	Prattville Male and Female Academy‡	Non-sect....	5	293
Talladega, Ala........	Talladega College	Cong	18	427
Sacramento, Cal	St. Joseph's Academy	Cath........	10	300
Jacksonville, Fla	Cookman Institute	M. E........	7	241
Key West, Fla........	Convent of Mary Immaculate *‡	Cath........	13	120
Live Oak, Fla..........	Florida Institute	Bapt........	5	92
Athens, Ga	Jewel Normal School	....	2	125
Do...............	Knox Institute	....	1	95
Do...............	Pierce Chapel	....	1	77
Atlanta, Ga...........	Atlanta Baptist Seminary	Bapt...	6	148
Do	Spelman Seminary	...do	30	551
Do	Storr's School *	Cong	9	589
Cave Spring, Ga	Mercer Female Seminary	Bapt........	1	25
McIntosh, Ga	Dorchester Academy *	Cong	4	248
Macon, Ga	Ballard Normal School	....	10	430
Do..	Lewis Normal Institute*......................	Cong	10	372
Mt. Zion, Ga	Mount Zion Seminary *	M. E........	4	124
Savannah, Ga	Beach Institute*............................	Cong	8	321
Tullehassee, Ind. T ...	Creek Freedman School	Bapt........	....	....
Lexington, Ky.........	Lexington Colored Normal School	Cong	7	300

* Statistics of 1887-'88.
†169 students not included here were attending schools designed for whites.
‡This institution is open to both races, and the figures given include some whites.

TABLE 13.—*Statistics of institutions for the instruction of the colored race, for 1888–'89*—Continued.

Location.	Name.	Religious denomination.	Instructors.	Students.
Louisville, Ky	State University	Bapt		307
Williamsburg, Ky	Williamsburg Colored Academy	Cong	8	299
Winsted, La	Gilbert Academy	M. E	12	229
Clinton, Miss	Mount Hermon Female Seminary	Nonsect	5	185
Meridian, Miss	Meridian Academy	M. E	3	82
Ashborough, N. C	Friends' Academy*	Friends	2	224
Concord, N. C	Scotia Seminary	Presb	14	100
Leicester, N. C	Brown Seminary*	M. E	2	127
Greensboro, N. C	Bennett Seminary *	do	5	300
Wilmington, N. C	Gregory Institute*		8	282
South New Lyme, Ohio	New Lyme Institute		8	427
Philadelphia, Pa	Institute for Colored Youth*	Friends	8	74
Oxford, Pa	Oxford Academy	Nonsect	6	651
Charleston, S. C	Wallingford Academy	Presb	7	236
Columbia, S. C	Benedict Institute	Bapt	14	240
Frogmore, S. C	Penn Industrial and Normal School	Nonsect	10	92
Grand View, Tenn	Colored Academy*	Cong	3	112
Jonesboro, Tenn	Warner Institute*	do	3	257
Knoxville, Tenn	Knoxville College	U. Presb	12	149
Mason, Tenn	West Tennessee Preparatory School	M. E	3	282
Morristown, Tenn	Morristown Seminary and Normal Institute	do	6	76
Pleasant Hill, Tenn	Colored Academy*	Cong	3	48
Hearne, Tex	Hearne Academy	Bapt	3	209
Marshall, Tex	Bishop College	do	8	230
Do	Wiley University	M. E	13	107
Waco, Tex	Paul Quin College	Af. Meth	4	223
Walnut, Tex	Central College*	Nonsect	5	220
Abbyville, Va	School of the Bluestone Mission*	U. Presb	3	453
Norfolk, Va	Norfolk Mission School	do	10	95
Richmond, Va	Moore Street Industrial School		4	100
Do	Hartshorne Memorial College	Bapt	7	
Total			354	11,480
	UNIVERSITIES AND COLLEGES. †			
Selma, Ala	Selma University	Bapt		187
Little Rock, Ark	Philander Smith College	M. E	7	356
Atlanta, Ga	Atlanta University	Nonsect	‡21	68
Do	Clark University	M. E	12	59
Washington, D. C	Howard University§	Nonsect	9	334
Berea, Ky	Berea College	do	18	170
New Orleans, La	Leland University	Bapt	10	240
Do	New Orleans University	M. E	9	360
Do	Southern University	Nonsect	9	432
Do	Straight University	do	17	201
Holly Springs, Miss	Rust University	M. E	8	
Jackson, Miss	Jackson College	Bapt		216
Rodney, Miss	Alcorn Agricultural and Mechanical College	Nonsect	7	138
Charlotte, N. C	Biddle University	Presb	7	
Raleigh, N. C	Shaw University	Bapt		180
Salisbury, N. C	Livingston College	Af. M. E	13	‡24
Wilberforce, Ohio	Wilberforce University	do	13	241
Columbia, S. C	Allen University	do	9	946
Orangeburg, S. C	Claflin University	Nonsect	20	244
Nashville, Tenn	Central Tennessee College	M. E	‡24	451
Do	Fisk University	Cong	17	63
Do	Roger Williams University	Bapt	8	
Total			238	5,010
	SCHOOLS OF THEOLOGY. ‖			
Talladega, Ala	Talladega College	Cong	1	16
Tuscaloosa, Ala	Institute for Training Colored Ministers	Presb	2	26
Washington, D. C	Theological Department of Howard University	Nonsect	6	38
Do	Wayland Seminary	Bapt	8	43
Atlanta, Ga	Atlanta Baptist Seminary	do	5	147
Do	Gammon Theological Seminary	M. E	4	70
New Orleans, La	Gilbert Haven School of Theology (New Orleans University)	do	3	9
Do	Theological Department of Leland University	Bapt	2	30
Do	Theological Department of Straight University	Nonsect	4	20
Baltimore, Md	Centenary Biblical Institute	M. E	15	195

* Statistics of 1887–'88.
† Not including professional departments.
‡ Number of instructors in all the departments.
§ 55 white students are enrolled in the different departments of Howard University.
‖ 40 colored students of theology not included here were attending schools designed for whites.

TABLE 13.—*Statistics of institutions for the instruction of the colored race, for 1888-'89*—Continued.

Location.	Name.	Religious denomination.	Instructors.	Students.
Charlotte, N. C.........	Theological Department of Biddle University	Presb......	3	13
Raleigh, N. C	Theological Department of St. Augustine's Normal School.	P. E	6	15
Do...............	Theological Department of Shaw University.....	Bapt........	2	40
Wilberforce, Ohio	Theological Department of Wilberforce University.	Af. M. E ...	2	8
Columbia, S. C	Benedict Institute.............................	Bapt........	7	236
Do...............	Theological Department of Allen University.....	Af. M. E	3	9
Orangeburg, S. C	Baker Theological Institute (Claflin University)..	....	....
Nashville, Tenn	Theological Department of Central Tennessee College.	M. E	2	4
Do...............	Theological Department of Fisk University......	Cong	1	9
Do...............	Theological Department of Roger Williams University.	Bapt........	1	....
Marshall, Tex	Bishop College	Bapt........	8	17
Richmond, Va	Richmond Theological Seminary	...do	4	63
	Total	....	89	1,008

SCHOOLS OF LAW.

Location.	Name.	Religious denomination.	Instructors.	Students.
Washington, D. C......	Law Department of Howard University	....	5	22
New Orleans, La.......	Law Department of Straight University	....	4	8
Columbia, S. C	Law Department of Allen University	....	1	5
Nashville, Tenn	Law Department of Central Tennessee College...	....	5	7
	Total	....	15	42

SCHOOLS OF MEDICINE, DENTISTRY, AND PHARMACY.*

Location.	Name.	Religious denomination.	Instructors.	Students.
Washington, D. C......	Howard University :			
	Medical Department	....	11	109
	Pharmaceutical Department.	....	1	16
	Dental Department........	....	3	11
Raleigh, N. C	Leonard Medical College (Shaw University) † ...	....	.....	39
Nashville, Tenn	Central Tennessee College:			
	Meharry Medical Department	....	9	55
	Dental Department.........................	....	6	11
	Total	....	30	241

SCHOOLS FOR THE DEAF AND DUMB AND THE BLIND. ‡

Location.	Name.	Religious denomination.	Instructors.	Students.
St. Augustine, Fla	Florida Institute for the Deaf and the Blind §.....	....	2	10
Danville, Ky...........	Kentucky Institution for the Education of Deaf Mutes (colored department).	....	‖14	36
Louisville, Ky	Kentucky Institution for the Education of the Blind (colored department).	....	‖11	19
Baltimore, Md	Maryland School for Colored Blind and Deaf Mutes. †	....	5	18
Jackson, Miss	Institution for the Education of the Deaf (colored department).	....	‖8	44
Raleigh, N. C	North Carolina Institution for the Deaf and Dumb and the Blind (colored department).	....	‖7	87
Cedar Springs, S. C ...	South Carolina Institution for the Education of the Deaf and Dumb and the Blind (colored department).	....	2	17
Nashville, Tenn	Tennessee School for the Blind (colored department).	....	‖8	12
Austin, Tex	Institution for the Deaf and Dumb and Blind Colored Youth.	....	3	44
	Total	....	60	287

* 30 colored students not included here were enrolled in schools designed for whites.
† Statistics of 1887-'88.
‡ There were 106 colored pupils not included here in institutions designed for whites.
§ Has 3 white pupils.
‖ For the white and colored departments.

TABLE 14.—*Summary of statistics of institutions for the instruction of the colored race for 1888-'89.*

States and Territories.	Public schools.		Normal schools.			Institutions for secondary instruction.		
	Colored school population.	Enrollment.	Schools.	Teachers.	Pupils.	Schools.	Teachers.	Pupils.
Alabama	226,925	105,106	6	71	1,445	4	28	906
Arkansas	106,300	56,382	2	12	261			
California						1	10	300
Delaware	‡7,070	†4,587						
Florida	‡52,865	34,008	1	3	54	3	25	453
Georgia	‡267,657	‡120,390	4	17	730	12	86	3,105
Kansas								
Kentucky	‡109,158	42,526				3	14	607
Louisiana	‡§176,097	‡51,539	2		57	1	12	299
Maryland	68,409	34,072						
Mississippi	‖273,528	172,338	3	14	413	2	8	414
Missouri	48,478	32,168	1	7	168			
North Carolina	‡216,837	†125,844	6	23	707	5	31	833
Ohio						1	8	282
Pennsylvania						2	14	501
South Carolina	¶180,475	104,503	3	17	738	3	31	1,127
Tennessee	162,834	†94,435	6	35	1,141	6	30	968
Texas	139,939	**96,809	2	21	374	5	33	817
Virginia	††265,347	119,172	2	74	977	4	24	868
West Virginia	10,497	6,209	1	9	194			
District of Columbia	‡18,200	13,004	2	13	203			
Indian Territory						1		
Total		1,213,092	41	316	7,462	53	354	11,480

States and Territories.	Universities and colleges.			Schools of theology.			Schools of law.		
	Schools.	Teachers.	Pupils.	Schools.	Teachers.	Pupils.	Schools.	Teachers.	Pupils.
Alabama	1			2	3	42			
Arkansas	1	7	187						
California									
Georgia	2	33	424	2	9	217			
Kentucky	1	18	334						
Louisiana	4	45	1,202	3	9	59	1	4	8
Maryland				1	15	195			
Mississippi	3	15	417						
North Carolina	3	20	318	3	11	68			
Ohio	1	13	124	1	2	8			
Pennsylvania									
South Carolina	2	29	1,187	3	10	245	1	1	5
Tennessee	3	49	758	3	4	13	1	5	7
Texas				1	8	17			
Virginia				1	4	63			
District of Columbia	1	9	59	2	14	81	1	5	22
Total	22	238	5,010	22	89	1,008	4	15	42

* In 1886.　　　　‡ In 1888.　　　　‖ In 1887.　　　　** Approximately.
† In 1887-'88.　　§ Estimated.　　¶ U. S. Census of 1880.　　†† In 1885.

8819———14

TABLE 14.—*Summary of statistics of institutions for the instruction of the colored race for* 1888–'89—Continued.

States and Territories.	Schools of medicine.			Schools for the deaf and dumb and the blind.		
	Schools.	Teachers.	Pupils.	Schools.	Teachers.	Pupils.
Florida				1	2	10
Georgia						
Kentucky				2	25	55
Maryland				1	5	44
Mississippi				1	8	18
North Carolina	1		39	1	7	87
South Carolina				1	2	17
Tennessee	1	15	66	1	8	12
Texas				1	3	44
District of Columbia	1	15	136			
Total	3	30	241	9	60	287

TABLE 15.—*Number of schools for the colored race and enrollment in them by institutions, without reference to States.*

Class of institutions.	Schools.	Enrollment.
Public schools		1,213,092
Normal schools	41	7,462
Institutions for secondary instruction	53	11,480
Universities and colleges	22	5,010
Schools of theology	22	1,008
Schools of law	4	42
Schools of medicine	3	241
Schools for the deaf and dumb and the blind	9	287
Total	154	1,238,622

TABLE No. 16.

We close this essay by a table copied from the New York Independent, compiled from several reports by Prof. James H. Blodgett, of the Census Bureau.

Statistics of public, private, and parochial schools in the United States.

States.	Teachers.	White pupils.	Colored pupils.	Private pupils.	Parochial pupils.
Alabama	6,291	186,794	116,155	22,953	1,150
Alaska	18	903	741	....	....
Arizona	233	7,828	....	462	418
Arkansas	5,016	163,603	59,468	11,070	1,118
California	5,434	221,756	....	17,720	7,123
Colorado	2,376	65,490	....	4,631	2,421
Connecticut	3,226	125,073	1,432	8,355	13,459
Delaware	701	26,778	4,656	1,126	1,712
District of Columbia	745	23,574	13,332	5,509	2,402
Florida	2,577	54,811	36,377	5,059	756
Georgia	7,503	209,330	133,232	48,187	287
Idaho	389	14,311	....	1,104	....
Illinois	23,296	773,265	5,054	28,164	75,958
Indiana	13,285	507,264	....	17,968	25,537
Iowa	26,567	492,620	647	15,633	20,335
Kansas	12,260	389,703	9,616	1,382	9,018
Kentucky	8,722	352,955	54,612	26,969	12,328
Louisiana	2,673	74,988	49,282	17,627	7,148
Maine	6,080	139,592	87	7,330	4,015
Maryland	3,826	148,224	36,027	11,153	8,943
Massachusetts	10,324	370,893	599	28,629	38,143
Michigan	15,990	425,691	1,341	16,216	34,779
Minnesota	8,947	281,678	181	7,575	29,332
Mississippi	7,386	157,188	193,431	20,072	1,311
Missouri	13,795	587,510	32,804	27,237	31,400
Montana	549	16,718	89	1,038	384
Nebraska	10,555	239,556	744	5,278	9,426
Nevada	251	7,387	....	78	325
New Hampshire	3,104	59,813	....	2,603	4,940
New Jersey	4,465	221,634	12,438	15,250	27,827
New Mexico	472	18,215	....	4,093	571
New York	31,703	1,035,542	6,618	56,787	103,093
North Carolina	6,865	208,844	117,017	25,651	1,320
North Dakota	1,894	30,821	....	578	1,608
Ohio	25,156	797,439	....	35,864	57,905
Oklahoma	14	537	....	....	....
Oregon	2,566	63,354	....	4,143	616
Pennsylvania	24,493	965,444	....	47,761	60,923
Rhode Island	1,378	54,170	....	3,814	5,940
South Carolina	4,321	90,051	113,410	13,623	634
South Dakota	4,356	66,150	....	2,042	1,537
Tennessee	8,376	354,130	101,602	41,827	2,391
Texas	11,097	312,802	98,107	22,310	4,573
Utah	680	36,372	....	10,258	536
Vermont	4,400	65,500	108	4,284	2,461
Virginia	7,523	220,210	122,059	12,831	2,005
Washington	1,610	55,432	....	3,328	954
West Virginia	5,491	186,735	6,558	3,498	1,189
Wisconsin	12,037	350,342	....	5,176	52,200
Wyoming	259	7,052	....	140	190
Total	361,273	11,236,072	1,327,822	686,106	673,601

APPENDIX.

The following essays have all been prepared as public addresses or magazine articles. Several of them have been widely circulated in pamphlet form, chiefly in the Northern States. I have always regarded the Northern side of my "Ministry of Education in the South" as of equal importance to its Southern department. For, even in educational circles, the knowledge of the actual condition of the Southern people in respect to the schooling of their 6,000,000 children and youth of school age is of just that confused description that the most absurd exaggerations, favorable or adverse, everywhere prevail. These essays are a selection from a large number of similar character, through which, in addition to a large amount of writing in the educational and popular press and constant public speaking, I have labored in the past twelve years to keep at least the Northern educational public informed of the real condition of affairs in the sixteen Southern States. They cover the entire period of my Southern ministry, and indicate my growing confidence in the thorough soundness of the Southern educational public and the increasing hope that the majority of the Southern people will consent to be guided by it in building for the children. As an introduction to the more mature and extended discussion of Southern educational affairs in the main essay of this "circular of information," the addresses and articles in this appendix may be useful.

A. D. MAYO.

I.

THE SOUTH AT SCHOOL.

An address delivered before the American Institute of Instruction, at St. Albans, Vt.,
July 6, 1881.

The word of the Lord (which in my copy of the "improved version" includes the command of our honored president of the American Institute of Instruction) came to me last week, resting under the maples of Wellesley, saying "Gird up the loins of your mind and go to St. Albans to stand in the place of one whom everybody is always eager to hear, and try to make the people forget that he is away." The foremost virtue of a good schoolman is a reasonable consent to be "supervised," and after ten years' training by Secretary Dickinson, who is said to have supervision on the brain, I have at least learned the art of swift and gracious obedience. So I am here not to stand in anybody's place or to make anybody's speech, save that which is given me to deliver on my own account.

It was suggested by our president that I should "tell my experience" concerning my journeyings during eight months of the past year through nine of the Southern States, on what I hope it is not vanity to call "A ministry of education." Certainly there is enough to tell about this, the most interesting and the happiest year of my life. But when I begin to collect my recollections, I realize that you have been instructed this afternoon by one of the most distinguished representatives of education in the South, Dr. J. L. M. Curry, one who knows all that is worth telling of its past schooling, and who must know more than all of us concerning its present condition, aspirations, aptitudes, and pathetic necessities. I certainly shall not presume to repeat his word and shall not attempt to speak in any positive or compendious way on the mighty theme—Education in the South.

And when I would tell the little story of my own wanderings up and down a land which, even under the leaden skies of last winter, had always sunshine enough to build a pathway of light for one of its visitors, I am more at a loss than ever what to say. For, on looking back over these months of pleasant occupation, I feel that much that I heard and saw, and was permitted to do, was of a nature so confidential, sacred, and involved in the personality of myself and those who met me with such friendly welcome, that to write it out in the press or shout it from a summer-convention platform would be like rushing to the housetop and proclaiming a year's history of my own family.

But there is one line of remark which I may be permitted to follow to-night without presumptious interference with the theme of our distinguished absent or present friends. Possibly I know as much of Northern school men, including school women, as either of these eminent gentlemen. And, though I know very little yet of the South in general, or the South at school, I am sure I know a great deal more than the multitude who are daily rushing to the front with loud and infallible prescriptions for all the ills that afflict that vast and various community. Governor Seward told me that the most profitable investment ever made by the State of New York was the geological survey that demonstrated there were no coal beds within its imperial boundaries. Henceforth no more fortunes would be wrecked prospecting for coal in

214

New York. It will richly pay several years of observation by more competent observers than myself if the Northern schoolmen and Northern people can learn what can not be done in this vast enterprise of schooling the South by anybody outside itself or virtually identified with its home life. But there are some things which we Northern teachers, representing especially the old North, can do. And these few things can be better told us perhaps by one of ourselves than by any man south of the Potomac or the Ohio. So I have concluded to occupy your attention during this evening hour by a very free, possibly a rambling, talk ; trying to keep in sight of the landmark I set up as my theme, "The South at School."

I am aware that the educational public, North and West, is now intensely preoccupied with local educational questions which, like a silver dollar held before the eye, may shut off the whole universe outside the world at home. But the experience of the past year has brought me to the conviction that however important may be such local controversies and interests, neither one of them nor all together compare in importance with this radical question of the new education through that imperial domain we call the South. I do not underrate the importance to New Boston of its chronic controversy on the proper administration of its splendid system of schools. I feel the great importance of the discussion, not yet closed, in the great Middle States, between private, corporate, and church education on the one hand, and the public school on the other ; a discussion that certainly touched bottom in the late deliverance of Mr. Richard Grant White. I wore out ten continuous years 47 in the vain effort to prevent the capture of the grand educational system of the most cultivated Western city by a politico-ecclesastical "ring," and I realize that for some years yet the Western and Pacific States will be vexed by the persistent attempt of these pernicious combinations to administer the public school in the interest of ecclesiastical power and political plunder. Still I am as sure of this as of anything, that if the education of the people goes wrong through that vast assemblage of States that stretches from Philadelphia to San Antonio, it will be comparatively of small importance who is superintendent in Boston, what university leads in New York, what methods of instruction prevail in St. Louis, or whether some monster of pedagogic depravity steals the examination papers in San Francisco.

The besetting weakness of American school men is the notion that the school of each master or the system of each locality or State is a little world in itself with which no stranger may intermeddle. But we are all finding out that American education, however various and in some ways antagonistic, is all embarked on one steamer bound for one port. I have a vivid recollection of a scene on board a European ocean palace, when a raging discussion in the cabin was suddenly suspended by a tremendous lurch of the good ship that brought every disputant's stomach, if not his "heart, into his mouth ;" and I noticed that the very exclusive Beacon street family that so far had hardly realized the existence of anything outside its own double stateroom gave unmistakable indications, through the partition walls, that it was stirred in profound sympathy with the sorrows of the colored cooks in the kitchen and the sooty salamanders that fed the fiery furnaces down below. American school life, underneath all its varieties, must be the training of American children and youth for that intelligent and righteous manhood and womanhood which is the absolute condition of good American citizenship. If Massachusetts or Louisiana is captured by any power hostile to this idea of education, the great school ship of the Republic will spring a leak and we shall all be summoned from our little berths and graded seats at the table to toil at the pumps to keep the ocean from coming in.

Of the American children and youth now in or out of school it must be said, as of humanity by the great apostle, "There is neither Jew nor Greek, there is neither male nor female, there is neither bond nor free: for ye are all one " in the glorious union and boundless hope of the new Republic now coming to pass, and, we trust in God, to endure long enough to be the normal school of self-government for all mankind. I can not discuss this radical position—that no phase of education is to-day half so important, so worthy of intense observation, as the spectacle of the South at school—so I shall confine my remarks to suggestions of what our teachers and our people can do for the encouragement and help of our brethren and sisters in those States in their present enterprise of putting their children in training for the momentous years which too soon are sure to come.

As I look at this matter it seems very evident that the first and essential duty of our Northern schoolmen is to cultivate the most friendly and intelligent sympathy with all educational workers and especially with the younger people and children of these Southern States. .There are certain cold facts concerning the status of education in these commonwealths which can be gathered from the new census, or even in more vital shape from the reports of the various public, private, missionary, and home ecclesiastical schools. Of course, in any general estimate and comparison with other parts of the country, the South must be judged by these facts. But I know from personal contact how small an element these tables of statistics, even added to the whole past of Southern history and supplemented by what anybody can see of the opinions and policy of a considerable portion of its people who represent the old past, really are in any fair estimate of this question. What the education of the South shall become depends less and less every year on what all these things stand for in the national life. My son, born on the first presidential election day of Abraham Lincoln, remembers nothing of the great war save a vision of soldiers marching in Cincinnati to repel the raid of Johnny Morgan from over the border. The most brilliant young university man of the Southwest was a boy under 15 in Virginia, while the Old Dominion was rocking to its base with the wrestling of mighty armies between Washington and Richmond. The teachers of the South, outside a few dozen colleges, are largely young men and women, under 35. The children, in these swift years, read of the great conflict as some of us heard of the old war of the revolution ; and, more and more, the management of Southern education is passing into the hands of a generation that, in all essential things, represents the new Republic. The man who has not visited the South and in a sympathetic and friendly spirit met that portion of its people most deeply interested in education, talked with its teachers, looked into the faces of its children, and seen for himself the absolute inability of its people to do much that is expected of it, can have but little valuable knowledge in this matter.

Gen. Lee said to his soldiers at Appomattox, "Let us go home and cultivate our virtues " He went home to become a schoolmaster. Every prominent school man of the North, for the next ten years, should visit the South to cultivate his sympathies with Southern teachers and children. If anybody can do this without prejudice, with charity and common justice, and come back with any feeling save the most profound and brotherly interest, asking the Lord " what wilt Thou have me to do ?" he is a man I am unable and do not care to understand.

In all great popular movements, like the present educational movement through the South, the most vital force is, after all, a mighty tidal wave of sympathy, overflowing all bounds, breaking in at every crevice, irresistible as the motions of the providence of Almighty God. Down in Kentucky one stormy day last winter, as I stood in the dripping station waiting for the train, a haggard, feeble old gentleman accosted me : "I hear you are down South visiting the schools. I was a rich man in Mississippi twenty years ago. The great war flung me up, a wreck, upon my relations in old Kentucky. I am almost through, but I thank God for this new boom in education and I want to shake hands with a man that has come from New England to help it along." I find it not easy to explain to comfortable ladies in luxurious parlors ; to sharp merchants after their per cents ; even to ministers of the gospel buried up to their eyes in little parish worriments, the things amid which I have lived for the past year. But I know if I could persuade a thousand teachers to do what I have done there would be a revival in their own souls that would make them behold "all things new." Nobody ever yet estimated the irresistible power of intelligent and educated sympathy in human affairs. The school public of the North includes the upper strata, God's aristocracy, among its people. If that public could really know the whole truth about the South at school as it can be seen by any friendly and wise observer who goes there in a spirit of love, the cause of education would be lifted up through all its borders; as one of its great Mississippi steamers would be speeded on its downward voyage on a full river swollen by the melting snows of Minnesota and the mountain slopes of the the far-off wilderness that holds the springs of the father and mother of mighty waters.

And if anybody asks me, "Are the teachers, the children, and the school public of the South prepared for such a visitation?" I answer, "Go and see." As for myself, I can say that I have met nowhere in any country a welcome more hearty, a confidence more affecting, an openness of mind and heart more hopeful, an appreciation, even of the most ordinary effort, made in a good spirit more cheering, than among these people; and I can, moreover, assure our friends that there is no field in the world now so valuable for the observation of thoughtful teachers and administrators of school work as the South to-day. Far more valuable to us than European school-keeping is the study of the great South, waking up through all her borders to send her children to school. A people so practical and intelligent as the school public of the North can not be greatly moved without incalculable results for good, and for that great revival my prayer goes up continually to Him who alone can move the soul of the people by the sweet influences of His holy spirit of wisdom, beauty, and love.

Regarded in this way, with a sympathetic and thoughtful spirit, these Southern States present the most encouraging field for educational enterprise now in the world. Our friends in the Southland have their own conceits of superiority; as the good people of New York, Ohio, and California, are in the habit of thinking well of themselves. One day, last summer, I was "mounted" in the cars, running down the lovely valley of the great Miami, Ohio, by a fine old fellow who had been brought there from Pennsylvania, seventy-five years ago, in an emigrant wagon, and had "grown up with the country." All this information he volunteered, in advance, and then turning upon me, said, "Where are you from?" "From Boston," I answered, I trust with becoming modesty. "Boston! Boston!" he replied, looking at me with open eyes; "Do you like to live way down there?" I have never found a place so new or so crude that its people didn't talk of some famous city as "Way down there." But be that as it may, the Northern schoolmaster or mistress, going southward, will do well to heed the advice of a jolly Texas Senator to a visitor from New England, "Now, don't go to Texas, as so many of you great scholars do, with the notion that it is inhabited by a pack of fools." Yet I am inclined to think that a habit of discouragement and a sort of hopeless way of looking at the possibility of success in school work is a greater obstacle, just now, "away down there," than any little habit of self-glorification which the Southern people share, not only with native Americans, but with resident foreigners as well. I have been called, a hundred times, in my wanderings, to encourage a despondent community where I have been moved once to smile at the conceit of pretentious ignorance.

A moment's reflection on both the white and colored divisions of the population of these 16 States will inspire the careful observer with a most reasonable and lively hope for the results of vigorous and well-directed school effort. I speak of the white and colored children and youth as separate divisions, with no political or social significance, but simply as a practical schoolman trying to apply the first principle of education; to take children as they are, and treat them, not as object lessons to illustrate a theory, but as human beings to be developed into good American citizens and sons and daughters of God. At present I am convinced it would be the great pedagogic mistake of the age to attempt to educate the masses of white and colored children in the South in the same schools.

The white children of the South are far more exclusively of English and Scotch descent than the people of the majority of the Northern States. The Huguenot and the Creole, even the Texas German, are but a slight exception to this rule. Indeed, the peculiarities of the different classes in Southern society are chiefly British traditions rather than native inventions. Here, as in Great Britain in the past, the education of the superior class was largely a training for executive and public life in young men and society life in young women. As in Great Britain, a numerous class there in the old days was permitted to grow up uneducated in schools into an obstinate and strong individuality, making one of the most stubborn and forceful sets of people that ever trod the earth. Apart from the class of degraded and stupid white youth that fringes the average Southern railroad station and figures at the cross-road whisky mill, the Southern white school children of all classes that I have seen (and I have faced a good many thousands of them) are just the boys and girls that would drive 48 Col. Parker wild to initiate in the open mystery of the "Quincy method;" perhaps even better material to be educated in the natural way than the little people that come to school bundled up to their lips in the wrappings of an elaborate metropolitan life, or hardened by the awful city demoralization that crushes out the offspring of so many of the descendants of our European immigrants. I have never seen brighter children, room after room, than in the public schoolhouses of several cities in Texas. I looked out upon 250 children in the school of Amy Bradley, in Wilmington, N. C., gathered from families that twenty years ago were accounted the most hopeless of "poor white trash," and I should be willing to leave Dr. Philbrick, Rickoff, or Harris to pass judgment on their brightness, beauty, and liveliness at their books.

We must remember that even the most neglected class of white people in the South, the inhabitants of that vast Appalachian mountain world, the central fortress of the old republic, as well as the lowland farming class of the central South, have received a training by the experiences of frontier life best of all calculated to develop independence and originality of manhood, and lay the foundation of a race that shall excel in whatever direction it may concentrate its force. The men who threaded these mountain trails; subdued the wilderness of the southwest; followed Andrew Jackson from Lexington, Ky., to Pensacola and around to New Orleans; wrenched away a vast empire from Mexico and established a new republic in Texas, and who, going forth, on either side in 1861, made the name American illustrious by almost superhuman valor and endurance, were the grandfathers and fathers of the white children who are now marshaled to tackle the "blue-back spelling book" and overthrow the despotism of ignorance and superstition through a realm as wide as Europe west of Russia, the future home of countless millions of freemen. I heard of one regiment from the hill country of South Carolina that began its campaign in the late war by opening a school during a winter encampment from which every man graduated in the spring well up in his "three Rs." The white children and youth of the South are in just the condition to be taught by the beautiful methods of the "new education," and we can help them to obtain that instruction which shall bring them forth the joy and pride of the Republic.

On the other hand, the 2,000,000 colored children and youth in the South present one of the most interesting fields of observation and experiment ever offered to the schoolmen of any land. The country is full of theories concerning what the Negro can not do and be. One of them will survive—that the Negro neither can nor ought to be an imitation white man. If ever a race of people had reason to be hopeful over its own achievements in its first two centuries out of the woods, surely the American Negro is that race. Only seventy-five years ago Northern slave-traders were landing African savages on the seacoast plantations of the South, and two hundred and fifty years ago the ancestors of our 7,000,000 of freedmen were roaming the jungles of "the Dark Continent." When I remember what I have seen in the admirable Southern missionary colleges and elementary schools established and taught by devoted Christian people from the North; what I have witnessed in churches, schools, and homes wholly under the influence of Southern discipline; what the most careful Southern observers who have always lived with them, like Dr. Haygood and Dr. Ruffner, say about them, I feel that if any class of people has earned the name American in so short time, under such disabilities, I do not know that class. I doubt if the history of the world records a more wonderful progress than that of the colored people of Georgia, who, fifteen years out of bondage, now possess one-twelfth of the live stock of that State and are taxed for $10,000,000 of property. At any rate I know what I have seen of the colored South at school. If their teachers will only begin at the beginning, be content, with the masses, to drive piles and form an educational mind for one generation; remember that every child of Anglo-American parentage inherits a thousand years of race discipline, while the Negro citizen is the world's last comer in the arena of civilization; throw wide open the "steep and rugged way" to the higher education, but insist that the colored youth who treads it shall be sure of every step and all the time lay deep foundations of moral discipline and marry brain and hand every moment of the journey, the country will have no cause to be ashamed of its colored school boys and girls in the days to come.

And it is now high time that the school men and women and the superior educational public of the South should come frankly to the front and join hands with the noble men and women of the North who have already established such munificent foundations in all these States for the education of superior colored youth. I do not now speak to bigots, devotees of fashion, or political fomenters of sectional strife, whether in the North or the South. I am not disposed to censure and want to forget all of unhappiness and misunderstanding that has separated honest, sincere Christian people in this work. I find the legislatures and the municipalities of nearly every Southern State now contributing to the support of these schools. I find the most intelligent and influential men and the most enlightened teachers in the South in substantial sympathy with this great work. I feel that most of the mistakes now being made in these institutions would be avoided could there be a larger mingling of Northern and Southern elements in the class room and in the administration of their affairs. The Northern managers of these schools need have no fear of complete honor and gratitude in due time from the white South. They can afford to go a good deal more than halfway and, by the might of sympathy, compel the superior Christian people of these States to come in and share with them in one of the noblest philanthropies of this age, illustrious for works of mercy among all the ages of the world.

One of the most encouraging omens of educational success that fell under my observation was the present attitude of a large body of Southern young women, especially in the central South and in Texas, revealing the most intense desire for a superior culture and the intention to take up the work of teaching, with a will, in city or country, in the white or Negro schools. We shall do well to make a large discount on the average Northern summer correspondents' account of young ladyhood at Southern watering places, or in the drawing-rooms of the ultra-fashionable class in cities. Even in old days of slavery the planter's wife always lifted the heavy end of the log, and occupied one of the most laborious and distracting positions ever cast upon the shoulders of American womanhood. That such an experience in a climate so trying, often quite broke down the health of the mother, and reacted, as overwork in the mother always does, upon the daughter, making her less able and willing to face the tremendous ordeal that American domestic life in the past generations has always been, is not surprising. But the class of female imbeciles and butterflies is only the fringe of any large group of American women, like the cloud of mosquitoes and flies around the edges of an Adirondack lake. The wise thing is not to linger on the beach fighting insects, but to paddle your canoe bravely out into the deep crystal waters, among floating gardens of blossoming lilies, a world of azure mountain sublimity crowding your horizon overhead. No class of women in Christendom has been tried by such overwhelming disaster, so tested and searched in every way in which God's providence can deal with woman, as our sisters of the South within the past twenty years. The schoolman is chiefly interested to know what has been the effect of the training upon the generation of young women and girls now under thirty years of age.

I had little time for the pleasures of polite society during my late tour among the Southern schools, and not being a society expert have no intention of writing up the drawing-rooms of New Orleans or New York; but I was constantly brought in contact with great numbers of schoolgirls and young women in public schools and private seminaries, as teachers and students of normal schools, and in the great normal institutes that are becoming a notable feature in Southern sunny life. I found the average schoolgirl responding reasonably to proper encouragement and good instructions, failing oftener from injudicious interference at home than from any other cause. With the superior schoolgirl I was always charmed by an enthusiastic and swift response to generous appeals and an undoubted sympathy with the highest ideals of American life. The superior young women of the South are not sitting in sackcloth and ashes, pondering or pouting over any dismal past. They are " up and coming," as thoroughly determined to gain front seats in American life as the maidens of "down East " or " out West;" they are crowding every open door of good education and are not going to be satisfied with the regulation of the fashionable boarding school, the superficial imitation of foreign training in the convent, or the pretentious instructions of sectarian "female colleges " for infants in short clothes. Every good public high school is thronged by them in much larger numbers than similar schools for boys. The few good normal schools contain a splendid body of enthusiastic girl students. As fast as their means will permit, they are filling up the few best seminaries for girls in the northern South and are doing excellent work. It is really affecting to see what sacrifices are cheerfully borne by great numbers of impoverished families to afford their daughters the opportunity for good schooling. The teachers of these higher female seminaries are making a record for devoted and unselfish work of which the world knows little. I found the instruction in white and, to a large extent, in colored schools falling more and more into the hands of these young women, often the daughters of families that twenty years ago were among the wealthy and influential people of these States.

Multitudes of as noble young women as live in any country are now cheerfully at work in Southern schoolrooms on the slender wages of the Southern teacher, often chafing under a sense of imperfect preparation, praying heaven that some good providence will swing open for them the " gates of pearl " to the higher cultivation, now the ideal of young American womanhood.

Off on a Texan prairie I fell upon a crowd of small boys who told me they went to school every forenoon at home to their oldest sister. In one of the largest cities of that State I found the two elder daughters of a judge of the Federal courts teaching their younger sisters. A United States senator-elect from Louisiana told me that in his last political campaign through the northwestern part of the State he was captured at every spare moment by a wide-awake young woman and compelled to examine her little class of uproarious youngsters in a home school.

For the next generation the South will have most admirable material for teachers in these multitudes of superior young women who must have a career. I believe, for the present, outside a limited class of college graduates, the young men of the South will be largely drawn away from instruction to build up the rising industries of the country or to seek their fortune in the great Northwest. This will bring the young womanhood of the South to the front in its education and vastly increase the power and influence of women in all regions of Southern life. The past twenty years in the South has been in itself the grandest possible university for the development of young American womanhood. While it has crushed many of those who entered too late to learn new lessons, it has summoned the younger generation as by a voice from heaven to " go up higher " and confront the mighty issues of the years that are to come. Whoever trusts and works for American girls down South in a spirit of sympathy and hopefulness may be assured of his great reward before this generation shall pass away.

Now here is a state of affairs providentially adapted for that working together of the educational public of North and South which, more than all statesmanship, will knit the hearts of our people in one. The immediate duty of the school public of the South has been seized by the quick instinct of the new secretary of the Peabody education fund, Dr. Curry, who tells us that the Southern people must be waked up, through all its borders, to realize, not only its educational needs, but its magnificent educational opportunity. Educational opportunity is not chiefly a lofty building, a pile of money, apparatus too elaborate for use, and vast libraries that no schoolboy has time or knowledge enough to read. The radical educational opportunity is a generation of bright children, pushed onward by the sharp goad of straitened circumstances from behind, beckoned onward and upward by a future so splendid that it makes the head swim even to think of its possibilities.

The white youth of the South must be told that the poverty of their parents is not their misfortune, but rather a good providence that summons every brave boy and girl to the full activity of the highest faculties and makes life an inspiring race for the noblest prize. The white people of the South must be told that they can educate their children with the means they have, if they will put themselves behind every dollar and bring their hearts, heads, and hands to the glorious work of giving their children the education which is the great American chance in life. The colored people must be told that no 7,000,000 of people in any land was ever, on the whole, so marvelously led by Providence as they for the past two hundred and fifty years. Indeed, all the good there ever was in slavery was for them. It was that severe school of regular work and drill in some of the primal virtues which every race must get at the start ; and American slavery was a charity school contrasted with the awful desolation and decimation of the centuries of war and grinding tyranny by which every European people has come up to its present status of civilized life. But no nation can long afford to keep school in a schoolhouse whose walls are barrels of powder and whose corner stone is a chunk of dynamite. Our African university exploded twenty years ago, leaving Young America of African descent unsinged, amid such a wreck as never yet came upon human university since the world began. If the Southern freedmen fail to recognize this wondrous providence of the past and the boundless opportunity before them and lie down, in stolid or trifling indifference to their future, they will deserve all that their most contemptuous critics say of them. But they will not so disappoint the world's expectation if their duty and their destiny be pointed out to them. Their own wisest leaders are telling them this already, and they will respond in reasonable time, if we furious Anglo-Saxons, a thousand years ahead, will only have the Christian patience to bear with the blundering steps of the last child of the centuries, standing on the threshold and facing the fierce electric light of American life.

Of course this stumping of the South must be done chiefly by Southern men. Every rising young lawyer, teacher, minister, merchant, every aspirant for civic honors, every man of culture, every woman of social influence should take the field and in every way appropriate to the locality wake up the people, as Horace Mann in Massachusetts and the great school statesmen of every Northern State have done in times past at home. And although the most brilliant and willful of Southern editors blurts out that "the South needs no missionaries," the Southern school public, wiser than its adviser, welcomes every man or woman who comes in the only way that any Christian man of sense cares to approach any community of American people.

This great work has now begun in earnest. Our Northern folk have no conception of the rapidly growing power of the educational movement in the South. It is polarizing political parties, shaking up religious sects, exciting the drawing-rooms, pulverizing " bosses, " civil, ecclesiastical, and social, and bringing mighty senators to their knees with the cry to the people, "What shall we do to be saved ?" And when we reflect on the power which a " solid South " has wielded in the past, that its old aristocracy twenty years ago was the most powerful body of people in Christendom, that its armies even without the help of the Negro and the loyal mountaineers held at bay for four years the tremendous power of our Government and enlisted the sympathy of the greatest empire on the globe, and how soon that people has risen above a complete overthrow of its old order of society, we may begin to estimate what the South will be when within the life of most of us here it will become practically "solid" for the new education and swing into its place in the grand onward movement for the republic that is to come.

But there is a work in this majestic enterprise which can be done by the school public and people of the North, which every consideration of patriotism, Christian brotherhood, and common justice loudly commands us to undertake. If we fail to do it, the South will not fail, at the end of weary years and prolonged bitterness of soul, to work out its salvation. But if we now come to the front and cheerfully and wisely do our part, the good time prayed for will come so soon that we shall be compelled to locate a national asylum for sectional politicians, reduced agitators, and the whole crowd of national buzzards who flourish on fields strewn with the corpses of the noblest and the loveliest of the land. Let me briefly sketch the outline of this field of operation as it lays outspread before me after a year's observation and travel between the Potomac and the Rio Grande.

First of all, the Northern school public and people can help the South to train its teachers for the work so swiftly crowding upon them. Nowhere is it so important that public and private schools should be taught at once by the best methods and organized according to the best models as there. A Southern country school, from two to four months long, fumbled over by an old schoolmaster "gone to seed," or fretted by a nervous school mistress who has not gone beyond the methods of the "blue-back spelling book," only breeds mischief with the children and despair in every parent endowed with common sense. Especially among the Negroes and the ignorant whites must the schoolmistress be able to stand her ground and insist on making her school a vital reality. A three months' school session, in which the children are thoroughly aroused and trained to gather knowledge for themselves, is a better education than a college term of ten months, where the soul of the student is overlaid by the stupidity of a professor whose teaching faculty was never born. A body of thorough teachers for the next generation means everything in Southern schoolkeeping. A good teacher can educate children under a tree, behind a stone wall, in the swamps of the Teche country with alligators "on the rampage" and moccasins for object lessons, can inspire the children, wake up the parents, "create a soul under the ribs" of the deadest county superintendent, and make the dreariest wilderness of ignorance blossom like the rose. The Peabody education fund has done wisely in concentrating itself on the training of teachers, but its gift is only a little rill flowing into a mighty hollow among the hills.

This work so far has been largely done for colored teachers by the great mission schools established by Northern funds and worked by Northern instructors. There are probably a hundred institutions of this kind, supported by religious denominations, or by private benevolence, where large numbers of superior colored youth are more or less qualified for instructing in the public schools. The best of these seminaries should, at once, be enlarged, munificently endowed, sifted in their teaching force, which should have a fair proportion of Southern-born teachers, placed more largely than now under the management of wise native trustees, while in each should be established a powerful professorship of the best methods of primary instruction. Thus enlarged, there is little doubt that, with reasonable safeguards against sectarian propagandism, they might claim State or national aid, as now, in several cases, they do receive. The South can not hope to establish colored normal schools to rival these and the union of North and South in their development would only be productive of the happiest result.

Indeed the arrangements for the normal training of Southern white teachers are at present far below the opportunities for the Negroes. There are not a half dozen genuine normal or training schools for white teachers in the whole South. The mass of these teachers are graduates of public, academical, or collegiate establishments, often taught by obsolete methods and not pretending to deal with didactics as a distinct science and art. No gift of money would now tell so quickly on Southern education as a contribution that would support in every State a dozen centers of normal instruction, or put into a score of high schools and academies an expert in the art of teaching. If the three million dollars for which Harvard College is said to be dying could be hurried up, and another three millions, within five years, planted in this way for the training of white teachers for our Southern common schools, every American university would vibrate with a new life, and American society would feel an electric thrill to its finger ends. To talk about the higher education, with the public school system in its cradle, is like an order for ship timber upon a country bare as the bald pate of a professor who never dreamed that the people must build the American university. It is the bright boys and girls that are waked up in the log schoolhouses and stung into insatiable longing for wisdom in the little cross-roads academies that will crowd the halls of the Vanderbilts, and lift up the drooping heads of the despairing colleges of the South. The first need of Southern schooling is that thousands of these splendid young people (no better anywhere) should be trained in the best methods of instruction. Then the public school system can be put on the ground and will fight its way to certain victory sooner than any of us believe it possible.

I speak of this home training of Southern youth for teachers because it is both impossible and impolitic, if possible, that Southern children in any large degree should be taught by teachers from the North. Our superior teachers can not afford to work under the disadvantages of a strange climate for the wages there paid. They do not understand the situation and can not handle the children in any such way as teachers reared in the locality. There is plenty of the very best material for teachers at home who need occupation and will be more deeply interested in the schools than strangers can be. Of course the North will be drawn upon for experts in this work of training teachers. Our Western cities welcome Southern girls of ability as instructors, and Harvard has just called a Southern professor to an important chair. Our friends in the South must keep open doors for such of our superior teachers as naturally drift their way. But no American State or community ought to rest till it raises its own teachers for its own public schools. O, if one-half the money that will be wasted in senseless luxury at Northern watering places during this summer could find its way to a thousand centers of education in the land now blazing with fierce sunshine, what a new and blessed life might be born out of this marriage of soul and gold for the uplifting of the nation and the glory of Almighty God.

It is true this development of Southern education under its own teachers may result in some changes there in the Northern regulation type of school. But I do not regard this an evil to be deplored. There is but one essential principle in American education; that a highway shall be opened from every man's doorstep to the summit of American life and every child shall be invited to walk therein and, if need be, assisted by the State, provided his education is a genuine walking in the common highway to wisdom and not a pretentious "cutting across lots" to earn the prize while shirking the toil. Any State that attempts to fence up any portion of its people so that it is practically impossible for its children to aspire to the best things, has violated the radical American idea of a school. But, this condition assured, I believe it only foolishness to insist that the Southern people shall imitate the schools of the North any farther than these schools are proved best for the locality. The beauty of our public school is that it accommodates itself so easily to the needs of a community. The fine adjustments of the city graded school are absurdly out of place in the red schoolhouse in the country. A teacher at Leadville, with a mixed multitude of all tribes and tongues on the benches, must cover more ground than the mistress of a crowd of children gathered from good families in an old Eastern town. What an absurdity is the long-drawn argument for "purely secular instruction" to a teacher of 50 Negro children on a Louisiana plantation; a moral cypress swamp of rank vegetation, gaudy flowers, poisonous snakes, and without perceptible bottom; demanding that nine lessons out of every ten should be a search for a moral and religious hardpan without which knowledge is a curse and mental sharpness the devil in paradise. It will be impossible, for years, for the South to develop the country district school after the type of the crowded farm country of Connecticut, or to work up that elaborate system of secondary education which from the first has been the special glory of Massachusetts; or to a dozen things which pedants in the school room declare absolutely necessary to "a thorough education."

Our Northern school public must understand that the Southern schools must be in many ways different from ours, if their children are to be as well educated as our own. I believe this independence of management will foster vigor and originality.

There has been no broader thinker on education in America than Thomas Jefferson. His ideas of an unsectarian religious university with an elective curriculum, supported partially or wholly by the State, have prevailed everywhere west of the Hudson and will finally conquer a place in the most stubborn New England State. His plan for a free school organization in Virginia, with some adaptations, is still the best for the South, and after a hundred years new Virginia is doing for the Negroes, at Hampton, what Jefferson advised at the close of the Revolution. We should encourage our friends in the South not in any superficial, sectional, or sectarian conceit of schoolkeeping, but in every wise effort to adapt the great settled principles of education to the actual necessities of their peculiar life. If we do that the time will come when the South may give to the North as many valuable methods as the West has already given to the East, and every State of the Union develop some beautiful variety in the national university—the public school.

The good work of building up the university life of the South and of reinstating the secondary preparatory schools for its colleges by Northern donations of money has already begun. Peabody, Vanderbilt, Corcoran, Hopkins, Brooks, and Seeney are all household names with the young men of the South, and it is greatly to be hoped that this good work of patriotism and philanthropy will gather strength with the growing years.

I have never believed in the policy of building up a few overshadowing university corporations in our country to the neglect of that class of respectable colleges that meets the wants of the great majority of our young men. There is one thing more important than profound scholarship in America, and that is a broad and lofty type of national manhood. Since the day when George Washington, at the age of 40, educated by the frontier life of provincial Virginia, drew his sword under the elms of old Harvard College as commander-in-chief of the armies of the thirteen revolting colonies, the most illustrious names in American statesmanship, literature, arms, and arts have not been the graduates of the few greater universities in sufficient proportion to warrant the lofty educational airs sometimes put on by their over-zealous friends. So far "the weight of the meeting" has been on the side of the smaller colleges and the open university of American life and "the scholar in politics," if that means the doctrinaire professor, is only thus far a lecture-room success. This does not imply that eminent scholarship is not an eminent good; only that it is an open question what style of training in this Republic turns out eminence of any sort so often as to justify the pretensions of any to educational infallibility. At any rate the South now needs the endowment of many good academical and collegiate schools which, at a reasonable rate of tuition, can give its young men a thorough start, far more than millions poured into one of its universities. Young men are greatly educated by noble men in college chairs rather than by narrow experts trying to maneuver a realm of science, like a little spitfire of a steam tug floating a great, sluggish raft from St. Paul down to the Gulf.

Especially do the superior young women of the South demand the most earnest interest in all who have money to give for the thorough academical and collegiate education of Southern youth. I think they are just now more eager for the higher education than their brothers, who are tempted by the brilliant prizes of secular life. The opportunities for them, with a very few exceptions, do not compare with those enjoyed by young men, and coeducation does not seem to be the fancy of the Southern people. It would be a national blessing if a hundred wealthy women or wives of rich men would each adopt some worthy school for girls in the South and endow it, with only the conditions that a genuine educational training of the higher academical sort should be furnished at the most moderate cost, with scholarships for meritorious girls with slender resources. And I am confident that in due time the wise millionaire will be found to plant at Atlanta, the gate city of the mighty Southwest, a Southern Wellesley, Smith, or Vassar, administered by a corporation that shall represent the whole country and both sexes; its lady president chosen from that group of admirable Southern women who are now toiling to lift up the scholarship of Southern girls, furnished with everything needful, without a flaw of sham education from its foundation stone to the weather cock on its tallest spire; so well endowed that for $200 a year a thousand students may throng its corridors and no good girl because of her poverty be left out in the cold. And along with this endowment of colleges the wealthy people of Southern birth now living in Northern cities might plant in many a city or county town a good library, with funds for lectures on topics of general culture, both of which are needed beyond measure in every State of the South.

It has been said that the railroad is the first university of a new country. I found the whole southwest in a fever of railroad building and its mountain slopes throbbing with a strange excitement of mining and manufacturing life. Every great planter or intelligent farmer I talked with was bewailing the low state of agriculture. Every wise observer of its new city life was asking for somethimg for the rising generation of white and colored youth to do. Industrial education is a necessity in the North, but it is the life blood of society through every State of the South. The railroad kings, the manufacturing princes, and the great merchants of the whole country should back the General and State Governments in munificent provisions for the thorough training of Southern blacks and whites in skilled labor around the whole circle of American industry. Without it the Negro will be shut out from mechanical employments and kept as a tenant or a farm hand, to his own injury and the incalculable harm of the South itself. Without it the poor white man will remain a poor fellow, while every post of lucrative labor will be seized by adventurous emigrants from foreign lands or more favored States. By the help of the National Government, which should be given at once in the most effective way, the Southern people can be left to establish the common school, first for the elementary and, in time, for the secondary training of all its children. But this most imperious necessity of endowments for industrial education should be met at once by that numerous class who are growing in wealth by their connection with Southern industrial life.

It may seem a little absurd for me, an humble minister of education, whose daily bread, for a year past, has been the kindly contribution that has enabled him to preach the gospel of light up and down the land, to be talking in this large way about money to a convention of teachers, most of whom have probably thought twice before facing the small expenses of this annual gathering of the American Institute of Instruction. But civilization has always been and always will be in the hands of poor men who make bold to "speak up" and demand the largest things of men who have everything to give.

The real privilege of wealth in this new land is not with people who waste their thousands in ridiculous aping of the expensive follies of European fashion or wallowing in a slough of base and vulgar luxury of the home-made sort. It is with that numerous body of wealthy men and women whose splendid gifts have made our land already a wonder of Christian public spirit and the leader in the charities of the world.

8819——15

As I come North, after a six months' working through the South, I am amazed at the show of vast wealth, the universal comfort, and the brimming prosperity of all classes of the Northern people. Our foreign-born mechanics and operatives, who are now training under démagogues in trades unions, are better off than several millions of respectable people of native birth between Washington and San Antonio. I deplore the awful waste of Northern substance in senseless pleasure and sinful excess of meats and drinks and dress, to the infinite harm of Northern children and youth. I have no words to express my abomination for that loud and boastful crew who are trading in politics, running a wicked race for power and plunder, and maneuvering "the machine" as if they wielded the destinies of mighty States. If our great statesmen have no occupation more honorable than throwing political fireballs and hand-grenades, showing up the foulness of each other's rival barbarisms and branding each other with sectional and partisan nicknames, in heaven's name let them come home and leave the Capitol for one session to the people who are praying and working for the children that even now are the expectant heirs of the world's great Republic. The glory of American statesmanship is to deal decisively with new issues as they arise, and "leave the dead to bury their dead" while following the Lord into the kingdom of heaven materialized in this new world.

As I rode, last April, over the flowery prairies of Texas, I saw all along the road the carcasses of horses and cattle and sheep, starved in the past awful winter. But I did not see even the most stupid cowboy down in the mud trying to blow the breath of life into the nostrils of these dead creatures that cumbered the ground. Even he knew well enough that the thing for him to do was to bridle the frisky colts, break in the stubborn little mules, and fold the tender lambs in his arms. These moldering skeletons, if let alone, would be fleshed by carrion birds, ground into compost, or trodden into the ground. Other springs would awaken them into new life and they would reappear, not in ghastly shapes of slaughtered hecatombs, but in a new and glorious birth of foliage and flowers, blue and scarlet and pink and tender green and cloth of gold, in the light and warmth of the kindling sunshine, shimmering out to the dim horizon line. O! friends of South and North, have we not already lived long enough amid the tombs, chanting "the doleful sound" of sectional hatred, bewailing the follies and sins of the past, perpetuating the wreck of fratricidal war? Now let us awake, for it is sun-up on the morning hills of the Republic; "work while the day lasts," and, when for us "cometh the night, in which no man can work," pass on and up to our better task beyond the shining shore, leaving behind a Young America trained for the glorious destiny that beckons from the heights to the generation now at school.

II.

THE SOUTH, THE NORTH, AND THE NATION KEEPING SCHOOL.

An address delivered before the National Education Assembly held at Ocean Grove, N. J., August 9-12, 1883.

I suppose myself invited to address this assembly of eminent school men and friends of education because of some unusual opportunities for observation of Southern affairs as related to the rising school life of this portion of our country during the past three years. Without enlarging on the details of this interesting experience, or even quoting authorities for my conclusions, I will confine myself to a plain statement of some opinions that have been forced upon me through the entire period of my investigations, and which have now assumed, in my mind, the form of established convictions.

I shall speak of what has been done in the sixteen States, which include our former slave territory, since 1860; endeavor to show how this marvelous work has been accomplished, in the only way it could have been, by the combined effort of the South, the North, and the Nation keeping school for the children; and from this estimate of these several educational forces, and the prodigious work that still remains to be done, I shall try to outline the true method of success in the future.

If I were required to present to a European audience the most forcible illustration of the working of republican institutions in our country, I should certainly select the history of the development of what we may call the New Education in our Southern States, from the breaking out of the civil war in 1861 to the present date.

I speak of the New Education in this connection. Up to 1860 the slave States had a system of education well adapted to perpetuate the dominant form of Southern society. It consisted of a reasonably thorough and extended system of collegiate, academical, and military schools for the sons of the superior class and such recruits from the lower orders of the white people as gave promise of unusual ability, with a large development of the ordinary female seminary of a generation ago for the corresponding class of girls. A considerable number of the sons and daughters of wealthy people were also expensively educated by private tuition at home, attendance on northern schools, or at institutions abroad. There was also a good deal of the sort of family and church instruction in political, religious, and social ideas that is always going on in a concentrated and aristocratic order of society. The result, as we all know, was the training of perhaps the most intelligent and forcible aristocratic class in Christendom, which displayed an energy in revolutionary politics and on the battle-field, which, for four years, held the fate of the Union in suspense, and arrested the attention of the civilized world.

But, of course, in this scheme of education, all but 2,000,000 or 3,000,000 of the 12,000,000 of the Southern people were left with no systematic or persistent attempt at schooling.

The 4,000,000 of slaves were almost completely shut out from every sort of school; although American slavery itself was perhaps the most effective university through which any race of savages was ever introduced to civilization. In that severe training school the African Negro learned to work, acquired the language of a civilized people, and took on at least some apprehension of the only religion that ever proposed to break every yoke and proclaim all men the children of God.

227

The several millions of nonslaveholding white people were not left entirely destitute. Many of the better sort were partially educated with their superiors. Almost every Southern State had a periodical experience of waking up to the importance of a system of common schooling for all white children. And especially in Virginia, the Carolinas, Kentucky, Alabama, and Louisiana, this was attempted, though, outside a few cities, always with imperfect success. But the Southern nonslaveholding white people, outside the rim of " poor white trash," corresponding to our Northern tramp, had the schooling which comes from discipline implied by the settlement of a new country and the enjoyment of citizenship in a republican State. It was a training that brought the Southern masses up to the point of that astonishing military efficiency which, along a line of battle of a thousand miles, held this mighty Union at arm's length through four terrible years.

I linger over this picture of the old Southern education because ignorance of it has created many false notions of the educational problem among our Northern people. In 1861 the South was not that abode of mental imbecility and dismal ignorance which many an enthusiastic teacher going down there has imagined. On the contrary, it was a country where, perhaps, one-fourth the white people were thoroughly trained for leadership in the aristocratic form of society, and where the Negro and the poor white man had received a discipline in the university of American life which was the best possible preparation for the new era of education, through schools, teachers, and books, upon which the South entered the very year of the outbreak of the civil war.

History will record that never before was such a spectacle witnessed as the sudd n waking up of Christian and patriotic zeal for the education of a people in a state of revolt against national power. It is true that the missionary of religion has often followed an army of subjugation to change the faith of nations of savages and barbarians. But, in our case, the Northern people displayed at once their immovable faith in the Union for which they were fighting, and their confidence and radical respect for their Southern brethren in revolt, by taking the schoolhouse as the most prominent article in the baggage train, and leaving the teacher to build up the waste places in the track of desolating war. The most thoughtful of our Northern people, from the first, believed that a good system of popular education of the Southern masses would have prevented the war and opened a way for the peaceful abolition of slavery. But, since that was not permitted, they believed that the only security for the restored Union would be that general enlightenment of both races which would bring the vast majority of the Southern people to a condition of intelligent citizenship. And, having no doubt of the success of the war, the same class " took time by the forelock," and within a year from the firing on Sumter had established the school for the "Contraband" along the Atlantic coast, from Washington to Beaufort, down the Mississippi, through the inland southwest, and at the city of New Orleans. In short, the schoolmaster and mistress followed the army during the progress of the war; instructing thousands of the Negroes of every age ; expending large sums contributed by the benevolence of the Christian people of the North; everywhere supported by the military power and, to a considerable extent, aided indirectly by the Government.

In 1862 the National Government voted a munificent donation of public lands for the establishment of agricultural and mechanical education in all the States. Anticipating the immense value of this donation to the South, the lands of these revolting States were religiously held in reserve against the time when they should be claimed in a restored Union. It is impossible to estimate the present and prospective value of this gift to the Southern people at their present crisis of agricultural, manufacturing, and mining industry.

In 1865 Congress took up this educational work, which had already outgrown the resources of private benevolence, and, through annual appropriations continued for six years, the gift of national property, and the diversion of confiscated lands, under the direction of the Freedmen's Bureau, gave an impetus to the work of Southern education, especially among the freedmen, which it has never lost. In the ten years, from 1860 to 1870, it is probable that not less than $20,000,000 were thus expended by the North and the Nation for education in the South.

Meanwhile, the Peabody Educational Fund of $2,000,000 had been devoted to the building up of the public school through the entire South. And this magnificent benefaction has been followed by many large contributions, like those of the Vanderbilt family, Mr. Corcoran, Seney, and Slater, Mrs. Stone, and Mrs. Hemenway, with great numbers of others, which have poured a constant stream of helpful aid southward for the past fifteen years. Neither should it be forgotten that the great majority of Northern teachers who have wrought in this field have virtually made their work a "labor of love;" the compensation, even of presidents of colleges, being less than the wages of Northern mercantile bookkeepers, and of the majority of subordinate teachers not above that of reliable servants in Northern cities.

For the last ten years, outside a few prominent institutions for the education of the white people, the great effort of the North has been made, through the mission organizations of the several churches, toward the establishment of all grades of schools for the freedmen. When the history of the educational work in the South by the Christian people of the North is fairly written, it will be, in itself, the most conclusive answer to the whole impeachment of our modern Christianity by its enemies of every grade. The history of the world can not produce a more affecting spectacle than the growth of this mighty Christian philanthropy, which, beginning amid the din of battle, has steadily marched on, through all sorts of misunderstanding, neglect, opposition, and disparagement, with amazing patience, forbearance, and wisdom, to its present state. To-day there are probably not less than a hundred important schools, twenty of them bearing the title of college, with ample buildings and excellent facilities for religious, mental, and industrial education, established for the Southern colored people, chiefly taught by Northern men and women, a body of instructors not inferior to any similar class in the country in general capacity for such a difficult work. In these schools not less than 15,000 of the superior young colored people are being prepared, not only as teachers and professional characters, but, what is more significant, trained for leadership of the 7,000,000 of American colored citizens. The whole problem of negro citizenship is involved in the formation of a genuine leading class—an aristocracy of character, skilled industry, and intelligence that shall, at once, give direction to the millions of these people, and become their true representative in all dealings with the white people of the Republic.

And it is not too much to say that the colored people, the South, and the Nation will be indebted to the Christian schooling in these institutions for the beginning of this prodigious undertaking. Perhaps the most gratifying feature in this work is the fact that, at the end of fifteen years, it has conquered all vital opposition among the leading classes of the South. Half a dozen States now make annual appropriations to these collegiate schools. Southern gentlemen are included in their boards of management. The State of South Carolina, first in secession, has been the first to include a colored college in the organization of its State University. Many of these schools of lower grade are now being included in the new system of public schools. The graduates of the higher seminaries are in constant demand as teachers. In short, it seems as if within a generation all these great seminaries will become virtually Southern universities, largely controlled by the Southern people of both races, endowed by Northern munificence, the most splendid offering in behalf of "peace on earth and good will to men" ever made under similar circumstances by the Christian church, in any age and land.

Thus, within the past twenty years, the people of the North, in connection with the Government of the United States, have shown their confidence, respect, and affection for the Southern people by a mighty work of educational beneficence, conducted on lines of operation where it was hardly possible that the South could help itself, involving an outlay probably, all things considered, of not less than $50,000,000. And the point we wish to press is, that this has been done in the characteristic American republican way. The Nation has not gone into these States to establish schools, antagonizing their people, and paralyzing home effort, but has simply given twenty-five millions of property to aid in a good work, and established in the Bureau of Education one of the most potent agencies for inspiration, encouragement, and in-struction possible under our form of government. The Northern churches and people have not gone down South to build fortresses of propagandism. They have wisely adjusted their educational work to the condition of the freedman, trained him to pay money and labor for good schooling, and sent him forth a superior person for all the uses and duties of Southern citizenship. And, although I have no right to speak for any church engaged in this great work, I believe, after careful observation, that nothing would be more satisfactory to the Northern Christian people than to see this splendid cluster of schools, with their investment of perhaps $20,000,000, past and present, lapse gradually into the hands of the Southern people as a permanent gift to their new educational life.

But we shall greatly mistake if we suppose the most important work in Southern education, during the first fifteen years, has been this friendly demonstration from the North and the Nation. No people can be educated permanently by another people. As far as concerns its educational life, every State of this Union is practi-cally a separate people. Although much can be done, at certain critical periods, as in our new States of the West, by material aid and the inspiration of superior teach-ers and advanced methods introduced from abroad, yet each of those great States to-day has built up its own system of education, in some respects better than corre-sponding systems in older commonwealths. So must it be with the South in the building up of the vast enterprise of the New Education. If these sixteen States, or those of them which were involved in the experiment of the Confederacy, had laid dormant through these fifteen years just outlined, or if they had wrought in an obstinate spirit of opposition to education, the prospect now would indeed be hope-less. For there is not power enough under our system of government, in the Nation, the Church, or the people of the North to force the American type of edu-cation even into Delaware against its will, to say nothing of the gigantic folly of attempting to school a region larger than Europe, with eighteen millions of people, at arm's length, across a hostile border-land, in the face of political, social, and ecclesiastical disagreement, intensified by a race problem more complex than was ever presented to any civilized land. Thus we can only understand the real sig-nificance, and predict the outcome of what has already been done by the North and the nation in Southern education when we understand what has been going on through these sixteen States during the time already described.

How should we expect the home educational movement to begin in a country so prostrated, demoralized, and socially turned upside down as the South in 1865 ? And here I record my opinion that the Northern people have never realized and can not understand the widespread ruin of every vital interest that fell upon the revolting States in 1865.

The Confederate resistance to the overwhelming power of the Union was like the heroic, almost preternatural, attempt of the inhabitants of a new Michigan village to fight off an all-consuming fire that is steadily advancing its awful circuit, only to close in with more fatal destruction at the end. No people in modern history had been left so thoroughly prostrate as every class in these revolting States at the close of the war. And in such wholesale overturn the school always goes first. In 1865 there were probably not a hundred of the old academies and colleges in these States in actual session. Many of their buildings were destroyed and all dilapidated ; their endowments had vanished ; their teachers were dead or scattered, and their patrons were at work driving the wolf from the home door, with no ability to send their growing children to any school, or to establish any thing to take the place of their former system. The effort of the provisional governments to place the Northern scheme of free elementary education on the ground, continued in some States for ten years, deserved far more respect than it received and more success than it attained. The radical weakness of this movement was the attempt to establish an expensive system of popular education among a people who had never tried it, had not come to believe in it, were not able to pay for it, and, naturally, looked upon it as a hostile movement of the victorious party in the civil war. Yet the South to-day will agree with us that even this experiment had its uses, and left on the ground a large number of schoolhouses and a growing desire for popular education among the masses of both races which has been a powerful stimulant to the home effort of the past ten years.

But only an educational enthusiast will believe that a permanent educational movement can be inaugurated until the educated and responsible class is convinced of its importance, and prepared to take it up in a practical way.

And, just here the leading class of the Southern States displayed that wonderful common sense and "gumption" which is the rarest outcome of our republican order of human affairs. It is possible that a French populace of a century ago might have been fired up with a prodigious enthusiasm to undertake the schooling of the ignorant masses while the whole upper story of educational life was a hopeless wreck. Fortunately for our country, the superior class of Southern people began their new educational work in the plain common-sense way of first rebuilding the school by which their own children could alone be saved from a lapse into the barbarism of ignorance. The most pitiful spectacle on earth is the reverting of an educated people to ignorance; and that was the most imminent peril that faced the Southern school man in 1865. The 3,000,000 or 4,000,000 of superior and variously educated white people of the South in that year found themselves in hopeless poverty, scattered over an area as large as Europe, outside Russia; the vast majority sparsely distributed through an open country; their homes swarming with children and youth, and no established system of schools to give them that mental training which would be their only outfit in the struggle for success.

In this emergency it would have been unnatural if the people had proceeded in any other way than they did: to get on the ground, at least, a temporary arrangement for the education of their own children and those of their white neighbors more destitute than themselves. To this work they bent themselves with a singleness of purpose and a pertinacity thoroughly American and deserving of all praise. Whatever they may have thought of the great effort of the North and the Nation in behalf of the Negro, they knew that it would be a questionable gain to give the crude elements of knowledge to the children of the freedmen if the offspring of the only educated class in the country was permitted to lapse into barbarism. I have studied carefully the progress of this prodigious effort of the upper strata of the Southern people within the past fifteen years, to reëstablish the upper side of education. We must remember that, in States where the vast majority of respectable people live in the open country, the establishment of even the secondary public school must be the work of years, and the first generation will be fortunate if it gets an effective elementary education fairly on the ground. For fifty years yet the academy in the county town and the college, as we now find it, will be the chief opportunity of all classes of white people for anything beyond the mere elements of schooling, through at least a dozen of these great States. So, for the past fifteen years, these people have toiled, as nobody can know but themselves, through sacrifices almost incomprehensible to our wealthy Northern communities, to rehabilitate their little colleges and academies, and to furnish the small amount necessary to give their children such education as they might in these schools. I undertake to say that this effort alone entitles the South to the profound interest, even admiration of all thoughtful school men eveywhere. The effort has been a most gratifying success. Leaving out the **great drift** of worthless and indifferent private schools that have sprung up with a mushroom growth, thirty-five of them, as I found, in one little city of 5,000 or 6,000 white people, the academies and colleges that have been actually organized, newly founded, or put in working order, are now, perhaps, sufficiently numerous, if well endowed, to meet the present wants of the people.   But to do this it has been necessary that the most eminent teachers should be overwhelmed with work and live on starvation wages; that great numbers of women of the highest social position, and the daughters of the leading families, should give their lives to the work of instruction; that families strangely impoverished should contrive to pinch themselves for the schooling of their young people; and that great numbers should still be dependent on the benevolence of neighbors and school corporations for what they obtained.   It is impossible, of course, to say how much this great rehabilitation has cost the Southern people in money.   Outside an occasional gift from the North, and two or three munificent endowments—like Vanderbilt, Tileston, and Emery—this money has been a home contribution, by a people just struggling up to comfortable living, in behalf of the secondary and higher education, always under Christian influences, and everywhere reasonably progressive.   To understand what this effort means, even to-day, is to suppose a State like Connecticut suddenly reduced to poverty; school funds and endowments swept away; with the ability, at best, to keep afloat a three or four months' district school for the masses; with an occasional graded school in the cities; and the upper third of its youth gathered in schools where the widows of its governors and judges and the daughters of its proudest old families are teaching, in overcrowded classes, at wages ranging from $300 to $500 a year, with an occasional prize of a $1,000 salary at the top; and the vast majority of its enterprising boys compelled to leave school at 14 to "keep the pot boiling" at home.   I know well enough the characteristic defects of this, the upper side of the new education in the South, and appreciate the great advance that has been possible in Baltimore, Washington, and St. Louis, and now in New Orleans, through the gift of several millions of dollars by Southern men like Hopkins, Pratt, Tulane, Corcoran, and the noble group of men who have founded the Washington University of St. Louis.   But until I see how a Northern State would do better things for the children under similar circumstances, I must be pardoned for my unaffected admiration of this prodigious undertaking of the leading Southern people since the close of the great war.

But the Southern people have not paused with this attempt at the reconstruction of the secondary and higher education for the white race.   Beyond this, of their own notion, in every State, within the past ten years, the people's elementary common school for white and colored children has been placed on the ground, defended through the dangers of its infancy, made better every year, until it has become a vital institution of Southern civilization.   And when we consider that even England waited until within twenty years before she seriously undertook to be responsible for the education of the masses; and that all Europe, outside Germany and Switzerland, has been even more tardy in this respect; that the free public schooling even of white children was practically unknown in the South, on any large scale, previous to 1860, while all instruction was forbidden to the Negro; that the whole education and entire political, religious, and social training of the leading classes was opposed to the common school; that, in most instances, all public-school funds were sunk in the war, and all the money, save a few hundred thousand dollars yearly from the Peabody and other funds, must be taken from communities where there is everything to be done and so little to do with; that in several States more than half the amount is given to the freedmen, while little comes back from their taxation; also the almost insurmountable difficulties of climate, and the condition of the open Southern country during half the year; this effort assumes a magnitude worthy of all respect.   In every Southern State the establishment of the public school has been fought through in the face of every enemy that threatens its existence at the North.   Widespread poverty has been the standing argument against taxation.   Sectarian narrowness and clerical zeal, Catholic and Protestant, have raised the cry, "Godless," "secular," "immoral," "communistic." Social exclusiveness has turned the cold shoulder and, as Gen. Grant said to me at the White House, " there is too much reading and writing already to suit a good many statesmen in the Capitol." In certain districts, and perhaps in the State of Louisiana, to-day, this bitter conflict between the people and their adversaries still goes on. Yet it can be said that in every one of these sixteen States the battle for the people's common school, in its whole range of development, from the country district to the State university, has been won. Every Southern State, this year, is doing a little better for its children than last year. Say every thing that can truly be said in disparagement of the new public schools of the South ; their establishment and support, to this date, is the most notable educational fact in Christendom within the past ten years. We must understand just how far this is a home work to appreciate its magnitude. The $100,000 or $200,000 of annual appropriation, and the labors of the agents of the Peabody fund, have been a great help. The training of colored teachers in the mission colleges, supported by the North, has been even a greater assistance, although partially kept up by the tuition paid by the colored people themselves. The influence of the Bureau of Education and its apostolic secretary, John Eaton, has been good and only good through all these years. The support of a superior system of public schools in Washington, partly at the expense of the General Government, has furnished an excellent model for the whole South. But all these influences, together with the friendly encouragement of Northern teachers, have been but a small element in this vast undertaking of the organization of the Southern common school, which is even more truly the work of the Southern people, unaided from abroad, than the establishment of the Western public school has been the work of the people of the West.

For three years past my own time has been engrossed by travels, studies, and labors, largely bearing on the present condition of the public school in the Southern States. I have done a great deal of work in twelve of these States, and think I understand pretty well what is going on in all of them. Their schools range from two to three months, in Louisiana, to five months, in the country in Virginia, and in many localities the school goes on for a longer time by private contribution. In all the larger cities, and in many smaller towns, the graded school is established for both races, and, in many cases, handled with great ability, by the best methods, for eight or nine months of the year. In every State the county institute for the training of teachers, in several the summer normal institute of several weeks' duration, and in some the proper State normal school for white and colored pupils, are established. Outside a certain class of fossil and antiquated pedagogues, and the usual drift of incompetent youth working for pay, these schools are taught by the choice young people of both races. A better class of people, more earnest, more determined to improve, more self-denying, working on wages painfully and sometimes pitifully inadequate, can not be found in any Christian land than the majority of the public-school teachers of the South. The State superintendents of education, and many of the city and county supervisors, are the same sort of people as our leading educators in the North. With occasional exceptions, I believe school funds are honestly and economically applied, and, in all but two States, divided with reasonable fairness among all the children. It is not possible to give the average colored child as good a school as the white child, because he can not take it ; but the colored public schools are everywhere improving, and are hindered as much by the ignorance and jealousies of their own people as by any other cause. The charge that the Southern public schools, except in very occasional individual instances, are schools of disloyalty, I know to be untrue. The attempt to publish series of sectional or even Southern schoolbooks has broken down, and the Northern educational "drummer" is on the heels of every school trustee and superior teacher from Delaware to Texas. Our Northern summer schools are crowded with these teachers, and thousands more would come if they had the money.

In short, the Southern common school is the American common school in all re-

spects, save its bitter need of more money, longer sessions, and more thoroughly-
trained teachers. It has already saved thousands of the children of respectable white
people from ignorance and, for the first time, brought the lighted candle of knowledge to other thousands of homes where mental darkness brooded before. Its graduates are not the lazy and shiftless, but the superior, skilled working class in all their
communities. And if any man, however eminent, honest, or Christian, declares that
these schools are godless, immoral, or even unmoral, I must be pardoned for telling
him that he does not know what he is talking about. If anybody can look at the
colored children and youth of Washington, graduates of the public schools, and contrast them with the awful crowd of untaught negro humanity that swarmed the
streets of any Southern city before the schoolmistress came in; or will compare the
white school children of Atlanta, Richmond, and Savannah with communities where
ignorance still prevails; and will then deliberately prefer this charge, I can only say
his make-up is so different from my own that there is no common basis for an argument in the premises. And I would remind my objector, on this ground, of the fact
that there is one plot of "holy ground" in every Southern community, where the
whisky bottle, the smutch of tobacco, the pistol and knife, profane and obscene speech
can not enter, by common consent; and that spot is the schoolhouse and lot, public
even more than private and collegiate, established by the Southern people within the
last fifteen years. Beside this, the whole subject of the superior and industrial education of the colored people is being debated in every Southern community. The State
and the church are both beginning to move on lines of advance. And in all Southern
cities there is a hopeful movement for the æsthetic and the higher industrial training
prophetic of valuable results in the near future.

Thus, while the North and the Nation have been at work, chiefly on the lower side
of this vast educational Southern problem, during the past twenty years, spending
perhaps $50,000,000, a large part of it for the elementary training of the colored peo-
ple, and testifying their confidence, respect, and faith that the South will appreciate
their work; this confidence, respect, and faith have not been misplaced. The Southern people have responded to this magnificent demonstration, not by flinging up the
hat in applause so much as by taking off the coat and working at the other end of the
problem as no other people ever wrought before. The result is that, during these
memorable years, the Southern people have not only restored their secondary and
higher education to a condition, in some respects, better than before 1860, but have
also established in every State the American system of public instruction, and committed themselves to its support, according to their ability, in every grade. It is impossible to estimate the money investment in this enterprise during all these years.
Last year the South paid not less than $15,000,000 for education, and this year the
sum will be increased. At least as much money and far more labor has been given
by the South, out of its poverty, than by the North and the Nation, out of their
abundance, for Southern education since the war. More than $50,000,000, meaning
to that people many hundred millions, judged by Northern standards, have thus been
laid upon the altar of the children's hope.

And now the traveler through the Southland finds himself everywhere in the presence of an educational revival as marked as in New England in the days of Horace
Mann. And the blessedness of this revival is that it is bringing together the children
and youth, their teachers, the younger parents, and the more thoughtful people of
North and South, as no movement in the political, the ecclesiastical, or even the industrial sphere of national life can possibly succeed in doing. It is easy enough for
stalwarts, sectarians, sectionalists, and soreheads of all descriptions to find food for
denunciation and gloomy foreboding in Southern society; and our Northern municipal life, to say nothing of certain ugly tendencies in other regions of society, will still
provoke the return fire of the diminishing Southern "old guard" that holds the fort
against the North and the Nation. But the time has come when, in behalf of the
children, all Christian men and women should call a halt in such recriminations, and

hold counsel together in the interest of that education of the head, the heart, and the hand which can alone make us one. For twenty momentous years the American people, in sixteen Southern States, have been laying the foundations and raising the opposite walls of the massive temple of the new education. While the North and the Nation have been toiling, on the one side, "all orders and conditions" of Southern men and women have worked, according to their light, each on his own angle, but all on some section of the mighty building where the children shall be gathered in. That these workmen have sometimes mistaken the beat of rival hammers and the clink of rival chisels around the corner for a new tramp of hostile forces, is not surprising. But one thing will be not only surprising but disgraceful and disheartening beyond compare; if, when these rival workmen have really built up the walls and met each other around the dome that crowns their common work, they should fall out, fling their tools at each other, and fight over the miserable wrangle of precedence to the bitter end while they should be clasping each other's hands, and running up the old flag with prayers and songs of dedication and ringing shouts of joy as of a people whose most devious ways have been along providential paths, all ascending to the summit of the Nation's hope and a new triumph for the human race

But all that has been done, on the whole so well done, is only the overture to the mighty work of educating the whole people, to which the South is now waking up Our Southern friends are fortunately gifted with a boundless faculty of hopefulness in all matters pertaining to their own future. It will be fortunate if a laudable satisfaction at their present achievements does not blind them to the fact that, after all, this prodigious coöperative effort of the past twenty years has barely placed on the ground the machinery for educating the coming generation, while the work to be done is so vast as to be almost appalling. Massachusetts began to educate her people two hundred and fifty years ago, and has stuck to it more persistently than any civilized people. Yet, to-day, there are nearly a hundred thousand people in Massachusetts unable to read and write. Only a practiced schoolman can estimate the terrible obstinacy of chronic ignorance; how it fights and runs away, and skulks and shirks to escape detection, and, when "brought to the book," goes through another dodge of masquerading through all the phases of sham knowledge; and how short a time is required for a generation to lose its grip and begin to revert to its old estate. The South will do well to turn a deaf ear to all educational flatterers and optimists for the next half century, and pay good heed to what its own wisest men and women are all the time telling it; that the enormous work of instructing its whole people, even in elementary knowledge and mental discipline, is only begun, and that it needs a redoubled effort at home, with all legitimate help from the North and the Nation for a generation to come, to do the work that patriotism, Christianity, and a wise self-interest demand.

The first point to be aimed at is to get the children actually into school and extend the the term of instruction in the country districts to at least six months in the year, while the city and village graded school should be sustained at least eight months. The superintendent of instruction for Kentucky reports that one-third the children of that State are in no school, and great numbers of the public schools are thoroughly inefficient. It is doubtful if one-half of the children of North Carolina are receiving even three months of reliable schooling. Louisiana, Florida, and Arkansas are even worse off, and all the Gulf States but little better. Thousands of ignorant people are keeping their children out of school for the pittance obtained for their work, and vagrancy and absenteeism from the schoolhouse in the open country greatly impair the value of the schools. Too many unbelievers are filling the country with the absurd cry that schooling makes the Negro lazy, and that the ignorant workman is alone reliable. But the fact is, that out of certain favored localities, chiefly in towns, the experiment of thorough, continuous, intelligent schooling has never yet been fairly tried on these dense masses of white and colored ignorance. A poor school, poorly attended, badly taught, neglected by the best people of a community, is a hotbed of many vices. When the South succeeds in getting her illiterate millions actually in range of the educational forces that make up the American system of education, it will realize that such training will treble its industrial power and lift up the whole basement story of its life into the life and warmth of modern times.

But two conditions are necessary for this achievement. The first is a resolute determination, in every Southern State, to strain every nerve to increase the amount of money appropriated for the public schools; and especially to establish the habit of local taxation for education. At the most, $100,000,000 may have been expended for every sort of education in these sixteen States since 1860. But the State of Massachusetts has expended nearly that sum during the same period. New York State spends $100,000,000 in ten years. Cincinnati pays as much every year as the State of Georgia, and Boston more than any Southern State, with perhaps two or three exceptions. Our new Northwest, besides its vast landed endowment, imposes the State tax, and then often shoulders a local assessment beyond any portion of the country.

Second. If anything has been proved in educational matters at home and abroad it is, first, that the church never succeeded in educating a people; second, that the family has always failed more decidedly than the church; third, that private enterprise never did more than educate a favored class; fourth, that in our country the common school, to be respectable, must be free to all; fifth, that neither the Nation nor the State can be relied upon for anything more than the most general supervision, encouragement, and partial support of the people's school; sixth, that no community succeeds in educating its children until it faces the hard fact of local taxation, and trains itself to the persistent and generous assessment of all its property for the common good. The most dangerous weakness of education through vast regions of the open Southern country is the fact that the people of both races do not understand this, and are looking to the State or to private benevolence and various other expedients to keep their schools alive. Another valuable result of this habit will be the training of the Southern people in that local self-government which has been so effective in the history of New England. Already this result has been marked in many localities. The present year North Carolina has passed a valuable law empowering school precincts to tax themselves, and the people of Texas have indorsed a constitutional amendment proposing the same thing.

Third. There must be a concerted effort at the training of teachers suitable to handle the common school by improved methods. A great deal of the school-keeping of all sorts in these States is inefficient and almost useless from the lack of teaching skill. Just now the South has the best material in the world for good teaching, for the best class of both sexes among the colored people, and the superior young women of the white people are thronging this profession. But even this will not save the school unless these young people can have not only academical but professional training. So far, the word normal school in the South is little more than a name for an academical grade of any sort. Even our universities and colleges for colored youth, with a few exceptions, have given no effective training in the art of teaching to their pupils. The Southern people need skill in the schoolroom, especially on account of the absence of many outside helps to the average child. The Peabody fund has struck the keynote in giving nearly all its income for the training of teachers in its own school at Nashville, in sumner institutes, and paying the salaries of skilled superintendents. The Slater fund should give no money to any institution for training teachers except on condition of a thorough normal department under an expert, with a practice school annex. Every Southern State should make haste in some effective way to push on the training of teachers, and every Southern academy and college should establish a department for the same purpose. It is in the schooling of such masses of children as are now brought into their classes that skill is especially required, and it is not a moment too soon to begin the gigantic work which half our Northern States have not yet compassed, but which every wise school man everywhere knows to be a prime condition of success.

Fourth. There is a great field for industrial education in the South, while there is danger that, in handling this complex matter, great and fatal mistakes may be made. There are two specious un-American notions now masquerading under the taking phrase "industrial education." First, that it is possible or desirable to train large bodies of youth to superior industrial skill without a basis of sound elementary education. You can not polish a brickbat, and you can not make a good workman of a plantation Negro or a white ignoramus until you first wake up his mind and give him the mental discipline and knowledge which come from a good school. The first thing that the illiterate classes need everywhere in our country for their permanent industrial elevation is six months of thorough elementary training in schools handled by good teachers for five or six years of their lives, and only a generation so taught can ever learn to work in connection with the labor-saving agencies which are revolutionizing every sphere of human industry. Second, that it is possible or desirable to train masses of American children on the European idea that the child will follow the calling of his father. Class education has no place in our order of society, and the American people will never accept it in any form. The industrial training needed in the South must be obtained by the establishment of special schools of improved housekeeping and the various styles of artisan work that its new manufactures will open for girls, with mechanical training for such boys as desire it, and a general improvement of agriculture through local associations of farmers and their wives. This will open into larger provisions for the higher form of technical schools. And this training should be given impartially to both races, without regard to the thousand and one theories of what the colored man can not do. But any attempt to recast the public school into a semi-industrial institution, in my opinion, will fail of both the ends proposed in the present state of Southern education.

Fifth. The time has come to call a halt in the establishment of new academies and colleges for both races until those on the ground are better endowed and made more effective. The educational scourge of these States now is the great army of broken-down people who are forcing themselves on the public as teachers of private and semiparochial schools, with no real qualification for the office of instructor. In more communities than is known this wasteful practice deprives the people of anything like thorough education, and fills the community with children and youth wretchedly prepared for the duties of life. There are now good secondary and collegiate schools in the South, enough to educate the people, if the people will give them fair support, and their communities will work persistently for their endowment. And with this should go on a general movement for the establishment of free libraries in every community. It will be a questionable advantage to teach a million Southern children to read if they turn to the dime novel, the lower side of the press, or the horrible trash with which every railroad is flooding the country. Every schoolhouse and church should have its children's library, and every community its collection of books suitable for general reading open to all.

Sixth. The Southern people will do well to give every child the great American chance of a fair elementary education and see how he will turn out. That is the only rational, scientific, practical, or Christian way to educate a people. The opposite way is to predict in advance what any set of children can not do, and then see to it that they have no chance given them to do it. And just here, if my words could reach every school district in the Southland, I would say : Give no heed to this noisy crowd of Northern educational cranks who are now filling the press with their preposterous, false, and silly denunciations of the American system of public schools. The American public school has great defects, like everything else, public or private, in the country ; but its defects are only those common to every American institution, and it is to be judged like the American family, business, politics, society, literature, and the church, by understanding its better features, marking its direction, and observing its spirit of progress. Judged in this way, our American education of all grades, in the North, is fully abreast of anything in the country, and is, perhaps, on the whole, more thoroughly alive to its own defects, and more earnestly striving for improvement than any other region of our national life. So I would say to our Southern friends—when Richard Grant White and Gail Hamilton denounce the common school as a failure all round; when ultra scientific experts ridicule it as superficial and misleading; when Bishop McQuade declares it godless, immoral, and communistic: when Dr. Nathan Allen tells you that New England manhood and womanhood are physically going "out the little end of the horn;" when 50 Zachary Montgomery and the crowd of journalistic scribblers declare that the schools are the nursery of laziness; when international novelists and literary lights sneer at our popular education as a nursery of vulgarity; when venerable college presidents and academical principals publish the high school and normal school a failure,—it will be perfectly safe to turn a deaf ear, and to go on building up every sort of good school in the South that now exists in the North; for while cranks die and go to their own places, good schools abide.

And out of this review of the educational outlook in the South comes to my mind the unanswerable argument for a wise, generous, and immediate policy of national aid for the people, especially of a dozen of these States, against the appalling illiteracy which is the one great bar to their prosperity. In my view this aid should be immediate and generous, graduated with the sole view to stimulate the energies of the people, kept sharply outside sectarian, religious, and partisan politics, left to the State authorities for administration—of course, under all proper safeguards—and supplemented by judicious continuation of private and Christian beneficence from the North, with a universal effort to make it the occasion of a great revival of kindly feeling through all sections. I believe the time has come when all this can be achieved, but better wait longer than have any imperfect, partisan, or partial attempt that will fail and leave misunderstanding and new jealousy in its wake.

Several results of such an act of eminent statesmanship I am confident would be assured.

First. The obstructive class in every community, whose greatest leverage now is in the acknowledged defects of the schools, would become a feeble minority as soon as public education took on the form of respectability and efficiency which such aid would assure.

Second. It would enable thousands of bright young people to obtain the elementary education at home which would fit them for a successful term in the secondary or collegiate school, and lay the foundation of professional success. Now the Southern academies and colleges are clogged with multitudes of students who have grown up with no elementary education, and are therefore unable to use the opportunities obtained by so much sacrifice and toil. A considerable per cent of national aid should be given for the training of teachers by the most practical methods that can be devised by the school authorities of these States.

Third. It will be a mighty encouragement and stimulant to local effort. Hang up a sum of money, to be obtained by any community on the sole condition that it strains every nerve of home resource, and every public-spirited man, every anxious mother, and every aspiring and eager youth besets that community to do its best. There are thousands of neighborhoods in the open Southern country and hundreds of little villages and settlements where such an offer would stimulate the people and, for the first time, bring them together in a hearty movement for the common education of their children.

Such aid, continued for a reasonable time, would root the people's common school in all except peculiar communities, and educate their inhabitants to its permanent support. I have never heard of a community which has enjoyed a good common school for a term of years giving it up for any cause but such as would destroy every public institution. The reason is that a good public school is the most potent stimulus to every other good institution. While in itself it is a powerful agency for mental growth and intelligence, a potent disciplinarian in the common moralities, a nursery of industry and patriotism, it is, all the time, stirring up the family and the church to new efforts, and in a variety of open and secret ways refreshing the social, industrial, and civic life of the people. The American people know a good thing when they have it, and the Southern people can be trusted to take good care of the school thus rooted and confirmed by national aid.

I leave to others the large and important sphere of argumentation that enforces this imperative duty on the ground of justice, political policy, Christian philanthropy, or defense against impending national calamities more threatening even than any peril of the past. And I must be excused for taking but little stock in the gloomy predictions and dismal apprehensions of many good people in all sections of the country in regard to Southern and national affairs. I do not think I have been deceived in my widely extended observations of the Southern educational situation, or have been blinded by the uniform kindness of these people to the difficulties still to be overcome. I can understand that even wise men, viewing Southern life from a local and limited angle of observation, can differ widely from me in their estimate, or even that eminent educators and social philosophers may be oppressed by anxious doubts concerning the outcome of American society as a whole. But, looking at this Republic along the line of historical perspective, it seems to me that for the past hundred years our new country has been maneuvering for position among the nations of the earth, and that now it stands before the world in an attitude more hopeful, with greater possibilities for a Christian nationality, than any people in Christendom. I can not discover any defect or danger in any section which will not yield to a true education of the head, the heart, and the hand, continued through a few decades, supported by the abundant means, pushed by the united executive capacity, and sanctified by the Christian spirit of our people. And, because I believe in this; believe in the possibilities of human nature; believe in the outcome of our American way of dealing with man; believe that the Southern people, even in its most illiterate regions, is at heart thoroughly American; believe that all foreign, obstructive, and un-American classes will either be finally absorbed or cast out from American society; believe that the vision of the fathers will be realized in the glory of the children, I have given my life to this glorious " ministry of education," and have come here to bear my own humble testimony in the great enterprise in which you are embarked to-day.

III.

FOUR YEARS AMONG THE CHILDREN OF THE SOUTH.

Preached at the Church of the Unity, Boston, Mass., December 12, 1884.

Text: "A little child shall lead them."—ISAIAH xi 6.

Early in the year 1863 I went, as a minister, to the city of Cincinnati, Ohio, then the borderland of our great civil war. For ten years I remained there, occasionally journeying through the Southwest, and observing carefully the state of affairs in the adjacent portion of the former slave States. Unable to go to the field, I was all the time asking myself what was to be my work in the upbuilding that I was sure must follow the complete wreck of the old Southern order of society, and how I could best meet the call of God to every patriotic heart.

It was not long before I came to a very distinct opinion that, after the politicians, the ecclesiastics, and, possibly, some other sorts of people, had reached the end of their favorite plans of national reconciliation, the real work must begin at the foundations, by establishing among the children of the South, of both races and all classes, a system of universal education which in time would lift up the very ground floor of society and develop everything there according to the ideals of our new American life.

This opinion slowly consolidated to a resolve that, when the call should come, I would go over and try to help these people in the beginnings of this mighty work. I could see it was to be a work difficult beyond expression; for up to 1860 there had been, through a large part of the South, no very serious or sustained attempt to establish a system of education for any but the superior class of white folk, and their five millions of slaves were, of course, in almost complete ignorance. So for fifteen years, till 1880, in the Northwestern, Middle, and New England States, I prepared myself industriously for a ministry of education by services and studies in educational affairs, tracing the relations of universal education to American history, and forming a large acquaintance with educational and public men.

Before I was half through with this preparation I heard the big horn blowing for me down in Dixie, and made haste to answer the call. I went forth and, with such support as a few benevolent people of the North and the hospitality of the South gave me, representing no party in politics or sect in religion, have traversed this Southland now for more than four years in this ministry of education. During these crowded years, besides a great deal of work in behalf of the cause done at the North and constant occupation with the press, I have visited fourteen of the Southern States. And so satisfactory has been this experience that I have resolved to keep on doing the work of this ministry as long as God grants the strength and good people furnish me the opportunity and means to do it.

By invitation of the pastor of this church I appear before you this morning to tell a plain story about things I have seen and a part of what I have been able to do in these deeply interesting journeyings among the children and youth of the South. My talk will be in answer to these three questions:

First. What is the actual state of affairs through this vast region, as I have seen it?

Second. What opportunities have been afforded me for such work as mine, and just what have I been able to accomplish?

240

Third. What can we all do in behalf of the present movement by the Southern people for universal education—I do not mean alone by aiding the effort the North is making to establish and support schools in the South, but rather by helping the Southern people carry forward the great system of free, popular education which they, of their own will, have begun within the past fifteen years—a movement incomparably the most interesting and far-reaching of anything that has happened in our country since the close of the war in 1865 ?

And, first, a word upon the situation.

You can read for yourselves the figures of Southern illiteracy that appear in the national census of 1880. There you will see that in the sixteen States once the fifteen slave States there are nearly 6,000,000 white children and youth under 21, with little more than 3,000,000 enrolled in any school; that not one-half of the 2,000,000 colored children and youth are even enrolled in schools; that the average attendance on schools is far below the enrollment; and that the vast majority of these pupils are in public schools, which at best, in Virginia, give five months, but in several of those States do not represent three solid months of annual instruction; that the teachers in those schools are paid more poorly than the servant and nursery girls in any large Northern town; that the city of Boston, with 400,000 people, pays yearly once and a half as much for education as the great State of Georgia; that one-third the voters even of Kentucky can not read or write, and one-third of her children are in no school; that not one-tenth of the colored voters or two-thirds of the white voters of the whole South make any appreciable use of reading and writing, even when they can read their ballot or write their name. You can also look upon the shrinkage in the valuation of these great States and cities in the years that followed the war, and understand how powerful Commonwealths like Virginia and Tennessee are convulsed even now by the question of paying a State debt which at least three of our new Western cities could carry on their back as easily as a soldier his knapsack. I need not repeat all this, which is public record, disputed by no man who reads. All this I confirmed in the fourteen States visited in my journeyings through more than four years.

But, friends, it is one thing to sit in your parlor at home, in this city, and read these columns of dead figures out of the census, and quite another thing to look through and through the state of society represented thereby, as I have seen it in the shape of living men and women and children.

Imagine, if you can, an old State as populous as Connecticut, more than half her people emancipated slaves and their children; another great multitude, white people, dwelling in such ignorance and aloofness from the higher influences of our time as no native-born class can possibly experience in an old Northern State. Now fancy what we, who regard ourselves an intelligent Christian people, should do in such case, if, after a twenty years' struggle, we found ourselves where the superior class of white people in one of these States, South Carolina, for example, is found to-day.

I have come to understand how, in 1865, the whole upper story of Southern society was overturned as completely as the roof of a house was ever blown away in a cyclone, and how the foundations of society were represented by 5,000,000 freedmen, largely without knowledge, without property, the prey to every sort of vice, their very religion a half pagan superstition, suddenly shot up into full citizenship, to do the work of legislation, to hold every office of honor and trust through sixteen States. And opposed to them, the other part of the foundations—another multitude of white people, in every grade of ignorance, full of race prejudice, accustomed to the violent life of a border civilization, ready to break out at any emergency into something worse than ordinary civil war. All that can happen in such a state of things I now understand from what I have seen.

I stood one day in a village of northern Alabama, and looked at a typical group, a family of these poor white mountain folk journeying toward some new home; a wretched scarecrow of a beast dragging a shaky wagon, loaded with the miserable

8819——16

effects of the household, and a woe-begone, aguish man, sprawled in front, driving the team. Behind came the wife, bareheaded and barefooted, her skirts in strings below her knees, leading the lean and sickly looking family cow. Then tramped the children ; two or three wild-looking boys romping with the inevitable crowd of dogs that is the annex to every poor Southern family ; two pairs of girls, with hair in snarls and bare feet heavy with the red mud of the roads, and such strange looks in their faces, with arms thrown over each other's shoulders, slouching in the rear. There may be a larger number of such folk in these sixteen States than there were people in the United States of America when Washington became our first President, and not immigrants, all of them homemade, descended from original English, Scotch, Protestant-Irish, or good Continental stock.

If anybody has really looked upon the sort of crowd that 75 per cent of the colored people of the South is to-day, as these people toil in the fields of its vast, lonesome country, or swarm the streets of every village on a holiday, he will understand what it means to have a State governed by such a majority, and how probable it is that any large body of Anglo-Saxon people in any part of America will consent to be so governed. I have seen how multitudes of these poor people must live, how loose must be the whole *morale* of their social life, how they behave under religious excitement, how helpless many of them are to meet poverty, pestilence, even a change in the weather ; and I marvel not at the social chasm that yawns between them and the white race, and am not surprised at anything that happens.

I have seen how improbable it is that these awful rivalries and repulsions should be kept out of the drawing-rooms and the churches ; how impossible there should be, just now, any widespread practical manifestation of democratic society and fruitful coöperation between classes, and large and beneficent public spirit in some of these States.

Of course, I have seen the best side of Southern society ; for my ministry has carried me through all regions of its higher as well as lower life. But, the more I see of the superior people of the South (and a more attractive people does not exist upon earth), the more I feel its utter helplessness to deal with the tremendous difficulties that involve the whole lower region of society. The class itself is comparatively small in numbers. Its families, with growing exceptions, are still struggling with poverty, just getting on their feet from under the wholesale wreck of twenty years ago. Their young men are scattering to seek their fortune ; and their young women facing life against more difficulties than confront any set of Northern girls I ever knew.

And how all this tells on every form of industry and enterprise ; making the laborers on the land the dullest peasantry in Christendom, making progress in the development of that vast region slow and unstable, keeping down manufactures and skilled mechanics, throwing all classes of people into the hands of sharpers, wicked moneylenders, and plunderers, who hover over the country like buzzards over a battle field ; and how all this must unsettle the very foundations of private, State, and municipal credit you can easily comprehend. Add to this the awful flow of bad whisky and a frequent loose administration of the criminal law, and the dark side of the picture is faintly outlined before you.

But I have seen, also, a bright side—so bright, indeed, that it has always kept me above discouragement, and brought me out, at the end of four years' observation, full of hope and confidence for the future of the South of our beloved land.

Beginning at the foundations, I have seen how wonderfully God has wrought in the history of the freedmen. Two hundred and fifty years ago the first slave ship landed the first cargo of African savages on the beach of old Virginia, in plain sight of the spot where now rise the towers of Gen. Armstrong's Normal and Industrial Hampton Institute. Only seventy-five years ago slave ships from New England and Old England were landing thousands of the same people in all the seaports of the South. These people were often slaves at home, degraded beyond the degradation of any race we have known. But they were scattered among the families of a Christian country that became a republic nearly one hundred years ago. They learned, in their estate of slavery, the three fundamental lessons in the progress of any similar people: first, the art of steady, profitable work; second, the language of a civilized country; third, the religion of Jesus Christ, which is destined to break every yoke on body or soul, and redeem every son and daughter of God. In this school of bondage they multiplied like the leaves on the trees, till now they number more than six million; and last year every soul of them was represented by a bale of cotton in the bounteous harvest fields of the sunny South.

Never was such a spectacle before as this development, so rapid from savage life to citizenship in the world's chief Republic. Spite of all that is discouraging in the life of the freedman to-day, no such great work was ever before wrought on so vast a scale in the annals of civilized man. The colored people of Georgia last year represented at least $8,000,000 of property earned and saved within fifteen years, and owned one-twelfth of the live stock of that enterprising State, and these people own $100,000,000 in the whole South. I have spoken to several thousands of their young people within four years, gathered in the great schools supported by the Northern Christian people, with occasional aid from their State governments; and, when I see how easily they take to good schooling in letters and in manners, and mark their slow but sure growth in good morals, I have no fear of the future of the colored man if he can be kept out of the hands of his foolish and wicked friends and guided by the best wisdom of the whole American people in the years to come.

I have marked this, that the various classes of the poor white people of the South (and there are many grades of intelligence, character, and industry comprised in the several millions of this class) still hold fast the bottom quality of the old British stock, and are developing every year in productive work, in *morale*, in the desire for education, in thoughtful attention to public affairs. We shall do well to put in all possible good work among the children of the poor white man of the South for the next fifty years, for he is bound to become a prodigious power in those States, and can be educated up to a mighty power for good. Every little white girl in the beautiful school of Amy Bradley, at Wilmington, N. C., would have grown up as wild, as unkempt, as hopeless as that group I saw in Alabama, had not the Lord come by in the form of a good schoolmistress and made of them all such a kind of children as we might not be ashamed to call our own.

And I have seen that, as fast as education lays its forming hand on these poor children, colored or white, they begin to draw near each other in justice, peace, and harmony. I have no enthusiastic anticipations of a Southern social millenium, but I can believe that a generation of good schooling, better churching, intelligent industry, and improved homes will at least enable these classes to dwell together in the unity of a common citizenship in the land we love. The war was also a revolution of emancipation to the poor white man of the South, and henceforth his way is open to the summit of American life, and already he is beginning to walk vigorously therein.

I have seen, with an interest I can not express, the present attitude of the higher classes of the Southern people. Of course, we are not to look at people past middle life, the survivors and sufferers from the awful wreck of war, for the most hopeful view. Yet even they are often bearing themselves with a patience, dignity, and spirit of returning friendliness, to which some of us, I fear, have not yet attained. But my ministry has been chiefly among the children, the youth, their teachers and friends—the young South; and there I have found little to deplore and almost everything to hope. I have spoken to thousands of the daughters and sons of the men we were fighting less than twenty years ago, many of them children of the leaders in that great conflict; and never have I spoken of the grandeur and hope of our common country and the opportunity of our new American life without a response as ready as I would expect here in Massachusetts. The young men of the old upper class of the South are doing just what our young men did in my boyhood, getting such schooling as they can, and going forth to seek their fortune in the new cities and towns of their own States, in the great Northwest, swarming in all the Eastern cities south of New York, and everywhere showing themselves as men. The class of stay-at-home, do-nothing, vicious, lazy boys is not half so great as we have been told. The young women of the best families are teaching the new public schools, pushing out in every direction toward new employments, so like our own good girls as I remember them in the past years that I can not see any real difference between them and our "sisters, cousins, and aunts." Our own young people, with all their splendid opportunities, will do well not to count on the stupidity, laziness, or any other defect of their companions of the South, for a generation of such work as many of them are now doing will bring them abreast of us in every good word and work.

I have seen how earnestly a large band of the Southern clergy are toiling at their sacred work; how faithfully the majority of their teachers are caring for the children in their schools; how the Christian people of both races are pondering the awful social problems that beset them; how the public men of their State and municipal governments are generally working on lines of progress; how every man that is anybody seems to be moved with a desire to be at harmony with us of the North. And I am astonished at the amount of building up in education that has been done by these people themselves within the past fifteen years; more than was ever done by any people in so short a time before. This year the South will pay $15,000,000 for education. And, now, I note everywhere among these people the waking up of this mighty desire for the educational and industrial uplifting of the young. It is the most powerful and profound inspiration of the new Southern life. If we meet it as we ought, it will bear this Southern people out into calm water, over all breakers and rapids, in the lifetime of many who hear me to-day.

In short, I sum up all I have seen in this : The Southern white people are Americans, trained in American republican institutions. A chronic social disease, slavery, preyed on their vitals for two hundred years. But, spite of that, so powerful is the schooling of our American republican form of society that, now this malady is cast forth, they are springing up, eager to run the race with us, chiefly needing that we will give them the hand of fellowship and the Godspeed of love and reasonable confidence through the years to come.

There is nothing inconsistent between these two pictures I have drawn. The darkness is of the night that is far spent, and the radiance is of the glorious dawn which already kindles the sky with omens of peace and good will—for our beloved America at first, and then for all the children of men round the world. For let us always remember, our triumph here in vanquishing the foes of republican society in America means the emancipation of Europe, the conversion and civilization of Africa, the unlocking the gates of the Orient, the social and political redemption of mankind.

You may now divine, in answer to my second question, the way I was received and the work I have been able to do in the past four years.

I went, of course, as any man should, thoroughly indorsed by the best educational and civic authorities in North and South, but with no official, ecclesiastical, or any other entanglement, as an independent, friendly minister of peace and light and hope. I carried nothing in my carpet bag but the New Education, mighty to bless all sorts and conditions of women and men. My one method of operation was to blow on every live coal I came across, and waste no time stirring up ash heaps or scolding at piles of burnt-out cinders. And because of this, far more than because of any special ability above other men (thousands of whom could do this work better than I, if they felt the same call), I have been met in a spirit of welcome of which I can not trust myself to speak in public and hardly can realize in the recollection. In all my public and private meetings with every class of people under every variety of circumstances I have heard scarcely a word of private discourtesy or public opposition.

But you may ask, "Just what have you been doing in these four years journeying through fourteen Southern States, and in what interest are you at work?"

In the interest of nobody save the children and youth, and the general good of the American people as it will be promoted by the abolition of the fearful illiteracy that now oppresses all these sixteen Southern States, and the general uplifting of their lower white and colored populations by the education of the head, the heart, and the hand. I go forth upon my own individual responsibility, and offer my work as "a labor of love" wherever I go. I probably owe a great deal of my success to this fact of my perfect independence of operation, nobody being able to assert that I have any purpose in view save the desire to help the Southern people in their great effort to help themselves in the education of the children. Although my labors are largely in the interests of public schools, yet I am constantly and most warmly received by the collegiate, academical, and private seminaries in every region that I visit. Indeed, so far as I am concerned, the Southern educational "latch string" is always out, and all doors fly open at my appearance. I have been accorded the most ample freedom of speech, as great as any man could use unless he desired to appear as a partisan political or sectarian religious missionary. And the hearing accorded to me by both races has been uniformly good, often enthusiastic and numerous, while without exception the press and the public men of all these States have most heartily coöperated in my ministry of education.

My vocation is that of a "man of all work" in the advocacy of education. While not attempting to establish schools or place teachers, I visit all sorts of institutions of learning from the college to the plantation district school; talk to the children and youth, meet their teachers, lecture at institutes and to groups of instructors, address legislatures, and coöperate with legislative committees and boards of education; labor with the influential classes of towns where the public school is not well established, make frequent popular addresses to the people of both races, use the press on every occasion for furtherance of my views, and almost every week preach in white or colored churches, Christian and Hebrew, on the moral and religious aspects of the great theme. And all the time the endless "talk by the way" goes on, the people everywhere being far more eager to question than I have strength to answer. With the single exception of teaching, I am doing everything that a friendly minister of education can do for the cause I have so much at heart.

Such is a brief statement of the work in which I have been engaged the past four years. I have no words to express my gratitude to God that I have been spared to give the closing years of a long Christian ministry to this ministry of education to the children and youth of our Southland. I can not trust myself in public to speak what I feel of the kindness and personal friendship of thousands of the best Southern people; of my obligations to public authorities, State and national; to the press, the churches, and the clergy, for their hearty countenance and too favorable estimate of what I have done. It is worth living half a century to look into the kindling faces of these many thousands of American boys and girls, of every class and both races, as they have shown before me like a mighty sunrise of hope and promise upon this great land of the future, for no part of the civilized world has a grander outlook than these Southern commonwealths. And I can not express what I would about the generosity of my friends who have helped me to be in at this sunrise of a great hope through a realm so late beneath the cloud. It is, indeed, a glorious opportunity to be with a people who have "walked in darkness" when first they "behold a great light," prophetic of brighter years to come.

And now I will briefly answer the third question: "What can we do to help on this work of the Lord, this beginning of the good time which, if we are faithful, is sure to come?"

First. Tell your members of the House of Representatives, in Congress, speedily to pass the bill for national aid to education which has come down to it from the Senate, where it received almost a two-thirds indorsement, without respect to partisan divisions or sectional lines.

This bill proposes to distribute some seventy millions of dollars, during the next eight years, in annual installments of seven to fifteen millions, among all the States and Territories, on the basis of the actual needs of the people. While every State will receive something, the object of the measure is to afford temporary aid and encouragement to the Southern States in overcoming the heavy burden of illiteracy, which is the greatest danger now threatening them and the nation from that direction. Eighty per cent of the colored people of the South are to-day abiding in an ignorance which implies all other personal, social, industrial, and civic disabilities. While the Southern States might be able to grapple with their white illiterates, which in some States constitute from twenty to thirty per cent of their class, I am confident, from four years' observation, that they can not overcome that black cloud of semibarbarism—the combined ignorance, superstition, shiftlessness, vulgarity, and vice of both races—without immediate and generous help from the people of the United States.

The Senate bill proposes to distribute this money only for elementary education in public schools, and for the instruction of teachers through the agency of the State governments; giving to no State more than it raises itself, and withdrawing the appropriation in case of abuse. It is believed by its authors that this national aid will be such an encouragement and stimulant to the people of the South that these States will be able, in ten years, so to establish their public school system that henceforth it can be supported by themselves, as all States eventually must.

I do not argue this question to-day. The argument was so thoroughly presented in the great debate in the Senate last winter, calling forth the greatest efforts of all its foremost men, that nothing can be added. It was shown there that this appropriation is in the line of the policy of the Government since its foundation ; that the South, within the past fifteen years, has shown a commendable disposition to help itself, by rebuilding its old system of collegiate and academical instruction, and establishing for the first time a system of public schools for both races in every State, improving every year, although unable to meet the pressing need because of the continued poverty of the masses of the people. It is proved that the public school funds in these States, with scarcely an exception, are fairly distributed among all classes and both races, and the safety of giving such moneys to the State authorities vindicated. The great and growing desire of the leading classes of the people for popular education is another assurance that this bounty will not be abused; as indeed it can not be, with the checks and safeguards incorporated in the measure.

I can bear testimony, from wide and careful observation, to the correctness of these views. And, more than this, I believe such a gift from the people of the United States to these States would do more to bind the Union together and attach the children and youth of all States and sections than any one cause, save the reuniting of the three great churches now separated on sectional lines. This bill now awaits action in the House of Representatives, and an earnest letter from any man or woman to the district Representative in Congress may expedite its passage, as during this very week the topic may be launched upon the House.

Second. While we continue to give freely to the educational establishments for the colored people in the South in charge of our great Northern churches and missions, let us not forget that the great work of educational uplifting must be done by the Southern people themselves, and largely in their common schools. Nothing better can be done by any benevolent man or woman than to send a library, support a teacher, give or loan money to superior young people, aid an impoverished Southern neighborhood to build a better schoolhouse, and generally put in material aid whenever and wherever it is evident it can be used wisely to encourage, stimulate, and help the people. A great deal has already been done by the Government and Northern churches; by great donations like the Peabody and Slater funds; by women like Mrs. Hemenway and Mrs. Stone, and by thousands of similar gifts, since the beginning of the great war. Probably $50,000,000 have thus gone South in twenty-five years past, largely for the colored people. I am convinced that no money has been better spent, and that the South to-day shows the result of what has been done for it in the revival of its industries, the improved conditions of society, and the great awakening of its educational life. But this sum, great as it may be, is so little for the education of 18,000,000 people, with more than 3,000,000 children and youth of elementary school age. Within that time the South itself has expended more than seventy-five millions from its own poverty. It will require the uttermost effort at home, reënforced by the national bounty and encouraged by all that the benevolence of the North can furnish for a generation to come, to place these people within sight of the least favored of our Northern States in that education which is the soul of every good institution and the security of the nation. And no money, public or private, can be so well invested for a generation to come as that which helps lift up the lower side of American society everywhere to intelligence, industry, religion, and patriotic devotion to the new life of the Republic.

I make this claim, because I know from actual observation the wide spread poverty and the great necessities of at least ten of these States, as contrasted with the marvelous prosperity of every portion of the North. Within the past four years I have journeyed through every Northern State from the Atlantic to the Mississippi; have skirted its Atlantic coast, sailed upon its lakes and rivers, penetrated its open country on all its great lines of railroad, and visited almost every city of 50,000 people in its imperial domain. I know and see with what lavish hand our people are spending for their own comfort and for all good and noble causes; and I deplore the awful waste of money in our new Northern luxury—millions wasted every year only to curse our children and youth and blight every sacred interest of the land. Oh, could one-half the money that has been thrown away in useless, almost criminal self-indulgence, by our Northern people during this past summer be used for these perishing minds and clouded souls, what a glorious expansion might be given to God's kingdom of light and peace and love through half these United States.

And finally the humblest of us can pray and talk and help create a public opinion that will speed this good work of reconciliation, and hasten the day when all our people shall be as one in the common hope and heritage of a Christian patriotism, the final bond of the union of hearts and of States.

But now, dear friends, are you still incredulous of the truth of my story and the wisdom of my counsels? Do you say, "It is impossible that a people so lately our bitter enemies should have come into any such accord as this, should be really so eager for the building up of American society, or at heart be ready to welcome the ministry of education with its prophecy of the new time?" Let me answer by a little picture of what once befell me in my wanderings up and down these broad Southlands, "all of which I saw, and part of which I was."

Late in the autumn of the doleful year 1862 I went out from Albany, N. Y., where I then lived, with a party of friends, to make speeches for the Union and persuade young men to enlist in the Army, depleted by the disastrous peninsula campaign. We came to a pleasant village under the shadow of the Catskills and were welcomed most heartily by the young Presbyterian parson of the place. He opened our meeting with a mighty prayer for the Union, and closed it with a solemn consecration of himself to the cause and an appeal to his young men to fall in, and a whole rank of them did fall in, and he went with them to the field. We left him, and his very name had long been buried out of sight under the avalanche of twenty revolutionary years. One rainy day in February, 1882, my feet first touched the soil of the State of South Carolina at a village up in its northwestern corner. The bottom was out of the muddy little town; but a deputation of friendly men were there to offer me the "freedom of the city," establish me in the chamber of honor at the hotel, and escort me to an evening reception by the master of the public white school,—a pushing son of Pennsylvania who had built his own schoolhouse and cottage for a private school, but, when he saw the public need, had turned it over for the people's use. Next morning the sun came out; and we went, all together, for a forenoon with the white children. After the round of ceremonies that always follows a stranger's visit and the regulation speech to the assembled crowd from the stranger, the boys and girls were dismissed for the day, partly as a compliment to the "visitor from Boston," and partly that the group of ladies and gentlemen and the teachers might wait on him to the colored public school.

So, crowded in a procession of spacious vehicles, we slowly navigated the red-mud sea across the town to the colored school. All the way the people were filling my ears with praises of the famous schoolmaster from the North, who had come there after the war, gathered the little colored folk in a shanty, and so wrought himself into their hearts that, when the Presbyterian Church, North, built for him a great schoolhouse, they paid his teachers and used his seminary as their public colored school.

In the midst of their praise the omnibus came to anchor in its last rut, and we all streamed out to where the wonderful master stood to bid us welcome. A moment of startled recollection, groping down through the crowded past, and my hand was caught in both the hands of my young parson of twenty years ago. There he was. He had fought it out in the line of battle to the end, then taken up the grander campaign of peace, bound for the kingdom come. So, through that sunny afternoon, we all sat on the platform in the big schoolhall together, the son of our friend conducting recitations worthy of any school, himself already known as a rising young naturalist in the North. The children sang their pathetic songs, the "stranger from Boston" made as good a speech as the choking in his throat would let him, and we were all of one mind and heart together.

Think of this! Twenty years before that good man and I were praying to the God of battles to go down with lightnings and thunders to overwhelm that furious chivalry who were flinging fire into the very magazine of the Nation, and boasting that the Union was gone and slavery should abide. Now, in that room, the minister of education from New England, the schoolmasters from New York and Pennsylvania, the schoolmistress from the West, the homebred teachers, and the best group of people in a South Carolina village were making a spring holiday together, with no shadow over their heads and no rock of stumbling beneath their feet; and the hand that led us up to this mount of union together was the dusky hand of a little negro child. Verily, in this "grand and awful time" in which we live to-day is once more verified the word of ancient prophecy from the far-off past: "A little child shall lead them."

IV.

THE EDUCATIONAL SITUATION IN THE SOUTH.

A lecture delivered in Washington, D. C., 1889.

For more than seven years I have been engaged in what it may not be vain to call a Ministry of Education through the sixteen Southern States of the Union, including visitations for observation, public lecturing, and private labors in the cause of education, especially of the whole people in common schools. Your attention is invited to an account of the actual educational situation of the Southern people. The situation is presented as the result of wide experience in every department of Southern school life, after many years of observation through all portions of the North.

The object of this address, while correcting some false impressions, is mainly to enforce the duty of the whole American people as private citizens, members of churches, and represented in Congress, to extend the helping hand to this portion of the country while in its present condition of imperative educational need.

Up to the year 1860 Northern public opinion undoubtedly failed to appreciate the educational status and the general mental power and social force of the Southern portion of the Union. Nothing is so difficult as the attempt of an aristocratic and a democratic order of society to understand each other. In 1860 the North was the most powerful democratic and the South the most concentrated and formidable aristocratic social order in Christendom. Although Southern society was greatly modified by our republican form of government, the institution of slavery was practically an aristocratic and military organization. No 2,000,000 of civilized people, in 1860, were so powerful in national affairs as this body, never including more than one-fourth the white and one-sixth the entire population of the fifteen Southern States. Its educational training for a century, though inferior in letters, had perhaps been superior, as a drill in political and social executive ability, to that of the North. Its schooling was modeled on the old English idea—colleges and academies, with a few notable exceptions of the denominational religious type, largely administered by the Protestant clergy, for the superior class; supplemented often by the best schools in the North and European study. This education was absorbed by the executive, political, and social life of a class which monopolized the wealth of an imperial realm, and had leisure, not only for home administration, but, from the first, largely to control the policy of the national government. There was no schooling, save occasional private teaching of the elements, for the 5,000,000 slaves.

For the several millions of nonslaveholding whites, there was no established system of education like the Northern common school. From the days of Thomas Jefferson, many of the most eminent Southern educators labored with the difficult problem of common-school education for the white " common people "; and, in almost every State, more than one attempt was made to establish it. In several large cities a respectable system of common schools existed; and in 1860, in a few States, there seemed a better hope for the masses. Doubtless a good deal was done by private effort and the church, especially among the bright children of poor families. But there was no general success in dealing with this department of popular instruction.

There were no reliable statistics of Southern illiteracy before 1860, although occasional glimpses show it to have been very extensive. Still, the nonslaveholding Southern white man had developed under the severe training of border life for a century. He had colonized eight immense new commonwealths in the South, and 1860 found him as good revolutionary war material as existed in the world. While it firmly holds together, no form of society is so powerful for concentrated effort as the high aristocratic. In 1860 the eleven seceding States represented one of the most effective public forces of Christendom; capable of being clenched in an iron fist whose persistent blows almost wore out the courage and patience of the mighty American Nation, extorted the admiration of foreign lands, and made every intelligent Northern statesman realize that the only safety for republican institutions on this continent was in keeping the South inside the Union. No thoughtful scholar will disparage the training that shaped such a people amid the hardships and deprivations of a new country.

But the year 1865 witnessed such an overthrow of Southern society as was never seen in modern times. The leading class was plunged in financial ruin, with nothing left but the land on which it stood—a prostration of all material interests such as our prosperous Northern people neither did nor could understand. And, although during the past twenty years new industries have been developed, new resources discovered, capital somewhat attracted, a vigorous immigration directed to the Southwest, and the whole population placed in a more comfortable state, yet the Southern people to-day, in comparison with the Northern, are very poor. Several millions of respectable white folk are living there in a way which must be seen to be appreciated.

The entire educational side of the South went down in this general wreck. For ten years school-keeping among the white people of the eleven seceding States went on in the face of almost insurmountable difficulties. In these troubled years the North and the Nation began the good work of schooling the freedmen, with occasional attention to the poorer whites. The provisional governments all put on paper, and some of them in operation, the Northern system of common schools. But not until 1870, in several States not until 1876, did the responsible white people really face the great question of free public education—the fundamental question in a democracy—the question which, after a thousand years' experimenting with other schemes, the liberal statesmen of Great Britain are compelled to face to-day.

One of the most deplorable results of this educational interregnum was the launching of a generation of white people into active life with the most meager schooling. Multitudes of Southern children of this period are now wrestling with active life with a most inadequate outfit from the schoolroom. The sudden conferring of the ballot on the Negro also made his absolute ignorance of letters both a local and a national peril.

The result of all this is that, spite of such efforts as will be described farther on, the eleven ex-Confederate States found themselves in 1880 involved in an illiteracy that no man who knows its extent and quality will attempt to ignore or underrate. We can read these startling figures in the census. There we learn that eight Southern States have over 40 per cent of illiterates; that in several of them, this illiteracy involves nearly half the people; that scarcely one-half the legal school population of the South are even enrolled in schools; that the average attendance is largely below the enrollment; that the schools in the open country, where nine-tenths the people live, probably do not average a four months' session in the year, with teachers often incompetent and always poorly paid, and the whole school arrangements frequently of the most primitive sort.

We must remember that the census classes as literate every person who can read and write in any degree, with a prepossession towards a favorable showing. But between the absolutely illiterate class and an intelligent American citizenship there abides a large section of the Southern people that makes small use of the little reading and writing that it has. Outside the educated class, the white masses of the

South, though doubtless advancing, are not yet a reading people. The free library is rising only in a few cities, and the vast majority have no access to collections of books. Outside a few dozen leading newspapers, the average Southern journal is meager, local, and read by only a portion of the people. Vast numbers of both races are educated chiefly by preaching and political speaking. The presence of these large bodies of illiterate people, especially among the Negroes and lower whites, is also a great hindrance to the good schooling of the children. Thousands of worthy families are too poor to give their youth more than this very imperfect country-school train-ing, with possibly a year at the nearest academy.

Any reliable and intelligent observer of American affairs can see how all this in-volves industry, religion, social life, public order and morals, and political virtue in difficulties that no statesmanship can at once relieve and no direct exercise of national power suppress. Every thoughtful Southern man understands that this condition, commonly named "Illiteracy," is a most alarming portent. These people tell us that nothing but a mighty and persistent educational movement, which shall lift up the lower strata of the Southern people to the level of a progressive American citizen-ship, can save this region from greater calamities than have yet assailed it. A great deal of popular misapprehension yet prevails among friendly and well-informed peo-ple in the North regarding the Southern situation in general and the condition of the eleven ex-Confederate States in particular. It would greatly help all estimates of Southern affairs to remember that the ruling race in the Southern States is almost exclusively of Anglo-Saxon descent, only modified by American life. For the last twenty years these people have behaved as an Anglo-Saxon people, with an aristo-cratic form of society modified by democratic tendencies, has always behaved under similar circumstances. The Anglo-Saxon man, in practical affairs, while slow to sur-render old opinions, for which he has long toiled and greatly suffered, is quick to dis-cern the limit at which the struggle must end, and hastens to seize on the vital ele-ments in the new situation and work on the line of progress at whatever sacrifice of sentiment or apparent consistency. The Southern people who lived through the great war are not ready to fall on the neck of Mr. Sherman or Mr. Edmunds with the con- 51 fession that for a hundred years their fathers were all wrong in their faith in the dominant sovereignty of the State and that they themselves were treasonable in fighting out the extreme form of that theory to its final decision.

But no influential portion of the active Southern people is to-day working on a line of hostility to the American Union. Were any foreign power to threaten the nation, the star-spangled banner would go up as soon in Charleston and New Orleans as in Boston and Chicago, and the first young men to shoulder the musket might be the sons of the soldiers who laid down their arms in 1865. The Southern people cer-tainly share the defect of the national character in not being an ideal people. Like the population of every portion of the country, they are afflicted with their own local infirmities and sins; but if history records any people who, with all their mis-takes, have done more things worthy of mark in the past twenty years, under cir-cumstances in any way similar, we have not read that page.

With the usual exceptions, these people are now at work, in a fairly vigorous and practical way, to get a living, develop their wonderful material resources, attract capital and immigration, and deal with affairs as they come up with the best wisdom and virtue at hand. Especially do I find the more energetic class of Southern youth working on the same lines, inspired by the same hopes as our Northern young peo-ple; leaving or staying at home, pushing to the front, appreciating the great advan-tages of American citizenship. And, if the Southern women of 1860 were distin-guished for their zeal in the great revolt, it may as truly be said that multitudes of their daughters are to-day coming to the front in the new upbuilding in a style that gives new luster to the young womanhood of the republic.

The educational movement in the South since the war has been largely the work of the Southern educational public, as the educational public is always the soul of this movement in all countries. And the southern educational public is in no essential way different from any similar public elsewhere, especially in the older Northern States. The new West, thanks to the marvellous bounty of the Nation, to Eastern money and the inflow of multitudes of the most intelligent and vigorous young people in the world, has known little of the slow growth of an educational system as it was known to the original States north of the Southern States to-day. Fifty years ago Horace Mann in Massachusetts, and the leading public school men of the Middle States, were fighting the same battle for universal education of an improved type that Drs. Ruffner and Haygood, Governor Thompson and President Johnston are fighting to-day.

There is the same class of excellent people who are still unbelievers in the free education of the masses in the South as in England, where even Mr. Gladstone does not dare to make free education a plank in the liberal political platform. There are plenty of "old-fashioned people," and now and then a college professor, who have no faith in the capacity of the Negro, and believe the public safety consists in keeping him an ignorant peasant, attached to the soil. There are churchmen who denounce the common school as "godless," and distrust all education separated from the control of their own priesthood and religious sect. Of course, the ignorant class there, as elsewhere, is at the mercy of educational demagogues, and, with a general desire for schools, is often the greatest hindrance to good schooling. There is no lack of small politicians, sometimes called "statesmen," of the type described by General Grant while President: "There is too much reading and writing now to suit a good many men up in the Capitol." And the South is not free from the class "we have always with us," people so inflated with local pride that any school with a big name is "magnificent" and can hardly be improved from abroad. It can not be denied that there is a powerful party in every Southern State still holding back from the hearty indorsement of the American common school, of which they have little reliable knowledge, and that in more than one of these States the system of universal education has hardly yet passed the crisis of its final conflict.

But there is also an educational public in each of these Southern States which, for intelligence, patriotism, ability, courage, and hopefulness has never been excelled in any land. That educational public began, more than fifteen years ago, to build up the American system of free, unsectarian, public education for the whole people to the full extent of the people's ability. It is in perfect sympathy with the educational public in the North. Its leaders' names are household words in every Northern center of education, and its good works are becoming known everywhere. It has been the great missionary body of the South in the new educational development of that realm; and the writings of its ablest educators should stand on the same shelf with the works of Henry Barnard, Barnas Sears, and Horace Mann.

Through evil report and good report this educational public has wrought until it has persuaded the Southern people to establish the American common school in every Southern State on the same basis of public support as in the North. In all States save two both races are admitted to the equal enjoyment of all permanent school funds. In every State the common school is established in all grades, including the free State university and the normal training of teachers. Probably every neighborhood in the South has something that may be called a free school. In Virginia, still the leading Southern school State, the towns are generally supplied with graded schools, and the country with a district school, in session perhaps five months in a year. But in the vast Gulf region, extending from Charleston, S. C., to the eastern border of Texas, outside a few cities, it is doubtful if there is an average of more than three months; and in the great central mountain world, inhabited by 2,000,000 people, the school partakes of the general type of society. It is doubtful if, leaving outside the four States north of the Potomac and Ohio rivers, the remaining twelve to-day can offer to such children as attend more than four months of schooling a year.

In regard to attendance on the public schools in these twelve States, my observation is that it is impossible to arrive at any such definite conclusions as form the basis of some of our recent Northern journalistic estimates. The educational statistics of several of these States are still far from complete. The science of educational statistics is the last result of a thorough system of schools, long a vital part of the community. New England, after 250 years, is just coming to reliable knowledge concerning the attendance in her schools. But in a dozen of these Southern Commonwealths, with nine-tenths of their people widely scattered through an open country, much of their territory away from railroads, their population unaccustomed to the public school, their officials often incompetent and always poorly paid, it is impossible that any such reliable estimate should be formed as is put forward in recent statements in the North. Even distinguished citizens, public men and journalists, at home, outside of school work, may think such estimates reliable, and be deceived in regard to the true aspect of educational affairs. In general it may be said that the attendance on Southern public schools is increasing—increasing largely wherever large additional facilities are offered. But the words " Enrollment," " Regular Attendance"—the whole technical vocabulary of our Northern school life—have a meaning far more variable and uncertain in the South. This is apparent : That the common school public is doing valiant service and the Southern people are becoming proud of their new education. The school age in many of these States is prolonged almost during minority ; a public necessity where multitudes of young children in the open country can not reach distant schools or attend with regularity. There are now not less than 6,000,000 of persons of " legal school age " in the whole South, of whom not more than one-half are enrolled, and a much smaller number actually attending a tolerably effective school four months in the year. And the years of school attendance in the South are fewer than in any Northern State.

The old-time system of denominational colleges and academies has been revived, and is to-day more extended and in many respects better than a generation ago, save in its endowment and the ability of the people to school their children. I have only sympathy and admiration for a large body of the superior teachers in these higher Southern schools. They are doing double work on half pay ; giving free tuition to needy students ; using their small earnings for their own improvement in summer ; often working on the edge of peril to health, with uncertain prospects ahead. Many workmen in the skilled manufactures of the North have an income much larger than the salaries for which hundreds of educated young men are now teaching in Southern colleges and academies, and thousands of accomplished young women teachers are living on incomes incredibly small. But these schools are crowded with pupils ; and, altogether, the upward push, especially of the better class of girls, for education is greatly encouraging. In the sixteen States, a few great benefactions—like the Vanderbilt, Johns Hopkins, Pratt, Peabody, Corcoran, and Tulane funds—have become the foundation of institutions that have a great future, and in a few cities the free library and lectureship are rising. The best graded schools of the larger towns are thoroughly good, often managed by experts, and are growing in favor with the people.

The sixteen Southern States will possibly expend this year for private and public schooling from $15,000,000 to $18,000,000 for their 6,000,000 children and youth. As the State of Massachusetts alone spends half that sum yearly on less than half a million of her children, one can judge if the South is yet in a condition where her friends can reasonably decline aid from any quarter to overcome illiteracy. During the past twenty-five years the North and the nation, in all ways, have probably invested for education in the South some $50,000,000. It can at once be seen that, while the school public of the South, since the war, has really done what no people ever did under similar circumstances, and that there is a gratifying progress in all these States, yet the Southern people only stand on the threshold of the mighty enterprise of lifting their section into permanent equality of intelligence with the rest of the country.

At the present moderate gain, with the swift advancement of the North, it will be a century before this can be done; and, although there are educational theorists who see no harm in this, the responsible people of the South do not propose to wait a whole or half century, provided they can show the North and the Nation that the safety, progress, and glory of the Union are bound up with the success of the New Education through this immense region of the republic.

This Southern school public has repeatedly during the past ten years placed these facts before the people, and any man may inform himself thereof and learn what it is saying to the people of the United States.

The Southern school public says that the Southern people, in ten or a dozen States, are not able to shoulder the prodigious burden of founding a system of public education, which at least should give country children six months a year of an effective district school, place a graded school for eight months a year in every considerable village, aid the State in training competent teachers, and enable the people to furnish school accommodations for the rapidly increasing multitudes of children. Our Northern States, in their present condition, have little comprehension of the burden of doing this work, for the first time, in the face of such difficulties as now environ the masses of people in these States. Unless the present generation can be reached in ten years, this curse of illiteracy will go on fastening itself on millions of youth and perpetuating all the peculiar evils of Southern life. The New England States, or the two States, Massachusetts and New York, have a larger property valuation than the whole South. The people of Massachusetts could buy Mississippi and Florida with their investments in the savings banks. Southern valuations are necessarily low, because based so largely on unsalable property ; and additional taxation there always means a new burden on country people unable to bear it. Too much of the village and city wealth is piled up at the expense of the open country. In short, a dozen of these States are in just that financial condition where taxation for the necessities of government is burdensome ; and education is always postponed to fundamental social necessities. In the new South everything is to be done, the whole section to be rebuilt, industries readjusted, civilization supported on a far more expensive scale than under the old dispensation. There are a dozen imperative public uses for every Southern dollar that reaches the tax-gatherers. The school tax is paid by the few comparatively well off, and almost wholly by the whites. In scores of counties I find the better sort of families largely supporting public schools to which they can not send their own children. The Southern people may be pushed, every year, to a moderate increase of home effort; but it would require twice the money now expended to give the children of the South six months of good schooling a year, and that is now a financial impossibility.

When we speak of the common schools of the South—especially of the vast *low country* the Southern people call by that name, extending along the coast from Norfolk, Va., to the Rio Grande in Texas, sometimes hundreds of miles inland, besides the more destitute realm, the mountain world, from Harper's Ferry, West Va., almost to Montgomery, Ala.—we must bear in mind the environment of the schoolhouse. Some of our Northern newspapers have compared the educational opportunities of the South with those of rural New England, to the disparagement of the latter. But they forget that the significance of educational statistics for such comparisons hinges on the environment of the school. No man really acquainted with these portions of the country could make the grotesque blunders into which these journalists have fallen. Every intelligent Northern man, born and reared in rural New England, knows what the common school, working in close connection with a group of powerful agencies of enlightenment and discipline, has done for all these States. With this picture of the average New England township in mind, let him go to an average 6 miles square, carved out of these portions of the Southland referred to, and the real status of school life will become apparent. In the low country, the most characteristic part of the South, swarmed by the negro population, he will find the overwhelming majority of adult people, freedmen, nine-tenths of whom do not read, doubtless improving after a fashion, but living as no considerable class of country people live in the North. A considerable portion of the white people either read little or not all, even when of some degree of general intelligence and worth. The vast majority are in no state to shoulder additional financial burdens. The few well off, thoroughly awake, and active in good works support a three month's common school, to which they often are not willing to send their own children. Yet these schools, defective as they may be, are often the highest influence for the uplifting of the majority of the people, though like an island in a surrounding sea where so many things oppose and so few support. Such comparisons between the educational opportunities of Southern and Northern children are wildly misleading, for they ignore the conditions of society amid which the school is established and in which it must be worked.

My own conclusion, from wide observation during the past seven years in all these States, in constant communication with the public school authorities, the only Southern people who have reliable knowledge of the state of popular education, may be summed up somewhat in the following suggestions, including my mature opinions of the duty of the remainder of the country in the premises.

First, the Northern people, at present, should in no way relax their private and church contributions for the education of the colored folk and such portions of the poorer whites as may be reached by the peculiar system of mission schools now largely supported by them. Indiscriminate giving to the crowd of private solicitors from the South for irresponsible school work is not wise. The effort of a considerable section of the Southern colored clergy to establish the parochial church system of schooling, everywhere the weakest side of American education, should receive no countenance from the common school public anywhere. The colored people should be urged, for ordinary purposes, to concentrate their means on the improvement of the common school. The higher mission schools for colored students should rather be endowed, enlarged, and improved than multiplied. There are now enough of them, if properly managed, to supply the demand for the secondary and higher education of the ablest colored youth, to train teachers and clergymen—the two greatest forces in the moral improvement of their people—and furnish the opportunity for industrial, agricultural, mechanical, and housekeeping service. A good deal might be done by judicious private student aid to Southern academies and colleges for white youth and by helping normal schools and institutes for training teachers. In many ways, the private capitalists and moneyed associations now coming in possession of vast areas of valuable Southern territory can aid in developing that popular intelligence which alone insures general material prosperity.

Our Northern teachers need little urging to show a friendly interest in Southern education; for, already, the Northern and Southern school men and women are the closest professional fraternity in the Republic. It would greatly help if the press of our Northern cities would inform itself more thoroughly concerning this feature of Southern life. One month's presentation of this, really the front view of the South, in place of the back-alley view so often given by the partisan, political, and religious press, would awaken a wholesome and healthful interest through the whole country. As it is, the ignorance of many of our leading Northern journals on this subject is stupendous, and their deliverances on Southern educational affairs have no claim to respect.

But that man must be poorly informed who thinks this vast work can be done by private aid alone. If the South is to get a real lift, that will enable at least twelve States to offer anything like the average American opportunity to this generation of her children, it must be by a speedy and generous system of temporary national aid. After the most careful observation I am convinced that without such help for a dozen of these great States they must go on slowly floundering through a bog of illiteracy in all the lower regions of society, that will more and more involve them, and finally the whole country, in such calamities as it is not wise to encounter.

In a general way, such a system of national aid, wisely guarded by the national and administered by the State authorities, confined to the building up of the common school, training of teachers, and the like, in ten years would plant the country district school firmly and with tolerable efficiency through the whole South ; and that is the fundamental need of this section.   Southern towns, though wearing the name and assuming the functions of cities, are few in comparison with the population. Virginia has not one-fifth of her people in towns of two thousand and upwards. North Carolina, with a population of a million and a quarter, has hardly a hundred thousand people in this style of towns.   The National Cemetery above Vicksburg, Mississippi, where sleep the bodies of 16,000 Union soldiers, has been the most populous city of that great State.   While many of these towns, especially the county seats, which are the vital centers, need assistance, it is in the open country, where the children chiefly live and the masses of people are slowly rising above the wreck of war, that this aid is most valuable.   The country schools are too often so poor and brief that they seem to many of the superior people to stand in the way of something better.   The problem is to give a tolerable six-months country school, in a comfortable schoolhouse, with teachers as good as the community can furnish, to the children of both races through all the States.   It will need twice the money the people now feel able to raise to do this.   In case of national aid, their utmost ability will be taxed to build schoolhouses and furnish additional schools for the great influx of pupils thus brought upon them. If the public-school party in every such community could be strengthened in this way, it would take heart and finally overcome all obstacles.   It could make schools that the people who now pay the taxes could use for their own families, which their educated sons and daughters would be glad to teach, and would thus lift the common school from an arrangement for " the lower orders " to what it should become, the people's common seminary.   Thus encouraged, the influential class would become the advocates of increased taxation, and everywhere the common school would come to the front as the great uplifting force in communities now blighted by ignorance and all which goes therewith.   Ten years of such work would leave the Southern people so much better able than now to support public education that in reasonable time national aid could be withdrawn and these States left to themselves.

It is almost impossible for a man who has spent his life in any portion of our Northern States, where the school is but one of many powerful agencies of popular training, to realize the great importance of a good country district or village school in such a region as more than half the South is, even to-day.   It takes the place and does the work, especially among the ignorant adult people, the majority of the colored folk, of half a dozen institutions and agencies in a more advanced community. The colored graduate of Hampton or Tuskegee, with a wife from Fiske, Atlanta, or Raleigh, is not only teaching the colored school, but the twain become the center of a new life for the colored people.   They persuade them to send their children to school, break up the awful vagrancy which is the curse of colored childhood, teach the children to work, instruct their mothers in decent housekeeping and their fathers in mechanics and improved field-work, shame the people out of their brutal herding together, lift them above their pagan superstitions, keep them out of the hands of the sharpers who plunder and the politicians who use them, teach them to avoid contention, encourage clean family life, establish a good Sunday school with a library, and persuade the young people to "bounce" the blatherskite preacher who is the bottom nuisance of the colored folk.   I know hundreds of white Southern teachers who are the most influential professional people in their communities, holding the hearts of the children and through them greatly helping the parents, attracting capital and good people to the town, pushing forward the temperance reformation, and becoming the soul of the church in a revival of intelligent and practical religion. No American community is hopeless where the children can be gathered into a common school that represents the educational training of the head, heart, and hand, and is the instructor of every family and the inspiration of every movement for better things. Now, the Southern common-school public entreats the Nation to help plant in every district in this illimitable realm this peculiar American institution and make it so good that it may become the center of a true American civilization and the pride and joy of millions yet unborn.

Some of our Northern people believe that national aid, as described, would injure the South. A class of social theorists oppose the common school itself on this ground, and the most specious arguments against national aid come from this quarter. I do not here argue the fundamental question, on which the American people has made up its mind. But the theory that self-help is the mainspring of public prosperity, though true in general, in this application is the right theory in the wrong place. It would help a good many ambitious and dogmatic social theorists in our country to follow their books less and study the American people more. They would learn that the American people is not to be judged by the estimate, reasonable enough, of a European peasantry, demoralized by centuries of paternal despotic government, so childish that manhood must be shot into it from a Krupp cannon or punched into it by a soldier's bayonet. The American people has a mighty digestion for every sort of material aid, and so far has grown strong and self-reliant as such aid has come. Chicago burns up in a day, takes all the money the world will give or lend, and in twenty years becomes the wonder of the continent. If our social science philosopher will get a pocketful of excursion tickets, for an outing through the fourteen Northwestern States between Niagara Falls and Alaska, he will confront an original object-lesson in national aid to American civilization that may convince him " there are more things " in the United States of America " than are dreamed of in his philosophy."

In 1788 the new American Republic accepted the gift of the vast territory now included in the five older Western States, and began that system of persistent national aid to American civilization which, stimulating the self-help of the people, has made Ohio, the oldest daughter of the Union, the rival of New York as the pivotal political State and the new West the dominant power in the Republic. The Nation offered a farm to every man who would go West, and a generous grant of lands for common schools and colleges. In 1803 the nation purchased Louisiana, from the Gulf to the crest of the great mountains, and in 1850 went into an expensive war to gain the Pacific Coast and the empire eastward. Thus, beyond the Mississippi, the Nation obtained by trade or the greater outlay of war every foot of ground to the Pacific, with new millions for Alaska. The Nation has spent who knows how much in clearing this wide realm of savages, subsidizing the great avenues of travel, lifting the valleys and leveling the mountains, over which countless swarms of people have gone in to possess the new paradise. In the civil war it made new grants for agricultural and mechanical colleges, and gave millions of money and valuable public properties for the schooling of the freedmen. More than one Western State has bottomed its school fund on the distributed surplus revenue of 1836. The old East has poured money into the West for half a century, to build churches and schools. In every way American enterprise and Christian philanthropy could suggest, the new West has been crammed and rammed and coaxed and prodded with material aid from this and every land. Now, our philosopher will, of course, expect to find these fourteen States the most thoroughly " demoralized " portion of the Union. He will learn that Western American life does not adjust itself to the little formulas that seem so comprehensive to a portion of our speculative " scholars in politics," for these fourteen States, which have received more outside aid for education than any people on earth, have done and are now doing more than any other people for the training of their youth. Their common-school system, with its upper-story high and normal school and State university, spite of its defects, is the broadest system of public instruction and training for free citizenship in Christendom. Where would our imperial Western country have been had this petty crotchet of the new social philosophy, now the favorite dogma of some of our circles of exclusive culture, been the law of public economy for the past seventy-five years? The moving power of American civilization is self-help, generously aided by public encouragement, to deal with the broadening opportunities of American life.

Our sixteen Southern States are becoming the new opening land of the Republic. The original settlement was chiefly in the garden spots, and left the amazing mineral, manufacturing, and other resources of these mighty Commonwealths almost untouched. The supreme need of the South is a big lift from the whole country to get on the ground an educational arrangement that, in due time, shall hoist its laboring class to something like the intelligence and skill of the rest of the Union. Till that is done the South is a strong man chained to a live-oak tree in a Louisiana swamp. That achieved, immigration with capital flows in; and the splendid drama of Western civilization is repeated to the inspiring strains of "Hail Columbia," from Washington to California.

This is the Southern educational situation, its achievements, necessities, and prospects as I see it. I need not repeat that it forces upon us a problem too great for solution by any spasmodic effort. No famous man, no religious sect, no system of private aid can do for the South what its progressive educational public assures us must be done. This mighty work—the gradual uplifting of the lower story of civilization in sixteen States—has already been well inaugurated by the Southern educational public. It is because that home public has done and is doing so much that I plead with the people of the North and the Nation to extend the helping hand. For, in all these movements that involve the national life, we shall lean on broken reeds while we depend on sects and parties, the low self-interest of commerce, or the amiable whims of society for deliverance. Under the gracious Providence which has never forgotten this Republic we must rely on the American people, moving all together, to do a work so immense in extent, at best so gradual in its results on the Nation's life. And by the people in this connection I mean the whole American people, slowly instructed, elevated, and guided in the ways of justice, freedom, religion, and intelligent power by that growing public everywhere that discerns the real signs of the times. Then, from State and Nation shall come up a sublime response to the majestic words, written in the memorable ordinance that gave civic life to the new Northwest: "Religion, morality, and knowledge being essential to good government and the happiness of mankind, schools and the means of education shall be forever encouraged."

V.

THE NEGRO AMERICAN CITIZEN IN THE NEW AMERICAN LIFE.

An address delivered at the conference on the Negro, Lake Mohonk, N. Y., July, 1890.

During the past ten years of a ministry of education among the Southern people in all the Southern States, I have been often challenged to formulate my opinion concerning the present condition and future outcome of the Negro. My invariable answer is: I have come to this portion of the country as an out-and-out advocate of the universal education of the heart, the head, and the hand possible for all orders and conditions of the American people. I believe the Christian religion, as it lay in the mind and shone forth in the speech and life of the great Teacher and Savior of man, includes this idea of education. All the progress this world has seen out of old pagan conditions of race, caste, society, and government, has been the work of this mighty regenerating influence. I hold it the deadliest treason and revolt against the Christian civilization, a backing down into paganism, or a worse lapse into the slough of despond of absolute atheism and secularism, to impeach the power of this divine agency to cure all our American ills.

I began my present ministry of education ten years ago, in the Southern States, in full faith in this gospel of the reconstruction of the whole Republic from "the remainder of wrath" that still vexes its progress and looms like a black despair over its least advanced portion. And, although I can not pretend to have converted or convinced anybody, I have seen with what an uplifting of the soul the better sort of the Southern people welcome any man who, in honesty of purpose, love of country and of all his countrymen, endeavors to get down to the bottom facts of the situation, with a just appreciation of the position of all true men, and with an invincible hope and a holy obstinacy in standing by the bright side of God's providence in American affairs. The fact that one man can go through all these States, among all classes, everywhere testifying to the grandeur of the full American idea and urging the people to live up to the vision of the fathers, with all but universal acceptation, so that the discords in this ministry have hardly been enough to emphasize the harmonies, is to me an assurance that the same line of work, assumed by a greater man and finally adopted by the influential classes of our people, will shape the highway out of the present complications.

My only recipe for the solution of all these problems that still divide the country is the putting on of that judicial and resolute Christian attitude of mind that insists on looking at all the facts of the case, setting them in their proper relations, all the time searching for the elements of progress which are the vital centers. It seems to me that a great portion of the misunderstanding and conflict at present is the result of a practical inability in the masses of the people to rise to this position and the mischievous pertinacity of too many leaders of public opinion everywhere in keeping the national mind engrossed with the temporary and unessential facts of the case. With no disposition to misrepresent or misunderstand anybody, I respond to your call to tell my experience as an observer of the Southern situation, especially as it concerns the Negro citizen in the sixteen Southern States of the Union, as I have seen him during a virtual residence in these States for ten years past.

259

It would seem that thoughtful Christian people might at least endeavor to realize the simple gospel rule of "doing as they would be done by" in the judgment of each other in an affair so momentous, where mistakes are fraught with such mournful possibilities as in this great discussion. It is easy to see how much of the difficulty comes from this inability to "put one's self in the place" of his opponent.

Would it not be possible for a larger number of our foremost Southern leaders, in church, state, and society, to try to appreciate the motives and temper of the loyal people of the North in the great act of conferring full American citizenship on the Negro, after his emancipation, 25 years ago? I do not defend any injustice, tyranny, reckless experimenting with government itself, that followed that act; no thoughtful man defends such things to-day; but I do hold that no true conception of this matter can be had by any man who honestly believes that this exaltation of the Negro to full American citizenship was either an act of sectional revenge, a narrow and ferocious partisan policy, or the reckless experiment of an excited sentimentalism. If ever a people, in a great and national emergency, acted under a solemn sense of responsibility to God, humanity, patriotism, and republican institutions, I believe the conviction of the loyal Northern people, that shaped the acts of reconstruction, is entitled to this judgment, and will so abide in history. It was the most memorable testimony of a national government, just rescued from desperate peril, solemnized by the death of its venerated leader, to its faith in popular institutions recorded in the annals of mankind.

But it must be acknowledged that the very nobility of the act that conferred the highest earthly distinction of full American citizenship on a nation of newly emancipated slaves, of an alien race, involved the penalty of great injustice to its object. It was inevitable that the Nation, having committed itself to this daring experiment, would watch its success from an ideal point of observation. So, for the past twenty years, one misfortune of the negro citizen has been that the portion of the country that won his freedom and lifted him to this proud eminence could do no otherwise than judge him out of its own lofty expectation, piecing out its almost complete ignorance of any similar people or situation by repeated drafts on a boundless hope, an almost childlike trust, and a deep religious faith, proven by the cheerful giving of $50,000,000 and the sacrifice of the service of noble men and women of priceless value in the effort to realize the great expectation of the Nation.

Again, is it more than plain justice that the leading mind of the loyal North, that saved the Union to nationality and freedom in 1865, should endeavor to represent to itself the actual point of view of the Southern people concerning this act of reconstruction then and, to a great extent, in the present time? I know that the most painful lesson of history is the difficulty of such comprehension of an aristocratic form of society by a people for a century trained in the school of a proud and successful democracy. Not one educated man in a thousand in the United States can put himself in the place of one of the great Tory leaders or scholars of Great Britain or listen with anything but impatience to the account that any European government or the Catholic Church can give of itself. How much more difficult for the average New England or Western citizen to understand the attitude of mind with which an old Southern planter or a modern Southern politician must contemplate this sudden and portentous upheaving of 5,000,000 freedmen to the complete endowment of American citizenship at the close of the great war.

For surely, at first sight, no body of 5,000,000 people could be imagined less qualified by its past to justify such expectations than the negro freedmen. Three hundred years ago the Negro was a pagan savage, inhabiting a continent still dark with the shadow of an unrecorded past. A hundred years ago the ancestors perhaps of a majority of the 7,000,000 Negroes now in the United States were in the same condition. Of no people on the face of the earth is so little known to-day as of the African ancestors of the American Negro. Of various tribes, nationalities, and characteristics, perhaps with an ancestry as varied as the present inhabitants of the European nationalities, these people were cast into a state of slavery which confounded all previous conditions and only recognized the native ability of each man or woman in "the survival of the fittest" in the struggle for existence on the plantation and in the household.

Once more: It has never been realized by the loyal North, what is evident to every intelligent Southern man, what a prodigious change had been wrought in this people during its years of bondage, and how without the schooling of this era the subsequent elevation of the emancipated slave to full American citizenship would have been an impossibility. During this brief period of tutelage, briefest of all compared with any European race, the Negro was sheltered from the three furies of the prayer book—sword, pestilence, and famine—and was brought into contact with the upper strata of the most powerful of civilized peoples, in a republic, amid the trials, sacrifices, and educating influences of a new country, in the opening years of "the grand and awful time" in which our lot is cast. In that condition he learned the three great elements of civilization more speedily than they were ever learned before. He learned to work. He acquired the language and adopted the religion of the most progressive of peoples. Gifted with a marvelous aptitude for such schooling, he was found, in 1865, farther "out of the woods" of barbarism than any other people at the end of a thousand years. The American Indian, in his proud isolation, repelled all these beneficent changes; and to-day the entire philanthropy, religion, and statesmanship of the Republic are wrestling with the problem of saving him from the fate of the buffalo.

I find only in the broad-minded and most charitable leaders of our Northern affairs any real understanding of the inevitable habit of mind which the average Southern citizen brings to the contemplation of the actual condition or possibilities of the negro American citizen. With a personal attachment to the Negro greater than is possible for the people of the North ; with habits of forbearance and patient waiting on the infirmities, vices, and shortcomings of this people, which to the North are unaccountable and well nigh impossible of imitation; with the general willingness to coöperate, as far as the comfort and the personal prosperity of its old slaves are concerned, is it strange that this act of statesmanship should appear to him as the wildest and most reckless experiment in the annals of national life? Even the most intelligent and conservative parent finds it difficult to believe his beloved child is competent to the duties of manhood or womanhood, and only with a pang does he see the dear boy or girl launch out on the stormy ocean of life. What, then, would be the inevitable feeling of the dominant Southern class, to whom the Negro had only been known as a savage slowly evolving into the humbler strata of civilization as a dependent chattel, when, at the end of a frightful war, it found itself in a state of civil subjugation to its old bondmen ? No subject race ever reveals its highest aspirations and aptitudes to its master race, and it is not remarkable that only the most observing and broad-minded of the Southern people, even yet, heartily believe in the capacity of the Negro for civil, social, or industrial coöperation with any of the European peoples.

Now, say what we will, this obstinate inability and sometimes unwillingness to put one's self in the place of the opposition have been the most hopeless feature of the case, the real "chasm" between the leading minds of the North and South. So to-day, while even partisan politics seems to pause in uncertainty on the steep edge of a dark abyss, when noble and humane people all over the country seem to be falling into despondency, when an ominous twilight, threatening a storm, is peopled by all the birds of ill omen, and "the hearts of men are shaken with fear," I am glad that we have been summoned here to look things squarely in the face, to bring a varied experience to bear on a new and more careful consideration of the whole matter, and by the guidance of a Christian insight endeavor to see the hopeful elements of the situation. We do not need to rehearse our separate knowlege of the shadowy side of the new South. The shadows we have always with us, everywhere. But, if we can locate the center of the new "Sunny South," we may go home with the conviction that, while the shadows in human affairs are always on the move, the sun shines on forever and is bound to bring in God's final day of light.

The pivotal question on which this vast problem turns is, has the Negro, in his American experience, demonstrated a capacity for self-developing American citizenship? I leave out of the estimate, at present, the exceptional people of the race, and look for the answer to the average Negro, as I see him in the Southern States; for I suppose nobody believes that full American citizenship is possible as the permanent condition of any people destitute of this capacity for self-dependent manhood and womanhood. The child race must be cared for by a paternal organization of society, and that element of paternalism is just what every good American citizen declares he will not have in his Government. In lieu of that, an extemporized or permanent social public opinion or an unwritten law will take its place and do its work.

If the Negro, as so many Southern people believe, is only a perpetual child, capable of a great deal that is useful and interesting, but destitute of the capacity for "the one thing needful" that lifts the subject of paternal up to the citizen of a Republican Government, then the thing to do is to leave him to the care of his superiors in the South, who certainly know this side of him far better than the people of the North, and, whatever mistakes on the side of occasional severity may be made, will in the end do the best for his permanent estate. In fact, nothing seems more evident to me than the practical inability of the National Government to essentially change the status of its seven millions of negro citizens, except through national aid to education. There is no power at Washington that can hold up for a series of generations any people in the permanent state of illiteracy in which the majority of the Southern Negroes are at present found. This illiteracy is simply a mixture of ignorance, superstition, shiftlessness, vulgarity, and vice. The General and State Governments, aided all the while by private benevolence and missionary zeal, can surround these people with an environment of valuable opportunities. Indeed, in many respects, they are now environed with such helps and encouragements as no race of European lineage has enjoyed at a similar stage of its history. But the test question is, has the Negro, on the whole, during his entire life of three hundred years on American soil, indicated his power to appreciate and use such opportunities for full American citizenship as are now vouchsafed to him by a gracious Providence?

To my mind he had vindicated his capacity for indefinite improvement in this direction even before he received the precious boon of citizenship of the American Republic. Remarkable as his progress in some ways has been during the past twenty-five years of freedom, I would be content to refer to his two centuries of slavery for proof of a remarkable aptitude for civilization. The best evidence for such capacity is a certain unconscious tact, a habit of getting on in a tolerable way under unfavorable circumstances, the turning his sunny and adaptive side to a hard bondage, the eager adaptation to and taking on of all helps to a better state of living. Contemplate, for a moment, this people, landing from an African slave ship on our shores, and contrast with that the status of the American Negro, with all his imperfections, in 1865, when he appeared, the last comer that has stepped over the threshold of the higher civilization and begun the upward career. How can that amazing progress in practical ability, in adaptation to the habits and manners of civilized life, reception of a Christian faith, be accounted for on the theory of perpetual childishness, as a race characteristic? Did any people, under a similar strain, realizing, as the negro did, the awful issues of the mighty Civil war, amid which his closing years of servitude were involved, ever bear itself with such personal fidelity to present duty, with such remarkable wisdom and tact, with such complete reliance on Providence for the result?

Bishop Haygood says the religion of the Negro accounts for his bearing during those tremendous years, when the home life of the South was virtually in his hands.

That a race, less than two centuries out of the jungle of African paganism, was found so imbued with the central element of Christianity, is evidence that it is not the perpetual child of humanity. Grant the failure of the Negro, during the fearful years that followed the war, to govern States rocking in the throes of a defeated rebellion, exasperated to the death by all the passions that wreck the souls of men and communities. Still, what a display of ability of many sorts, the practical faculty of getting a living, often the higher faculty that has thrown up thousands of shrewd, successful people, there was! Radical that he is, the Negro has shown himself the most politic of peoples in his endurance of what could not be overcome, and his tactful, even crafty, appropriation of all opportunities. He has pushed in at every open door, listened at the white man's table, hung about church and the stump, taken in the great public day, looked on when he did not vote at the election. He has been all eyes and ears, and every pore of his skin has been open to the incoming of his only possible education. Deprived of books and the ordinary apparatus of instruction, he has used all the more eagerly the agencies of God's supreme University, human life—used them so much better than several millions of "the superior race" that, in proportion to his opportunity, he has made more out of the Southern American life than any other Southern people.

On the eve of the day when the great assembly of Confederate veterans at Richmond solemnly buried their old cause in the unveiling of the statue of their great military commander, I sat on a platform, before a crowded congregation of Negro citizens, in the city of Washington, gathered at the commencement exercises of Wayland Seminary. Eighteen young men and women, all from Virginia, received the diploma, and ten of them appeared in the usual way. As I looked over that audience of well-dressed, well-mannered, appreciative people, and listened to the speeches of those young folk, so marked by sobriety of style, soundness of thought, practical views of life, lofty consecration of purpose, and comprehensive patriotism; as I read their class motto, "Not to be ministered unto, but to minister," and remembered that only two hundred and seventy years ago the first cargo of African pagan savages was landed on the shore of the Old Dominion, and all this was the outcome of that—I wondered where were the eyes of men that they did not behold the revelation of Divine Providence in this little less than the miraculous evolution of the new citizenship of a State destined yet to praise and magnify the ways of God in American affairs. Say that this only demonstrates his "power of imitation." But what is this mysterious faculty of "imitation," that everybody says the Negro has to the last degree, but another name for a capacity for civilization? Nine-tenths of our human education is imitating what a superior person does, from the child repeating its mother's words, to the saint "putting on the Lord Jesus Christ."

It may be granted that, in one respect, slavery was a help to this progress. It protected the Negro from his lower self, on the side of vagrancy; and that is "the terrible temptation" of every people in its rudimentary years. He was protected against vagrancy, laziness, drunkenness, and several temptations of a semitropical clime which are too much for thousands of his betters. But here has been a sore obstacle to his success in his new estate of freedom. A great wrong that has been done him during these years has been the neglect to enforce order, decency, and industry, along with the observance of the common moralities of every-day life, by the people among whom he has lived. What would be the condition of New England to-day had her people tolerated, in the multitudes of foreign-born peasants who have landed on her shores, the vagrancy, laziness, shiftlessness, dependence on common charity, with the perpetual violation of the minor morals which confront the observer, from every part of the civilized world, in his travels throughout the Southern States? Here was the place for the Anglo-Saxon to assert his superiority, by insisting on the common observance of the common order, decencies, and moralities of life, in and out of the household, by the freedman. For lack of this, the vagrant class has been left virtually at large, like a plague of frogs and lice over all the land, choking up the towns and villages, making good housekeeping for the Southern woman the most trying human lot, and surrounding childhood of every condition and class with such temptations as no people can permanently resist.

If the well-disposed class, the majority, could have been aided by the law of the land and public opinion to move on unhindered by this intolerable impediment, the last twenty-five years would have told a far different tale. Of course, the white people of the South do not realize this. Slavery was a police that made vagrancy impossible, and the lower slave element was securely locked up under the Argus eyes of the old-time system of labor. I am not here to defend any denial of the suffrage, or social or industrial disability, inflicted on the negro citizen; but I give it as my deliberate conviction that all these things have not been so harmful to the Negro as this strange neglect of the Anglo-Saxon South to enforce the recognized policy of all civilized lands on its vagrant colored and white class, at the very time when this race specially needed the primary lessons of sobriety, obedience to law, everyday morality, and of that hard work without which "no man shall eat." Yet, spite of this drawback (and only an observer from a differently regulated community can appreciate what a drawback), the better-disposed class of the Negroes has signally vindicated its capacity for civilization within the limitations of personal and race impediments, and in the use it has made of its opportunities.

I observe, also, in the average Negro, an amiability, a patience and forbearance, a capacity for affectionate devotion, sacrifice, and unselfishness, that separate him decisively from the savage and the savage side of civilized life. What an element of civil, social, and industrial lubrication this may become, has already become, in our grating, pitiless, ferocious Anglo-Saxon greed of power, gain, and all kinds of superiority, any man can realize who sees the working of it in a thousand ways. I I can understand why the Southerner feels a certain loneliness amid the splendors and well-ordered regulations of our higher Northern life. He misses the atmosphere of kindliness, broad good humor, real belief in human nature that the Negro always diffuses around himself. I feel it the moment I touch a Northern city on my return from every annual visit to the South; and I thank God that the Negro "man and brother," especially the woman and sister, were sent by heaven to teach our proud, restless, too often inhuman civilization some of the amenities that outlive the inhumanities and finally bring in the kingdom of God.

Another quality the Negro displays, of great promise in the future, though so often turned to his disadvantage in the present—a love of approbation, self-possession, and an ability to "put his best foot foremost" and show for all he is worth, the perpetual assertion that he is going to be somebody some time. "Why did you sell that corn you promised to me?" said a white parson to his negro "brother in the ministry." "Well, boss, I got a bigger price for it." "But was that honest?" "No, it warn't that." "Why did you do it?" "Because, boss, I warn't the man I took myself to be."

It is well to "take yourself to be" a man of parts and character, even at the peril of disappointment. And that persistent pushing to the front, crowding in at every open door, "claiming the earth," which now makes the life of the most sensible and considerate white citizen of the South often a weariness, sometimes a despair, in his dealing with the Negro, is the prophecy of an aspiration for better things and a loftiness of manhood and womanhood of vital importance.

Along with this is the eagerness for knowledge that is still a characteristic even of the ignorant classes, though less apparent now than in the years following the war. Spite of the neglect of the proper conditions and the means of gaining this precious boon for the children the average Negro, in humble estate, believes in the school with a vigor that in the lower European classes is not developed, more than in the corresponding class among the Southern whites. Discontent with a low estate is the movement power of American civilization, and no class in America is less content with its own infirmities than the better sort, the majority of the freedmen.

Another valuable characteristic is the good taste, love of beauty, native capacity for ornamental art, which always appear in the Negro when suitably encouraged. The handwriting in the colored schools is often remarkable, the drawing uniformily respectable, the taste in dress, the arrangements of flowers and ornaments, above the average of any corresponding class in the country. In the negro the new South has its most valuable deposits of " raw material" for the best operative and mechanical class for that clime and country. Already he is domesticated in all these mechanical and operative industries, with the exception of the cotton mills, where the labor is still monopolized by the poorer white class, greatly to its own advantage. Here is a great work being done by the numerous mission schools of the higher sort, supported by the Christian people of the North, in the organization of industrial education. In this important branch of schooling the superior class of negro youth has, so far, enjoyed greater opportunities than the corresponding class of white youth. And, although the graduates of these schools will not be day laborers or servants, yet, as teachers, housekeepers, and general leaders of their people they will exert a prodigous influence in the years to come. The introduction of a simple and practical annex for industrial education, for both sexes, in the school system of the South, especially for the negro children, would be a movement of incalculable value to the whole people of that region, so much in need of intelligent and skilled labor in the uprising of its new industrial life.

All these qualities tell in the steady progress of large numbers of these people toward a more comfortable, wholesome, and respectable way of living. This is evident especially to a regular visitor not involved in the wear and tear of 7,000,000 freedmen getting on their citizen legs, as are our Southern white brothers and sisters. I see everywhere, every year, a larger number of well-looking, well-dressed, well-churched, housed, well-mannered colored people. One reason why our Southern friends are not so impressed with this upward movement is that as soon as a colored family gets above the humble or vagrant class it somehow disappears from ordinary view. One inevitable result of the social boycott that shuts down on every negro family that attains respectability is that its white neighbors are put out of connection with this class and left to the tender mercies of the class beneath, where their patience is worn out and, too often, the impression taken for the whole race. The estimate of the increasing wealth of the Negroes is often disputed, but at the most reasonable figure it is a significant testimony to the growth of practical enterprise and steady improvement in the upper strata of the whole body.

While the acknowledged vices of the race are still a terrible weight on the lower and a constant temptation and humiliation to the better class, it is not certain that any of them, save those "failings that lean to virtue's side," are especially " race defects." A distinguished physician of Alabama has shown that the illegitimate births among the negro population of the black belt of that State are in the exact per cent of the Kingdom of Bavaria. Certainly the vices of the lower class of the south of Europe people that are now swarming the shores of the Gulf States are not less common and far more dangerous than those of the Negro. Human nature in its lower estate, especially when shot out from its barbarism into the devil-side of civilization, is fearfully deficient in its appreciation of the ten commandments. But I believe no people of the humbler sort are making more progress in overcoming the weakness of the appetites and getting in sight of the Christian moralities than the better sort of the Negroes. In the church, the home, and the school I see the growth of a self-respecting manhood and womanhood that in due time will tell.

Though differing from many whose opinions and experience I respect, I do not regard the temporary isolation of the Negro in the Southern church, school, and society so much an evil as a providential aid in gaining the self-respect and habit of self-help absolutely essential to good citizenship. Spite of the hard side of slavery the Negro has not had his fair share of the rough training that brings out the final results and the determination that tell in history. A habit of dependence, even to the extent of servility, in the lower orders is still one of his most dangerous temptations. He has also been greatly tried by being for a generation the romantic figure of American life, the especial object of philanthropic interest in church, state, and society, everywhere outside the sixteen Southern States. It is well that he should be relieved for a while from these temptations. In company with the white boy, the negro boy on the same school bench would all the time be tempted to fall into his old position of an annex to the white man, and in the church would be under a strain that would sorely tax his manhood. Where he is he grows up with a wholesome confidence in himself. His own best people are teaching him with no hindrance the law of responsible manhood and womanhood. The result is that when he emerges into active life, if he has well appropriated his training, he is in a position to treat with a similar class of white people on terms that insure mutual respect.

I am struck with this feature of Southern society—the constant "working together for good" of the better class, especially of the men of both races in all communities. The outrage of a drunken rabble upon a negro settlement is published to all the world, while the constant intercourse of the respectable classes of men of the two races, that prevents a thousand such outbreaks and makes Southern life, on the whole, orderly, like the progress of the seasons and the hours, goes on in silence. It is not necessary to project the social question into the heart of communities in this state of transition. The very zealous brethren of the press and the political fold, who are digging this "last ditch" of social caste, away out in the wilderness, half a century ahead of any present emergency, may be assured that nobody in the United States will ever be obliged to associate with people disagreeable to him, and that, as Thomas Jefferson suggested, "if we educate the children of to-day, our descendants will be wiser than we, and many things that seem impossible to us may be easily accomplished by them." At present, the office of colored teacher and preacher is the noblest opportunity for general usefulness granted to an educated, righteous, and able young man or woman in any land. That teacher or preacher becomes the man or woman of all spiritual work to a constituency singularly appreciative; if instructed in industrial craft, all the more valuable. I am amazed at the assertion of some eminent people that the superior education of the negro youth has been a failure. If the destiny of the Negro is only that of a child-peasant forever, this is true; but, if his range of possibility is what we believe, no such result of even a modified form of the secondary and higher education, with industrial accompaniments, has ever been seen in Christendom, as is evident to any man who regards this side of the life of this people with open eyes.

All that I have said bears on a fundamental truth concerning the uplifting of the American Negro citizen. The Northern white man, especially if a philanthropist, regards the Negro as an annex to the Northern, the Southern white man regards him as an annex to the Southern, white citizen; but the Negro is anything but an annex to anybody. He is an original element, providentially injected into American civilization; the only man who did not come to us of his own will. It may turn out, for that reason, that he is to be the "little child that shall lead them," and finally compel a reconciliation of all the distracting elements of our national life. Every race that has any outcome finally demonstrates its capacity by throwing up a superior class by which it is led, stimulated, and gradually lifted to its own highest achievement of civilization. Tried by this test, the Negro is not behind.

I have spoken so far of the average man and woman of the race, but that observer must be strangely blinded who does not see the evidence of the formation of a genuine aristocracy of intelligence, character, industry, and superior living among these millions. I do not refer to that unfortunate class who assert a superficial superiority by separation from their people and an uneasy longing to be recognized by their white superiors. I mean the growing class that is trying, under a solemn sense of gratitude to God, love to the brother, and consecrated patriotism, to lift up its own race. Among the 7,000,000 of this people in the United States there must be several hundred thousand of this sort. They are found everywhere, all the way from Massachusetts to Texas. They already form a distinct society, and the most American of all our great newspapers, the Cincinnati Commercial Gazette, has already recognized the fact by the prominent "Colored Society Column" in its Sunday morning issue. This class is becoming a distinct power, and its influence on the classes below is one of the most important elements of the race problem. It is already on good terms with the corresponding class of white people, though differing in politics and often grieved by what it regards public, social, and industrial injustice.

One significant fact in this connection is that now the Negro is the most determined Southerner. The young Southern white man, relieved from the attractions of the old aristocratic position of slaveholder, like all American young men of parts, is on the lookout for the main chance. The South is less and less to him a name to charm with. His own State no longer seems to him a "nation" which claims his uttermost devotion. A million of these young men, it is said, have left the South for the North and Northwest since the war. Whole regions of these older States are as steadily drained of this important population as the older portions of the Northeast. The Southern young woman will follow as soon as her call is heard. At present she is the "mainstay" of the rural South, the good angel of its coming civilization, getting more education and having more to do with the upper story of Southern life than her average male companion who stays at home. But the Negro loves the sacred soil, the old home, the climate, and its surroundings. In due time he will become the dominant occupant of large portions of the lowland South. He has no more idea of going to Africa than the Southern Jew of going into business in Jerusalem. He will move about as he becomes more intelligent and understands his own interests, but he is the Southerner of to-day, and all persuasions or threats that would dislodge him are vain. As the political issues of the past fade into the distance, he will more and more act in all public affairs with the leading race, with whom his companionship and interest belong. He must be educated where he is, and, as the years go on, he will rise to the call of his own superior class and find his own place—a great and beneficent place in our wonderful American family.

Education is the lever that will raise this great mass of humanity to the high plane of full American citizenship. I believe it would be a great blessing to the whole South, could the suffrage, educational, labor, and vagrant laws of Massachusetts be incorporated into the legislation of every Southern State. Protection to the child, suppression of vagrancy, enforcement of industry, and educational test of suffrage, better churching, improvement in the home, reading of good books, all the influences that are so potent in any respectable Northern community, will in good time achieve the success of every class and race of the American people. For the Negro, two-thirds of this education must be, for a generation, outside the schoolroom, in the broad university of the new Southern American life. If we only knew it, this is one of the richest educational opportunities God has ever vouchsafed to any people.

What a call is this opportunity for missionary service, in its broadest and loftiest aspect, to the whole American people. Every theory of despair on the race problem proceeds from a pagan or atheistic estimate of human nature and destiny, and leads down to despotism or anarchy. Without the blessed gospel of Christ our American race problem would be too awful to contemplate. Thank God, it did not come to us in an age of pagan darkness, of mediæval violence, in a land crowded with people, in a civilization cursed by the bitter results of a long and stormy past. It came to us in an opening age of light, when all the celestial forces are at an upward slant, when the Church is getting itself together to work for man while God takes care of the creeds, in a country so large and bountiful that hundreds of millions would not crowd it, and "every man may sit under his own vine and fig tree, with no one to molest and make afraid."

As I am borne through the vast spaces of our marvellous Southern land, and stand in amazement before its revelations of resources, hitherto unknown, I ask myself—

Is this only to become the theater of a greater greed of gain, "a hazard of new fortunes," its only outcome a semitropical materialism, an inevitable temptation to a dismal era of "booms" and "syndicates" and "trusts," with a new insanity for the almighty dollar, so powerless to satisfy the deeper need of the humblest human heart? May it not, rather, be God's summons to such an awakening of our overworked and materialized American people as will compel them, in sheer self-defense, to give mind and heart and hand to that lifting up of the lowly, and that preaching the gospel of self-help to the poor, which is the end of Christian charity? I look for the day when the divided churches of our three great Protestant denominations will be brought together by the growing sense of this "home mission" claim, and the whole church and the adjacent realm of the world be polarized in one supreme effort to solve this old caste puzzle of the nations and ages, by showing that the simple gospel of Christ means peace on earth and good will to all men.

But now comes the final question, on which not so much the destiny of the Negro citizen as the very existence of Southern American civilization depends. Will the Anglo-Saxon Southern people, at present nine-tenths of the entire white population, in due time appreciate this opportunity and join hands with all good men and women at home and abroad in this the grandest crusade of all the ages?

I have no doubt that the race problem will finally be solved in the South largely through the agency of the Southern Anglo-Saxon people; not over their heads, but with their thorough coöperation. I see already, amid superficial indications to the contrary, the converging lines of this tendency, and below hostile theories the inevitable drift of the common life of all these great Commonwealths towards the American type of society.

I see the positive indication of this great convergence of opinion especially in what may be called the educational public of the South. By this I mean that portion of the Southern people of all classes and both races which within the past twenty-five years, amid difficulties and complications almost unconquerable elsewhere, has quietly and persistently laid the foundations of the American system of universal education in every State, county, city, and neighborhood in these sixteen Commonwealths.

The common school is so much the habit and unquestioned postulate of republican government everywhere in the North that we have never done half justice to the people of the sixteen Southern States for this, by all odds, the most significant movement of the past generation this side the water. That a people, in 1860 the most aristocratic in the organization of its society upon earth, who fought through a bloody war and only fell in "the last ditch" of the absolute ruin of their old social order, should have risen up from this awful overthrow, cleared the ground of rubbish, and with scarcely any aid that they could use, of their own will have planted on the soil the one institution that is the eternal foe of everything save republican government and democratic society, is the wonder of the age and the complete vindication of the essential Americanism of the Southern people. It would be well for our cynical scholars and self-confident politicians who dilate on the imperfections of this system of education, to remember what Massachusetts was fifty years ago, when Horace Mann drew his sword; what Pennsylvania was thirty years ago, when Wickersham took command; what even to-day some portions of the older Atlantic States are declared by the testimony of their own educational authorities to be. Doubtless there has been exaggeration of the achievement of the South in popular education, partly through ignorance, more in the way of home advertisement, most in the inierest of the defeat of the Blair bill. But with all this drawback, the Southern people have taken "the first step that costs," and established the free school for all classes and both races, unsectarian, but practically one of the most potent moral and religious forces of this section, growing all the time, already beyond the peril of destruction or serious damage from its numerous enemies, and it "has come to stay." True, the educational public has not half converted the average Southern politician, for whom, as Gen. Grant said, "there is too much reading and writing now." It has not yet entirely swung the Southern clergy and the church over to its hearty support as against the old-time Protestant parochial and private system of instruction. It is still a social outsider in some regions, and through vast spaces of the rural South it is so poor that it seems to have hindered more than helped the better-off classes who shoulder its expenses. But it has for the first time gone down into the basement story of the Southern household, bearing that common schooling to the lower orders and the "plain people," which means modern civilization and progressive Christianity, involving the full committal to the new American order of affairs. It is a wonder that the leading classes of the North—the press, the political organizations, the industrial leaders, even the philanthropists—are still so imperfectly informed concerning this, by all odds, the most vital and significant end of Southern life. The splendid mission work of our Northern churches, which indirectly has so greatly aided the growth of the schools for the Negroes by training their teachers, has sometimes obscured the magnitude of the home work. But this, with the remarkable rally of the whole secondary and higher education, is a demonstration that the South has no intention of remaining permanently in any second place in the great educational movement of the time. Imperfect as the common school is, the Negro has been the greatest gainer therefrom, for through it and all that goes along therewith he is laying up a steady increase of self-respect, intelligence, and practical power, which will astonish many good people who still go on repeating the parrot cry that education has only demoralized the younger negro generation for the industrial side of life. But it is not what the common schools have done, but what the Southern people have failed to do to reënforce them, that still holds thousands of negro youth in the bonds of a vagrancy, shiftlessness, and debasement that deserve all things that can be said against them. The cure for this is more and better education, reënforced by the policy of every civilized land in the suppression of the devil side of society that will ruin the greatest country under the sun.

But, below and beyond this open and evident work of education, I see more clearly, every year, that the logic of the new Southern life is all on the side of the final elevation of the Negro to the essential rights and opportunities of American citizenship; and, beyond, to the generous coöperation with the nation in aiding him to make his own best use of that supreme opportunity. We, at the North, are constantly misled by the press, which is a very poor representative of this most important element of Southern life. We hear the superficial talk and read of the disorder that is the inevitable accompaniment of States in the transition from a great civil war to their final adjustment to the national life. An eminent educator of the South writes me: "Ask 100 men at the street corner what they think about the education of the Negro, and 75 of them will demur, and some of them will swear. The next day every man of them will vote for the higher school tax that gives the Negro a better schoolhouse and the permanent establishment of his education." Our Southern friends are no more logical than other portions of the country, and the superficial life of all countries is constantly adjusting itself to the logic of its undertow. I can see in more ways than I could explain, even to a Northern community, that these people are "in the swim" whose tide can only drift them off into regions of life which seem almost impossible to them to-day.

The test of this drift is that, spite of all obstacles and embarrassments, there is, in every respectable Southern community, no real hinderance to an intelligent, moral, industrious, and prudent negro family getting all out of American life that anybody expects, save that social and, in some localities, political recognition, that are the last achievements of long periods of social evolution in national affairs. In all essential respects the negro citizen is better off in the South than in any Northern State. The outward opportunities for full association with the white population in the North are, after all, of little value in comparison with the substantial opportunity for becoming the great laboring agricultural class and of capturing the field of mechanical and operative labor. It will be his own fault if he permits the insolent naturalized foreign element that now dominates our Northern industrial centers to elbow him off into a peasantry or a menial and subordinate laboring population.

As I look at the way in which these 7,000,000 people are gaining all the vital opportunities of life among the 12,000,000 of their Anglo-Saxon neighbors, I am amazed at the way they seem to go on, only half-conscious of what the rest of the world is saying about them, "working out their own salvation" by the power that is in them, in the only way by which an American people can finally succeed. The only fit symbol of this mighty movement is the Mississippi River, after it has become "the inland sea" of the Southland. States and their peoples, Congress and the Nation, scientists and cranks, debate and experiment on the way to put the "Father of Waters" in harness, to tie up this awful creature that holds the fate of 10,000,000 people in its every-day whim. But all discourse, legislation, and experiment at last run against the question, what will the Mississippi River do with us next week? So, while the Southern people and the Nation are wrestling with what they choose to call the "race problem," this inland, Southern human ocean, searching and spreading and pushing into every nook and corner of the lowland, is going on its way; and every deliverance of the scientist, the socialist, and the statesman, brings up against some new and unexpected thing that the Negro has really done. "How are you getting on with your neighbors down here?" said I to a deputation of fine-looking colored men, who stepped out of a carriage and presented me with a well-written address of welcome to the city of Vicksburg. "Well, we used to have trouble; but we have finally concluded the white man has come to stay, and we adjust ourselves to that fact." The white man has indeed come to stay all over the United States of America; but he will stay, not always as the white man proposes, but as God Almighty disposes. And, wherever he abides, he will finally be compelled, by the logic of American events, to stay in peace and justice, in freedom and order, in Christian coöperation with all the great elements of a republican society, shaped from all the peoples that a beneficent Providence has called to abide together in this, God's morning land.

VI.

THE THIRD ESTATE OF THE SOUTH.

An address delivered before the American Social Science Association, Saratoga, N. Y.,
September 2, 1890.

From the beginning of the European settlement even to the present year of our Lord, the most prominent object of interest and observation in what we used to call the Southern States of this Republic has been the relation of the upper and under classes of Southern society—the slaveholding Anglo-Saxon, and the lately emancipated Negro. Not only abroad, but at home, it has scarcely entered into the calculations of statesmen and economists that a great change in Southern affairs was impending that would bring another dominant class to the front. It was known that even in 1860 there were 6,000,000 white people in these Southern States who had no immediate connection with slaveholding, and that a number of people, smaller than the present population of Boston, representing, possibly, a population of 2,000,000, comprised the ruling class. It was expected that this middle class would be felt in arresting the movement for secession in 1861. And I believe that a decided majority of these people had neither the desire nor intention of striking for a new nationality. But, with the exception of the action of West Virginia and the stubborn loyalty of the mountain populations of the central South, this expectation was disappointed. We met these people on the battlefield through four dismal years, where they earned a reputation for good fighting which has made the name of an American soldiery illustrious.

But now, like a mighty apparition across the Southern horizon, has arisen this hope or portent of the South—the Third Estate—to challenge the authority of the old ruling class, and place itself where the "plain people" of every Northern State was long ago established, as a decisive influence in public affairs. South Carolina, the head and front of the old South, is now swept by a political revolution as radical as the emancipation of the slaves in 1865. Texas, where the old order never got complete foothold, is now passing under the same control, so easily that it is not half understood what weighty concerns are involved in the coming political movements of this growing State. Other States, especially on the Gulf, are rent by the same movement from below. It is evident that this is no surface or temporary affair. Its present political and financial theories will be largely modified by the rough discipline of responsible power. But the movement is in the line of American civilization, and, however checked or misdirected for the time, will finally prevail.

The wise observer of Southern affairs will greatly mistake if he insists on the exclusive observation of the old conflict of races and the political condition of the Negro. For the coming decade the place to watch the South is in this movement of the rising Third Estate. What it demands and what it can achieve in political, social, and industrial affairs; what changes can be wrought in itself by the great uplifting forces of American civilization—by education, including the influence of the family, the church, and the school—on these things will depend the fate of this important section of our country for years to come. And on the outcome of this movement hangs the near future of the race question—whether the swarming millions of colored citizens in these sixteen States will gradually reach their fit position in the body politic, or the whole South be plunged into the horrors of a race war, which will once more demand the strong arm of the Nation to save that section from suicide.

The present essay, the Third Estate of the South, is an honest attempt to give my own opinions concerning this, one of the most important movements in the history of the Republic. The assumption of infallible wisdom and the ventilation of wholesale theories, North and South, in the discussion of Southern affairs is the misery of our public life. A virtual residence of ten years in this region, including all the sixteen States, with good opportunities for observation, has deepened the impression that, of all the social and civic puzzles that confront the American social scientist and statesman, no knot is so tangled, so difficult to be undone, so dangerous to be cut by the sword, as this. To-day the South, as a section, has passed into a permanent minority of sixteen of the forty-four States. But it is still possible to array these States again in a conflict that would inflict a wound on the Southern member through which the Republic would bleed to death. It is "easy as preaching" to embroil and exasperate whole commonwealths, great classes and races, in a permanent misunderstanding that not even another Washington or Lincoln could reconcile. Even as concerns the South itself the question is one of vital interest. The spectacle of the 500,000 white people of South Carolina split into hostile clans by a political campaign now foaming on the ragged reef of violence is inexpressibly painful and discouraging. I shall not try to deal with this question by the ambitious methods of grand analysis, abstract theorizing, or inflated prophecy. If I can cast a little side light upon this procession as it moves on its twilight path it may not be in vain that I occupy the time of the reader.

In the European sense, there never was a Southern aristocracy. The descendants of the few European families of the favored class who drifted to the colonies never had a perceptible influence after the war of the Revolution. The abolition of all special privileges reduced the superior colonial class to the condition of the leading class in a republic of white men. There was a social "upper ten," in the original Southern Atlantic colonies, that held on indefinitely. But that largely disappeared, as a family affair, beyond the Alleghanies, where the new leading class made its way upward by personal power and solid service as certainly as in the Northwestern States.

But, in the American political sense, there was and has been, up to the present time, a dominant class in this portion of the country more powerful for all the issues of public life than any order of nobility in Europe since the French revolution. It was, primarily, a combination of landholders; practically, an aristocracy of the dollar. From the peculiar condition of the country and its monopoly of certain industrial products, the people of the South adopted and tied itself to the system of slave labor, cast off by the North as unprofitable, impolitic, and dangerous at the formation of the Republic. Whatever of anti-slavery sentiment—and there was a great deal—lingered in the early history of these States was swept downstream by the gathering tide of the dominating industrial and political interests. So it came to pass, in time, that a great combination of men, separated from each other by abysses of social, religious, and educational repulsions, found common cause in the protection of slavery in the old and its introduction to the new Southern and Southwestern States. The diaries and correspondence of Judge Story and John Quincy Adams, during their early years in Washington, are full of this observation of the formidable power of this combination—its skillful handling of Congress, its invariable success in every conflict with a half conscious and divided North.

And without indorsing the exaggerated rhetoric of our Southern college commencements concerning the splendor of this class during "the golden age" of Southern society, we may grant to this combination the praise of remarkable ability and, on some lines, of broad foresight in national affairs. It was composed almost wholly of the ablest, most politic, and persistent class in modern history—the British upper middle class—modified by the influences and interests of its peculiar position on the edge of Christendom. It made all things subordinate to the chief end of favoring the Southern ambition to become the ruling power of the country. The professional classes became its spokesmen and allies. The leisure of its landed proprietors fostered a universal ambition among its young men for political activity as the be-all and end-all of life. Its schools were a reproduction of the British system of education a century ago—universities, colleges, and academies for the upper white class, more completely under the administration of the Protestant clergy than the schools of Catholic Europe are now under the control of that astute priesthood; well adjusted to lift up the promising youth below to companionship with his betters, and elbow off the "common herd" into a widespread illiteracy. Its women, among the most brilliant and capable in the world, were no such tribe of imbeciles and idlers as we fancied in the North. The Southern matron in her plantation life was one of the most overtaxed and devoted workingwomen of her sex. Outside this domain female culture gravitated to the social ability which gave her the lead at Washington, and till a late period made her the nation's best social foot put foremost on the shores of Europe.

This political aristocracy, in all vital affairs, governed the Republic till it was moved to rise up and divide the nation in 1861. It instigated and brought on the condition of war against the Indians, Great Britain, and Mexico, by which the country was distracted through its first seventy years. It was the author of the magnificent scheme of the expansion of territory which gave us the empire of Louisiana, Florida, Texas, the Pacific coast—all the additions to our territory except the latest purchase, Alaska. It led in the settlement of the West, following the sagacious policy of Washington, whose eye was always glancing over to the wilderness beyond the Alleghanies. Tennessee and Kentucky were in a blaze of Indian border war, while the Northwest slumbered almost undisturbed.

It is difficult to understand why a class so able and astute in many ways was led on to the hazardous experiment of dividing the Union in 1860. With the Constitution on its side, with an indefinite power of congressional obstruction, it could have kept slavery for a long generation, and made the country pay the cost of a modified system of emancipation. The reasons seem to be found in the absorption of a powerful society, engrossed in the work of self-preservation, in a strangely isolated position. Pushed off to the border of civilization with only a half barbarous Mexico and a boundless wilderness on the Southwest, and a vast and lonely seaboard all around, shut off by its own theory and purpose from contact with the rising tide of progressive modern life, its literary, professional, and social influences all captured and held in subjection by the political intolerance which is the most unrelenting form of tyranny, it was not strange that this group of accomplished statesmen fell into the delusion, not only of their own sectional invincibility, but honestly believed that their political allies in the North would, in the last event, consent to their demand of virtual permanent control of the General Government, or a separation on sectional lines. A distinguished citizen of Boston, during the summer preceding Mr. Lincoln's election, was for a time in daily confidential communication with Jefferson Davis. He reports that he found his distinguished acquaintance completely possessed with the idea of the military and civic superiority of the South, and the willingness of the dominant party in the North to consent to whatever it should demand.

How this came out we all know. The world has acknowledged the prodigious ability and matchless devotion with which the dominant class went through this desperate programme, to the terrible end of its own destruction. Its military commanders have furnished many forcible and picturesque and one noble figure to American history. Its statesmanship, now disparaged, was probably as competent as a cause so at odds with the trend of modern civilization would admit. But we do not yet recognize fairly the great services rendered to the South and the Nation later on by this class, even in the demoralized state in which it was left by the war, when not one in ten of its families was found upon or has since stood on a solid financial footing. Its young men were scattered to the Southwest, to the Northwest, to the growing cities, leaving the open country in charge of a class that, in the old time, had little influence in affairs. Its women gathered up the wrecks of a great destruction, in true American style; and to-day the young women of the better sort of Southern families are the hope of the country, rehabilitating the homes, the soul of the Church, the best school teachers, the leaders in the temperance reform, on the lookout for all industrial opportunities that can be used.

The leaders in the war naturally became the leaders of reconstruction politics. And, whatever may be the verdict of history concerning the way in which the eleven ex-Confederate States have been placed in line to receive a share of the progressive life of the country, the display of ability has fully borne out their old reputation. The South to-day owes about all it has of order and law, the common school for all classes and both races, the restoration of its religious and educational affairs, to the administration of this class. The great obstacle to the progress of the Negro is not his old master class, for among these people are often found the wisest and most Christian views concerning the development of their old bondmen, and an amount of personal sacrifice and patience that only a constant observer can appreciate. I do not know what New Boston, with her 500,000 people, would do if suddenly overwhelmed by an avalanche of the 700,000 South Carolina negroes, marshaled by our redoubtable friend, Gen. B. F. Butler, in a solid colored contingent, to capture the city government, administer its vast interests, handle its twenty million debt, and, in public affairs, represent it to the world. I fancy the "weight of the meeting" would there prevail, by some of the numerous methods by which an Anglo-Saxon community everywhere, in the end, manages to put inferiority on the back seat and land the management of vital affairs in the upper story.

But it was inevitable that this long lease of power by the Southern dominant class should come to an end. In New England and New York, the aristocratic States of the old North, this change was gradually wrought by the educational influences that prepared the humbler classes, native or foreign born, for the responsibilities of power. Eighty-five per cent of the men worth $100,000 or more, in these States, began with nothing but this outfit. But in the South the progress of the Third Estate has been slow; indeed, until the past twenty years, it had hardly begun. But all things hasten, even in the piney woods or mountain realms of our southland, and now, under the simple name of a "Farmers' Alliance," this mighty army of the common people has been revealed, like a frowning mountain world uncovered by a rising mist. Already it may be predicted that the old order, as far as it depended on the European qualities of family and class training, has gone by. Hereafter, the South follows the North in the rush to the front of the fittest who survive. And the contest for place will be on industrial lines there as here.

For a time to come I believe the Negro question is to be held in partial subordination by this great uprising of the Third Estate. Certain it is, that the attempt to lift the negro citizenship of the South out of its natural place, the rear column of its civilization, will be a stupendous blunder. The child in a family, however bright and promising, can only play at being the equal of his elders; though he can make a big disturbance, break the harmony, and mar the peace of the household. To suppose that 7,000,000 citizens, in the condition of our Southern Negroes, twenty-five years out of personal slavery, can by any device be wrenched from their present position and shot ahead of the 12,000,000 plain white people who have been on the ground for two hundred years, and must become the dominant power of the South for generations to come, is only to indulge in the dream of an enthusiast.

But whether the white man of the Third Estate can rid himself of the old theories of race and caste, and adopt the American idea that all men shall be fairly tested by what they can do, depends on many contingencies. Is it possible or probable, in a period sufficiently brief to avoid the danger of a disastrous race conflict, that this vast constituency can be brought over to the practical American view of giving to every child the great American chance in life? I do not know. But I greatly hope; and the sources of my hope, or some of them, I now declare.

When the history of the South descends from the realm of romance, where it still lingers, to the solid ground of fact, it will be seen how absurd everywhere outside the domain of legend is the impression of a radical difference between its original population and the old Northeast. Nobody pretends that the Southwest, beyond the Alleghanies, was peopled by a line of "gentler" descent than the Northwest. About all the South had to show in Revolutionary days of great statesmanship and eminent patriotism was, like the similar class in the North, a descent from the respectable middle estate of Great Britain. But, when we turn to the Third Estate— always the majority, and now rising to the head and front of the new South—we find the source of its power, as in the North, in the mixture of population from a dozen sorts of vigorous European people. The Catholic churchman and dissenting Englishman of various social degrees, the Scotch and the North Irish Protestant, the early German of the valley of Virginia, the Huguenot of South Carolina, the Highlander, Hebrew, and other miscellany of old Georgia, the Creole, Frenchman and Spaniard in Louisiana, all went into the seething caldron of the early colonial life. Up to a generation before the war came in a steady immigration of excellent people from New England and the Middle States. I rarely visit a town in the five old Atlantic Commonwealths that I do not find the descendants of these people—always glad to renew the old-time associations with home. The accident of a change of residence alone prevented the Rhetts of South Carolina from being a Boston, and the later Winthrops of Massachusetts a Charleston, family. Along with this uniformly good stock drifted in at an early date a baser element, brought to the colonies on indenture—the lower sort of the English cities, whose descendants even now in Maryland and Delaware rank low in the social scale. The growing power of slavery intensified the separation of the respectable sort from the common lot. The illiteracy of whole regions of the country wrought its perfect work in the "poor white trash," resembling the Northern tramp, except that he is not only too shiftless to work, but too lazy to tramp.

How the strange population of the great central mountain world—near two millions at present—was formed nobody seems to know. This region was a mysterious "no man's land" till the enterprise of the last twenty-five years revealed it, with all its natural sublimity and beauty and its industrial importance, to an astonished world. Perhaps from the Revolutionary Tories of the adjacent States, from criminals, outcasts, eccentrics, and broken-down people in general, with a sprinkling of more ambitious blood, was made up that people which, even now, seen among the mountains overlooking the valley of Virginia, but better observed in east Kentucky, Tennessee, western North Carolina, and northern Georgia, sends forth a louder cry for the missionary of civilization than any portion of the Republic.

So far as variety of material is concerned, the old colonial South had an equal mixture of blood with the old North. Of late the trend of European immigration has not taken a southern direction, and the per cent of foreign-born population in all the Southern States east of the Mississippi is very small. A most interesting fact for the historical inquirer is the explanation of the origin of the Southern white people, and the romance of the reality will eclipse the glamour of rhetorical mist in which the origin of this section has been involved.

So it has come about that the present population of this grade in the South is far more homogeneous than in the North. The rough training of the pioneer life welded these various elements into one people. Even the Louisiana Creole is yielding. A leading merchant of New Iberia, the heart of the Teche district, told me that twenty years ago only one in five of his country customers attempted to speak English, while

now only one in five is compelled to trade in French. A brisk colony in the Northwest has invaded the prairies of southwestern Louisiana, and a Congregational college, with a Yankee president, is established on the old domain of the padres. Yet
there are still great differences in education and efficiency in the different elements
of this people. The coast country, including the immense piney woods empire, still
produces a considerable population of a sort less hopeful than any other of whatso-
ever "previous condition." The lovely Piedmont region, surrounding the great central mountain realm of the old South, has a farming population greatly resembling
the New England country people of my boyhood. The States beyond the Mississippi—
Missouri, western Arkansas, and Texas, the new Southwest—have received more immigration since the war than all the rest of the South: of the best and common sort
of its own; somewhat from abroad; from the Northwest, whose people seem inclined
to edge down into a milder clime; perhaps also a considerable return wave from the
crowd that settled southern Ohio, Illinois, and Indiana in bygone days. It is said a
million young men from the Southern country districts have gone to the cities, the
Northwest, and the Southwest since 1865. They have left on the ground, in some
portions of the old South, a white population, so far as the men are concerned, inferior to the old-time occupants—less capable of reclaiming the country, less inclined
to deal fairly with the colored folk.

But it is almost hopeless to draw a diagram of the Southern Third Estate as it now
exists. Nobody, even to the "manner born," can do it to the satisfaction of the Southern people; for the pride of State, locality, sect, and social condition—what Mr.
Breckinridge calls "the provincial flavor"—are "solid" against any decided estimate of matters so delicate. Before the war, lines were more sharply drawn. While
alert to capture and lift up to companionship and position the rising talent of the
lower class, the old-time ruling set drew hard and fast lines between themselves and
the ordinary non-slave holding people. My first experience of South Carolina was in
1859—in a stage coach bound for the Catskill Mountain House, New York, filled with
a brilliant Charleston group, chiefly ladies. Completely ignoring my presence, the
only man of the company entertained his fair companions all the way up by his ad-
ventures on a tour through the upper counties of "his nation," talking of the people
there, amid peals of laughter, in a way that reminded one of Dr. Johnson and the
literati of London a century ago, defining a Scotchman as "a good fellow, if caught
early." Till the war, a property condition of representation in the South Carolina
legislature gave a power to the lowland slaveholders which was used in a way that
has come back to plague the Commonwealth in the new upheaval of affairs.

The civil war was the great university of the lower masses of the Southern white
people. The Grand Army caught them up in its all-inclosing net; locked them up in
its fierce conscription; marched them all over their own country, with occasional visits
to Northland, outside and inside a Union prison camp. To a people so preternaturally
eager to see and hear and talk, this was a God-send—the beginning of the blessing
that has come to the Southern poor white man equally with his colored brother from
the collapse of the rebellion. The break-up of the old estates, especially in the Gulf
region, brought large numbers of these people down to the lowlands as owners of
farms. The opening up of central Florida sent a wave of immigration from the piney
woods people that still contests the Northern and Western occupation. The mighty
development of the railroad system has remanded the coast country of the Atlantic
and Gulf to a secondary place, and brought up the Piedmont region, in which a large
number of thriving towns have arisen, and which, with the mining and timber lands,
is the seat of the new Southern prosperity. The new Southwest is growing almost as
fast as the new Northwest—an exception to the old South, outside of special districts.

The marvelous growth in the South, of which we hear so much, is largely a development of the mining country bordering the mountains, where a number of new
towns have sprung up and capital is being invested, of the lumber country and special
agricultural districts. But much of the old landed realm is still in no condition to be

rejoiced over. There are more people at work than of old, black and white. The division of farms has stimulated production. In certain quarters skilled agriculture is taking the place of the old-time fumbling with the soil. New fields in Florida, Mississippi, and Texas are opening for the culture of cotton, fruits, truck, and staples. The country people are living somewhat better than ten years ago. But the intolerable "lien system," whereby the town merchant practically owns the land and enslaves its occupants, is a dispensation such as afflicts no large body of civilized people besides in our country. How multitudes of good folk can live at all under such a systematic plunder is only accounted for by their moderate demands for living and the impossibility of getting out of the deadlock alive. The attempt of a class of Southern politicians, in the interest of their pet economic theories, to compare the condition of this portion of their people with that of the farmers of New England and the established portion of the West is simply ludicrous to an observer of the different portions of the country. More than half the people in whole regions of the South outside the better class in the cities are compelled to live in a way that is unknown in these States, except to the lower class of the foreign-born, with little outlook for better times. But this country is capable of recuperation by capital, skill, and especially the occupation of small farms by industrious and thrifty people. In time the better class of the Negroes will come into possession of a great deal of this open country and reclaim it.

It would greatly change the Northern estimate of Southern affairs could the fact be understood that confronts the traveler through the length and breadth of the Southland—that through vast regions, even of the older States, the people are living under the conditions of a border civilization. Not a border country in the sense of our new Western frontier—a vanishing "out into the West," with a furious civilization, armed to the teeth with all the implements of modern progress on its heels. Not the terrible border life that railroad extension and the mining boom make in the new villages extemporized in a howling Southern wilderness. Hundreds of these new towns in the South, where the iron horse reins up and the great steam leviathan wheels round, are a refuge for the drift and diabolism of the whole surrounding country, which appears regularly on "dress parade" in the new city. One little metropolis of this sort in East Tennessee has enjoyed the luxury of a hundred murders since it was struck by the "boom." But this is the old-time border life, where people lived far away from each other and the world, with meager privilege of travel, rarely used, the only town the county seat, and that not often visited. Here is developed an obstinate type of personal independence that stands out, like the iron handle of the town pump, in either sex. But what is not done that can be done in such a life? The man attends to his own little world; defends himself as best he can against wild creatures and wilder men; makes a sharp practical code of the neighborhood, that underlies the law of the land, and is administered far more thoroughly than the latter. These populations, once polarized by the plantation families, which made a center of superior living, are now often left adrift by the decay of this class and the breaking up of the old order generally. The census of Virginia in 1880 showed not a quarter of a million of her people even in villages. And, although the growth of what are called "cities" has been more marked during the past ten years, yet, outside of occasional districts, the vast majority of the Southern white people live in an all-out-of-doors style, not easily understood in the crowded communities of the old East and large portions even of the new West.

While this sphere of life is favorable to some of the primitive virtues—hospitality, good feeling, and sociability—and to the absence of some of the vices of great cities, yet the dearth of the agencies of the higher civilization is a fact almost incredible, unless experienced. Even Texas, the most prosperous Southern State, has yet no system of roads; and only 3,000 of her 8,000 country schools have a schoolhouse over their heads. The appalling loneliness of the "Lone Star" empire has already driven more than a third of its people into villages and cities. But in the older States a full half of the people of both races live outside the opportunities for schooling, reading, churching, and the use of a tolerable press—most of the modern agencies of social uplifting that are the commonplace of the North. The South in winter outside the towns lies under a fearful embargo of mud, which shuts up the people to such a homelife as can be enjoyed under the circumstances. The average country school does not last a full four months, is placed at inconvenient distances, often kept in an unfit schoolhouse—a peril to the health of the children of the poorer people. Less than 60 per cent of Southern children in the open country, where three-fourths their whole number live, represents the average attendance on school less than four months in the year. Probably not a hundred "cities" of the South now have a free library, or a good circulating library accessible to the masses of the white people. The city daily journals have a limited circulation away from the towns and railroads; and the country press is too often, at best, feeble and misleading. Thousands of people do not read that, but depend upon common report for news. The significance of the Scripture phrase—"wars and rumors of wars"—is apparent in a community largely dependent upon rumor and what the popular leaders choose to tell of public affairs. A considerable portion of middle-aged men are of the class that obtained little or no schooling during the war and the ten succeeding years, and have come up, a degenerate race from their parents, to shoulder the weighty responsibilities of the present. Here is the seat of the negrophobia that often blazes out into violence and outrage. It is not the deliberate purpose or feeling of the better class of the Southern people, but the inevitable result of the friction between the races, where a considerable element of the dominant race is so removed from the higher influences of American life.

Yet the vast majority of this great population is of "native American" birth, and is all the time affected by the training school of American life. The political speakers and preachers, the visit to the county town, the coming and going of the emigrating youth, the temperance agitation, the yearly revival meeting, the "boom," that is heard a great way off, like the thundering oncoming of the chariot of the sun, the awakening eagerness to make money, which Dr. Johnson pronounced " about the best thing an honest man can do"—all these influences keep the drowsiest realm somewhat astir, and form a sort of education to several millions of these people—on the whole, better than schools without common sense. Even the mountain world is stirred to its silent depths. Twenty-five years hence the class of people described in Miss Murfree's novels may be as difficult to locate as the bison of the Western prairies.

I rode a whole day in South Carolina with the son of an old Connecticut River railroad president, who was stumping the region along the line from Charleston, S. C., to the Ohio River, soliciting grants of money and land for the route that will give the shortest access to the ocean from the Northwest. A dozen lines of travel are penetrating this marvelous wilderness, so long an enchanted land in the heart of the old republic. In half a century this section of mountain country will become one of the most attractive portions of the United States—much of it more fit for occupation and agreeable in climate than a good deal of New England. These mountain people were loyal in the late war. Wherever the Union Army penetrated they fell in with vim. A hundred and forty thousand white soldiers were enlisted from this country— 24,000 more than from Vermont, New Hampshire, and Connecticut, 7,000 more than from nine of the present Northwestern States. Eastern Kentucky gave more white soldiers to the Union Army than its entire number of voters.

In short, the Third Estate of the South is chiefly of good original stock, though for two hundred years content to sit on the back seat and rise up at the call of a superior class. But that drama is well on toward the fifth act. Radically sound, good-natured, energetic, looking in with all its eyes at the great, wide-open front door of the new American life, with the first enjoyment of the common school and the hunger and thirst for more, hearing afar off the loud sound of the "forging ahead" of the grand new

South, earnest and devout in religious faith—here is a material for American citizenship such as nowhere else can be found in this world. We may well consider what a conservative force in national affairs is here in training, only needing the education of the time to bring to the front a people that will close up with the best elements of the Republic, and "hold the fort" of an Anglo-Saxon progressive civilization against all raids from home or abroad.

What can be done by the whole country to aid in the evolution of this people in the Southland? How can this great uprising be so directed that justice will be done, not only to its superior class, which it will gradually displace and reconstruct, but to the 7,000,000 of colored folk alongside of which it must live?

The first condition of social advancement is an understanding of the favorable elements in the problem. Even the "less favored" of this great population, the higher strata of which are well up, have several characteristics that deserve mention.

First, this body of the Southern people is not hopelessly committed to the fixed theories concerning government, social arrangements, and American affairs in general which thirty years ago opened the "bloody chasm" we are all trying to fill up to-day. The exaggerated ideas of State sovereignty, the antiquated philosophy of eternal race distinction, the prejudice against modern ideas of education and industrial matters which characterized the old leading class and still somewhat affects its rising generation, are not "to the manner born" with them. Indeed, a new State of the Union was formed in 1862 from the breaking out from these ideas by an important district of the Old Dominion. That the masses of the South have followed the leading exponents of these views, even through the destruction of civil war, is not decisive, since there had been little open discussion of such matters among them previous to 1860. But there are significant indications that, wherever the broader American ideas are fairly presented, without partisan or sectional animus, there will be found in this quarter a hearing that prophesies a hopeful future. The eagerness with which the country people have turned to the common school—the special anathema of the old order in the old time—and now for twenty years have supported it, bearing the chief burden of its colored department, almost to their full ability, and the constant demand for its improvement, is a case in point. Coeducation of Southern boys and girls has always been unpopular in respectable Southern circles; but in the common schools it is well-nigh universal, and is now introduced in the State universities of three States. At the Miller Manual Labor School in Virginia, under the shadow of the university, 400 youth of the humbler white class are schooled together with a respect for womanhood worthy the higher ideal of the chivalry that interprets the Golden Rule. The special horror of the Southern upper class is the education of the colored and white races together. But at Berea, on the edge of Old Blue Grass Kentucky, I found one of the best collegiate institutions of that State, where a large number of white mountain boys and girls were "improving their minds," and making manhood and womanhood, with a third as many lowland Negroes, with absolutely no friction. Of course, the old-time notions concerning labor have passed out of sight of this, the rising industrial class of the South. I do not know what political policy or party in national affairs is to prevail in the future. But I am sure that another twenty years of fair opportunity to present the broad-gauge American idea of affairs to this people would result in a state of opinion that would leave the country safe, whatever party might dispense official "pie" at Washington.

Second, I believe in this people will be found a mine of enthusiastic and intelligent patriotism. The war against the Union was not an uprising of the Southern masses, but a deliberate policy of the class that had its confidence—never seriously contemplated by three-fourths of the Southern people. Once in, they fought, as American men always do when that is the business on hand. But, long before the bitter end, it was understood that the hearts of great numbers of the Confederate soldiery were no longer in the cause. I was informed by a distinguished gentleman in Richmond that months before the end, on a tour through the mountains of Virginia, he met great numbers of deserters and disaffected people who did not propose longer to fight for a cause that boded so little good for their kind.   The nonslaveholding class has no such prejudice against the Negro as the master class ; indeed, this prejudice is far more a repulsion of caste and a memory of " previous condition," than a theory of race. They do not especially love the Negro ; the lower strata look upon him as a dangerous rival in many ways.   But it will not need a miraculous conversion to convince them that the welfare of an American State consists in standing by equal rights, justice, and fair play all round, leaving vexed questions of social import to regulate themselves, as they invariably will.

Third, another special trait that has attracted my attention from the first is the teachableness of the children of this class with a reverence for superiors and confidence in those they believe friendly and unselfish.   There is no better material than great numbers of these youth for the natural methods of teaching, which wake up the desire for improvement, spite of untrained manners and habits of living.   I live among boys and girls who are making such efforts to gain a scrap of the opportunity so bountifully flung into the streets before all the children of our Northern cities as makes this one of the most pathetic spectacles of American life.   All the stories that have thrilled the churches of the North concerning the eagerness for knowledge of the young Negro can be paralleled among the children and youth of the humbler white class, with the important difference that the average white child of Anglo-Saxon parentage, even of illiterate descent, seems to have at the bottom of his mind a pair of pincers by which he takes fast hold of what goes in, and generally reveals the power of heredity in a people for centuries the leaders of the progressive society of the world.

All these and other elements of hopefulness encourage the apostle of the new American life in his dealing with the most needy of this class, and insure the hearty coöperation of the upper strata.   And, now, what can the North and the Nation do to hasten the coming of this great uprising among 12,000,000 of white American people, on whose future relations to American ideas the fate of these great Commonwealths depends ?

First, it can aid, in all public and private ways, to put on the ground a good working system of country common schools, of at least six months' duration a year, where all children can receive the elements of education, with the moral and social discipline which is " half the battle " in the training for American citizenship.   As fast as the simple elements of industrial training can be imparted, it will be well.   But the great need of the third estate youngster of the South is a revival of brains that will open his eyes to the wide world outside the home lot, and form a habit of good reading and sound thinking on what is ahead of him.   That itself will be a great industrial uplift, and in time revolutionize the methods of unskilled labor which are the chief hindrance to Southern advancement in material things.   I still hold to the deliberate opinion that the country people of the South are doing about all they can for their common schools.   Special districts will be able to approach the cities and villages in their ability for local taxation.   But for two hundred years the common people of the South have been taught that " taxation is tyranny," and that " economy," even pushed to public stinginess, is the ideal of good government.   Even were this pestilent heresy exploded, and the people convinced that wise and generous taxation is the life-blood of Republican society—since, of all things, American civilization is the most expensive in the outlay, though the most economical in the income—the power to bear taxation for putting on the ground the vast educational plant required for the white and colored schools, chiefly at the expense of the white population, burdened as at present, is not there.   The persistent denial of this fact by a portion of the Northern metropolitan press, in the interest of the land agents and the investors in Southern capital, has gone far to publish a report that Dr. Curry pronounces a " stupendous humbug."

To my mind the defeat of the Senate bill for national aid to education, last winter, was such a mistake that, could it be fathered on either party, it would entitle that combination to a retirement from power for a quarter of a century, on the ground of political incapacity. No critic of New England, however malignant, has drawn a bill of impeachment of Yankee statesmanship so formidable as was furnished by the votes of five New England Senators that accomplished that defeat, representing three States that lead the Union in the enjoyment of educational opportunities. A cause so manifestly just and wise and essential to Southern progress as some form of national aid for the time needed to put the educational affairs of these Commonwealths on their feet is sure to come up for renewed action. The bill of the venerable Senator Morrill for additional aid to agricultural colleges, including those for colored people, which has passed both Houses of Congress, is fraught with positive good. These schools are among the most valuable in the South, especially for the youth of the poorer classes. With the reënforcement of $15,000 to $25,000 a year they can be greatly improved, becoming everywhere, as they have become in Mississippi and Texas, an important element in the movement for skilled labor for all people. A generous system of national aid for education, administered, as it could and would have been, by the State educational authorities established at the close of the war, would have saved us from the bitter antagonisms awakened by the election bills of the present day. Said a radical politician to William H. Seward concerning the fugitive slave law—one of the most mischievous ever enacted by Congress—" What would you have done, as President of the United States, had that bill come up to you from Congress ?" " If I had been President of the United States that bill would never have reached the White House." The statesmanship that will save our country is that which works at long range, on the lines of the great uplifting agencies of civilization, in hope of gradual and permanent advancement, dispensing, as far as may be, with the old bungling rule of the sword and constable beyond the line of personal disobedience of the law.

Third, industrial education, in its broadest and most practical form, with good schooling in the elements of English, must become a great factor in the uplift of the new South. All the arguments used for its application to the Negro have full application to the children and youth of the Third Estate. Especially is this true of the young women of this class. The lower forms of woman's work, with an increasing push into the operative and other modes of profitable labor, are falling into the hands of the colored women. Large numbers of these girls, in the excellent industrial mission schools of the South, are becoming successful workers in a variety of occupations for women. Whether the white girl of the South is to "lie off" and "play lady," while her colored sister "toils and spins," or take her part in the rising sphere of profitable industry, the three hundred and fifty ways by which an American woman can get a respectable living, is to be decided by this movement for the training of the hand of the rising womanhood of the South. Several of the Southern States already admit girls to the agricultural colleges. But the Mississippi plan seems the most popular. This State supports a great industrial and normal school, with free tuition for white girls—a sort of college "of all work," where a young woman can get a good academical education and be trained for teaching while compelled to take some branch of industrial training. Though somewhat hindered by political interference in its administration, this school is becoming a positive success and reflects great credit on a group of admirable women who pushed it through the legislature, and are still watching by its cradle. Georgia is about to establish a similar school at her old capital, Milledgeville. The plan is so feasible that I look to its establishment in all these States.

Bishop Atticus G. Haygood, the foremost educational and religious leader of the whole Southern people, has inaugurated his elevation to a bishopric in the Methodist Church South by a wise and noble plan for a great school of a similar class for Southern white girls in the Alabama mining country, on the border between " down

south" and the north where the daughters of the impoverished rich and the ambitious poor can be educated at a rate that will enable thousands of good girls to
obtain their great and only chance for education. The next million that goes down
that way from Northern benevolence should be given to Bishop Haygood, in whose
hands the vanishing surplus of the United States Treasury would have been wisely
invested in "the building for the children" of the people of all conditions in these
States. It is one of the delusions that still abide in too many minds that the great
industrial need of the South is cheap and unskilled labor, the toil of an ignorant
peasantry. The desperate need of the South is intelligent labor in the masses, under
the leadership of trained commanders of industry, an army that will go forth "conquering and to conquer" into this marvelous world of opportunity.

The white masses of the South need to be brought in range of that system of agencies of the higher American civilization now in operation even in the most remote
Northwest, and which are the glory of the more prosperous States. It is impossible
to describe the difference in the mental atmosphere in which a bright boy or girl in
an average county in South Carolina, Alabama, or Louisiana is brought up and
that amid which his cousin lives in Massachusetts, Ohio, or Wisconsin. It is all the
difference between living in a country where the whole environment is educational
and a country where education is a special thing, and the youth is all the time compelled to push out of his ordinary surroundings to gain it. A free library in every
neighborhood, a better class of newspapers, a movement to "add to faith knowledge"
in the church—all these, now rapidly coming to the front in the prosperous cities,
still wait for their day in the open country. Yet here is the place, almost the only
place left in American life, where is yet leisure from engrossing work. Oh, what a
boon to us hurried and wearied mortals would be that precious leisure, flowing like
a great quiet river through these rural districts of the Southland! Here is the place
where all these beautiful and beneficent agencies would be best appreciated by the
the children and youth, who would accept them as eagerly as the children of New
England fifty years ago, springing to them as to a bounteous feast.

And is not the group of men and women already known who can bring the philosophy of social science down from heaven to abide upon earth, and put into simple
statement, in leaflets or short readable tracts, the knowledge that makes for good living
and true prosperity? The South is now drugged with the theories of professional
politicians. Now the tariff, now the Negro, now the railroad, now the distant millionaire, is paraded up and down as the cause of "agricultural depression," the
source of all Southern woes. Now let the social scientists "take an inning," and tell
the people what wasteful housekeeping, bad cookery, unskilled labor, unfit dress,
ignorance, superstition, shiftlessness, vulgarity, and vice have to do with the undeniable trials of these, with other multitudes of the less favored of our American people. A railroad conductor, with a big head on his shoulders, said to me: "All along
this route of 500 miles the people would read tons of leaflets, tracts, anything containing good, sound information and advice on common things. I could distribute
all that anybody would give me."

But why go on? Here is a people, not inferior in capacity to any upon earth, of
the best original stock, appearing for the first time as a controlling element in sixteen great States of the Republic, in whose hands is the destiny of other millions
just introduced to American citizenship. On them will depend the the outcome of
Southern affairs for the coming generation more than upon all the rest of the country. What an appeal to the patriotism, the justice, the Christian spirit of the whole
American people. But alas for the sin, the shame, and the discouragement which
stand between such a people and all that come to them in friendly coöperation. I
live all summer in sight of money enough thrown to the dogs and to the devil to
place on the ground, in many of these States, the agencies which their own noblest
people are all ready to use for the public good. When the great Protestant churches,
that still work at cross purposes along the border, learn the wisdom of Christian

statesmanship, close up their ranks, and pour a stream of Northern money into this the most fruitful mission field on earth, there will be more hope of the coming of the kingdom for which their prayers go up day and night before the Lord.

The conviction forces itself upon a careful observer of these States that the time has passed when any set of leaders, any political or ecclesiastical party, can solve the difficult problems now set before them. It is doubtful if the foremost men, North and South, who were once arrayed as enemies in war, can ever "see eye to eye," or repose that confidence in each other without which all dealing with matters so delicate involves an ever-recurring exasperation. Napoleon said, "When a great thing is to be done in public affairs, keep away from the leaders and go to the people." "The people" that will finally bring peace, confidence, reconciliation, through all our borders are the children and youth now being trained all over the land for the grandest effort of Christian administration that ever confronted a generation of men. And the Southern children, on whom we are to largely depend, thirty years hence, for this glorious work of reconstruction and reconciliation are the boys and girls of this rising Third Estate and the Negroes, the youthful millions that now swarm this land of the South. The best we can do is to hold things as good as they are, with the hope of making some little headway year by year against sectional prejudice, provincialism, and all the enemies of the new republic. But greater than all other things is the work to which we are called—the education of the head, the hand, and the heart of the twenty millions of Young America. Then, as Thomas Jefferson said, "if we educate the children aright, our descendants will be wiser than we, and many things impossible to us will be easy to them."

VII.

OVERLOOK AND OUTLOOK IN SOUTHERN EDUCATION.

An address delivered at the University of Tennessee, May 12, 1891.

I am aware that he who offers to speak on a subject so vast in itself and so involved in social, political, industrial, and religious questions as the present condition and future prospects of education in the South should present some credentials on his right to demand a hearing. My own conviction of the right so to speak is founded on an eleven years' experience in the journeyings, observations, consultations, and labors in the Southern States implied in what I hope it is not vain to call "a ministry of education." Eleven years ago, after many years of deep interest and connection with the educational life of the North, I heard the call to go over the border and give myself for my remaining years to this ministry. Encouraged by leading authorities, educational and public, including many of the most eminent statesmen in Congress and the national administration, I entered upon this mission.

During the past eleven years I have visited every Southern State, labored in every department of education with special reference to the development of the common school, made large acquaintance with the Southern educational public, and kept myself in close connection with the Southern people of both races and all classes, really living with the children and youth, the young parents and teachers, with constant opportunity of consulting with the leaders of religious, public, and educational affairs. In this way, not so much from superior ability as extensive and unique opportunities of observation, I have obtained an overlook of the educational situation which I believe is nearer the facts of the case than the general impression gathered from the press, the churches, or partial private observation. Such observation goes below the imperfect statistics that figure in the census, or even the brief and often unsatisfactory reports of the State and local educational officials of the South.

In matters educational everything depends on the meaning attached to current terms, the quality of the school and the teacher, and the social environment of the school itself. My estimate of this region of Southern life differs from many estimates which I find in the press or the educational public. I present it as the result of my best effort to obtain a truthful notion of the "lay of the land;" and I am encouraged by the practical indorsement of my general view by the foremost educational authorities of that section.

With this brief introduction, I now ask your attention to some remarks on the Overlook and Outlook in Southern Education.

In the year 1865, to an outside observer, the whole fabric of Southern education lay prostrate in the appalling wreck, disappointment, and despair of the great American civil war. The majority of leading institutions of learning had been suspended or were only partially at work during the four years of conflict. Buildings had been destroyed or had fallen to decay, students and teachers were in their graves or just emerging from the smoke of battle, endowment funds of every sort had gone the way of all earthly riches, and the impending bitter conflict of politics during the troubled years of reconstruction served to postpone the revival of letters to a far-off generation. To-night, in briefest possible outline, I tell the wondrous story of the

284

great enterprise of the Southern educational public, leading the people of every Southern State in that awakening and organizing of the educational spirit which has rebuilt on the old foundation better than before and beyond all former ambition the work of universal education, which in due time shall bring a good American common school to every man's door.

How that mighty enterprise in this latter day was undertaken, and how it has gone on for the past twenty-five years, is one of the most wonderful things in the marvelous history of our country.

The South more than any other portion of the Republic is the land of tradition. Nowhere is loyalty to the memory and the achievements of great men so powerful a motive for the action even of the more intelligent classes as here. And happily the highest traditions of the South and the testimonials of the fathers were largely on the side of the education of the people. A hundred years ago Thomas Jefferson had outlined one of the most complete systems of general education then published to the world, and through his life with the full indorsement of the greatest men of his State had he labored with the people of Virginia for its adoption. Failing in all but its university upper story, he bequeathed the glorious vision to a coming generation.

All along the years the foremost statesmen and educators of the South had periodical awakenings to the absolute necessity of a more thorough schooling of the white masses. One of the best educational volumes for popular circulation would be a compilation of the eloquent, wise, and practical sayings of the greatest leaders of Southern life on popular education up to the outbreak of the civil war. And in several of the States attempts had been made to realize this idea, though outside a few cities, nowhere except in North Carolina, with any considerable measure of success.

So when, at the close of the war, the great effort was made by the National Government, private benevolence, Northern church activity, and the Peabody educational fund, to establish the common school for all children, in every Southern State, it found great numbers of the people prepared for it. · The necessities of the higher and the aspirations of the lower classes of society conspired with the desire of thousands of cultivated women for employment, and the common school appeared even before the decisive years of 1864–'65.

It is not necessary to defend all that was attempted in the next ten troubled years, even with good intentions, for the schooling of either race. It was inevitable under the circumstances, that great mistakes should be made, and that the people should sometimes revolt against a good deal that was well meant and wisely done. Enough to say, that no money was ever better invested for education than the $50,000,000 sent southward by the North and the Nation during the past twenty-five years. It has stimulated the desire for knowledge in several millions of youth; aided hundreds of communities to establish a useful system of schools; gathered teachers and students in seminaries of peculiar merit; introduced industrial education among the freedmen, and built several thousand schoolhouses between the Potomac and the Rio Grande. And, best of all, has been the coming together of schoolmen, children, and people, for the first time known to each other. "A little child shall lead them." State after State, class after class, have been found grouped around the schoolhouse door, beautiful prophecy of the coming "day of the Lord," when the educational and religious forces of the whole country shall be marshaled like an angelic host, with flaming swords, against that barbarism of ignorance and unrighteousness which is the Satan in the fair Eden of the new Republic.

It would require more than one discourse to do faint justice to the corresponding movement of the Southern people during the past twenty-five years in behalf of the education of their 6,000,000 children and youth. It is only the truth to say that never in the history of the world has a more notable work been attempted and carried beyond the first point of danger under anything like similar difficulties and complications than in our Southern States. I need not here speak of those difficulties and complications to an assembly of Southern friends of education, who are even to-day confronted by them all, like a stout traveler beating against a teasing wind.

It was fit that Virginia should lead in this great enterprise and, under the masterly superintendency of Dr. Ruffner, the Horace Mann of the South, take up the work that fell from dying hands at Monticello fifty years before. The New Dominion of 1891 now supports every feature of the system outlined by Thomas Jefferson, from the State University to industrial training for the freedmen in the Old Dominion of a hundred years ago.

In these memorable twenty-five years the American system of common schools in every department has been established in fact and incorporated in the constitution and laws of every Southern State. Almost every district in these sixteen Commonwealths has now something that can be called a district common school. Every city of the first class, with an increasing number of smaller towns, has established the graded school system according to the organization and methods that prevail in the superior school-keeping everywhere. Nearly half of the 6,000,000 Southern children and youth of both races and all classes of the legal school age between 6 and 21 are enrolled, and more than 50 per cent of the actual school age, from 6 to 14, are in regular attendance from three to four months in the year. And outside, through the influence of what is done inside the schoolroom, by the press, books, home, private, Sunday school and church instruction, many thousands of youth and adults of all ages are reached.

This year the entire South will appropriate $23,000,000 for every sort of education, a sum greater than the British Parliament allows for the common schooling of 30,000,000 people. A majority of these States have established the State or city normal school, and the normal institute for training teachers is in operation in every Commonwealth. The development of literary and educational lecturing has been steady, and the Southern press speaks out for the children, with a few insignificant except tions, generally on the right side. In all but two of these States the colored folk have equal share in the distribution of the public school funds, while their contribution to these funds is still far below what it might be made. Industrial training, the most notable advance of the present era in popular education, has been planted in every State, in the higher schools, for the Negro and in an increasing number of excellent seminaries for white youth.

The original munificent gift of the General Government for agricultural and mechanical education, last year repeated by Congress, has been made of use in all and of great service in several of these States. The introduction of great numbers of superior young white women and the lifting up of several thousands of the better sort of colored youth to the most vital of American professions, the teaching of the people, has been one of the most remarkable features in the history of education in modern times.

And, spite of a great deal of direct and more indirect opposition and a fearful amount of indifference, Southern public opinion is now so firmly set towards universal education that the most dangerous experiment by any aspirant for civil office is even the underhand opposition to the people's common school. Every year the appropriation for education is somewhat larger. Thrice during the past six years only five or six of the twenty-two Senators, representing the ex-Confederate States in Congress, have thought it either wise or prudent to speak or vote against national aid to education.

Even more honorable has been the record of the recuperation of the secondary and higher education in all these States. With the aid of perhaps $10,000,000, donated by benevolent persons of both sections for colleges and academies, the Southern white people have rehabilitated these schools till, in all but endowment funds, they are, on the whole, superior to any former period. In the skill and devotion of large numbers of their teachers; the improvement in organization, discipline, and modes of instruction; the convenience of buildings; the broadening of the whole idea of the secondary and higher education,—in all that brings the upper realm of the educational life of a people in line with the best thought and practice of the age, the university, collegiate, academical, and professional schools of the South are now well in advance of any previous time; and were their pressing need of money relieved and the ability of elementary education to prepare fit material more largely developed, a more decided advance could be made along the whole line. Several important foundations—like Johns Hopkins University, the Peabody Institute, and the Pratt Free Library, in Baltimore; Washington University, at St. Louis; Vanderbilt, at Nashville; Tulane, in New Orleans, and the State University of Texas; with a number of excellent agricultural and industrial institutions for men and women—have been positive additions to the higher education of the South.

The most unique feature of this movement is the building of a score of great schools, largely by Northern gifts, for the superior training of colored youth in connection with an annual subsidy from several of these States. No competent educator now questions the vast importance of this enterprise. At present these schools are training, probably, 20,000 of these youth for leadership, not only of the education but of the entire higher life of the 7,000,000 of their people. They are all normal and industrial and several of them professional schools, and their worthy graduates now occupy a position of singular opportunity as missionaries of the higher American civilization. Eventually all these seminaries may be handed over to the Southern people and become permanent colleges, of a broad and practical type, for increasing numbers of the aspiring youth of their race.

One result of this vast educational movement has been a remarkable development of literary, artistic, and musical ability in this section within the past ten years. The group of new Southern authors now occupies an honorable place in American literature. The Chautauqua assembly inaugurated by Bishop Vincent, a Southern man; the reading circle, and the free library are developing with increasing support. In short, within the past twenty years greater progress has been made, in these sixteen States, in popularizing all varieties of education than was ever made under similar circumstances in any age or land.

This wonderful work has been accomplished by what may be called *the educational public of the South ;* leading, sometimes compelling, the masses. Nowhere are the people so loyal to able leadership in all good things as in these States. It would astonish the country to learn how small a number of resolute men and women have often lifted whole communities and States from the educational discouragement of 1865 to the hopefulness of 1891. Nowhere has there been a grander display of heroic, even daring courage, executive ability, patient endurance of trial and skillful dealing with opposition, with more triumphant success than in this portion of the Union.

Herein is a source of chronic misapprehension of the Southern educational situation by the average outside observer. Seeing everywhere through these States undeniable evidence of popular indifference and cultivated hostility, the observer declares that education is not in the saddle, but under the feet of the "solid South." These critics forget that in the condition of affairs that for twenty-five years has prevailed in these States, a few resolute, able, wise, and consecrated leaders have been able to swing a whole section upon the right track and hold it there till aid shall come from abroad or opposition be worn out at home.

And the time has come to do justice to a large body of the Southern military men, often of distinguished rank, who have aided so powerfully, especially in the upbuilding of the higher education in the South since the war. The Southern brigadier in Congress has been well advertised in all Northern centers of political life. The Southern brigadier in the schoolroom, from Gen. Robert Lee, reorganizing education in old Washington College in Virginia, to William Preston Johnston, son of Lee's great military compeer, lifting up the banner in New Orleans, yet awaits fit commemoration in the mighty work of national development yet going on before our eyes. No more valuable service has been rendered to the country than by thousands of these young men of the South, who hung up the sword in 1865 to wield the "pointer" at the schoolroom black-board; stepping from the camp to the college professor's and president's chair, and who still remain, on the whole, the broadest and most forcible element in the higher education of their people. Their old field titles have been glorified by service in that grander warfare, "whose weapons are not carnal, but spiritual." They are now the lieutenants and captains, majors and colonels, generals and commodores in that noble "army of the living God," moving with resistless might to the decisive charge on the wavering host of ignorance, with victory already assured, amid the plaudits of the world, a victory over which all good men and women and little children in all nations " will rejoice and be glad all the days of their life."

Why, then, with this inspiring record, shall we not fall in with what it is becoming quite the fashion, especially in certain metropolitan centers of culture and journalism in the North, to proclaim, and say, "The South, educationally, is doing well enough now;" on the whole is, possibly, in a more healthy condition than some other parts of the country; at any rate is in no especial need of sympathy or aid from any quarter.

Because this vast work, so well begun, is only begun; and the sooner the whole country takes in the full length and breadth and depth of the Southern educational situation the better for everybody now and for the next fifty years. The Southern educational public has certainly well begun the most difficult educational work of the time, and perhaps its most valuable service has been to reveal the gravity of the situation to every competent observer.

The latest reliable enumeration places the legal school population of the whole South, between the ages of 6 and 21, in round numbers at 6,500,000; of whom a much larger proportion than elsewhere need the common school, from failure of opportunity in early childhood. Of these not over 4,000,000 this year will look in at any schoolhouse door, and but little over one-third (2,300,000) will be in regular annual attendance from three to four months on any school.

The real school age everywhere is from 6 to 14. In the most favored States hardly one youth in twenty, above 15, is in any school. In the North Atlantic division of States, 75; in the North Central, 77; in the Western division, 70 per cent of all children between 6 and 14 represent the average attendance on the common schools, with large bodies in the numerous Northern and Western cities in church and private schools. In the Southern Atlantic division 56, in the Southern Central division 52 per cent only represent the average attendance at this age on public schools, with about the same ratio of private attendance. Thus, in round numbers, only 54 per cent of the children of the South, between 6 and 14, are in regular school attendance, and the ratio beyond that age is smaller than in the North.

This comparison is only made to expose the claim that "things are well enough now;" also the other statement, that "illiteracy is chiefly confined to a generation that is dying out." In fact, illiteracy is steadily increasing though perhaps not relatively to increase of population.

The attendance in the majority of these States on public schools varies from twelve to twenty-three weeks of the year in school days, and is greatly hindered by distance or the absence or discomfort of school-houses (in Texas the 8,000 county schools having about 3,000 school-houses), and in many cases by the unsuitable condition of children. The majority of teachers are serving on an average salary of less than $30 per month, supporting themselves, while their receipts are for only the few months above stated.

Even were the Southern masses of every sort reasonably intelligent, this condition alone would involve a future peril. But, when we remember that this is only the foreground of the picture—the most favorable view for at least ten States—its real significance appears. In fact, in State after State, one-fourth, a third, sometimes almost one-half, in one State a majority, of the men who wield the ballot and a larger proportion of the women that make the men that make the Government are in this condition. When to this is added the dearth, even in most of the large towns, of libraries and the whole American apparatus of popular culture, with the other fact, that nine-tenths of the children of the South are dispersed through an open country as large as western Europe, where all means of culture outside the family must be comparatively scanty; and still another fact, the vast number of adult age whose small reading and less writing leave them practically strangers to books; we begin to measure the depth and breadth of this abyss we call "illiterary" over which the "gay and festive" politician in Congress and the high-toned literary "dude" of the Northern metropolis wreathe a rainbow of bombastic oratory and optimistic journalism, until "even the elect" fancy this enchanted foreground the gleaming gate to paradise, instead of a painted cloud-scene before the open mouth of the pit.

The State of Massachusetts has in her savings banks a sum equal to the present tax valuation of all but three of the ex-Confederate States, and is able this year, for her 400,000 school children, to afford nearly half as much money as the entire sixteen Southern States, including Missouri, Texas, and Maryland. No Southern State, except Virginia, Maryland, Missouri, and Texas, will this year be able to appropriate as much for schools as the one city of Boston with her 60,000 children. Ten of the sixteen will not exceed the city of Cincinnati with her school attendance of 35,000; and not one the city of Chicago, which calls this year for $5,000,000—$40 for each child. But the seven Southern Atlantic States, with less than 60 per cent of their children from 6 to 14 in average school attendance, are paying as heavily on their valuation as New England with her 85, and two of her States 95 and 98 per cent of similar age in average attendance. Facts like these reveal the nature of the claim that the South is fully able to fitly school her entire youthful population if she will.

The plain fact of the situation is that twelve of the sixteen Southern States, under present circumstances, can not educate this present generation without at least twice the money they now feel able to pay, and that to demand of people so circumstanced an effort twice as great as of wealthy New England even practically in sight of the great Northwest, buttressed on every side with bountiful national aid, is simply rhetoric with no base of hard cash.

What, then, shall we say? That the Southern educational public has failed and the schooling of these 6,000,000 of Southern children and youth is a dream of the educator, and the whole fabric of popular education, so painfully reared, so consecrated with toil and tears and prayer and lives slowly wearing out with endless work, like the houses and churches of Charleston at sunset of the awful day when "the earth trembled," may tumble any hour in hideous ruin? No, none of these things. Both my assertions stand. And the explanation is that no modern people yet has really measured the prodigious difficulty of building up an adequate system of public instruction and keeping it alive and effective from year to year.

Even Germany, with a government of iron and a policeman and a soldier at every door, has spent half a century in prodding the German peasant of a hundred years ago up to the average German immigrant as we see him to-day. New England, with her broad notions of individual independence, spent two hundred years before 1835 in working up her common schools to a condition little better than Virginia in 1891, and the last fifty years, with the ghost of Horace Mann flourishing his "scourge of small cords" over every obstinate schoolmaster, in crowding her native and foreign born population up to her present achievement. The mighty Northwest, with the whole world pouring in its supply of vigorous young people, and the Nation and the old East paving every step of her career with gold, has needed a generation to reach her present estate. Here in the South there has been barely twenty years of work, on the heels of the most overwhelming revolutionary epoch of modern times. Out of the wreck of property, the disruption of the established system of labor, the fearful apprehension of race conflict, and the thousand open and hidden complications that can only be appreciated by one who can "put himself in the place" of this people, the prodigious work of the reconstruction of the old and the creation of the new education has been carried to the point described.

Of course, not one in a hundred of the ablest schoolmen of the South, at the beginning, could compass the vastness of the enterprise or conjecture the hindrances that would spring up, like foes in ambush, at every step of the upward winding way. Of course the masses of the white people, on whose shoulders the burden must still rest for years, could not then understand very well what all this meant. To change the whole system of instruction and with it the old-time idea of education itself for 18,000,000 of people in sixteen great States, in education absolutely independent; to gather 6,000,000 of children and youth in schools, housed in decent buildings, taught by competent teachers, in session long enough to stamp even good instruction on the mind ; to do this a little better every year, with repeated calls for more money upon the small portion of the people who feel able to pay taxes for anything, while the demand is for constant taxation for everything; to push this enterprise in the face of ignorance, indifference, and the violent and secret opposition of the classes that everywhere in Christendom are now fighting the common school; what an undertaking was this at first; how much greater it seems every year; how positively awful it looms before us here to-day. The marvel is not that so much remains undone, but that so much has been accomplished in these swift and troubled twenty years. Nowhere but in the United States of America could such a work have been done.

For this is the most characteristic result of American institutions; that no American community, however stricken, falls on its back and howls abroad to the nations for sympathy; or breaks up into a mob to pull down society; or does anything but "pick up the pieces;" clear the ground of rubbish; receive with thanks whatever is given; and straightway begin to "calculate" how something shall be done so much better than what was destroyed, that the world shall think the kingdom has really come. It is perfectly credible that, one year after the earthquake summer a bishop of the Southern Methodist Church should have announced that the Garden of Eden was situated on the peninsula between the Ashley and Cooper rivers, just where new Charleston stands to-day, in her dress coat, inviting the country to her enthusiastic hospitalities.

The one thing that neither war, pestilence, nor famine; stormy winds, turbulent sea, nor shuddering earth can drive out of an American community or State is the notion that it is a shame to be content with anything less than superiority, not only to any of these "effete despotisms" abroad, but to every Commonwealth, however favored, at home. "Do you like to live way down there in Boston?" a jolly old fellow of ninety summers, with a quart of whisky in his face, and a peck of hayseed in his hair, sung out to us on a train in the superb valley of the Miami, in southern Ohio. "Come down out of the blizzard to the sunny South," shouts every lounging and laughing Southern American citizen of any descent, though shaking with the ague he caught invariably "somewhere over there," but never at home. This "glorying in infirmities," of which the apostle speaks, has first been realized in the land of the American eagle. South Carolina has done, for twenty years past, just what Massachusetts would have done under similar circumstances, with the blunders that inevitably attend any great thing attempted by a people so impatient of weakness, so swift to see the working point, so self-confident and hopeful as an American community. She has "picked up the pieces," and placed herself on the threshold of a grander future than Calhoun or Petigru ever discerned.

Doubtless the Southern educational common school public has been favored, on the one hand by the necessities of the superior people, and on the other by that popular loyalty to able leadership which still holds these vast and in many ways diverging Commonwealths in what we call "a solid South." But whatever may be the cause, here stands the South to-day. With a bravery, dash, skill, and endurance demonstrated on a hundred battlefields, the educational phalanx has marched from Maryland to Texas, has driven the enemy of universal education everywhere from the open field, and has gained virtual possession of the land.

Now comes the second and even more difficult phase of the war. The foe has gone into intrenchments; in every Southern State is a great fortified camp, provisioned and held by the enemy of universal education, and outside there is disaffection, which must be overcome and changed to active loyalty to the children before any notable advance can be made.

Within the past twenty years of American and European warfare no fortified city has been carried by assault. Vicksburg, Richmond, Charleston, Metz, Strasbourg, Paris only yield to patient siege by overwhelming numbers. The educational public of the South is now taking in this fact, that the time has come for a corresponding change in the conduct of the war against that illiteracy which is at the bottom of everything which blocks the way to success in every department of Southern life. Here and there a town, now and then a county, on a favorable "crop year" a legislature, can still be carried by a dash and some fine thing achieved. But the problem now is to invest the great open country, where 4 of every 5 of the children live, and where the Southern people must be educated, if at all, within the next twenty-five years. How shall that campaign be constructed? How shall the fortress of illiteracy in every State be surrounded; covered at every point; isolated from the rest of the world; bombarded, starved, worn out to the point of " unconditional surrender" to the triumphant hosts of knowledge, morality, prosperity, and lasting peace? I do not conceal the gravity of the enterprise. I would flatter nobody with the fancy that this is a holiday work. Rather would I say, with the valiant King Harry in the play :

> Proclaim it through my host,
> That he which hath no stomach to this fight,
> Let him depart ; his passport shall be made,
> And crowns for convoy put into his purse:
> We would not die in that man's company,
> That fears his fellowship to die with us.

Having now outlined the situation, " the overlook ; " let me proceed more briefly to present "the outlook" in the suggestion of a few of the more obvious lines of operation in this vast adventure, the education of the younger six millions of the Southern people into good American citizenship, a work in which we may all engage, if we will, but of which no one of us will see the end.

Leaving out all details of operation on local or State lines of policy, which must be varied by the circumstances of every case, there is one central, persistent, and absolutely essential condition attending the success of universal education everywhere in our country. That condition is a great awakening of the whole people to an intelligent comprehension of the perils of illiteracy, a just idea of the best way to educate the whole people, and an unconquerable determination to do this work in the shortest time and the best way possible under the conditions, any or every where present.

The more we study the growth of popular education in our country the clearer it seems that no power less irresistible than the awakened masses of the people will ever educate all the children. No social aristocracy, plutocracy, political party, nor the most devoted priesthood of the best church ever did or ever will do much more than educate for its own purposes, unless the whole people, led by an overwhelming majority, makes up its mind that universal education shall prevail by the help of these powerful agencies if they will, or in spite of them if they oppose.

Every Southern State will have a competent system of public instruction as soon as it is evident that its people demand it and will, if necessary, leave every ecclesiastical, political, social, or financial "upper class" on a side track, as it goes thundering on its resistless way thereto. Each Northern and Western State and city has fought through every battle that the educational public of the South is now called to encounter. There, as here, great bodies of churchmen have asserted the sole right of the Church to educate, and denounced the people's school as godless. An upper social circle has voted the people's school "vulgar" and " common." Financial potentates have denounced the education of the laboring classes as destructive to industry, and there never was a time when there was not too much reading and writing for large numbers of " great statesmen," who would straightway dwindle to small politicians if tested in a competitive examination by an intelligent constituency. As long as the masses anywhere are indifferent to education or so divided in their allegiance to these different kinds of leadership that they waste their energies in fighting each other, education will be the luxury of the superior sort and the people will be left to the crumbs that fall from their masters' groaning tables. This does not mean that the superior classes are necessarily hostile to the masses, but simply that it is the instinct of unregenerate human nature to "look out for number one" and leave the other numbers to keep up if they can. The only remedy this side of heaven for such a state of affairs is that the American people, first and last and all the time, should " look out for number one," especially in this fundamental matter of universal education. Superior classes will always succeed in getting their full share of the best things in this life without the people postponing any essential public good in their behalf. And in the end the church, good society, industrial prosperity, and civil order will all be better cared for by a sovereign people, trained in that threefold education of the head, heart, and hand which goes to the making of the true woman, the whole man, the thoroughly furnished citizen of the Republic and of every American State.

So the field is cleared for action in front of this educational public which has already done such splendid work and secured such permanent results in the past twenty-five years. It is now summoned in every State to do what the educational public of New England did fifty years ago, under Horace Mann; what New York did ten years later, under Page and May; what Pennsylvania did later yet, under Stevens and Hickox and Wickersham; what Ohio did, under Lewis and Guilford; what every one of these States has been compelled to do: organize a vast movement as intense as a church revival, as comprehensive as a political campaign, in behalf of universal education.

Here, as everywhere, this great propaganda must be laid out at first by the educational public, that is, the superior teachers working along with the influential friends of education. The most obvious way to do this has already been indicated in two Southern States. In Louisiana two societies, including many of the ablest and most influential friends of universal education for the past ten years, have been a powerful agency for holding the people to the support of the people's common school. Eight years ago a similar organization in Kentucky compelled a radical reconstruction of the public-school system, with an important revision of the school laws.

A similar combination in every Southern State, in five years would force the discussion of popular education in every corner of the Commonwealth, would silence the teasing and carping opposition of influential people who have nothing practical to offer, would demonstrate the fact that there is no natural hostility between public and any other form of true education, would make every newspaper an educational journal and compel every aspiring young public man to put all he knows into a speech in favor of universal education and " speak his piece" wherever a baker's dozen of any sort or condition of people could be gathered to hear him, and finally would make it the burning question in every school district from Maryland to California— how can the people's school be established and kept alive long enough and good enough to give to every man's child the great American chance, a fair education in the elements of the mother tongue, with a love for knowledge which will go before him like a lodestar through every year of his life.

The first point to be made in this " great argument" is to blaze into the popular mind the meaning of American illiteracy. Illiteracy in America does not mean simply ignorance of books by a people like the European peasantry of a century ago or the majority of the seven millions of the American people made citizens within the last twenty-five years. To understand this matter we must forget a good deal of the poetry and romance concerning " a contented peasantry" and the general blessedness of the "less favored" classes in Christendom. For a thousand years past, ninety-nine people in a hundred everywhere have been represented in literature by the one man who either was least informed of their actual estate or most interested in keeping them as they were. It is the old fable of the lion painted with the man on his back, because the man held the brush. In our time the people are turning artist and historian and, for the first time, the world is learning just what it means for the masses anywhere to be ignorant, and what that ignorance really signifies when it becomes the portentous fact we call illiteracy. For illiteracy is a compound fact, which, in its last analysis, includes the sum of all evils in an American State. It is the same in Massachusetts and Arkansas, in Ohio and Florida, in Oregon and North Carolina, in classic Boston and the last new "metropolis" extemporized on the prairies of Oklahoma or amid the canebrakes of Louisiana.

American illiteracy means, first, that ignorance, narrowness, and dullness of mind which shut every unlettered man or woman away from the great modern source of reliable knowledge concerning everything, the printed page. It leaves its subject dependent on his own narrow observation and experience, and, finally, compels him to "wait till the man comes round" to tell him what is truth and duty for him in his particular sphere of life.

Illiteracy in labor means that, in a country more bountifully endowed with resources than any and already the richest in the world, at least one-third the people are still enslaved by the primal necessities of life, compelled to toil all their lives, where they happen to be, to keep the wolf from the door, or to live on the leanness while the more favored feast on the fat of the land. And all this because they do not know enough to work according to the scripture ordinance, "with their might." They do work with all their muscle, with a fragment of their brain, a figment of their character, and a suggestion of their immortal soul. Because of this whole States still lie just "out of the woods;" the forest, the mine, the factory, the fisheries, the whole upper side of modern industrial life, languish while eloquent orators in Congress and professors of political economy in college rack their brains to devise a patent method of transferring money from the pockets of skilled and able into the wallets of unskilled and ignorant men. And when the illiterate class does wake up to its condition, too often it finds itself in the hands of some high-stepping organization whose blundering leaders, like the early volunteer generals in the late war, make havoc of their followers and wreck the very cause they would advance.

Illiteracy in the home means that the same classes of our people, living in the Eden of the world, still abide in a sort of existence that nobody tolerates an hour after he can get out of it, destroying half the material that goes into the kitchen and compelling their families to "eat and drink damnation" in what is preserved; to lose, in great cities, half, and everywhere a frightful percentage of children below the age of 10, and launch other millions into life weighted with all manner of bodily ailments, to say nothing of the exposure to the curses of intemperance, unchastity, vulgarity, shiftlessness, and the whole brood of incapacities and vices that swarm around the door of the illiterate household of any race, class, or condition that abides on American soil.

Illiteracy in religion means that here in America, as everywhere, an ignorant class will always be the prey of bigotry, fanaticism, and ecclesiastical despotism. Surely, after the experience of almost two thousand years, no intelligent man need wonder at the only partial success of pure and undefiled religion even in so-called Christian lands, while the majority of the human race is still outside the pale. Make all allowance you will for the sin, indifference, even native incapacity of man for righteousness, the hideous fact remains that, because the vast majority of nominal religionists in the Old World were in the bonds of illiteracy for fifteen hundred years, despotism in church and state and fanaticism in the masses deluged every land with blood, and to-day the revolt of these half instructed populations has filled Europe with atheism and every form of socialistic abomination. So is it here, just to the extent that the same causes are at work ; vast multitudes of people going wild over a religion which has no power to hold them to the common moralities of decent life, great religious bodies wasting in sectarian conflict the energy that should be turned towards emptying the American hells, and plenty of eminent leaders still enthralled by the delusion that in some way education, especially outside their own preserve, is hostile to the blessed reign of truth, love and beauty, which makes the kingdom of God on earth and the salvation of man in Heaven. Talk of "Godless Education !" Illiteracy is the champion infidel against that religion *which is the light of the world.* An illiterate American population is always a nursery of immorality, crime, and the discontented poverty that is one of the most fearful temptations of mankind.

Illiteracy in civil life means that every ignorant male citizen, whether his ballot be cast or withheld, is compelled to vote somebody up or something down of which he can have no reliable knowledge. It means that two-thirds of our American cities and three-fourths of our American States are to-day in the power of a vast army of ignorant voters; now captured by this "ring" and now by that; to-day "plumped" in one quarter, to-morrow concentrated on another strategical point, and always used for some other end than the country's good. Half a dozen great questions with which our country has caught up will be fought over for the next twenty-five years to the impoverishment, exasperation, and alienation of classes, races, and sections that should be in harmony, because great, shrewd, unscrupulous men know the art of muddling politics and maneuvering the host of illiteracy. So, directly or indirectly, this Republic is now largely governed by partisan politicians elected to office by the votes of people that every thoughtful man says are not fit to vote at all.

As soon as the people can be made to understand that American illiteracy is the bottom curse of American life, the great American slough, underlying every State, with an open death-pit in every neighborhood, into which empties the whole mental and moral sewage of the nation, they will cease to take counsel of false guides and turn to the educational public for the true leadership that will save the State. They will see that the question of universal education underlies all others in our country, as the geologic drift determines all that appears on the surface of the earth.

And the message of the educational public to the people is that, here, as always and everywhere, *no people can be educated in any other way than by itself; in a system of instruction, organized, supported, and supervised by the whole people, through competent agents, elected by and responsible to themselves.*

And by the people's common school I mean, not the European, but the American common school, organized in its elementary, secondary, higher, normal, industrial, and university departments in every State according to the wisest method possible at present, with a free field for its development as the years go on.

The people should be told that it is neither "good form" nor good sense to resist the inevitable drift of our new American life towards the thorough organization of at least the elementary education in the modern public school. Of course, every family must judge of the circumstances and opportunities that environ its own children ; and, for many years, the secondary and higher training of Southern youth must be largely provided for by private, corporate, and denominational zeal. But it is simple waste to keep alive inefficient agencies while a meager public fund is almost thrown away upon a three or four months' common school, badly taught, and altogether of very doubtful use. In a country like the South, where every dollar tells, the funds for the elementary education of children and youth should, as far as possible, be concentrated for the greatest good of all. I go from town to town where a dozen families are spending, for their own children, badly handled at home or banished away from parental charge, money enough, with the help of public aid, to establish a thorough graded seminary where their own can be better educated up to the academical or college age than at present, and all receive the blessings of good instruction. And if any man objects that "he does not believe in schooling other people's children," let him and such as he go on till their neighborhood is filled with illiteracy and then inquire if it is more profitable to "pay for other people's children" as paupers, criminals, unskilled laborers or voters banded together by the demagogue to plunder the rich for the relief of the poor.

The most economical way of using private wealth for education is to supplement public taxation or to build schoolhouses and erect libraries, and with true public spirit try thus to establish the bottom interest of every American State. The poorest sort of charity is to support an impecunious incompetent as a school teacher at the expense of your own children. Many a community almost hopelessly distracted by sectarian, social, political, and business differences, in the attempt to support the graded school, has taken its first lesson in that art of "working together for good" whose other name is American public spirit and whose loftiest title is American patriotism.

In many communities this fact is appreciated and in all but the poorest communities the hearty coöperation of the better-off people would greatly forward the universal education which is the mine of common prosperity. No doubt everybody knows somebody's child who is "a good for nothing" in spite of even a good school, as every celebrated family turns out its own "black sheep," every upper social set its reprobate, the best church often the champion scamp, and even the Democratic and Republican parties, politicians who are not Washingtons. Of course, a mob of wild children, from homes cursed by ignorance, superstition, shiftlessness, vulgarity, and vice, swarming in a schoolhouse unfit for a stable, with a stupid, rough, perhaps wicked teacher, is not to be changed into a crowd of model young Americans by three months' schooling a year. A prodigious amount of poor schooling is not education. Education is responsible, like religion, only for what it has the opportunity to do in a thorough, sensible, and persistent way. And, tried by this test, America is the richest of nations, because by her free schools, working with free labor, a free church, a free press, and free government, a greater proportion of her people than of any other land is trained to the self-help which is the moving power of good citizenship in a country like "ours."

A central point in this reform is to improve the teaching force in every sort of school. First, banish every mental, moral, or social incompetent from the schoolroom. The most dangerous tramp in America is the educational "dead beat" who stands ready to step into every vacant chair of instruction. Next, train every competent youth who desires to do this work and select the fittest therefrom. No country has a greater wealth of good material for teaching than the South, especially in the vast number of young women, often of the best lineage and the finest native fitness, who are crowding this profession for employment. For a generation the able young men of the South will be largely drifted into other professions, with scarcely enough to fill responsible educational posts, and, more and more, the young womanhood of the country must do the people's work in the people's school. No money will be so well invested as in superior seminaries and arrangements for training these daughters of the people, not only in knowledge but in pedagogy, the broadest of the sciences and the finest of the fine arts. Every college, academy, and graded school should at once undertake this work, along with the State normal, the summer institute, and the educational press. For never so much as now could it be truly said the teacher is the school.

And now it may be asked, "where is the money to come from to do this prodigious work of educating the whole people?" I answer, whatever aid may come from abroad, finally from the whole Southern people, awakened as they can and may be by the educational public in the way I have described. Do you say, "the Southern people can not do it now?" I reply, a great deal more can certainly be done in many portions of the South than at present.

The Southern colored folk handle more money than New England saw for the first seventy-five years after the landing on Plymouth Rock, and in those years every institution was established that makes New England what it is to-day. Coming from those States which have done so much for the colored folk in their higher education, I say to them in all kindness, you have money for amusements, for secret societies, for indulgence in things useless and harmful, more than enough to add a month or two every year to the public school, put a good teacher therein, and, if necessary, build a decent schoolhouse by the labor of your own hands.

In general, I hold that increased interest in education in these States, as everywhere, will be followed by a diversion of money from useless and harmful expenditure to that investment in the upper story of life which is "treasure laid up in heaven." I was never in a Southern State that did not drink and smoke and waste in superfluities and bad economies money enough, at least, to greatly improve its education in every grade. Now Boston thinks very well of herself, but Boston spends, yearly, for the devil's school, that goes by whisky and its environments, $3 for every $1 invested for education and religion. Cincinnati, the Queen City of the Ohio Valley, pours $10,000,000 a year down her thirsty throat for $1,000,000 spent in all her schools. The Southern people may be as much better than their Northern neighbors as Mr. Bill Arp, of Georgia, so confidently asserts, and still waste enough in the same way to bring a good school to every man's door.

I know some of the political gentlemen will tell me that this is drawing checks on the bank of the millenium which will go to protest in the legislature of to-day. Be it so. But this is solid sense, that there is always money somewhere for what a man, a woman, a family, a neighborhood, a State, has set its heart on doing. The small politician's art is to preach that "economy" which means knocking out the brains of things to save the people's money. The statesman's high vocation is to lead the people to spend on the upper side of life for everything that exalts, enlightens, and refines man and makes for the true glory of the Commonwealth. And just in proportion as the educational public can awaken the people to the overwhelming importance of true education, the people will respond by putting more money into the school, the church, the library, the superior press, and that industrial training which is the logical outcome of all that makes up universal education in the American sense.

But the people of the forty-four Northern States of the Republic need not fall back into a "comfortable assurance" that all I have said is a matter of local, almost of foreign interest, with which the American people and the Nation have no concern. In one sense it is a local question. The people of every Southern State must look forward to the time when it can offer a fit training for good American citizenship to every child within its borders. The schooling of the children can not be assumed by the General Government; and all private, church, and even moral assistance, to be effective, must adjust itself to local methods and work in coöperation with the highest wisdom of the educational public on the ground. From what I have said there is little doubt that the educational public in every Southern State is firmly and unalterably fixed in the determination to push the work of universal education so well begun. And it will move forward on the great lines of our American system of universal education. There is no foundation for the assertion that the Southern people are now educating their children into hostility to the Union or in anyway preparing for new national disturbance in the future. Every type of Southern school is adjusting itself as rapidly as circumstances will permit to the best methods and broadest ideas in favor with the foremost educators of all civilized lands. Its one difference, the separation of the races, is a temporary necessity, absolutely essential to any effective scheme of public schools, and at present, in my opinion, is of even more importance to the colored than the white people. I have no doubt that every department of education, even under present circumstances, will be a little better every year, and that in due time the South will be able by its own effort to come in sight of the rear guard of the great Northern army of the children.

But now the question that confronts every patriotic American is this: Can the people of the North, can the Nation afford to "stand and wait" through the long and troubled years while this mighty enterprise is slowly evolving to its consummation?

Do not the whole people owe an imperative duty to this Southern educational public which, in the face of such prodigious obstacles, has already vindicated its title to the confidence and admiration of the Republic, and laid the foundation of that great future we are all glad to prophesy for this portion of the Union? Is not the American people bound by every consideration of justice, of patriotism, of national policy, of enlightened philanthropy, and Christian brotherhood, to come to the relief of this heroic Southern educational public and, in every way consistent with American ideas and methods, expedite the work and speed the coming of the Kingdom through half the national domain?

The question resolves itself into this: Can the North and the Nation safely endure the strain of such a condition of affairs as we now attempt to cover by this polite phrase, "Southern illiteracy?" Leaving out of account the effect on the South itself, can the North and the Nation safely encounter the future of these sixteen States, involved in this, the bottom peril of American civilization? American illiteracy is only another name for the barbarism that everywhere is fighting our republican order of society, in New York as in New Orleans, in Chicago as in Charleston. Ignorance of letters is its least characteristic; American illiteracy is a condition of society in which ignorance, superstition, shiftlessness, vulgarity, and vice are rolled together in the most deadly disease that can beset a modern community; a disease that is not only a negative and passive hindrance to the growth of any community in American ideas, but the most malignant, persistent, and intolerant enemy of everything which all wise and good men regard essential to the nation's higher life. And, just as the most awful result of a physical epidemic is the selfishness and recklessness often developed in a portion of the leading classes, so the most hopeless outcome of American illiteracy is the indifference, insensibility, and skepticism concerning republican institutions through the whole Union, among great numbers of wealthy, cultivated, and powerful people, to whom the Nation looks for leadership in its higher estate.

The first condition of helpful coöperation with the Southern educational public is, that the whole American people realize the peril of Southern illiteracy, as it is seen in all its ghastly features by those who live along with it, comprehend its present significance, and glimpse ahead with "a fearful looking for of judgment" in a time near at hand. A State like Louisiana, with a majority of her voters in this slough of illiteracy, with at least ten States in which this class ranges from one-third to nearly half the population; where less than 60 per cent of the children under 14 are in average attendance on any school, and that not exceeding four months in a year, for the brief years possible, with all the disadvantages which I have enumerated, such a State or portion of the country is not to be redeemed from peril by the establishment of a few manufacturing cities, or a revival of prostrate commerce, or the burying of a lower class under an avalanche of Northern or foreign immigration, by the success of any political party, or any other of the superficial expedients with which a confiding public may amuse itself. Southern illiteracy is the great pestilent slough in which the basement story of society in sixteen States now rests, with the hideous malaria poisoning every nook and corner of its loftiest and loveliest sky parlor or most exclusive closet. And the slough itself is only the deepest depth of the same deadly marsh that underlies every Northern city and State, involving these powerful Commonwealths in perils we are only beginning to apprehend.

There is but one remedy for all troubles peculiar to our Southern civilization. Indeed, the South has no peculiar peril. It is true to-day, as a generation ago, when Dr. Bushnell, foremost of American churchmen, sounded the alarm, "Barbarism is our first danger." It does not help the matter to call barbarism by a more attractive name, any more than to call hell by translating its Saxon back into its Greek or Hebrew name. The one cure for all Southern, as American evils, is the same operation in social affairs as Chicago undertook a generation ago, when she put a screw under her basement story and lifted herself bodily above her prairie slough, to her present level. So must the whole American people and the Southern educational public work together to place this great American screw we call universal education—the training of the mind, the hand, the character of its younger third for good American citizenship—under the mud sills of Southern society, and then, with "a long pull, a strong pull, and a pull altogether," lift the whole house up into the light, safety and abiding glory of a Christian civilization.

Here I might pause. For "the one thing needful" in our country is to awaken the people to a true understanding of any local or national peril. No people on earth is so fertile in expedients, so decisive and swift and radical, and relentless in its dealing with any acknowledged evil when once challenged to mortal combat, as our own. Could the people of the United States realize the length and breadth and height and depth of Southern as the heavy end of American illiteracy, the log would be lifted, even though a mountain, and cast into the sea. No man can predict how the American people will deal with any national peril until the awful day of judgment is upon it. My only qualification for this outlook is an unusual opportunity for observation, in every American State, under the most favorable circumstances, now for these past twelve years.

The first duty of the North, not only to itself but to the South, is to force and put out of court, now and forever, the formidable attempt to change the American system of common schools—free to all, unsectarian in theology, moral through its whole organization and administration, supported and supervised by the whole people—to the European and Canadian system of subsidizing schools established and administered by the clergy of different religious sects. No one denomination is responsible for this pernicious crusade. It is the last kick of the declining ecclesiasticism that yet aspires to rule the State by monopolizing the training of the children for American life. To-day this is openly and secretly one of the most formidable obstacles to the growth of the Southern common school. A weakening here is a new peril to every Southern State. The Southern educational public watches this conflict in the North with an apprehension of which we have little comprehension. In proportion as the North does this and at the same time reforms, strengthens, and adjusts its system of common schools to the growing needs of the Republic, will the educational public in every State of the South take heart and resist more bravely and effectually this, the most dangerous assault yet planned on our republican civilization.

In general, the most important educational work of the North to-day is a thorough dealing with our system of country district school keeping. The country district school is now the only American institution that "wobbles" on without fit supervision; the one realm of American public life left to the caprices, whims, and obstinate conceits of unskilled labor. Nine-tenths of the children of the South are in the country district school, and that school is a generation behind the country school of the North. Every advance in effective country school-keeping north of the Potomac and Ohio will be felt as a thrill of health and a prophecy of life through sixteen Southern States.

The fit training of teachers is now an imperious need of Southern education. Here the North, through its great mission schools for the colored folk, and the Peabody, Slater, Hand, and other funds, is doing a work which can not be too much praised. Without these agencies the common schools for the colored folk would have been an impossibility, and the education of white children would have been far less advanced than at present. So far nine-tenths of the money that has built up these schools, amounting probably to $20,000,000 during the past twenty-five years, has come from the Northeastern States. It is high time the Northwest, so indebted to the older States and the Nation for the development of its own splendid system of education, should consecrate a generous gift from its abundant means to this work. Every important Southern school of the higher grade, especially for the colored people, needs a solid endowment as a protection against future contingencies. The Peabody fund should be increased by other millions, and the Northwest can and should do it.

It is time that the miscellaneous support of elementary schools for the Negroes by Northern contributions and the general giving to irresponsible Southern solicitors should cease, and every Northern dollar sent southward go "where it will do the most good;" and that place at present is strengthening the agencies and institutions that train the teachers for the common schools. This, with a judicious system of endowment of the most hopeful Southern colleges for white youth, is in the direct line of the most effective aid and comfort.

Our great financial bodies, that are now covering the South with their investments in the mine, the railroad, the factory, and the forest, are confronted with a moral obligation to coöperate with the Southern educational public in this mighty work of educating the children. No power on earth is so heedless and godless as the unsanctified, relentless love of money which now, as in Palestine eighteen centuries ago, is "the root of all evil." This vast money power from the North now invading the South goes weighted with a fearful responsibility. It can either strike hands with the Southern party of reaction, that would force back the rising power of the humbler Southern people, or it can stand by the common people in their first great opportunity to gain that intelligence which is the soul and the security of the American type of freedom. More than one Southern community has reason to bless its new prosperity for the gift of opportunity for its children. All rational hope of permanent material success in this region depends on the educational training which will change the unskilled labor, now the millstone around the neck of the South, to the intelligent and skilled labor which is the soul of the mighty industrial power of the North.

The Christian people of the three great churches still divided on sectional lines should speak up, loud and plain, to their clergy and church; preach it with an imperative command, in some practical way, consistent with mutual self-respect and Christian principle, to cast down that wall of sectional division which is the scandal of American Christianity. A hundred level-headed Christian laymen could evolve a plan of union that would open to the Southern people the great treasure-house of the money and Christian sympathy of these powerful churches of the North. The direct and indirect effect of such coöperation would be felt at once through every realm of Southern educational life. Every other set of people in the United States has gotten over the sectional malady save the influential churchmen of these three great religious organizations, and their delay is now one of the greatest obstacles to the spiritual and mental advancement of the masses of the Southern people.

Finally, every year of my Southern ministry of education enforces the belief that without some effective, generous, and speedy form of national aid, the present generation of Southern children cannot be educated, and the peril of Southern illiteracy will be perpetuated, more dangerous with every decade. The situation is this: More than a third of the children of the South are growing up to feed the slough of the present illiteracy. Another third are so poorly furnished with schooling as to make even what they have a serious question of results. The bottom need of the South is a tolerable country school of five or six months for all classes, a town graded school, with opportunity for training teachers, for eight months, and the expansion of the State agricultural and mechanical schools to the ability to inaugurate some practical scheme of industrial training. This year the two States of New York and Massachusetts will, without hardship, appropriate more money for education than all the sixteen Southern States. The present insufficient Southern appropriation for education is a heavier strain upon the white people of the South than the most generous appropriation of any Northern State. At least twice the present amount is needed there even to approach a moderate estimate of Southern needs. To say that the Southern white people, who must pay nine-tenths of this money, can lift this burden, is simply romance to a man who, like myself, has "walked around Zion" and knows of what he speaks. The West saved the Union a generation ago by the prowess of its arms and the breadth of its statemanship. This it did because that corner stone of popular education was laid by the nation a century ago in the magnificent land endowment on which it has built one of the most effective systems of common schools in the world; while Eastern money and the best blood of every good family, reënforced from over the sea, has flowed like a mighty river to fertilize the uplands of society from the Alleghanies to the Pacific. Now should the West again step forth to the final restoration of the South and in coöperation with the common school public of all sections, elaborate some practical scheme by which the General Government can do for these States what has been done so magnificently in its own marvelous history of the past 100 years.

Already has the overture to that grand union of the whole American people for the abolition of Southern illiteracy and the final salvation of the Republic been secured in the relation of the great body of the teachers and school men and women of the country. The Southern teaching brotherhood and sisterhood is already known and honored by the corresponding class everywhere, perhaps even more than at home. Indeed, one portion of the American people was never in special need of reconciliation or reconstruction north and south of old Mason and Dixon's line. While other men hung back and still weary the patience of patriotic people by their bitter recriminations or diplomatic maneuverings in behalf of national harmony, the superior teachers and school men and women only awaited the signal in 1865, from Washington, to flow together in a brotherly and sisterly fashion that declares them the most receptive, sympathetic, and broad-minded class in the outlook for the future in these United States.

And, finally, the entire American educational public must "renew its strength like the eagles," and summon the whole American people to come out from that narrow provincialism, sectionalism, and local selfishness which is the stamp of everything second-rate in every corner of the American Union. In this Republic no State, city, hamlet, family, or individual, however excellent, is great and good enough to fling off the sympathetic word, the helping hand, the patriotic arm-touch of the other. I always ask, when I hear the haughty message, "Let us alone," "What mischief is that man or that community plotting against the American people?"

Oh, believe me, American men and women, we all need each other, and we must all "hang together" or our great experiment of republican civilization will explode in anarchy, or close up in the iron fist of despotic power. For a few years now you of the South need the abounding sympathy, the helpful suggestion, the abundant means of the whole American people uniting for education more than you need immigration, capital, the success of your favorite politics, or any outward prosperity. Your 18,000,000, reënforced by its younger third, thoroughly trained by the American system of education will be enough to realize your wildest dreams of prosperity, and make you more than ever a commanding influence in the national life. Tell the American people what you need and the people will gladly give it you, with no lack of faith in its wise and honorable use. Before another generation New England, the Central, the Northwestern, the Pacific States, may need you in some national emergency where only a firm and enlightened patriotism can prevail. For, to every section and every State, as the years roll on, may come the providential opportunity in its turn to "save the Union," if not by weapons of war by those higher agencies and more potent forces that incline the delicate poise and shape the destiny of our glorious companionship of sovereign and united American Commonwealths.

NOTES TO ESSAY REPRINT

1. Johann Heinrich Pestalozzi (1746–1827), a Swiss educator, believed that the purpose of education was individual and social improvement. He stressed child-centered education through natural methods, by relating experience to knowledge through the object lesson, and by reducing knowledge to its simplest elements so as to build from simple ideas to complex. His theories were introduced into the United States in the early nineteenth century. Frank Pierrepont Graves, *Great Educators of Three Centuries: Their Work and Its Influence on Modern Education* (New York: Macmillan, 1912), 122–63.

2. A pioneer in educational reform, Horace Mann (1796–1859) focused on reform of common schools and teacher training. He founded the *Common School Journal* in 1839, and through twelve annual reports as secretary of the Massachusetts Board of Education, he advertised the deplorable conditions in the schools. The *Seventh Annual Report*, written after five months of observing European practices and innovations, became an important vehicle in the transmission of European ideas to America. *Dictionary of American Biography* XII, 240–44.

3. Hugh Miller (1802–1856) was a Scottish essayist, geologist, and lay theologian whose writings enjoyed great popularity during the middle and late nineteenth century. Mayo had probably read the American edition of Miller's most popular work, *The Old Red Sandstone, or New Walks in an Old Field* (Boston: Gould and Lewiston, 1858).

4. In 1883, Senator Henry William Blair (1834–1920), of New Hampshire, proposed that $105 million be given to the states over a ten-year period to improve public education. Because states having the highest illiteracy would receive the largest percentage of the fund, this legislation would have been of great aid to southern schools. In 1884, 1886, and 1888, the Senate passed the Blair bill, but it was always defeated in committee in the House of Representatives. In 1890, the Senate itself abandoned the bill.

5. Henry Barnard (1811–1900) was a pioneer in educational reform. He was secretary to the board of education in Connecticut, educational agent in Rhode Island, and first U.S. Commissioner of Education. Barnard believed that awakening a public conscience was fundamental to effecting reform. He founded the *American Journal of Education* in 1855 to promote support for public education. *DAB*, I, 621–24.

6. A chaplain in the Union army, John Eaton (1829–1906) served as superintendent of freedmen in the Army of the Tennessee, and his efforts became an important precedent in the organization of the Freedmen's Bureau. Appointed U.S. Commissioner of Education in 1870, Eaton strengthened the administrative structure of the department and emphasized educating the public through the collection and dissemination of information. *DAB*, V, 608–609.

7. Nathaniel Henry Rhodes Dawson (d. 1895), although a lawyer, was appointed commissioner of education by Grover Cleveland in August, 1886, partly to counter southern opposition to the office of education, which was perceived to be an instrument of federal intervention, and partly to reward his services in rebuilding the Democratic party in Alabama. See Kenneth R. Johnson, "N. H. R. Dawson: United States Commissioner of Education," *History of Education Quarterly*, XI (1971), 174–81.

8. For further details of Jefferson's plan, see his "Notes on Virginia" (Paris, 1784) in Adrienne Koch and William Peden (eds.), *The Life and Selected Writings of Thomas Jefferson* (New York: Random House, 1944), 262–66.

9. The Reverend James Henley Thornwell (1812–1862) had served as president of South Carolina College during the antebellum period, but he was hardly the kind of educator

Mayo would have preferred. Conservative in religious and political matters, he defended slavery as biblically sound and effectively eliminated freedom of expression at South Carolina College. See Benjamin M. Palmer (ed.), *The Life and Letters of James Henley Thornwell* (Richmond: Whittet, 1875).

10. Robert J. Breckinridge (1800–1869), a Kentucky Presbyterian minister, was the father of his state's public school system and served as superintendent of education from 1847 to 1852. During the Civil War, he was Kentucky's most distinguished Unionist. See Will D. Gilliam, Jr., "Robert J. Breckinridge: Kentucky Unionist," *Kentucky Historical Society Register*, LXXIX (1971), 362–85.

11. Calvin H. Wiley (1819–1887), the "Horace Mann of North Carolina," devoted his life to the development of a state-supported system of public education. He served as state superintendent of education from 1853 to 1866 and remained active in educational matters until his death. Edgar W. Knight, *Public School Education in the South* (Boston: Ginn and Company, 1922), 235–38.

12. Central Female College was a Baptist institution founded in 1853 for the training of young women. Mayo is in error in his reference to Dr. Walter Hillman. The Clinton, Mississippi, physician never taught at the institution, but he was a benefactor for more than twenty years. In 1891, in recognition of his generosity, the board of trustees changed the college's name to Hillman College. Dunbar Rowland (ed.), *Mississippi: Sketches of Counties, Towns, Events, Institutions, and Persons, Arranged in Cyclopedic Form* (Reprint of 1907 ed., 4 vols.; Spartanburg, S.C.: Reprint Co., 1976), I, 456.

13. Richard Cobden (1804–1865) was a prominent British liberal, best remembered for his articulate support of the Anti-Cornlaw League (1838–1846). He visited the United States in 1835 and on that basis published a pamphlet, "England, Ireland, and America," in which he argued that America must not be allowed to compete with British products and that sound British policy lay in the direction of free trade and nonintervention. He praised the American people, and Mayo may be referring here to his comment, "the insatiable love of caste that in England, as in Hindostan, devours all hearts, is confined to no walks of society, but pervades every degree, from the highest to the lowest." *The Political Writings of Richard Cobden* (2 vols.; London: William Ridgway, 1867), I, 131. For biographical information, see *The Dictionary of National Biography*, IV, 10.

14. Elected a bishop of the Methodist Episcopal Church, South, in 1886, Atticus Green Haygood (1839–1896) was a prominent Georgia educator. He believed that progress in education was vital to the South's material development. For a summary of his views, see Atticus Haygood, "The South and the School Problem," *Harper's New Monthly Magazine*, LXXIX (1889), 225–31.

15. Although born in the United States, George Peabody (1795–1869) gained a fortune as a London banker. In 1867, he created the Peabody Education Fund to promote learning in the American South. Thomas H. Johnson, *The Oxford Companion to American History* (New York: Oxford University Press, 1966), 622.

16. Edward Southey Joynes (1834–1917) was a professor of foreign languages at five southern colleges and universities between the end of the war and his retirement in 1908. While teaching at William and Mary, Washington and Lee, Vanderbilt University, the University of Tennessee, and the University of South Carolina he wrote several textbooks in French and German. For some insight into his educational philosophy see his letters to the editor in the *Nation*, LXXXIII (1907), 259, 458.

17. A leading southern educator, William Preston Johnston (1831–1899), served as president of Louisiana State University from 1880 to 1883, and as president of Tulane University from 1883 to 1899. He was a son of the Confederate general, Albert Sidney Johnston. Arthur Marvin Shaw, *William Preston Johnston: A Transitional Figure of the Confederacy* (Baton Rouge: Louisiana State University Press, 1943).

18. The Mississippi state legislature created the Mississippi Industrial Institute and College for Women in 1884 with a campus in Columbus, Mississippi. The first session began in 1885 with more than 250 young women enrolled, primarily in a teacher education program. *Bulletin of the Mississippi State College for Women*, LXXXVIII (January, 1973), 7–9. The Georgia Normal and Industrial School was established in Milledgeville two years later. Its purpose, according to the Georgia commissioner of agriculture, was to

prepare young women to teach or to train them in one of the "industrial arts suitable for females to follow." Georgia Department of Agriculture, *Georgia: Historical and Industrial* (Atlanta: Franklin Printing and Publishing, 1901), 375.

South Carolina's first state-supported college for education was an outgrowth of Winthrop College for Women, a private school established in 1886 in Columbia, South Carolina, with substantial assistance from the Peabody Educational Fund. In 1891 the state accepted control of the college, renaming it the South Carolina Industrial and Winthrop Normal College. Four years later, it was moved to Rock Hill. *Winthrop College Catalog, 1976–77*, LXVIII (August, 1976), 6–7.

19. Usually considered a herald of modern architecture, Henry Hobson Richardson (1838–1886) was born in St. James Parish, Louisiana, but followed his career in New York where he became famous for his "functional buildings," most of which were constructed in the 1870s and 1880s. During the same period, John Wellborn Root (1850–1891), born in Lumpkin County, Georgia, designed some of Chicago's finest structures. To a degree, his work was influenced by Richardson's. *Concise Dictionary of American Biography* (New York: Charles Scribner's Sons, 1964), 862, 887.

20. Susan Elizabeth Blow (1843–1916) pioneered early childhood education in the United States, founding the first public school kindergarten in St. Louis in 1873 and opening an institute for training kindergarten teachers the following year. Edward T. James (ed.), *Notable American Women, 1607–1950* (3 vols.; Cambridge, Mass.: Harvard University Press, 1971), I, 181–83.

21. Unquestionably a few favored slaves and a handful of free blacks learned to read and write, particularly in the urban areas of the coast and the border states. It is doubtful that more than two or three percent of the blacks of the Confederacy's eleven states could read and write in 1865. See for example, Ira Berlin, *Slaves Without Masters: The Free Negro in the Antebellum South* (New York: Pantheon Books, 1974), 303–306.

22. Hiram Rhoades Revels (1822–1901), a black, represented Mississippi in the United States Senate from 1870 to 1871. From 1871 to 1883, he was president of Alcorn University, located in Oakland, Mississippi. *Concise Dictionary of American Biography*, 856.

23. The American Tract Society school was later incorporated into the Institution for the Education of Colored Youth, chartered by Congress in 1863. Ellen M. O'Connor (ed.), *Myrtilla Miner: A Memoir* (New York: Houghton, Mifflin, 1885), 100–101.

24. Commissioned brigadier general in the volunteers in 1861, James Samuel Wadsworth (1807–1864) commanded the defense of Washington in the spring of 1862. He was later killed in the Battle of the Wilderness. *DAB*, XIX, 308–309.

25. John W. Alvord served as the national superintendent of education for the Freedmen's Bureau. Howard W. White, *The Freedmen's Bureau in Louisiana* (Baton Rouge: Louisiana State University Press, 1970), 172.

26. This was, of course, the Morrill Act, which granted every state thirty thousand acres from the public domain for each of its congressmen. States were then to use the money received from the sale of this land to establish a mechanical and agricultural college. Johnson, *The Oxford Companion to American History*, 585.

27. In 1899, Katharine Drexel founded the Sisters of the Blessed Sacrament to encourage missionary work among American Indians and blacks. The order established two schools for girls in the South: the Institute of St. Francis de Sales in Rock Castle, Virginia, and the Academy of the Immaculate Mother in Nashville, Tennessee. Katharine was the daughter of Francis A. Drexel, the Philadelphia banker and philanthropist. Charles G. Herberman *et al.*, *The Catholic Encyclopedia* (15 vols.; New York: Robert Appleton, 1907), II, 599.

28. Founded in 1867 by J. Britton-Smith, D.D., with a fifty thousand dollar endowment, the St. Augustine Normal School and Collegiate Institute was designed to educate black men and women to become teachers and clergymen. It opened in 1868 with 7 instructors and 140 students and in 1891 included 10 instructors and 164 students. See Charles Lee Smith, *The History of Education in North Carolina* (Washington, D.C.: Government Printing Office, 1888), 158–59, 161.

29. Founded in 1846, the American Missionary Association carried on mission work in the American West and Africa before the war. After 1865 it became the largest of the freed-

men's aid societies, supporting education throughout the South and working closely with the Freedmen's Bureau. Richard Bryant Drake, "The American Missionary Association and the Southern Negro, 1861–1888" (Ph.D. dissertation, Emory University, 1957).

30. John Fox Slater (1815–1884) was a Connecticut woolens manufacturer. In 1882 he created the John F. Slater Fund to promote the education of blacks. The Fund was principally used to train teachers. *DAB*, XVII, 205. For a useful look at the operation of the Slater fund, see Louis D. Rubin, Jr. (ed.), *Teach the Freeman: The Correspondence of Rutherford B. Hayes and the Slater Fund for Negro Education, 1881–1887* (2 vols.; Baton Rouge: Louisiana State University Press, 1959). For a critical view of the impact of the Peabody fund, see William P. Vaughn, "Partners in Segregation: Barnas Sears and the Peabody Fund," *Civil War History*, X (1964), 26–74.

31. A railroad president and shipbuilder, James McMillan (1838–1902) represented Michigan in the United States Senate from 1889 to 1902 and took a lively interest in southern education. *Biographical Directory of the American Congress* (Washington, D.C.: Government Printing Office, 1971), 1390.

32. *Leonard and Gertrude*, the most popular of Pestalozzi's works (see note 1, p. 301), was published in Europe in 1781. Gertrude, by her virtuous example, becomes the instrument of salvation for her husband, her village, and, ultimately, for the state. This story exemplifies Pestalozzi's belief in the mother as the natural educator and in the pedagogical power of the object lesson. Graves, *Great Educators of Three Centuries*, 124.

33. Friedrich Wilhelm August Froebel (1782–1852), a German educator and disciple of Pestalozzi, was interested in early childhood education. He believed that education, a process of self-realization and socialization, began at birth. Sound early education was the basis of subsequent success, he argued, and he experimented with toys and games as educational devices, advocated systematic training for mothers, and founded the first kindergarten at Blankenburg in 1837. Graves, *Great Educators of Three Centuries*, 194–233.

34. McFadden Alexander Newell (b. 1824) held various teaching positions until 1865 when he was appointed principal of the Normal School, Baltimore, and became state superintendent of schools. He founded "The Maryland School Journal" and, with William L. Criery, coauthored a series of textbooks, *The Maryland Series*. In 1877–1878, he was president of the National Educational Association. *The National Cyclopaedia of American Biography* (56 vols.; Clifton, N.J.: James T. White, 1892–1975), XII, 512, hereinafter cited as *NCAB*.

35. William T. Harris, a native of Connecticut, came to Missouri in the 1850s and was a crucial figure in the development of the St. Louis school system, ultimately serving as assistant to the system's school superintendent when Mayo knew him in the 1880s. Harris (d. circa 1900) succeeded Nathaniel Dawson (see note 7, p. 301) as United States Commissioner of Education and devoted his energies to pedagogical reform rather than encouraging federal aid to education. See his article, "The Necessity of Five Co-ordinate Groups in a Complete Course of Study," *Education*, XVI (1895), 129–34. Walter B. Stevens, *Centennial History of Missouri: One Hundred Years in the Union, 1820–1921* (6 vols.; St. Louis: S. J. Clarke Publishing, 1921), II, 749.

36. William Henry Ruffner served as Virginia's superintendent of public schools from 1870 to 1882. His father Henry Ruffner had been president of Washington College (later Washington and Lee University) and proposed a master plan for a state common school system in 1841. Edgar W. Knight, *Education in the United States* (Boston: Ginn and Company, 1935), 325.

37. James H. Binford (1838–1876), superintendent of Richmond city schools from 1870 to 1876, was one of the most effective promoters of the state's common school system in the postwar period. In the six years before his death, Binford made the Richmond schools a model for the South. Virginius Dabney, *Richmond: The Story of a City* (Garden City, N.Y.: Doubleday, 1975), 230.

38. When the District of Columbia schools were reorganized in 1901, one of the brothers, Winfield Scott Montgomery, was named "Assistant Superintendent of the Colored Schools." As an 1878 Phi Beta Kappa graduate of Dartmouth College with twenty years

of public school experience, Montgomery was qualified to head the black schools, but, for political reasons, a white was named his superior. Constance Green, *The Secret City: A History of Race Relations in the Nation's Capital* (Princeton: Princeton University Press, 1967), 173. Winfield Montgomery's older brother, Henry, served as a supervisor in the colored schools of the District of Columbia from 1882 until his death in 1899. House Documents, *Report of the Commissioners of the District of Columbia for the Year Ending June 30, 1899*, 56th Cong., 1st Sess., IV, 264.

39. Mayo is referring to the vote on the 1886 Blair bill, in which every southern senator either voted or paired. Of those who voted, fifteen voted yea and three nay. Four southerners paired, with two supporting the legislation and two in opposition. Thus, seventeen southern senators endorsed the bill and five were opposed. See *Congressional Record*, 49th Cong., 1st Sess., 2104–2105.

40. This series of monographs, edited by Herbert Baxter Adams, was published as Contributions to American Educational History in the United States, Department of Interior, Bureau of Information, *Circulars of Information*. For a complete list, see U.S. Office of Education, *List of Publications of the United States Bureau of Education, 1867–1910* (Washington, D.C.: Government Printing Office, 1940), 29–32.

41. After investigating working conditions in Georgia for the Department of Labor, Mary Clare de Graffenried (1849–1921) created a sensation with her exposé, "The Georgia Cracker in the Cotton Mills," which appeared in the February, 1891, issue of *Century Magazine*. James, *Notable American Women*, I, 452–54.

42. After the Civil War, Amy Morris Bradley (1823–1904), a teacher and a nurse, established institutions to aid poor whites in Wilmington under the auspices of the Soldiers' Memorial Society of Boston and the American Unitarian Association. With the aid of philanthropist Mary Porter Tileston Hemenway (1820–1894), she founded the Tileston Normal School in 1872 in order to educate southern women to meet the educational demands then filled by northern missionaries. James, *Notable American Women*, I, 220–22.

43. After teaching for some years in Atlanta, Laura Askew Haygood (1845–1900) journeyed to Shanghai, China, as a missionary for the Methodist Episcopal Church, South. There, in 1892, she established an excellent high school for girls called the McTyeire Home and School. Atticus Green Haygood was her brother (see note 14, page 302). James, *Notable American Women*, II, 167–69. In 1878, Clara Conway founded the Clara Conway Institute in Memphis, Tennessee. Frances E. Willard and Mary A. Livermore, *A Woman of the Century: Fourteen Hundred-Seventy Biographical Sketches Accompanied by Portraits of Leading American Women in All Walks of Life* (Reprint of 1893 ed.; Detroit: Gale Research, 1967), 201–202. From 1880 to 1926, Mildred Lewis Rutherford (1851–1928) served in various capacities, including principal, at the Lucy Cobb Institute in Athens, Georgia. Rutherford and the institute devoted themselves to the training of girls in the genteel traditions of southern womanhood. Rutherford was a leading member of the United Daughters of the Confederacy. James, *Notable American Women*, III, 214–15.

44. A pioneer in the education of blacks, Myrtilla Miner (1815–1864) founded the Colored Girls School in Washington, D.C., in 1851 at the urging of Henry Ward Beecher. Primarily a normal institute, the school functioned, despite local opposition, until 1879 when it was incorporated into the Washington public school system. See O'Connor (ed.), *Myrtilla Miner* and James, *Notable American Women*, II, 547–48.

45. Mary B. Briggs was the first black principal of the Miner school and served from 1879 to 1883 when she was succeeded by Lucy Moten. O'Connor (ed.), *Myrtilla Miner*, 105.

46. This is one of the few occasions when Mayo's bitter resentment of the Catholic hierarchy is revealed in *Southern Women*. As a life-long opponent of "sectarian" private schools, he was inevitably drawn into conflict with those Roman Catholics who supported parochial schools in the late nineteenth century.

47. Richard Grant White (1821–1885) was a popular New York journalist of the post Civil War era, whose articles appeared in many publications including *Putman's Magazine*, the *Atlantic Monthly*, and the *North American Review*. Mayo is undoubtedly referring here to White's scathing attack on the public schools which appeared in the December,

1880, issue of *North American Review*. For a review of the controversy it aroused, see B. J. Lovejoy, "Mr. Richard Grant White vs. the Public Schools of the United States," *Education*, I (1881), 335–48.

48. For Parker's influence on Mayo see Mayo's "The New Education and Col. Parker," *Journal of Education*, XVIII (1883), 83–88.

49. Mary Muhlenberg Hopkins Emery (1844–1927), a Cincinnati philanthropist, donated a number of buildings to Mount Berry School (later Berry College) in Rome, Georgia, and Berea College in Berea, Kentucky. *NCAB*, XXIV, 127–28. For information on Tileston, see note 42, p. 305. In 1873 Cornelius Vanderbilt (1794–1877), the New York railroad and steamship magnate, donated a total of one million dollars to Central University, located in Tennessee. The school was afterwards renamed Vanderbilt University in his honor. *Concise Dictionary of American Biography*, 1102–1107.

50. Gail Hamilton was the pen name of Mary Abigail Dodge (1833–1896). A popular journalist, Hamilton wrote articles for numerous publications, including the *Independent* and the *Atlantic Monthly*. Although she championed better education for women, she was opposed to women's suffrage. James, *Notable American Women*, I, 493–95. For information on White, see note 47, p. 305. Dr. Nathan Allen (1813–1889) was a Massachusetts physician noted for his work in phrenology and fertility. *DAB*, I, 201–202. A rigid canonist and prominent conservative, Bernard John McQuaid (1823–1909) was consecrated Roman Catholic bishop of Rochester, New York, in 1868. He established a number of parochial schools in his diocese. *Concise Dictionary of American Biography*, 625.

51. From 1866 to 1891 George Franklin Edmunds (1828–1919) represented Vermont in the United States Senate. He was a supporter of Radical Reconstruction. *Concise Dictionary of American Biography*, 263. John Sherman (1823–1900) represented Ohio in the United States Senate from 1861 to 1877 and from 1881 to 1897. He generally supported Radical Reconstruction. His brother was the Union general William Tecumseh Sherman. *DAB*, I, 949–50.

52. From 1877 to 1882, Hugh Smith Thompson (1836–1904) was superintendent of public education for South Carolina. His many reforms won him great acclaim, and in 1882 he was elected governor. In 1886 he resigned to become Grover Cleveland's assistant secretary of the treasury. He was appointed to the Civil Service Commission in 1889. *NCAB*, XXIV, 78. For information on Johnston, see note 17, p. 302.

INDEX

For further information on the contents of *Southern Women in the Recent Educational Movement in the South*, readers should refer to Mayo's detailed Analysis of Contents, pp. 3–13.